Microsoft® Works 6 F... For Dummie...

T0281642

Miscellaneous Spreadsheet Stuff

To Do This ...	Do This ...
Sum at end of column or row	Press Ctrl+M, or click Σ in the toolbar
Change column width	Drag edge to the right of column letter
Change row height	Drag edge below row number
Insert row above	Choose Insert⇔Row
Insert column to left	Choose Insert⇔Column

Quick Formatting in the Word Processor

To Do This ...	Press This ...
Add or Remove space	Ctrl+0 (zero) before paragraph
Double-space text	Ctrl+2
Single-space text	Ctrl+1
Indent	Ctrl+M
Un-indent	Ctrl+Shift+M
Hanging indent	Ctrl+Shift+T

Number Formats in Spreadsheets and Databases

To Do This ...	Press This ...
Dollars	Ctrl+4 ($ key)
Percent	Ctrl+5 (% key)
Comma at thousands	Ctrl+, (comma)

Navigating in Almost Any Document

To Do This ...	Do This ...
Scroll up/down	Use vertical scroll bar
Scroll sideways	Use horizontal scroll bar
Move right, left, up, down	Press arrow key
End of column/next paragraph	Press Ctrl+↓
Start of column, paragraph	Press Ctrl+↑
One screen up/down	Press PgUp/PgDn keys
Beginning/end of line or row	Press Home/End keys
Beginning/end of document	Press Ctrl+Home/Ctrl+End keys

For Dummies: Bestselling Book Series for Beginners

Microsoft® Works 6 For Windows® For Dummies®

Cheat Sheet

Quick Formatting Almost Everywhere

To Do This ...	Press This ...
Bold	Ctrl+B, or click B on toolbar
Italic	Ctrl+I, or click I on toolbar
Underline	Ctrl+U, or click U on toolbar
Center	Ctrl+E, or click Center Align on toolbar
Left-align	Ctrl+L, or click Left Align on toolbar
Right-align	Ctrl+R, or click Right Align on toolbar
Remove font styles	Ctrl+spacebar
Insert page break	Ctrl+Enter
Change page margins	Choose File➪Page Setup

Starting, Saving, Printing, Closing

To Do This ...	Do This ...
Start Works	Double-click Works Shortcut icon
Exit a program	Choose File➪Exit
Return to Task Launcher	Choose File➪New
Start a new document	Press Ctrl+N
Save a document	Press Ctrl+S
Open a document	Press Ctrl+O
Close a document	Press Ctrl+W
Print Preview	Choose File➪Print Preview
Print	Press Ctrl+P

Editing Almost Everywhere

To Do This ...	Do This ...
Select something	Click on it or drag across it
Select with keys	Press Shift+ navigation key
Delete	Press Delete key or Backspace key
Cut selection to Clipboard	Press Ctrl+X
Copy selection to Clipboard	Press Ctrl+C
Paste from Clipboard	Press Ctrl+V
Move	Select, drag to position
Copy	Select, Ctrl+drag to position

For Dummies: Bestselling Book Series for Beginners

Microsoft® Works 6 For Windows® FOR DUMMIES®

by David Kay

WILEY

Wiley Publishing, Inc.

Microsoft® Works 6 For Windows® For Dummies®

Published by
Wiley Publishing, Inc.
909 Third Avenue
New York, NY 10022
www.wiley.com

About the Author

David Kay is a writer, engineer, and aspiring naturalist and artist, combining professions with the same effectiveness as his favorite business establishment, Acton Muffler, Brake, and Ice Cream (now defunct). Dave has written about a dozen computer books, by himself or with friends. His latest new title is *Paint Shop Pro 7 For Dummies.* His other contributions to world literature may be found in various editions of *Microsoft Works For Windows For Dummies, WordPerfect For Windows For Dummies, Graphics File Formats*, and *The Internet Complete Reference.*

In his other life, as the Poo-bah of Brightleaf Communications, Dave writes and teaches on a variety of subjects. He and his wife Katy, and golden retriever Alex, live in the wilds of Massachusetts. In his spare time, Dave studies animal and human tracking and munches on edible wild plants. He also has been known to make strange blobs from molten glass, sing Gilbert and Sullivan choruses in public, and hike in whatever mountains he can get to. He longs to return to New Zealand and track kiwis and hedgehogs in Wanaka. He finds writing about himself in the third person like this quite peculiar and will stop now.

Dedication

This edition is dedicated to my wife, Katy, an environmental engineer extraordinaire determined to clean up the world, even if she has to ship dirt to Alaska.

Author's Acknowledgments

I would like to acknowledge the support and tolerance of my wife, Katy, and of my friends and family, from whose company I am sadly removed while writing these books. Thanks also to the folks at Waterside, and to the congenial editors at Wiley Publishing, including:

- ✔ Acquisitions editor Tom Heine for his finely honed acquisitiveness and pseudo-omnipotence
- ✔ Project editor Paul Levesque for keeping the book from exploding into tiny little unrelated bits
- ✔ Senior copy editor Kim Darosett
- ✔ Copy editors Teresa Artman and Nicole Laux
- ✔ Technical editor Allen Wyatt

Publisher's Acknowledgments

We're proud of this book; please send us your comments through our online registration form located at www.dummies.com/register/.

Some of the people who helped bring this book to market include the following:

Acquisitions, Editorial, and Media Development

Project Editor: Paul Levesque

Acquisitions Editor: Tom Heine

Copy Editors: Teresa Artman, Nicole A. Laux

Proof Editor: Jill Mazurczyk

Technical Editor: Allen L. Wyatt

Editorial Manager: Leah P. Cameron

Media Development Manager: Laura Carpenter

Media DevelopmentSupervisor: Richard Graves

Editorial Assistant: Seth Kerney

Production

Project Coordinator: Dale White

Layout and Graphics: Jackie Bennett, Brian Torwelle, Julie Trippetti, Jacque Schneider

Proofreaders: Laura Albert, Charles Spencer, Susan Moritz, Nancy Price, York Production Services, Inc.

Indexer: York Production Services, Inc.

Special Help
Kim Darosett, Rebecca Senninger, Sarah Shupert

Publishing and Editorial for Technology Dummies
Richard Swadley, Vice President and Executive Group Publisher
Andy Cummings, Vice President and Publisher
Mary C. Corder, Editorial Director

Publishing for Consumer Dummies
Diane Graves Steele, Vice President and Publisher
Joyce Pepple, Acquisitions Director

Composition Services
Gerry Fahey, Vice President of Production Services
Debbie Stailey, Director of Composition Services

Contents at a Glance

Cartoons at a Glance

By Rich Tennant

page 7

page 153

page 219

page 347

page 381

page 281

page 71

Cartoon Information:
Fax: 978-546-7747
E-Mail: richtennant@the5thwave.com
World Wide Web: www.the5thwave.com

Table of Contents

Introduction

ongratulations! You have already proven your superior intelligence. Instead of blowing several hundred bucks on the biggest and most muscle-bound word processor, database program, spreadsheet program, graphics, and communications software you can find, you're using Microsoft Works 6 — a program that can do probably everything you need for a lot less trouble and money. Heck, you're so smart that you may have bought a PC with Works already installed.

So then why, exactly, should you be reading a *For Dummies* book? Because *For Dummies* readers are an underground group of people smart enough to say, "Okay, so I'm not a computer wizard. So sue me. I still want to use this stuff." The *For Dummies* books are for people who

- Want to find out how to use their software without being bored silly.
- Feel as though there should be a manual to explain the software manual.
- Actually want to get some work done. Soon. Like today.
- Don't want to wade through a lot of technical gibberish.
- Don't think the way that computer software engineers seem to think.

What's in This Book

This book describes how to use all the programs of Microsoft Works 6, separately and together, plus includes some introductory information on Windows, disks, and other basics. In this book, you discover how to create good stuff without having to completely understand what you're doing. More specifically, you find out about the following topics:

- Window basics (opening, closing, and painting them shut)
- Word processing (like food processing, only messier)
- Spreadsheets (for soft, comfortable naps on your spreadbed)
- Databases (for storing all your baseless data)
- Graphics (for charting uncharted waters and general doodling)

- ✔ Calendarification . . . calenderizing? (for using a calendar program)
- ✔ Web browsing (for shmoozing the Internet's World Wide Web)
- ✔ Newsgroups (for ranting about your pet peeves)
- ✔ E-mail (for sending and receiving messages and files)
- ✔ Mail merge of letters, envelopes, and labels (for doing your very own junk mail)

What's Different about This Book

Unlike software manuals, this book doesn't have to deliver a positive message about the software, so it doesn't breathlessly try to show you everything you could possibly do. Nor does it describe, as a manual does, every button and command. Instead, it focuses on the everyday things you have to do, gives you some background, points you toward shortcuts, and steers you around some of the stuff you probably don't need to know.

This book doesn't assume that you already know about software or the jargon that goes with it. Heck, it doesn't even assume that you know much about Windows. If you're already comfortable with your PC and Windows, that's great, and this book won't bore you to tears.

Foolish Assumptions

Apart from thinking that you are a brilliant and highly literate person (evidenced by the fact that you have bought or are considering buying this book), here's what I assume about you, the esteemed reader:

- ✔ Your PC has Microsoft Works 6 installed on it.
- ✔ You don't necessarily have great familiarity with Works, Windows, or mice, except perhaps that you know that it Works to put screens on Windows to keep mice out.
- ✔ If you're on a computer network, you have a computer and network guru available — an expert whom you can pay off in cookies or pizza to solve network problems.

Apart from that, you could be darn near anybody. I know of mathematicians, computer scientists, business people, and daycare center managers who use Works quite happily.

How to Use This Book

Nobody, but nobody, wants to sit down and read a book before they use their software. So don't. Instead, just look something up in the index or table of contents and "go to it." Don't just read, though. Follow along on your PC, using this book as a tour guide or road map. I use pictures where necessary, but I don't throw in a picture of everything because you have the pictures right there on your PC screen, and they're even in color.

If you're already fully fenestrated (Windows-cognizant), just march right along to the part of this book that covers your favorite Works program. Because Works is an integrated package of several programs, you'll find that they have a lot in common. If you're still figuring out what the heck all this stuff is on your computer screen, check out Part I — Survival Skills.

This is mainly a reference book, so you don't have to read it in any particular order. Within each part, though, the earlier chapters cover the more fundamental stuff. So if you want, you can just read the chapters in order (in each part) to go from the simple to the more complex.

How This Book Is Organized

Unlike many other computer books, which are, say, organized alphabetically by gadget, this book is organized by what you want to do. It doesn't, for example, explain each command as it appears on the menu. No, what this book does is break things down into the following useful parts.

Part 1: Survival Skills

If you're currently beating your head against Windows, files, directories, mice, or disks, or you're just trying to get under way with Works, Part I is the place to turn. In this part, you find out how to start Works, make your various windows behave, and get basic keyboard and mouse skills.

Part II: Doing Anything Instantly (Or Almost)

If you're going to survive today's fast-paced world, you have to know the shortcuts. In this part, you discover what Works tasks and other automated features — address books, letters, envelopes, labels, mail merge, brochures, calculations, databases, charts, graphics, reports — can do for you; let Microsoft do the hard stuff while you just fill in the particulars. Microsoft's designers help you deliver professional appearances.

Part III: Pursuing the Wily Word Processor

The one program that nearly everyone uses — the word processor — can also be rather elusive. In this part, you discover its wiles and ways. This part covers everything from basics (such as how to type and delete text) to subtle and elusive facts (such as where paragraph formatting hides) to essential bells and whistles (such as page numbers, tables, borders, lines, headers, footers, and footnotes).

Part IV: Setting Sail with Spreadsheets

Yo, ho, ho! Stay the mizzen! Batten down the poop deck! Here's how to put the wind in your spreadsheets and computerize your calculations. Even if your feelings for calculation are more "Oh, no" than "Yo, ho!," this part shows you how to have a nice cruise. From the basics of entering stuff in cells and navigating around, to the secrets of creating and copying formulas, to the subtleties of date and time arithmetic, Part IV is your port of call.

Part V: Doing Active Duty at the Database

As some old soldier once said, "There's the right way, there's the wrong way, and there's the Army way." Well, in Works, there's the Works database way. If you've never used a database before, this part gives you your basic training. If you've already done a hitch with other database software, this part helps you understand the slightly quirky Works way of doing and talking about databases. This part explores fields, records, data entry, and views, as well as making changes, filtering, and creating basic reports.

Part VI: Being Online and On Time

Part VI drags you kicking and screaming into the fast-paced 21st century, where if you're not on the Web, on e-mail, and on time, you're left in the dust. Here's where you discover how to communicate with the world with Outlook Express, browse the Web with Internet Explorer, and still remember your kid's birthday with Works Calendar.

Part VII: The Part of Tens

The Part of Tens? Why not the part of eights? Who knows, but thanks to the perfectly ridiculous act of fate that gave humans ten fingers, every *For Dummies* book has a Part of Tens. In this part, you find two chapters — "Ten Things NOT to Do" and "Ten Solutions to Common Problems" — that offer suggestions and recommendations that will make your life easier.

Icons Used in This Book

You would think we were in Czarist Russia from the popularity of icons in the computer world. Everything from toasters to VCRs has icons instead of words now, which is no doubt responsible for all those sleepy folks sticking bread into the tape slot at breakfast time. (That's not a problem at your house?) Anyway, not to be left behind, this book uses icons, too — only these icons are much cuter than the ones on your toaster. Here's what they mean:

If there's an easier or faster way to do something, or if there's something really cool, you'll find one of these target-thingies in the margin.

This icon reminds you that you shouldn't forget to remember something — something that was said earlier but is easily forgotten.

This icon cheerfully tells you of something that may go wrong, with consequences ranging from mild indigestion to weeping, wailing, and gnashing of teeth.

You won't see too much of Mr. Science (alias the *For Dummies* guy) in this book. When he does appear, he indicates that he has a little inside information on how things work that you just may want to know. But, if you ignore him, you won't be much worse off.

The One Shortcut Used in This Book

This book always uses genuine English words to describe how things work! Well, almost always (sorry). There's one important exception. When you see an instruction that looks something like this:

"Choose Blah➪Fooey from the menu bar"

it means, "Click Blah in the menu bar, and then click Fooey in the menu that drops down." (The underlined letters in the words indicate "shortcut keys" — but if terms such as *shortcut key, click, menu bar,* and *menu* mean nothing to you, that's okay — see Chapters 1 and 2.)

This sort of instruction crops up so often that if I didn't use that shortcut, you would be bored silly by Chapter 3 — and IDG Books would have to slaughter another forest's worth of trees to get the extra paper to print the book!

(You may also notice another very minor typographic peculiarity of this book. It capitalizes first letters of certain Works features, even though Works itself doesn't. That habit makes sentences like "Click the Center Across Connection check box" theoretically readable, whereas, "Click the Center across connection check box" would be utter gibberish.)

Where to Go from Here

If Works is already installed on your PC, you're probably already perplexed, annoyed, or intrigued by something you've seen. Look it up in the table of contents or the index and see what this book has to say about it. If you're just trying to start a document in Works, see Chapter 1. If you're trying to master some of the basics, such as controlling windows and moving around, see Chapter 2. Otherwise, drag a comfy chair up to your PC, bring along a plate of cheese for your mouse, and thumb through the book until you find something fun.

Part I
Survival Skills

The 5th Wave   By Rich Tennant

"This Corel color scheme is really going to give our presentation style!"

In this part . . .

The old recipe for bear stew read: "First, catch a bear." This was great advice as long as the reader was pretty well informed about bears. Otherwise, the prospective stewer became the stewee more often than not.

If you think that most computer books, like that recipe, leave out some pretty important fundamentals, Part I of this book is where you want to start. Here's where you can find out how to start Works; how to use and control the windows on your PC; how to create folders and save files on your computer; and all those other fundamentals that some other books assume that you know all about.

"Though this be madness, yet there is method in't."

—*Hamlet,* William Shakespeare

Chapter 1

Wanna Start Something?

Microsoft Works is quite a collection of stuff — just what you might expect if the folks at Microsoft told you that they were going to give you "the works." Your question, then, is "Where do I start?"

In this chapter, I show you the easiest ways to get going in Works, depending on how you like to work or exactly what you're trying to do. Microsoft's Task Launcher, which leads to any of Works' different tools, is the main starting place for most people. But I also show you how to open a Works tool directly from the Windows Start button and how to open a document if you're already using a Works tool.

Finding and Starting Works

First things first — you need to wake Works up and get it running. Finding and starting Works is especially easy if, during installation, a *shortcut* icon found its way to your PC screen (called the Windows *desktop*).

Look on your screen for an *icon* (a tiny picture) labeled *Microsoft Works* and double-click that icon. Figure 1-1 shows the Works shortcut icon and some other things that are probably on your screen.

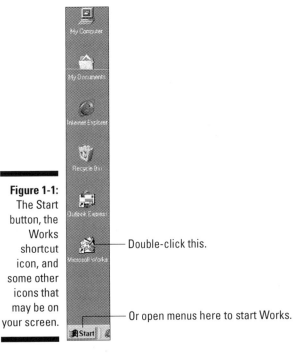

—— Double-click this.

—— Or open menus here to start Works.

Figure 1-1:
The Start button, the Works shortcut icon, and some other icons that may be on your screen.

If you can't find a Microsoft Works icon, here's how to find and start Works by using menus:

1. **Click the Start button (shown in Figure 1-1).**

2. **In the menu that springs up, point with your mouse pointer to <u>P</u>rograms and pause there.**

   Another menu appears next to the first one. (All such subsequent menus are called *submenus*.)

3. **Move your pointer horizontally until it's on the new submenu. Then move the pointer vertically to point to an icon labeled Microsoft Works.**

   Click that icon. Depending upon how Microsoft (in its finite wisdom) has decided to install Works, either another submenu appears, as shown in Figure 1-2, or Works launches, as shown in Figure 1-3.

   If Works launches at this point, you're done! Skip Step 4.

4. **Again, move your pointer horizontally until it's on the latest submenu. Then move your pointer down to point to another icon labeled Microsoft Works. Click that icon.**

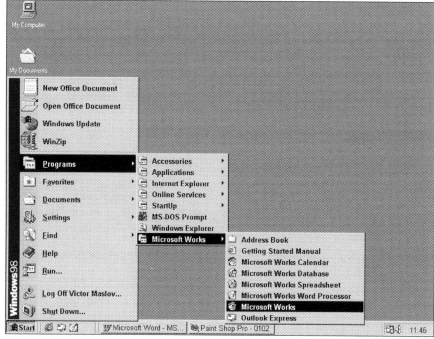

Figure 1-2:
Where
Works lurks:
menus
within
menus
within
menus.

Hey, you did it! You got Works running, and the Microsoft Works Task
Launcher window appears on your screen. You know that the window is part
of Works because the title Microsoft Works appears in text in the top line. (All
windows have a top line, called the *title bar,* which gives the name of the program or file that appears in that window.)

If you know which Works program you want to use, you can skip the Task
Launcher window and go right to your program. Use the Start menu as the
preceding steps describe. As you see in Figure 1-2, the final submenu lists
Microsoft Works Calendar, Database, Spreadsheet, and Word Processor. In
Step 4, choose one of those listings to go directly to the program you want.

You may discover that a tiny rectangle has appeared near the top of your
screen, sporting four tiny colored rectangles corresponding to Works features. That is the Works Gallery, and you don't really need it right now. In
Chapter 12, I explain how you click the Gallery and stuff drops down from it.
You can press Alt+F4 to make it go away.

The Works starting window is called the Task Launcher window because it
helps you get going. Specifically, it can find files you've worked on recently,
start up the program you need to create or work on a document, or create a
new document by using something called a *task* (an automated program).

You can call up the Task Launcher at any time while you're using one of the three main Works programs (the Works word processor, spreadsheet, or database program). Choose File⇨New from the menu bar at the top of the Works window you're using.

This book uses a shortcut way to describe choosing something from the *menu bar,* that list of words marching across your Works window just under the title bar. When this book says "Choose *Blah*⇨*Fooey* from the menu bar," it means "Click the word *Blah* in the menu bar; then click the word *Fooey* in the menu that drops down."

The Works Task Launcher window always gives you your choice of three ways to start working. Those three options (plus the option of taking a tour) appear in Figure 1-3. This figure shows the initial appearance of the Task Launcher; that is, the Home page that appears the very first time you start Works.

The three main ways to get started in Works from the Task Launcher window are as follows:

✔ **The Tasks option:** Not sure which program you want to use? Click this option to choose among predesigned documents (tasks) of various kinds, instead of choosing a program.

✔ **The Programs option:** Do you know which one of the main Works programs you want to use? Click this option.

✔ **The History option:** Do you already have a document on your PC that you want to open? Click this option to choose from a list of recently worked-on documents or to find any existing document that's on your PC.

(Another option listed on the Home page is the Take a Tour option. You probably won't choose this option more than once. Click this option to have Works give you a razzle-dazzle tour of its features. Because choosing Take a Tour is not really a way to do any work, I don't refer to this option again in the book.)

The Tasks, Programs, and History options are the ones you'll normally choose to do your work. You may click the words Tasks, Programs, and History in either of the two places that they appear in Figure 1-3: along the top of the window (in a horizontal list called the *menu bar*) or in big type in the center of the Home page. (You can return to the Home page at any time by clicking Home in the menu bar, but you don't really need to because the Tasks, Programs, and History options are always available to you on the menu bar.)

After you click one of these three options, the Task Launcher window changes its face! At that point, it displays one of three pages of the Task Launcher (Tasks, Programs, or History), described in the upcoming sections.

Now showing, the Home page

Choose which page to start from

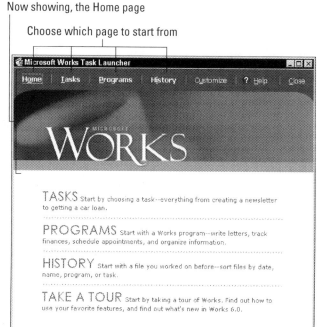

Figure 1-3:
The Task
Launcher's
menu bar
and the
Home page
give you
several
ways to get
started.

The page that you begin on, the one shown in Figure 1-3, is the Home page. To return here, click Home on the menu bar (along the top of any Task Launcher page). During the normal, workaday use of Works, you never see this page again. You always return to the Tasks, Programs, or History page.

To quit the Task Launcher altogether, click Close on the menu bar. When you later restart the Task Launcher, you return to whatever page was displayed (say, the Programs page) when you last closed this window.

Starting from the Programs page

Click Programs on the Task Launcher menu bar to go to the Programs page. A list of programs appears on the left side of the Programs page. (If a scroll bar appears to the right of that list, click the down arrow at the bottom of the bar to see even more programs.) Click a program in that list to see a brief description of what the program does. When you click, a list of the Tasks that use that program appears on the right side of the page.

After you choose a program, you can start it up in one of two ways:

- ✔ **Create a blank document:** To start a blank document in your chosen program (or just plain start the program), click the blue, underlined text with an icon next to it. (That text may read, for example, Start A Blank Spreadsheet or Start A Blank Word Processor Document or Start A Blank Database.) For more details on each program, see that program's section in this book. For an overview of these programs, see Chapter 2.

- ✔ **Create a predesigned document:** To have a Works wizard or template create a particular document for you, look at the list of available documents (tasks) on the right side of the Programs page. The list of tasks changes as you choose different programs. You can find the same tasks on the Tasks page of the Task Launcher, but here they appear with the program that they use.

If you can't see the entire name of a Task (if it ends in an ellipsis), pause your mouse cursor over it and the full name appears.

Confusingly, some programs listed down the left side of the Programs page may not really be Works programs! (I cover several of them in this book, anyway.) These programs may have come with Works as part of Works Suite (if that's what you have), or someone may have installed them previously. The Works Task Launcher links you to them, but they are their own separate programs. If the program name does not begin with the word *Works,* it's not really a Works program, and you should consider getting the *For Dummies* book on that program.

Here are a few of the programs you're likely to find listed:

- ✔ **Works Word Processor** is for typing and creating documents with text and pictures.

- ✔ **Works Spreadsheet** is for doing all kinds of calculations.

- ✔ **Works Database** is for keeping track of information.

- ✔ **Works Calendar** is a program that keeps track of your appointments.

- ✔ **Works Portfolio** is a program for collecting and organizing photo files and other images, documents, or sounds on your PC.

- ✔ **Word** is Microsoft's full-featured word processor. It is *not* the same program as the *Works* word processor. In fact, if Word appears, the Works Word Processor may not even be installed on your PC! (Look for it in the list of programs.) If the Works Word Processor does not appear in the list of programs, you probably have Works Suite. You can use Word as your word processor, and it's similar (but not identical) to the instructions you find in this book.

✔ **MSN** is The Microsoft Network, Microsoft's entry into the very competitive Internet Service Provider industry of businesses that connect you to the Internet.

✔ **The Address Book** is an accessory program that comes with Windows, which Microsoft hopes you will use to store your addresses.

✔ **Internet Explorer** is Microsoft's Web browser for viewing and interacting with the World Wide Web.

✔ **Outlook Express** is for sending e-mail and participating in newsgroups on the Internet.

✔ **FoneSync, Windows CE device synchronization, Palm compatible device synchronization** — or anything to do with *sync,* or synchronization — have to do with moving data (say, people's addresses) between your PC and some other device that you may or may not own (such as a cell phone).

Starting from the Tasks page

Tasks (also sometimes called *TaskWizards* or just plain *wizards*) are automated programs that automatically begin to build the document that you need. Tasks are great for keeping things simple, if you don't mind Works making some of your decisions for you. You can begin a Task only from the Tasks or Programs pages of the Works Task Launcher: Click Tasks on the menu bar of the Task Launcher window to go to the Tasks page.

Lots of Tasks await your bidding in Works, so to make finding them easier, the Tasks page lists them by category. (The Programs page lists them by program.) Categories include Letters and Labels, Newsletters and Flyers, Household Management, and more, listed down the left side of the Task Launcher window. To see more Task categories, click the down arrow at the bottom of the scroll bar to the right of that column. Take these steps to choose and launch a Task from the Tasks page:

1. **To see what Tasks are in a category (in the column on the left side of the window), click the category.**

   The Tasks in that category appear on the right of the window.

2. **To see a description of any of the Tasks listed, click its name in the center of the window.**

   A description appears on the right of the window, with a Start button.

3. **To start the Task, click the Start button that appears on the right side of the window.**

Understanding files, disks, folders, and directories

Here's an overview of the fundamental atoms and molecules that make up that mysterious substance called software:

✔ *Files* are how your computer stores programs, your documents, and other forms of information. Each file has a *filename,* given either by you or by the program that created the file, so that you and the PC can both identify it. In Windows, when you see a file listed somewhere, you can almost always double-click the file to open it. In many (but not all) places where files are listed, you can also delete a file, copy or cut and paste it somewhere else, or rename it by right-clicking it and choosing from the *context menu* that drops down. See *Windows 98 For Dummies* (or *Microsoft Windows Me Millennium Edition For Dummies*) for help.

✔ A *hard drive* is where your PC keeps files that live permanently in your PC. You can also keep copies of files on a removable diskette (a little flat plastic thing that is often simply called a disk), also called a 3½ floppy by Windows. Diskettes are used either for backup (in case your hard drive breaks) or to give files to other people. The diskette drives (the places you put diskettes) are called A: and sometimes B:. (You may have only A:.) The hard drive is called C:. If you have a second hard drive or a CD-ROM drive, this drive is usually called D:. (Why the colons? It's ancient PC tradition.) If your computer is on a network, you can store things on hard drives on someone else's computer; talk to the person who manages your network in order to find out how you can do this task. To see what hard drives and floppies you have available, look for an icon labeled *My Computer* on your Windows desktop and double-click it.

✔ *Folders* help you organize your files into groups. Folders are analogous to file folders in a file cabinet, so they appear as yellow file folders. These computer file folders (sometimes called directories or subdirectories) have names, too. Some folders are created and named automatically by Windows — other folders you must create and name yourself. Works lets you create a new folder at the same time you save a file so that you can easily organize your documents. Folders are usually within folders within folders on your PC — a hierarchy of folders. To go up the hierarchy is to open the folder that contains the currently open folder. To see the folders on your C: drive, double-click the My Computer icon on your Windows desktop; then, in the window that opens up, double-click the symbol labeled *C:*. To see what's in a folder, double-click it.

✔ Whenever you save your work in a file, you give your file a *filename.* You can give files nice, readable file names with spaces and punctuation in them, such as Letter To Mom About Cookies. (You can't, however, use any of these characters: * ? " < > | : / \.)

✔ Files also come in different types, depending on the program that created them. The type is indicated by an *extension* added to a file's name. An extension can be up to three characters long, preceded by a period. The extension is added by the program that you use, such as Works. When you click a file to open it, the extension tells Windows what program to use to open the file. When you save a file, you may, if you like, specify the extension yourself, but in general, letting Works (or whatever program you are using) take care of specifying the extension is best.

When you want to tell your computer in detail about a specific file in a specific location, you can put all the information together into one string of characters called a *path*. You start with the disk drive; then you add the directory (folder) name, any subdirectories' names (folders within that folder), the filename, and finally the file extension. To separate each piece of information, you type a special slash mark called the *backslash* (\). (The backslash key is usually near the Backspace key.) A path is written something like this:

```
c:\letters\mom\cookies.wps
```

A Task starts up a program and builds a document in that program. What program? Check the icon that appears next to the description in Step 2. For example, the Task for *letters* creates a document in a word processor program. If Microsoft Word is installed on your system, the Word *W* may appear; if so, that task will launch Word. If the icon depicts a pencil scribbling on paper, the Works Word Processor will appear.

After you start a Task, a document appears in one of Works' programs. A wizard screen may also appear on top of the program window and show you various alternative styles of documents you can choose. Make the choices the wizard gives you and — *poof!* — you have a document. See Chapter 5 for more about tasks.

Tasks generally just get you started — you still have to customize the document. Making changes can sometimes be tricky, so check out some of the specific task chapters in Part II. You may also want to refer to the chapter on the particular program that you find yourself in, such as the spreadsheet program.

Starting from the History page

If you have recently created or worked on a document in Works, Works remembers. When you get the urge to return to one of your recently created or recently worked-on documents, click the History option in the Works Task Launcher. The History page appears, displaying a list of documents, as shown in Figure 1-4.

To choose a document from this list, just click the document name. The document opens in its own window. If you see the same document listed more than once, you can click any of the listings. By listing the document several times, Works is just trying to help you remember your history of working on the document. All of the choices lead to the same document: the one you most recently created. They don't lead to different versions.

Click document name
to choose

Click column headings to sort

Click arrow to change sorting direction

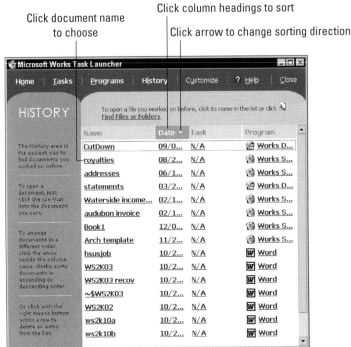

Figure 1-4:
History in
the making.

This History page offers several options. You can sort the list of documents by name (alphabetically), by date, or by which task or program created it. Just click the word Name, Date, Task, or Program in the column heading. To reverse the order of sorting, click the name again or the arrow next to it. You can also clear the history by clicking Customize in the menu bar and then clicking the Clear History button in the dialog box that appears.

If you are working in a Works program, not in the Task Launcher, you can find a short list of documents most recently worked on by that program. Click File in the Works menu bar. Click one of the documents listed at the bottom of the menu to open it.

Finding Documents Not Listed under History

It won't take too long before you're knee-deep in documents and folders, and you may need a little help finding the document that you want. Your buddy, the Task Launcher, can come to your rescue. Open the History page and then click Find Files or Folders.

The Find: All Files dialog box springs into view. The Find dialog box may look familiar to you if you have used the Find program in Windows — they are both the same program! (You get the Find dialog box directly from Windows by using Start⇨Find⇨Files Or Folders from the Windows Taskbar.) For the full, gory details of using the Find dialog box, see *Windows 98 For Dummies* or *Microsoft Windows Me Millennium Edition For Dummies* by Andy Rathbone (IDG Books Worldwide, Inc.).

The Find dialog box has multiple pages, sort of like the Task Launcher has, but in dialog boxes these pages are called tabs. They stick up like the tabs on file folders, and you click a tab to select it. Here are the things to enter, depending on what you know about the file you seek:

- **Enter a location:** Choose the Name & Location tab and make sure to select the Include Subfolders check box.

  Click the down arrow for the Find In drop-down list. If you don't know where (on what disk drive) the file lives on your computer, choose My Computer. If you think the file is on your computer's hard drive, choose the selection labeled *(C:)*. If you know what disk or folder the file is in, either choose it from the list that appears or click the Browse button to open that disk or folder. Click the + symbols displayed to access folders. When you find the folder you think your file is in, click it and then click OK.

- **If you know part of the name:** Choose the Name & Location tab.

  First, press the Delete key to delete what's there and type as much of the name as you remember in the Named text box. After you've typed one or more characters, you can substitute the * (asterisk) character for any other part that you don't remember. So, for example, if you're looking for an invoice, and you know that the file begins with *inv,* type **inv***. To look for only Works documents, add a Works three-letter extension to the end: `.wps` for a Works word-processing file (`.doc` for a Word file), `.xlr` for a Works 6.0 spreadsheet file (`.wks` for earlier versions of Works' spreadsheet files), or `.wdb` for a database file.

- **If you know any text that the file or folder contains:** Choose the Name & Location tab.

  Type the text into the Containing text box. This selection is *really* useful because you don't have to remember anything about the document's name or location! If you wrote a letter to Mr. Smith about condominiums, just enter either Smith or condominium into the Containing text box. Try to choose a unique word or phrase.

- **If you know roughly when the file or folder was created, last modified, or last accessed (opened):** Choose the Date tab.

  First, click Find All Files. Then click the drop-down menu and select Modified, Created, or Last Accessed. These terms refer to what action was taken on that date: when the file was last modified, when it was created, or when you last opened the file. Then specify the date, either by clicking the selection Between and then double-clicking and typing over the dates shown, or by clicking During The Previous and specifying a number of preceding months or days.

✔ **If you know the type of the file or folder:** Choose the Advanced tab.

Click the down arrow next to the Of Type box and select a file or folder type from the drop-down list that appears. (*Type* refers to the program that handles this kind of file on your PC.) Listings for types of Microsoft Works files begin with the words *Microsoft Works*.

✔ **After you have specified something on any or all of these tabs:** Click the Find Now button.

A list of documents appears at the bottom of the Find dialog box — just double-click the document you want in order to open it!

Clearing the Task Launcher from Your Screen

The Task Launcher is a separate program whose only function in life is to help you find files and start up the task or program you need. It doesn't do much on its own. After you have started working in a Works program window, you probably don't need the Task Launcher very often. Yet it stays on your screen, adding to the clutter and consuming some of your PC's computing resources. You can ignore it, if you like.

My suggestion for dealing with the Task Launcher (after you are done using it) is to minimize it to a button on the Windows taskbar. Click the tiny minus sign (–) button at the far upper-right corner of the Task Launcher window. The window shrinks to a Microsoft Works Task Launcher button on the Windows taskbar. To expand the Task Launcher window again, click that button.

You may also close the Task Launcher altogether. Click Close on the menu bar near the top right of the Task Launcher window.

When you are using the Works word processor, spreadsheet, or database program, you can always bring the Task Launcher back by choosing File⇨New. Note that pressing Ctrl+N (listed as a shortcut for File⇨New) does *not* open the Task Launcher, but opens a new, blank document in a separate window, in whatever program you're using.

Opening Documents When You're Using a Program

While you are running a Works program, such as the word processor or spreadsheet, you can open a document from within that program. You don't need the Task Launcher.

You can also open a document directly from Windows. First, you open a window to the folder where your document file is, and then you double-click that file. For example, double-click the My Computer icon to see the various hard drives; then double-click the C: hard drive icon to look in the hard drive, and so on. Look for files that say Microsoft Works in the Type column. Double-click your file when you see it, and the correct Works program launches, displaying your file.

If you are already using one of Works' three main programs (the word processor, spreadsheet, or database program), choose File⇨Open from the menu bar of that program's window or press Ctrl+O (that's the letter *O*, not the number *0*). This procedure takes you to the Open dialog box.

Browsing through the folders in the Open dialog box

The Open dialog box shows you the contents of a folder. It displays the name of this open folder at the top of the dialog box in the area marked Look In.

- ✔ To open any document you see, double-click it (or click it and click the Open button).

- ✔ To open any folder you see, double-click it.

- ✔ To open the folder that contains the currently displayed folder, click the Up One Level button at the top of the dialog box. Your PC has folders within folders within folders (a folder *hierarchy*). The top of the hierarchy is the hard drive (say, C:) containing those folders.

- ✔ To go more than one level up the folder hierarchy, click the down-arrow button to the right of the Look In box. Then click any folder in the list that appears.

- ✔ To look on a diskette (or to look at the very top of the folder hierarchy on your hard drive), click the down-arrow button to the right of the Look In box. In the list that appears, click hard drive C: for your hard drive and click A: or B: for your diskette. (D: is typically your CD-ROM drive if you have one, but you probably won't find any Works documents there.)

When you first start Works, it opens a folder called My Documents and shows you what's inside this folder. The My Documents folder is the same one you see on your Windows desktop, which you can open by double-clicking it.

Looking for different types of documents in the Open dialog box

If you can't find the file you want in the Open dialog box, you may be using the wrong Works program. Each Works program can open only certain types of files. File types are indicated by an icon that precedes the name.

For example, if you're using the word processor program when you choose File⇨Open to get the Open dialog box, you can't open database files. Works programs normally do not open anything but their own file types.

To open a file of a different type, first return to the Task Launcher window, open the right program from the Programs menu, and then choose File⇨Open. Or click the file on the History page, and Works automatically uses the correct program to open it.

If you want to try to open a file created by a different program (maybe somebody gave you a file), click the down arrow to the right of the Files of Type box (in the Open dialog box) and select one of the other types from the list that appears. If you are trying to open a file created by another program, your best choice is All Files (*.*). (To see All Files, you may have to press the up arrow on your keyboard while looking at the list, or scroll up that list.)

Chapter 2

Wrestling with Windows and Files

*I*f cars had as many gadgets and doodads as PC software does, we would all take the bus. Works tries to be helpful about all of its doodads, but sometimes even the help can be a little bewildering. In this chapter, I try to point out the stuff you need for day-to-day survival, including some basics of Works, Windows, and files that nobody may have pointed out to you before.

Understanding the Inner Workings of Works

Works is made up of smaller programs. When Microsoft built Works, the programmers put in a bunch of programs that they thought most folks would likely need at some time. No matter how you start a document — even if you start it by using a Task — you are using one of these programs. These programs include

- A word processor for writing letters and other documents
- A spreadsheet for creating tables and doing calculations
- A database program for storing large amounts of information and helping you find it easily
- A calendar program for helping you manage events in your life

Works also hooks you up with several programs that aren't specifically Works programs but are frequently found on PCs, including Internet Explorer, Outlook Express, and others.

In addition, Works contains what I call *tools,* which are mini-programs that don't get separate billing but can help you do various tasks:

- A charting tool for making charts out of the information in spreadsheets and tables
- A drawing tool: Microsoft Draw
- A tool — WordArt — for doing artistic things to words and letters
- A bunch of other little tools, such as a spell checker and a thesaurus

The word processor, spreadsheet, and database programs are what I call the Big Three; the others are sort of helper programs, like elves. I talk about each of the Big Three and the various elves in detail in Parts II through IV. Right now, I show you what the programs have in common.

Like the tools in a Swiss Army Knife, you usually have only one program in Works open at a time, although nothing has to stop you from having several programs open at once. Sometimes, having more than one program open at a time is helpful. You may, for example, want to create a spreadsheet (using the spreadsheet program) to be inserted into a word processor document that you're working on. You still use only one program at a time, but you want to be able to switch back and forth between them quickly and easily. (Read the section, "Controlling the Windows of Works," later in this chapter for more information on switching from one document to another.) Each program or tool is a specialist: It works only on its own kind of thing. The word processing program is for working on text documents; the spreadsheet program is for tables and spreadsheets.

The things that these programs work on are all called *documents* by Microsoft, which therefore forces me to discuss word processor documents, spreadsheet documents, database documents, and so on. What a bore. Most of the time in this book, I rebel and call the spreadsheet documents *spreadsheets* and the database documents *databases.* Radical, huh?

As with the tools in the Swiss Army Knife (and I promise to drop this analogy soon), the individual programs in Works are not the best — in the sense of being the most fully featured — of their kind. Just like a professional carpenter probably prefers a solid screwdriver to the folding one in the knife, a professional financial analyst would probably prefer a more fully featured spreadsheet program (such as Excel, Quattro Pro, or Lotus 1-2-3) to the one in Works. Nonetheless, the Works programs are perfectly fine for most of what the vast majority of people want to do, and they cost less and need less memory and disk space on your computer. In a way, Works' programs are the best because they don't have a lot of extraneous features that you don't need and that would only trip you up.

Because all these programs are part of the same Works package, they look and work very much alike. When you go to print a spreadsheet, for example, you do it almost exactly the same way that you would print a word processing document. Certain things may be different, but the similarities are very helpful. You don't have to relearn the basic commands for each program.

Controlling the Windows of Works

When you start working on a document, you're often confronted with a window full of confusing stuff. What's more, the window is probably an inconvenient size and is covering up something important on your screen.

Works' windows behave like those of every other program that runs under Windows. You can refer to *Windows 98 For Dummies* (IDG Books Worldwide, Inc.) for the full gory details on handling windows, but the basics are here.

Here are three important points to remember about using Works windows:

- ✔ The Task Launcher gets its own window.

- ✔ Every document you open gets its own window.

- ✔ Each window gets a button on the Windows taskbar — the thing that has the Start button on it. Clicking that button shrinks the window down to nothing, but doesn't close the window. Clicking the button again expands the window to its previous size.

At first, the windows don't fill your screen, so they're hard to read and use. You can enlarge them if you like, or you can shrink them to a button on the Windows taskbar. (Shrinking takes them out of the way when you're not using them.) Or, you can close them (get rid of them) altogether when you're not using them.

To shrink, enlarge, or move a window, belly up to the title bar. Every window in Windows has a bar (called the title bar) at the top that describes what that window is all about. The title bar contains (in the right corner) buttons useful for controlling the size of your program window, as shown in Figure 2-1.

Figure 2-1:
The Works
title bar
heads your
Works
windows
and provides
tiny buttons
to control
window size.

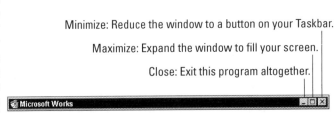

Minimize: Reduce the window to a button on your Taskbar.

Maximize: Expand the window to fill your screen.

Close: Exit this program altogether.

Refer to Figure 2-1 to check out how to minimize, maximize, and close a window. Here are a few other things you can do with your program window:

- ✓ **To shrink a maximized window:** When you expand the window to its maximum, Windows replaces the maximize button with a restore button.

  Click this guy to restore your Works window to an intermediate size.

- ✓ **To enlarge/reduce the window's width or height:** Click an edge or corner of the window (where your cursor turns into a double-headed arrow) and drag the edge or corner in any direction indicated by the arrow heads.

- ✓ **To restore the window after it has been shrunk to a button on the taskbar:** Click that button on the taskbar.

- ✓ **To move the window:** Click the title bar, but not any of the buttons or the Works icon at the far left. Hold down the mouse button, drag the window where you want it, and release the mouse button.

You can also control the Works window by clicking the Works icon at the far left of the title bar and then clicking a selection in the menu that drops down, including Minimize, Close, and Maximize.

If you open more than one window at a time, your screen may get a little more confusing. Look at Figure 2-2 to see the Works Task Launcher window plus a window for each program that is open simultaneously.

Your screen is less confusing if you don't have several windows open at the same time. The best approach is to minimize or close windows you don't need at the moment.

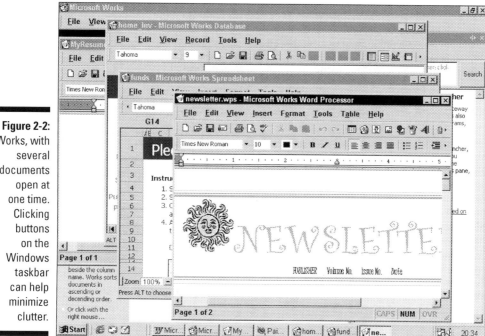

Figure 2-2:
Works, with
several
documents
open at
one time.
Clicking
buttons
on the
Windows
taskbar
can help
minimize
clutter.

Sometimes you want more than one window open. You may want to cut and paste between documents, for instance. In that instance, keep the following in mind:

✔ **Only one window can be active at a time:** The *active window* is the one with a title bar that is in some exotic designer color (such as blue); you find it on top of the other windows. The active window is the one you are currently typing in or giving commands to.

✔ **To make a window active:** Click anywhere on the document, or click its button on the Windows taskbar.

When you first open any Works window, a help panel appears on the right side. The help panel can be useful, but most of the time it just clutters things up. (I eliminated it in the windows of Figure 2-2.) For more on the help panel, see the section, "Getting — and getting rid of — Help," later in this chapter.

Zooming

"If you can't raise the bridge, lower the water." This saying has served many people well over the years, despite the fact that it is complete gibberish. Continuing in this vein, an alternative to making a window bigger (so that you can see more) is to make the document text look smaller — known as zooming out. (Or is it zooming in? Never can remember, but never mind; it's zooming, anyway.)

The important thing to realize is that zooming has absolutely no effect on your document. Zooming just makes the text look bigger or smaller. Your document prints the same. Here's a way to zoom that works in every one of Works' programs: Choose View⇨Zoom from the menu bar. The Zoom dialog box zooms into view and lets you choose a magnification expressed as a percentage — the smaller the percentage, the smaller the document. You can either click one of the standard percentages listed there, such as 75%, or type a percentage in the Custom box. Click the OK button in this dialog box when you're done.

In the spreadsheet and database programs, click the minuscule + or – buttons next to the Zoom button at the bottom-left corner of your document window. The + button enlarges your document; the – button shrinks it.

Taking a Stroll in Your Document

The smoothest way to get around in your document is to slide! At the side and bottom of each document window are scroll bars (which I think should be called sliders) that you use to move the document around within the document window.

To see farther up or down in your document, use the vertical scroll bar, as shown in Figure 2-3:

- ✔ **To slide the document up or down in little increments:** Click the arrows at the top and bottom.

- ✔ **To slide the document with a lot more speed:** Click and drag the box in the middle of the scroll bar up or down. (Or click above or below the box.) The position of this box on the scroll bar gives you a rough idea of how far down in the document you are. If the box is large — nearly filling the scroll bar — that means that most of your document is visible in the window.

- ✔ **To slide the document horizontally (in case your window isn't wide enough to display the entire width of the document):** A horizontal scroll bar at the bottom of the window works the same way as the vertical one.

Another easy way to get around in your documents is to navigate. For this technique, use the navigation keys on your keyboard: namely, the arrow keys plus the Page Up, Page Down, Home, and End keys. The navigation keys move the blinking cursor (that defines where editing takes place) around your document, keeping the cursor visible in the window. The arrow keys move one line or character at a time, but the Page Up and Page Down keys move one window's worth at a time.

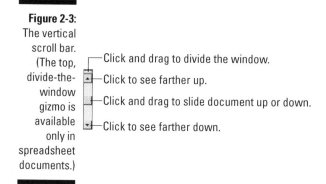

Figure 2-3:
The vertical
scroll bar.
(The top,
divide-the-
window
gizmo is
available
only in
spreadsheet
documents.)

Click and drag to divide the window.

Click to see farther up.

Click and drag to slide document up or down.

Click to see farther down.

If you use the scroll bars to move around in your document, make sure that you click in the new location before you begin typing or editing. The scroll bars move your viewpoint around, but the scroll bars do not move the blinking cursor that defines where the editing action takes place. Before you press a key, put that blinking cursor where you want it by clicking where you want to type or edit. Otherwise, your viewpoint snaps back to wherever you left the cursor as soon as you press a key.

Ordering from the Menu Bar

The main way to place your orders in Works is to use the menu bar, as shown in Figure 2-4. Click any of the words in the menu bar, and a menu of commands drops down. Then click one of these commands to execute it. Yet another menu may appear, or a dialog box may spring up.

The sequential process of choosing things from menus is pretty boring to write about (and even more boring to read about) without using some kind of shortcut notation. I could say, "Click File on the menu bar; then click Save on the menu that drops down," but this kind of talk would drive you batty after awhile. So in this book (and in *For Dummies* books in general), I say the same thing using this kind of notation:

Choose File⇨Save.

Just like the menu in your local sandwich shop, a large portion of the Works menu bar always appears the same. This regularity is true no matter what program you use — the menu bar for each program appears very much the same. However, each of the words on this menu bar leads to a set of commands, some of which change with different programs. So, if the commands on a menu ever look unfamiliar, you probably have different types of documents open in Works, and you switched from one type to another. This book goes into detail on the more important differences in the program-specific Parts III through V.

Dots indicate that a dialog box follows.

Underline indicates Alt + Key option.

Menu bar

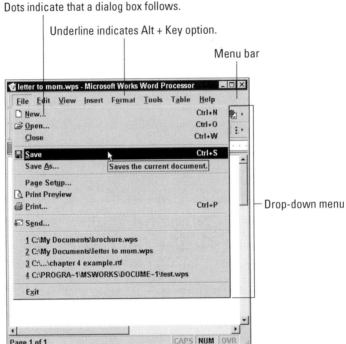

Drop-down menu

Figure 2-4:
Clicking a
word in the
menu bar
gives you a
menu of
yummy
commands.

Generally speaking, here's what you can do in each of these menu bar selections:

✔ **File:** Open, close, and save documents; set up the page layout; print.

✔ **Edit:** Copy text and numbers, move them, find them, replace them; also (and very important) undo whatever change you just made to the document.

✔ **View:** See things differently or otherwise change the way the screen looks (but without changing the document itself), such as by turning the toolbar on or off.

✔ **Insert:** Plug stuff into your document, such as illustrations from another document or file.

✔ **Format:** Change the appearance of text and numbers and how they line up.

✔ **Tools**: Use the spell checker or other little helpers to the Big Three tools.

✔ **Help:** Read help information about Works or turn the Help feature on or off.

Part I of this book deals with the commands that remain the same in each of these menus. For anything in these menus unique to a particular program, check out that program's part later in this book.

Keep your eye on the bottom line!

If, before you choose any of the commands in a drop-down menu, you would like a reminder of what the command does, keep your eye on the command as your cursor touches it. Don't click with your mouse; just highlight the command. You see a little box with a reminder of what that command does. Click to choose the command that you need.

Command Shortcuts Using the Keyboard

If you don't want to take the time to order from a menu, use a shortcut. Some commands in the drop-down menus have a key combination (such as Ctrl+S) shown on the same line. This means that you don't even have to make that menu drop down in order to use that command. Ctrl+S, for example, saves your document as a file. Just press the key combination: Hold down the Ctrl key, in this example, and then press the S key. You can find these shortcuts easily in a list in the drop-down menu whenever you click a menu selection. Refer to Figure 2-4 for examples.

If you're more comfortable using a keyboard than a mouse, Windows gives you another way to use menus. See all those underlined letters in the menu bar? Press the Alt key and the underlined letter key on the menu bar, and the drop-down menu springs up cheerfully (so to speak) under that word. To choose a command from the drop-down menu, just press the letter without the Alt key.

The Ctrl+key combinations work immediately, without going through the menu. The Alt+key combinations enable you to pick items off whatever menu is currently displayed so that you use the key combinations sequentially. For example, use Alt+F to open the File menu followed by S to save a file.

Toiling with Toolbars

The Works menu bar is lovely, full of genuine English words and lots of drop-down menus. Although the Works menu bar is quite nice, it's just a tad tedious to use sometimes. You click the menu bar, you click the drop-down menu, you click the dialog box . . . pretty soon your eyes glaze over and you just sit there and click . . . click . . . click — until you are found and revived, days later, by the Mouse-Induced-Stupor (MIS) Patrol.

After having had to resuscitate a few afflicted colleagues, the engineers at Microsoft did something about this grave problem. They employed the classic engineering technique of going to a bar. In this case, they went to a tool bar (known in Works parlance as the toolbar).

Toolbars, as shown in Figure 2-5, are lines of buttons, just under the menu bar; the toolbars are as full of icons as a Russian museum. The spreadsheet and database tools have only one toolbar. The word processor program has two.

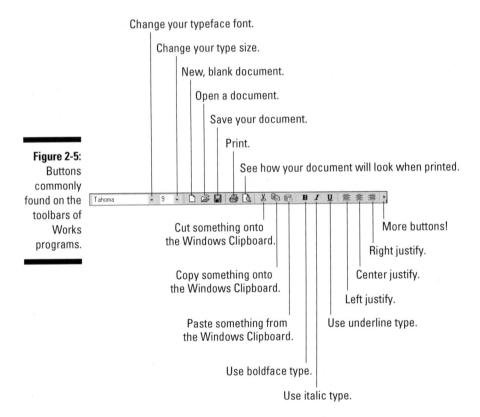

Change your typeface font.

Change your type size.

New, blank document.

Open a document.

Save your document.

Print.

See how your document will look when printed.

Figure 2-5:
Buttons commonly found on the toolbars of Works programs.

Cut something onto the Windows Clipboard.

More buttons!

Right justify.

Copy something onto the Windows Clipboard.

Center justify.

Left justify.

Paste something from the Windows Clipboard.

Use underline type.

Use boldface type.

Use italic type.

If you find the toolbars aesthetically displeasing or just plain don't want them around, you can click View⇨Toolbar to remove a toolbar from the screen. If you later decide that you want it back, do the same thing. Each icon is a shortcut alternative to some command in the menu bar — a command that the folks at Microsoft thought that you may use a lot. Just click the icon once, and stuff happens: You save a file, for example, or you print something out. No more click, click, click. Just click.

When commands go gray

One aspect of Windows that occasionally gives new users gray hair is when certain commands gray out in a drop-down menu or in a dialog box.

When commands are grayed out, they are temporarily inactive, not applicable, or otherwise unavailable for comment. Generally, you won't care, but sometimes, you really, really want Works to execute that command. Well, to do so, you have to figure out why that command is currently deactivated. Why doesn't it apply in this case? Generally, a command is grayed out for one of two reasons. One, the action that command is responsible for can't be done at that time; and two, the item the command relates to just isn't present in your document (or in the area of your document that you have selected).

The selection of icons in the toolbar changes a bit. Some icons appear in all of the Big Three programs of Works; others appear only for a particular program. For example, the Save icon appears in each toolbar because you always need to be able to save your work. On the other hand, the Insert Record icon appears only with the database program. That icon makes no sense anywhere else. The toolbar is different in each program.

The icons that appear most frequently are shown in Figure 2-5.

If you forget what an icon is supposed to do, just move your mouse cursor over it (don't click). A tiny square appears with a one-word description of the icon's function.

For more about the editing, formatting, and file operations that these buttons actually do, see Chapters 3 and 4.

Dealing with Dialog Boxes

Dialog boxes tend to crop up all over the place. On menus and submenus, a command that ends in three dots (. . .) warns you that you're about to have to deal with a dialog box. Those three dots are called an ellipsis. The dialog box's purpose in life is to let you specify important details about the command, such as what to name something you want to store and where to put it.

On the surface, dialog boxes look like windows, but you can't shrink or expand dialog boxes. (You can drag them around by their title bars, though, if they are in the way.) Internally, dialog boxes can look like darn near anything. Here, in Figure 2-6, is an example from Works. Fortunately, certain internal gadgets (I prefer the technical name, "thingies") reappear regularly.

Text box: Type something in.

List box (or scroll box):
You get lots of choices.

Explanation button

Drop-down list box:
Click the arrow for more.

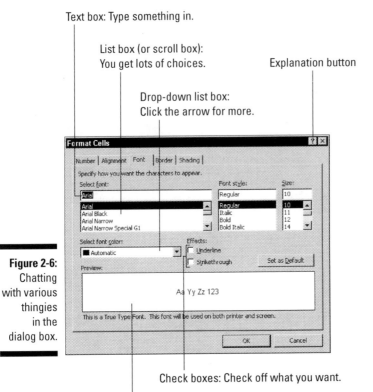

Figure 2-6:
Chatting
with various
thingies
in the
dialog box.

Check boxes: Check off what you want.

Preview window: Shows the effects of your changes
before you apply them.

The following is how this dialog box stuff works. Don't try to memorize all the names and distinctions of the thingies. I certainly don't use the names any more than I have to. Just refer back here if you get confused about a dialog box.

✔ **Explanation button (question mark):** Click this button in the title bar, and a question mark attaches itself to your mouse cursor. "Gee, how useful!" you say. But wait — the excitement is yet to come: If you then click a button or setting in the dialog box, you see an explanation of that item. Click in a plain area of the dialog box to clear the explanation off the screen.

✔ **Text box:** You can type something in a text box, but often a quicker way (such as clicking something in a list box immediately underneath the text box) is available to accomplish the same task. When you open a text box, it usually has something in it as a suggestion. You can delete that suggestion by pressing the Delete key, or you can change the suggestion by clicking anywhere in the box to get a typing cursor. Type new text or press the Backspace or Delete keys to erase stuff. Do not press the Enter key when you're done typing unless you don't need to do anything else in this dialog box!

✓ **List or scroll box:** List boxes or scroll boxes show you a list of choices. Click one of the choices, and your choice generally appears in a text box above the list. Double-click one, and the computer not only chooses that item, but it also tells the dialog box, "I'm done — go and do your thing!" If more text is in the list than fits in the box, a scroll bar appears alongside the list box. (Such scroll bars work like the scroll bars in your document window.)

✓ **Drop-down list box:** A drop-down list box is like a list box, but you have to act to make it appear. To make a drop-down list box reveal itself, click the down-pointing arrow alongside the box.

✓ **Check boxes:** Check boxes are like tax forms, but even more fun. Check off one or more things by clicking them or the box next to them. A check mark appears when an item is selected. Click the item (or the box next to it) again to deselect it.

✓ **Option buttons:** These buttons enable you to click only one thing in the list. The center of the button appears black when the button has been selected (if it's black, it's on).

✓ **Command buttons:** The most important command button is OK. Click the OK button when you're done with a task. If you want to back out of a command, click Cancel. Other command buttons may take you to yet more dialog boxes.

When I discuss a feature in a dialog box (say, a check box labeled `No header on first page`), I use initial capital letters for the feature's name, or else it appears in `a special font like this`. For instance, you'll see *Click on the No Header on First Page check box* or *Click the box labeled* `No header on first page`, rather than *Click on the No header on first page check box*, which looks like utter gibberish.

Pinky finger alert!

Touch typists, keep your pinky fingers under control. Pinky fingers tend to want to press the Enter key or the Esc key, either of which can make a dialog box go away. When you press Enter, the dialog box goes off and does its thing, even if you're not ready for that to be done. When you press Esc, the dialog box just goes away quietly, as if you never started the command. (Pressing Esc is the same as clicking the Cancel button.)

Hollering for Help

We all need a little assistance now and then. A little assistance, I say, not necessarily the squadron of very eager helpers that have been built into Works. The helpers are all very nice, but they can be a bit overwhelming if you don't know how to keep them under control. In this section, I try to sort them all out and make the Help features of Works a little more, um . . . helpful.

The Help feature is a little bit like having a manual in your computer. The nice thing is that Works can sometimes put you on the right page of Help automatically, based on what you're doing at the time. (This feature, called context-sensitive help, is found in most Windows programs.) Even when Works doesn't put you on the right page automatically, you can look through the equivalent of a table of contents or an index and zap yourself to the right page.

Kinds of help

Two basic kinds of help are available in Works:

- ✔ **Brief explanations of dialog box thingies:** When confronted with a dialog box that looks only slightly less complex than the cockpit of a jet fighter, here's how you can find out what the various buttons and settings do: Click the ? button in the upper right-hand corner of the dialog box and then click the button or setting. A brief explanation appears. To make the explanation go away, click a blank area of the dialog box.
- ✔ **Detailed documentation on how to do things:** This form of help appears in the panel that pops up automatically in Works whenever you start a new document, and it sets up shop in the right-hand side of the Works window. I describe this type of help in the rest of this section.

Getting — and getting rid of — Help

One of the first things you may want to do with Help is put it away! If you don't need Help, its pop-up panel takes up valuable real estate on the right side of your Works window. To put Help away, click the X button to the right of where you see *Works Help* in the Help title bar. To restore the Help panel, press the F1 key on your keyboard.

You can also resize the Help panel by clicking the double-arrow button to the left of the X button. Alternately shrinking and expanding the Help panel is a good way to follow the Help instructions without the Help panel itself getting in your way.

You can call the Help squadron into action by doing any of the following:

- ✔ Press the F1 key to get help related to whatever you're currently doing.

- ✔ Choose Help⇨Contents from the menu bar to choose help for a particular program.

- ✔ Choose Help⇨Index from the menu bar to get help on darned near anything.

- ✔ Click the ? button on the Standard toolbar in the word processor program.

- ✔ To clear the Help panel, click the X button to the right of where you see *Works Help* in the Help title bar. Press F1 to restore the Help panel.

The Help panel that appears looks like Figure 2-7 (although it's different for every Works program).

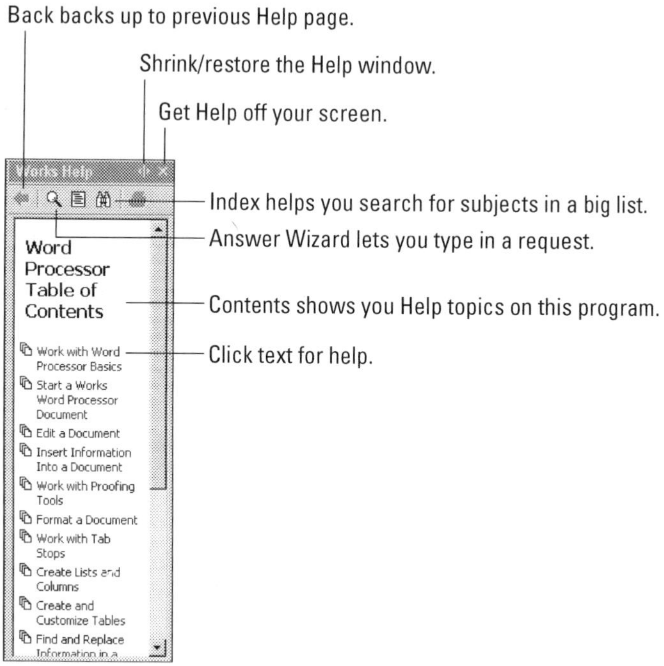

Back backs up to previous Help page.

Shrink/restore the Help window.

Get Help off your screen.

Works Help

Index helps you search for subjects in a big list.

Answer Wizard lets you type in a request.

Word
Processor
Table of
Contents

Contents shows you Help topics on this program.

Click text for help.

Work with Word Processor Basics
Start a Works Word Processor Document
Edit a Document
Insert Information Into a Document
Work with Proofing Tools
Format a Document
Work with Tab Stops
Create Lists and Columns
Create and Customize Tables
Find and Replace Information in a

Figure 2-7:
The Help panel being its usual helpful self.

The Works Help panel has a series of levels that you navigate by clicking the document-like bullets next to each topic or the text of the topic. In fact, whenever your cursor looks like a hand with a pointing finger, you can click to display the thing you were pointing at. Each item you click adds text to the screen or takes you to another page of text. Keep clicking until you get some explanatory text, or numbered steps to help you.

Besides browsing through the Help panel by clicking bullets, here are some other ways to work with the Help panel:

- ✔ **To ask Help a question:** Click the Answer Wizard icon (magnifying glass) shown in Figure 2-7. Click in the box where this text appears: `Type a question here and then click Search`. Type your question, and then click the Search button just to the right of where you typed.

- ✔ **To type in a subject you want help on or to select a subject from an amazingly long list:** Click the Index icon (binoculars) shown in Figure 2-7. Click in the topmost white box of the panel that appears, and type a word describing the subject you are interested in. The Help panel searches a list of topics (displayed in the middle of that panel) for the word you type; or, you can click a word in that list. A list of Help documents containing your text appears at the bottom of the panel; click the one that sounds like it may help.

- ✔ **To choose a topic from a table of contents:** Click the Contents icon (document), shown in Figure 2-7. A bulleted list of topics appears for you to choose from.

Saving Files and Creating Folders

Existence is fleeting and fragile, especially for Works documents. They flicker into life when you create them, but they cannot survive when Works is not running or your PC is off. To preserve Works documents, you have to save them as files on a disk, whether that disk is your permanent hard drive or a removable diskette (or floppy disk). Read through Chapter 1 for more on files and their residences.

Works won't let you exit the program without asking you whether you want to save your work as a file, so you don't have to worry about that. But you never know when someone's going to trip over the power cord to your PC, so save your work to a file often.

Works gives you three ways to save your document as a file. Choose your favorite:

- ✔ Choose File⇨Save from the menu bar.
- ✔ Press Ctrl+S.
- ✔ Click the button with the diskette icon (on the toolbar).

When you use these commands to save a document for the first time, Works gives you the Save As dialog box, as shown in Figure 2-8, so that you can give the file a name and a location. After you save the document for the first time, Works subsequently saves it with the same name and to the same location.

Create a new folder.

View Desktop. | Show file-names only.

Go up one level.

Show details about
a document or folder.

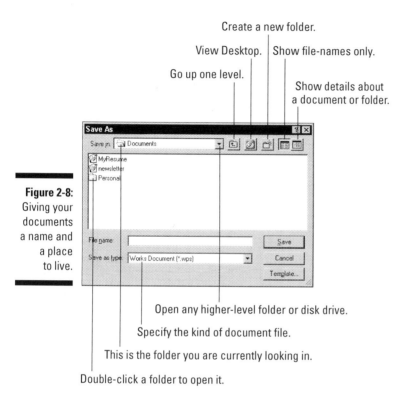

Figure 2-8:
Giving your
documents
a name and
a place
to live.

Open any higher-level folder or disk drive.

Specify the kind of document file.

This is the folder you are currently looking in.

Double-click a folder to open it.

To make a copy of the file and give it a different name, different location, or even a different file type, use the File⇔Save As command to get to the Save As dialog box. This procedure is helpful if you need slightly different versions of the same file (for example, if you are sending the same letter to three different people). Read more about this in the upcoming section, "Making versions and copies of your file."

The Save As dialog box is a close relative of the Open dialog box I describe in Chapter 1 — a twin, in fact (but fraternal, not identical). These two dialog boxes work in almost exactly the same way: You need to tell Works where the file is to go and what its name should be.

Telling Works where the file should go

Unless you tell Works otherwise, it puts all your documents on your hard drive, in a single folder. (What a program does unless you say otherwise is called its default.) Putting your documents on your hard drive is fine, but having all your documents in the same folder is, however, like the extended-wear diaper — not a particularly good idea. Both of these storage solutions result in a rather full and untidy situation. I'm sure you wouldn't put all your documents in a single folder in your file cabinet (although I might).

Unless you say otherwise, Works puts all your documents in the My Documents folder. (Its technical name, or *path,* is C:\My Documents.)

You can peer inside that folder at any time by double-clicking the My Documents icon that appears on your Windows desktop screen. (It usually lurks near the upper left-hand corner of your screen.)

You have the choice of putting your document in My Documents, or any other existing folder — or creating a new folder for your document. You can create folders within folders, if you like (a folder hierarchy). Here's how to specify what folder the document should go into:

- **To open any of the yellow folders displayed in the big white box:** Double-click that folder.

- **To open the folder that contains the current folder:** Click the Up One Level button, at the top of the dialog box (refer to Figure 2-8).

- **To go more than one level up the folder hierarchy:** Click the down-arrow button to the right of the Save In box. Click any folder shown.

- **To go almost to the top of the folder hierarchy:** Click the View Desktop button. (To get to the actual top, double-click the My Computer icon you now see.)

- **To use a disk or to open the very top of the folder hierarchy on your hard drive:** Click the down-arrow button to the right of the Look In box. Click the disk drive: *C:* for your hard drive; choose *A:* or *B:* for your diskette.

- **To create a new folder in the folder that's currently open (shown in the Save In box):** Click the New Folder button (refer to Figure 2-8). A new folder, cleverly named New Folder, appears; just type a name to replace this name.

Naming your file

To name your file when you save it, put a name in the File Name box in the Save As dialog box. Just click the File Name box and type in a new name. (Leave off the three-letter extension; Works supplies it automatically, according to the file type displayed in the Save As Type box.)

You can choose to use the name of an existing file; just click the existing file's name in the big white area of the Save As dialog box. If you use a file name that already exists, you overwrite the file, and its original contents are lost. Works warns you about this situation, however, and gives you a chance to change your mind.

You can use names up to 255 characters long, with spaces and some punctuation. You can use spaces or commas, but you can't use the \ / : * ? " < > or | characters.

Making versions and copies of your file

You may want several similar, slightly different versions of your file. For instance, you may want different versions of your resume. You may also want a copy of your file on a diskette, either for security in case your PC fries in a lightning storm, or to give to someone else.

To make a different version of a document file, first open the original document. (Head over to Chapter 1 if you need help with that.) Then, before you do anything else, save this document under a new name: Choose File⇨Save As, and in the Save As dialog box that appears, type a new name in the File Name box. Click OK to close the dialog box and create the new file. Now make your modifications, and after you do, choose File⇨Save to continue to save these changes under the new name. Your old document file remains unchanged.

To make copies of your document file, it first has to have been saved once as a file already. Having done that, follow these steps:

1. **Choose File⇨Save As and locate your file in the Save As dialog box.**

2. **Right-click the file, and choose Copy from the menu that appears.**

3. **Still working in the Save As dialog box, open the disk or folder where you want the copy of the file.**

   (For instance, if you want the copy on a diskette in the diskette drive, click the View Desktop button, double-click the My Computer icon, and then double-click the icon marked $3^1/_2$ Floppy (A:).)

4. **To make the copy, right-click in the big white area of the Save As window, and click Paste on the menu that appears.**

5. **Click the Cancel button to exit the Save As dialog box.**

Works Stoppage

Incredibly, the day may come when you want to stop using Works. To do so, you may have to close more than one window. Remember that each program you use in Works has its own window, including Works Task Launcher. You can use any one of the following ways to exit a Works window:

- Click File➪Exit from the menu bar.
- Click the button with the X in the upper right-hand corner of your Works window.
- Press Alt+F4.
- On the Windows taskbar, right-click the button for the window you are using, and choose Close from the menu that drops down.

Works stops running, and the Works window disappears from your screen.

Except . . . if you're working on something and haven't saved your work as a file, a dialog box pops up at this point. The dialog box asks whether Works should save changes to the file you're working on and gives you three choices: Yes, No, or Cancel.

- If you click Yes, whatever you're doing in Works is saved with the file name you gave in the Save As dialog box. (If you never named this document, Works presents the Save As dialog box now so that you can do so.) If you're making changes to an existing file, the changes overwrite the old contents of that file; the process is just like recording over a videotape.

- If you click No, whatever you're doing in Works goes to computer heaven (or a warmer place) and is lost forever. If you're working on an existing file, that file remains the way it was before you started working on it. If this is a new file and you click No at this point, you end up with nothing.

- If you click Cancel (or press the Esc key), nothing happens to your document. You don't exit Works, and nothing is saved.

This dialog box may appear several times, once for each different document you are working on. Each time this dialog box appears, it asks only about a single file. When all the open documents are saved, Works disappears from your screen.

Chapter 3

Basic Editing and Formatting

*Y*ou there, with the eyeshade and the ink stains. Yeah, you — you're an editor, believe it or not. In computerese (geek-speak), whenever you change a document, you have *edited* it. And, as it turns out, many of the basic editing operations are the same in the different tools of Works.

But before you whip out your blue pencil and go a-editing, you have to be able to do a couple of really basic things, like type and delete — or highlight certain text that you want to take action on.

Typing and Deleting

All Windows programs display a flashing cursor (a vertical bar) to indicate where you are about to type. To move that cursor, so you can type wherever you want, you can do a variety of things:

✔ **Click where you want to type.**

✔ **To move the cursor by the smallest possible step (one letter, one cell, and so on), press the left-, right-, up-, or down-arrow key on your keyboard.**

> ✔ **To move the cursor by a larger step, press the Home, End, Page Up, or Page Down key on your keyboard.**
>
> Exactly how far these actions take your cursor depends on the program and the circumstances. Holding down the Ctrl key as you press these keys may also change your destination (usually making your cursor go farther).

When you type, you normally insert text at the cursor position, pushing the following characters along. If you prefer to overwrite the following characters, press the Insert key on your keyboard. Press it again to return to inserting.

To delete, you can do any of the following:

> ✔ Press the Backspace key to delete the character before the cursor.
>
> ✔ Press the Delete key to delete the character after the cursor.
>
> ✔ Select (highlight) some text, and then press either the Backspace or Delete key.

Selecting (Highlighting)

Selecting is pointing out to Works exactly what element in your document that you want Works to operate on. For example, you select what text you want to make bold, what illustration that you want to delete, or what cells in a spreadsheet that you want to copy.

Selecting is really pretty simple. To select a bunch of stuff (text, spreadsheet cells, whatever) with your mouse, perform the following mouse-based highlighting process:

1. **Click at one end of the text that you want to select — but keep your mouse button pressed down; don't let up.**

2. **Move your mouse pointer to the other end of the text that you want to select.**

   As you move your mouse, a black, rectangular area extends in the direction you're moving, enveloping your text like an ominous fog. Incongruously, this fog is sometimes called the *highlight*. (In the word processor, the fog envelops one character at a time until you extend it beyond one word; then it hungrily envelops one word at a time!) If any illustrations are in the middle of your text, they're selected, too.

   When you select multiple lines of text, don't go to the end of the line and then back to the beginning of the next, and so on. Just keep moving your mouse over the text you want until you reach the end of your selection; move your mouse backward to un-highlight text if you captured too much. Like driving in Boston, just go directly toward your final destination, ignoring all intervening pedestrians and other distractions. If you overshoot your destination, just move your mouse backwards.

3. Release the mouse button.

The text is now selected (highlighted), and your mouse cursor is free to do other stuff, such as choose things from Works menus or click buttons on the toolbar.

If you didn't quite get the end point where you wanted it when you released the button, you can cleverly adjust the end point by using the arrow keys on your keyboard.

Here are a few special cases that you may encounter when selecting text. For more information on tool-specific special cases, see the chapter on that tool.

✔ **To select a word:** Double-click it. The word processor has even more click-tricks that let you select lines and paragraphs.

✔ **To select the entire document:** Click Edit in the menu bar and then click Select All in the menu that drops down. Or press Ctrl+A.

✔ **To select an illustration or chart or some other solitary chunk of stuff in your document:** Just click it once. Some sort of border appears around it.

✔ **In a spreadsheet, just click a cell to select it.** However, use the highlighting process to select multiple cells; a border makes a little corral around the selected area.

✔ **Likewise, to select a single field in a database, just click the field.** Selecting stuff in List view works just like in a spreadsheet.

Being Bold (Or Italic): Quick Text Styles

B/<u>U</u>? Or be I not you? That is the question. And if I *were* you, I would want to know what these **B**, *I*, and <u>U</u> buttons in the Works toolbar are all about. Here's the answer:

(Warning! The following text contains material that may be offensive to anyone with poetic sensitivities or other forms of good taste.)

> **B** is for bold, as all writers should be,
>
> *I* is for italic, from Italy across the sea,
>
> <u>U</u> is for underline, when emphasis is key, and
>
> ***<u>this</u>*** is what you get when you use all three!

(See what writing computer books does to your brain? You have been warned!)

Bold, italic, and underline are three really basic ways that you can change the appearance (format) of your text. This particular form of text formatting is called *character formatting,* or more specifically, *changing the font style.*

Changing the font style

To change the style of text that you type, follow these incredibly complex and sophisticated instructions:

1. **Click the B, *I*, and/or U̲ button on the toolbar to turn on formatting.**

2. **Type.**

3. **Click the same button again to turn off formatting.**

To change the font style of text you already typed, select the text first, then click the **B**, *I*, or U̲ button.

Changing the font style without using the toolbar buttons

If you don't like using the mouse, you can use the following key combinations rather than click the toolbar buttons:

✔ Press Ctrl+B for **bold**.

✔ Press Ctrl+I for *italic*.

✔ Press Ctrl+U for underline.

You can specify the font style in yet another way. For more on this, skip to the upcoming section, "Using the Font dialog box."

Removing font styles

To remove a particular style (say bold) and leave other styles (say, italic) intact, select the text. Then click the button in the toolbar (**B**, for instance) for the style you want to remove.

To remove all styles from a block of text, select the text first and then press Ctrl+spacebar. To begin typing with unformatted text, press Ctrl+spacebar; then start typing.

Ctrl+spacebar also changes the font and size back to the original, except in the word processor. The word processor offers no quick way to go back to the original font and size. You have to re-specify the original font and size by using the font and size boxes; these boxes appear both on the toolbar and in the Font dialog box.

Fooling with Fonts

You may have noticed a rather tedious consistency in Works. A lot of the type looks the same. The way type looks is called its *font*. (The way type looks used to be called the *typeface*, but the computer industry has transmogrified the terminology.) Works has a rather boring preference for using two fonts called Times New Roman (a truly dumbfounding name) and Arial (incorrectly calling to mind Disney's *The Little Mermaid*, if you're a parent). How can you bring a ray of sunshine into this dreary world of fonts?

Changing font and size with the toolbar

If you're using any of the Big Three tools (the word processor, database, or spreadsheet tools), take a gander at your toolbar. If you're not using any tools at the moment, redirect your gander — and any other waterfowl you may have lying around — to Figure 3-1, where you can see a piece of the toolbar with a drop-down menu.

Figure 3-1: Grab an interesting font from the toolbar's font area.

The font box on the toolbar — together with its sidekick, the font size box (the one with the 12 in it in Figure 3-1) — lets you brighten up your document with any font that's installed on your computer.

Here are two quick steps to change the font you're currently using:

1. **Click the down arrow next to the font box.**

   Works shows you each font by name. The name is written in that font to give you an example of what it looks like. To see more fonts, use the scroll bar on the right of the menu. (Check out Chapter 2 for more on scroll bars.)

2. **Click any font in the drop-down menu.**

To change the font of text that you've already typed, select the text first and then do the preceding two-step.

Changing font size works the same way. To change the size you're currently typing in, click the down arrow to the right of the font size box for a drop-down list of sizes. The font size is in points; bigger numbers mean bigger fonts. Click any size in the menu that drops down from the box. (Or you can click in the font size box, type a new size, and then press the Enter key.) To change the font size of text that you've already typed, select that text first and then change the font size box.

Using the Font dialog box

The main command for changing font, style, and all other type-related stuff is Format⇨Font (or Format⇨Font and Style in the database), which brings up a Font dialog box. Each program in Works has a slightly different dialog box, but you can see in Figure 3-2 the basic controls you find in each one.

(In the spreadsheet and database programs, it's technically not the Format Font and Style *dialog box,* but the Font *tab* of a dialog box — but it looks and works basically the same as what I describe here.)

The Font dialog box does the same things as the font, size, and style features on the toolbar, plus a little bit more. You can also

✔ Choose the ~~strikethrough~~ style here.

✔ Choose a color for your type.

✔ And if you're using the word processor, you can choose a position, such as subscript or superscript, or achieve various other effects.

Click a style or effect here.

Click a font here.   Click a size here.

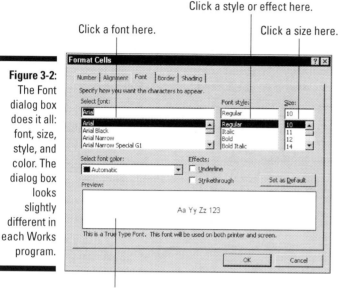

Figure 3-2:
The Font
dialog box
does it all:
font, size,
style, and
color. The
dialog box
looks
slightly
different in
each Works
program.

Preview window shows the effect of your choices.

Here's how to format characters using the Font dialog box (or tab):

1. **If you're formatting text that you've already typed, select that text.**

   If you just want to start typing in a new font or style, skip this step.

2. **Choose Format⇨Font (or Font and Style in the Works database program).**

   The Font dialog box arrives on your screen.

3. **Click the font and/or size that you want.**

   To see more fonts or sizes, click the arrows in the adjoining scroll bars. The preview area at the bottom of the dialog box shows the effect of your choices.

4. **If you want a special style, such as Bold, choose it.**

   In the word processor and spreadsheet programs, bold and italic (the styles you get using the buttons **B** and *I* in the toolbar) appear in a list box called Font Style. To get both, choose Bold Italic. To turn off bold and italic, choose Regular.

   In the database program, bold, italic, underline, and strikethrough are check boxes. Click to enable or clear the check mark for your chosen style.

   In the Works word processor, Underline is not a check box, but rather a drop-down list from which you can choose several styles of underlining. The word processor also includes a number of effects, such as embossing or engraving, that you choose by selecting their check boxes.

5. **For colored type, click the Color box.**

   Zowie! Color! Click the color that you want from the drop-down menu that appears. Choosing *Automatic* gives you black text unless you've fooled around with settings in the Windows Control Panel. (Click the down arrow in the scroll bar to the right of the menu for more colors.) Colors may give shades of gray on a black-and-white printer.

6. **If you want superscript or subscript, click it.**

   You can make characters superscript or subscript only while you're using the word processor. The area marked Effects in Figure 3-2, where these selections hang out, doesn't appear with any other tool. Clicking Superscript raises text above the normal line and is used for footnote numbers and exponents. Subscript lowers text below the normal line, as in H_2O, the formula for water.

   To remove subscripting or superscripting, click the box again to remove the check mark.

7. **After you set up everything the way that you want it, click the OK button.**

In the word processor toolbar, you can choose superscript or subscript right from the keyboard without using a dialog box. Press Ctrl and the = (equal sign) key for subscript, and press Ctrl+Shift and the = (equal sign) key for superscript.

The spreadsheet and database tools enable you to set the default font to your current font and style choices. The *default font* is what that program uses unless you tell it otherwise. After you make your choices, click the Set Default (or Set As Default) button in the Font tab of those dialog boxes.

Copying, Cutting, and Pasting

Finally, this sentence was written. Subsequently, this sentence. First, this sentence was written. Paragraph sense make does this? No? Then you (or somebody) need to edit it.

The particular editing features in Works that can make short work of such scrambled writing are the copy, cut, paste, and drag features. The first three features are practically universal among Windows programs. Employing, as they do, a Windows feature called the Clipboard, these features even let you transfer things between Windows programs, using that Clipboard as a vehicle.

The *Windows Clipboard* is a temporary storage area that holds only one thing at a time; you can copy text and illustrations and all kinds of things to the Clipboard. You can then paste the contents of the Clipboard into nearly any document in a Windows program.

Besides carrying things between Windows programs, the Clipboard also serves as a vehicle to move things around either within a Works document or between Works documents.

Copy and paste

You can copy any text or illustration onto the Windows Clipboard and then insert it (paste it) somewhere else. In fact, after you copy the text or illustration onto the Windows Clipboard, you can paste the text or illustration as many times as you like. This feature is very useful if you are repeatedly typing something lengthy, such as Dinglehausen-Schneitzenbaum Furniture Prefabrication Company.

Here's the procedure for copying:

1. **Select the text or illustration that you want to copy.**

2. **Press Ctrl+C, or**

   Choose Edit⇨Copy, or

   Click the Copy button in the toolbar. (The Copy button is normally next to the button with the scissors, and the icon on the Copy button shows two overlapping documents.)

   This procedure copies the selected stuff onto the Windows Clipboard. These commands do the same thing in most other Windows programs, by the way.

3. **Click where you want a copy to appear.**

   This spot can be in the document that you're working on, in some other Works document, or even in something that you're working on outside of Works, in another Windows program that's currently running. You can take your time opening documents or whatever you need to do.

   Whatever you copy stays on the Clipboard only until you copy or cut something else or turn off your computer.

4. **Press Ctrl+V, or**

   Choose Edit⇨Paste, or

   Click the Paste button in the toolbar. (The Paste button shows a clipboard with a document.)

   This procedure copies stuff from the Windows Clipboard and pastes it into the new location. The Ctrl+V (paste) command is the same in most Windows programs.

You can repeat Steps 3 and 4 as many times as you like, until you put something new on the Clipboard. Dinglehausen-Schneitzenbaum Furniture Prefabrication Company. Dinglehausen-Schneitzenbaum Furniture Prefabrication Company. See, it works!

If you want to make only a single copy of some text or an illustration, you may find it easier to use the drag feature, coming up soon in the "Drag" section of this chapter.

Cut and paste

If you want to move something, one way is to cut and paste it. This procedure is exactly like the copying and pasting just described, except that the original text is removed from your document and placed in the new location of your choosing. (Copying something leaves the original text in its original place because you copy it as opposed to cutting it.) The cut and paste method is particularly useful for moving something a long distance — over several pages or between documents. Within Works, you can also just drag something to move it, as I show you in a minute.

Here's the procedure for cutting and pasting:

1. **Select the text or illustration that you want to move.**

2. **Press Ctrl+X, or**

   Choose Edit⇨Cut, or

   Click the Cut (scissors) button in the toolbar.

   This procedure copies the selected stuff onto the Windows Clipboard while deleting it from your document. These commands do the same thing in most other Windows programs.

   The next two steps comprise the paste procedure, which is identical to the procedure you use in copying and pasting.

3. **Click where you want the text or illustration to appear.**

4. **Press Ctrl+V, or**

   Choose Edit⇨Paste, or

   Click the Paste button on the toolbar.

As with the copy procedure described previously, you can repeat Steps 3 and 4 as many times as you like until you put something new on the Clipboard.

Drag

As even Og the Caveman knew, dragging is often an easy way to move some-thing. In Works, you can drag text or an illustration to a different place within a document, or even to another document, as long as the document to which you are dragging the text or illustration is open in a window.

Dragging doesn't work well if you have to move or copy something a distance of many pages. The cut (or copy) and paste method is better in that event.

Here's how to move or copy something by dragging it:

1. **Select the text or illustration that you want to move.**

2. **With your cursor over that selection, press the mouse button (don't let go) and drag the selected text or illustration where you want it.**

   Your selection doesn't move yet, but a little box representing your selec-tion attaches itself, lamprey-like, to your cursor as soon as you press the mouse button.

   If you want to copy — not move — the selected text, press and hold the Ctrl key down at this point. The cursor with the little box now acquires a tiny + sign.

   If your destination is not visible in the document window, drag to the window's edge in the direction that you would like to go. When your cursor hits the edge, the window scrolls.

   If your destination is in another Works document, that document has to be open in a window; just drag to your destination in that window.

3. **Release the mouse button at your final destination.**

Now the selection actually moves to its new location.

Windows allows you to drag illustration (graphic) files from a My Computer window into a Works document. In Chapter 12, I discuss putting illustrations in your documents. You may notice that you can drag text between Works and other Windows programs, too, but because the result is more compli-cated than it appears to be, I don't recommend this technique.

Yikes! Undoing What Has Been Done

Yikes! You just accidentally pasted a double-cheesecake recipe into your nondairy diet book! What now?

One way that Works improves on real life is that it lets you undo your mistakes. Works doesn't enable you to undo all mistakes, mind you, but you can undo most editing mistakes, such as changes that you make to the contents of an open document. But Works doesn't undo mistakes that you make with files, such as deleting, replacing, and renaming files.

If you accidentally delete a file from your hard disk, you can undelete it using Windows (not Works). Find the Recycle Bin icon on your Windows screen, and double-click it to open the Recycle Bin window. In that window, find the file you deleted, click it, and choose File➪Restore from the menu in that window.

Works lets you undo up to 100 things that you have done to your document, one at a time, working backwards from the most recent action. Typing or deleting a succession of characters counts as one single mistake, not a bunch of them. If you type a sentence and then undo it, the entire sentence goes away.

To undo, choose Edit➪Undo *(something)*. The *something* that appears in the menu is whatever you last did: type, enter a number, delete, or format. A faster way to undo is to press Ctrl+Z. Repeat the command to undo the next earlier action.

If Works can't undo your mistake, it tells you so by graying out the Undo command line and displaying Can't Undo in the command's place.

To redo something you have undone, choose Edit➪Redo *(something)*. A shortcut is to press Ctrl+Y. If you undo a series of actions, you can redo steps in that series by repeating the redo command.

Checking Your Spelling

One of the helpful little gnomes that scurry around in Works is its spelling checker (or spell checker, although the idea of checking a spell sounds more wizardish than gnome-like). Specifically, the spell checker helps you eliminate typographical errors (typos) and misspellings. Actually, what the spell checker does is make sure that your document contains 100 percent genuine words (or words that it thinks are genuine).

The spell checker does not, however, make sure that you use words *write*. Like in that last sentence — the word *write* is absolutely and indisputably a word; it just happens to be in the wrong place at the wrong time. The spell checker doesn't turn up anything wrong with that sentence.

Automatic checking — and those wavy lines

Unless you change the way Works word processor works, it checks your text automatically (called background spell checking). This feature works only in the word processor. With a wavy red line, Works identifies words that it thinks are misspelled, repeated, mis-hyphenated, or otherwise defective.

To correct the problem, right-click the indicated word. If the word is misspelled, a list of words drops down, including (with any luck) the correctly spelled word. Click on any word that you want to replace the underlined one.

If Works detects some other kind of problem, the drop-down list offers you a correction. For a repeated word, for instance, Works offers you the choices of Delete Repeated Word or Ignore All. To make the menu go away without choosing a correction, click anywhere in the document. Ignore All means *ignore this and future problems identical to this one.* If you discover that you have correctly spelled a word but Works simply doesn't know it, choose Add to add the word to Works' dictionary.

Many people find automatic checking and all its wavy lines distracting. To turn it off, choose Tools➪Options. In the Options dialog box that appears, click to clear the check mark labeled `Background Spell Checking`.

Running the Spelling and Grammar checker yourself

If you don't like the automatic, background checking that Works does, you can run the manual Spelling and Grammar checker. This little helper gives you a few more options than the automatic version. Here are the details on snaring misspellings:

1. **If you are just going to check a single word or block of text, select the word or text block by highlighting it.**

   To check your whole document starting where your insertion point or spreadsheet cursor is, don't bother selecting: Go on to Step 2.

2. **Choose Tools➪Spelling and Grammar or press the F7 key on your keyboard.**

   In the word processor, you can alternatively click the Spelling Checker button on the toolbar (the check mark with ABC on it).

If the spell checker doesn't find any words that it can't recognize, a little box tells you that the spell-checking process is done; click the OK button in that box.

Otherwise, you get the Spelling dialog box, as shown in Figure 3-3.

3. **See whether the word that the Spelling and Grammar Checker found is really incorrect.**

   The word is shown at the top of the Spelling dialog box, where it reads `Not in Dictionary`. Works suggests a replacement in the Suggestions text box.

4. **If the word is okay, ignore it or add it to the dictionary.**

   If the word is okay this particular time (but may be a typo or misspelling if it appears again in this document or any other document), click Ignore. If the word comes up again during this spell-checking session, it is flagged again.

   If the word is okay in this document (the word *snark,* for example, in a document about sailboats) but may be a typo or misspelling in some other document, click Ignore All. The word is ignored until the next time that you use the spell checker.

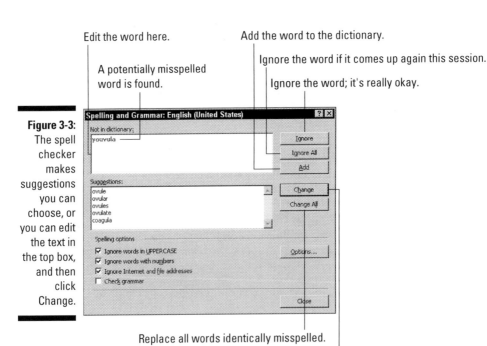

Edit the word here.

A potentially misspelled word is found.

Add the word to the dictionary.

Ignore the word if it comes up again this session.

Ignore the word; it's really okay.

Figure 3-3:
The spell checker makes suggestions you can choose, or you can edit the text in the top box, and then click Change.

Replace all words identically misspelled.

Replace the word with the word in the Suggestions box.

If the word is a real word (such as *uvula*) that you might use again and again, click Add. This action adds the word to the spell checker's Custom Dictionary and is thereafter and forever ignored in any document that you check. Be certain that the word is really spelled correctly before you do this!

After you act on any of the preceding tasks, the spell checker moves on to check the remainder of the document.

5. **If the word suggested by Works in the Suggestions box is not correct, edit it.**

If you know the correct word, click the Not in Dictionary text box (not the Suggestions text box) and edit the word directly. Click Change to apply the correction to your text.

6. **Click the Change button to replace the original word in your document with the one that you have highlighted in the Suggestions box.**

You don't get to watch this replacement happen because the action happens so fast. The spell checker moves right along to your next apparent blunder, and you're back at Step 3.

Eventually, the spell checker reaches the end of your document and puts up a little box letting you know that the spell-checking process is done. Click OK in this box.

If you didn't start spell checking at the beginning of your document, Works asks whether the spell checker should go back to the beginning and start there. Click OK in this box if you would like to check the first part of your document. Click Cancel if you're done.

Chapter 4

Putting Print on Paper

*A*ccording to some accounts, computers were supposed to lead to the age of the paperless office. No more of this cutting down forests, flattening them into paper, smearing ink all over them, and then dumping them into landfills where typos are preserved like mummies for the critical eye of posterity. Hah! As my fellow technology skeptic (and co-author of other books) Margaret Levine Young is fond of saying, "The paperless office of the future is just down the hall from the paperless bathroom of the future."

No, computers actually have increased paper consumption. And you, too, can join the parade with your own printer. Fortunately, features such as Works' Print Preview can at least minimize the amount of paper that you waste.

Printing is something that proceeds roughly the same way in each program. In each tool, the commands that have anything to do with printing (including page set-up parameters, such as margins and orientation) have been forced by Microsoft to live with evil relatives in the File menu. Perhaps, someday, some handsome royalty from the kingdom of Microsoft will rescue them and give them their very own Print condominium on the menu bar.

The special world of envelopes

Unless you really like figuring out the nuts and bolts of how things work, you probably shouldn't attempt to print envelopes without help from Works. Works has a special envelope tool (which also serves as the envelope wizard) that works with the word processor tool to take care of all your page setup and printing needs.

Because this special envelope tool uses the word processor to create the envelope, I put the discussion of how to print a single, simple envelope in Chapter 7. For a discussion of using the envelope tool/wizard to create multiple envelopes for a mass mailing, see Chapter 8.

Setting Up the Page

Ever since humankind progressed from scrolls to pages, things have been going downhill. Now we have to worry about top and bottom margins, as well as side margins. Even worse, now we can print the darn pages sideways! Back to scrolls, I say!

In the meantime, we have to deal with all this stuff. Fortunately, the controls for page margins, page size, and orientation work the same for the Big Three Works tools: the word processor, database, and spreadsheet.

You don't have to set up the page every time you print — just set up the page once for each document. Your page setup is saved as part of the document file. In fact, you may be quite happy with the margins and other page setup stuff that Works uses automatically (the default). In that case, you don't have to bother with setting up your pages at all! Skip ahead to "Previewing Coming Attractiveness," later in this chapter, which describes how to see what your document looks like before you print it. If you like the way your document looks, don't bother fooling with Page Setup.

Making marginal decisions

In Works, *margins* are defined as the spaces between the edge of the page and the regular body text and footnotes of the document. Headers and footers (including page numbers) go within these margins, and you specify their positions separately using the Header margins.

Choose File➪Page Setup to open the Page Setup dialog box. Then click the Margins tab, as shown in Figure 4-1. Here are your options on this tab:

The Preview image shows your changes as you make them.

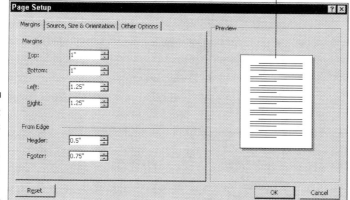

Figure 4-1:
The Margins
tab — a
place to do
marginal
work.

✔ **To increase or decrease a margin:** Click the up arrow or down arrow next to the value.

✔ **To type in a specific margin value:** Double-click that margin's white text box and type in a new number. If you want inches (or whatever your default units are), you can just type in the value and leave off the units (for example, type **2.5** for 2.5 inches). You can type in other units, too, such as **cm** for centimeters, **mm** for millimeters, **pi** for picas, and **pt** for points.

When you type a margin value into a box, the Preview image on the right side of the dialog box shows the resulting change as you type. (Refer to Figure 4-1.)

✔ **To set header or footer margins:** Headers and footers are text that can appear in the margins on the top or bottom, respectively, of every page. The header distance is measured from the top edge of the page to the bottom of the header text, so the header distance must be set to a value no larger than the top margin. In similar but reverse fashion, the footer distance is measured from the bottom edge of the page to the top of the footer, so the footer distance must be set to a value no larger than the bottom margin.

To return margins, page orientation, and all other settings in the Page Setup dialog box to their original (default) settings, click the Reset button.

Hooked on metrics

Let's face it: Inches are silly, but that's what we grew up with here in the good old U.S. of A. If you live in a country where people have discovered that they have ten fingers and toes, you probably prefer the metric system. Or perhaps you've worked in the typing, publishing, or printing businesses, where they have really silly measurements, such as the pica. (Maybe the pica is a small and fuzzy measurement named after the small fuzzy alpine bunny, *Pica D'Amerique,* or *Pika.*)

If you want Works to use your favorite *metrics* (units of measure), do this:

1. **Click the Cancel button in any open dialog boxes, such as in the Page Setup dialog box.**

2. **Choose Tools⇨Options.**

   The Options dialog box springs up. If it has multiple tabs, click the General tab. Look for the area marked Select units for page size and margins at the top of the dialog box and you find a list of possible measurement units.

3. **Click whatever unit you want Works to use by default (that is, the unit you want Works to use when you don't specify a unit, just a number).**

4. **Click the OK button to close the Options dialog box.**

Setting source, size, and orientation

Use the Source, Size & Orientation tab of the Page Setup dialog box to set where paper goes into the printer (source), what paper you want (size), and which direction you want to print (orientation.) Of those three concerns, your most common one is orientation, as you switch between, say, printing letters and printing signs.

You will probably print 99 percent of your work on standard-sized paper in the *normal,* or *portrait,* orientation. For spreadsheets, signs, certain kinds of flyers, and other work, however, you may want your printer to print sideways — in the *landscape* orientation. Set your Works program to print landscape-oriented pages (portrait is the default) on the Source, Size & Orientation tab of the Page Setup dialog box (File⇨Page Setup). See Figure 4-2. You can also configure specially sized pages here; many printers require you to manually insert special-sized paper.

Using landscape orientation does *not* mean that you insert the paper sideways into your printer! Most printers do not allow sideways paper. Instead, they *print* sideways on paper that is inserted in the normal way.

You can also tell Works that you want to use a special paper, such as card stock or labels, or a different-than-normal (8½ x 11 inches) paper size. Choose File⇨Page Setup to open the Page Setup dialog box; then click the Source, Size & Orientation tab. Here are additional changes you can make on this tab:

Figure 4-2:
Anything to
do with
paper —
paper size,
orientation
of the print
to the paper,
or where
paper gets
put into the
printer —
appears on
this tab.

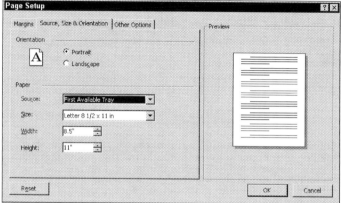

✔ **To set page orientation:** Click the Source, Size & Orientation tab. Then click either the Landscape or Portrait radio buttons. The page icon (with the letter A) illustrates how type will be printed on the page.

✔ **To tell Works that you want to use a special paper source on your printer:** On the Source, Size & Orientation tab, click the Source drop-down list. If you need to use a special paper-feeding place on your printer, such as a manual feed slot, you can click that source in the list. For manual feeding, when the time comes to put the paper in for manual feeding, Works reminds you. If you choose an automatic paper feed, Works tells the printer to use that special source.

✔ **To tell Works that you want to use a special paper size or an envelope:** On the Source, Size & Orientation tab, click the Size list box. Click the paper size in the drop-down list box. If you're using a paper size that's not shown in the drop-down list, double-click the Width box and type in a new value; then do the same for the Height box. When you're done, check the Preview image to see whether things look roughly correct.

Remember that you can click the Reset button to return to the default paper size, source, and orientation. This will also reset margins and all other options in the Page Setup dialog box.

Width always refers to the direction a line of text will run.

Starting page number and other options

Each type of Works document has certain special options for page setup, so see the individual tool sections in this book for more information on those options. One other option that they all have in common is the capability to specify what page number appears on the first page of your document. Use this feature when you compile a document with separate sections and chapters that each needs sequential page numbers. Suppose, for example, that your first section ends on page 19, and you want the second section to start on page 20. In that case, set the first page number of the first element to be 1, and then set the first page of the second (and subsequent) elements to follow sequentially.

Here's how:

1. **Choose File➪Page Setup to open the Page Setup dialog box; then click the Other Options tab.**

2. **Either click the Starting Page Number box and type in a value, or click the adjoining up arrow to increase the page number setting.**

3. **Click OK.**

Reusing the same setup all the time

Because your page setup only affects the current document, you can get frustrated if you want to use the same non-default (custom) settings all the time. You have to set up these settings each time that you want to use them. One solution to this problem is to create a custom template. A *template* is a sort of prototype document that contains specific settings you want to use over and over again. After you design a template, you can create a new document based on this template by choosing from Personal Templates, a category that now appears on the Tasks list in the Task Launcher. For more on templates, see Chapter 5.

Previewing Coming Attractiveness

You format your document, and you *think* that it will look quite attractive on paper. But how do you know for sure? Announcing a preview of coming attractiveness, coming soon to the Bijou near you! Specifically, it's time for Print Preview, which shows you how Works thinks your document will look in print — without wasting paper. See Figure 4-3 for a sneak preview of Print Preview.

You can get into Print Preview in any of three ways:

✔ **Choose File➪Print Preview from the menu bar.**

✔ **Click the button on the menu toolbar that looks like a document with a monocle.** (To see whether you're on the right button, place your mouse cursor over the button without clicking. You should see a tiny label reading `Print Preview`.)

✔ **Press Ctrl+P and then click the Preview button in the Print dialog box that appears.**

Next Page

Previous Page

Magnifier

Zoom

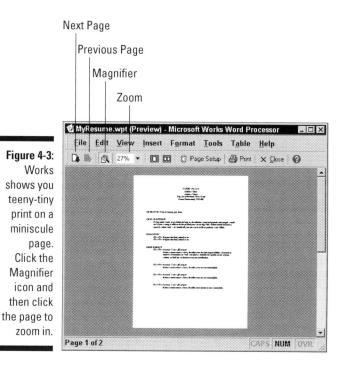

Figure 4-3:
Works
shows you
teeny-tiny
print on a
miniscule
page.
Click the
Magnifier
icon and
then click
the page to
zoom in.

Whichever way you use, you get a Print Preview dialog box that initially shows you a tiny, illegible picture of your document. (The picture may be illegible, but this initial bird's-eye view is actually helpful for checking margins and overall layout.)

Here are some of the things you can do in this dialog box:

✔ **To enlarge or shrink the view of the document:** Click the Magnifier icon on the toolbar (refer to Figure 4-3). The cursor changes to a magnifier with a plus sign in it. Click the document to enlarge it; click again to shrink it. Clicking the Zoom drop-down list to the right of the Magnifier icon (marked 27% in Figure 4-3) gives you additional magnifications and layout choices. Use the vertical and horizontal scroll bars to view parts of the document that extend beyond the window.

✔ **To see other pages:** Click the Next button to see the next page or click the Previous button to see the preceding page. If no next or preceding page exists, the buttons are grayed out. The Next and Previous buttons are at the left end of the Preview toolbar, as Figure 4-3 shows.

✔ **To see two pages at once:** Click the Multiple Pages button (the one with two white rectangles). To return to a single page, click the One Page button to the left of the Multiple Pages button.

✔ **To actually print the document on paper (what a stunning concept!):** Click the Print button. (When you print, don't worry about how big the document looks in Print Preview. The document prints at normal size.)

✔ **To return to the document window:** Click the Close button or press the Esc key.

Printing on Actual Paper!

What will they think of next? Imagine being able to actually see words and graphics on paper rather than on a computer screen!

The procedure for printing is nearly identical for the Big Three programs of Works (and very similar in the other programs). Printing is also pretty simple when things go right. Just follow these steps:

1. **Turn on your printer.**

   Some printers turn on automatically when you start to print, so if you can't find an On switch, try skipping to Step 3 or 4.

2. **Wait until the printer comes online.**

   Most printers have an indicator light somewhere that is marked On Line. If this indicator light lights up, the printer is telling you that it has had its morning coffee, has done its exercises, and is ready to roll.

3. **To print the whole document without further ado, click the Print button on the Works toolbar.**

   The Print button has a picture of a printer on it.

   At this point, you're essentially done. Skip the remaining steps in this list and read "Terminating Printing," later in this chapter, for those times when you change your mind about printing the document.

4. **If you want to print only a part of the document or print multiple copies, choose File➪Print or press Ctrl+P.**

   The Print dialog box comes to your aid. If you have more than one printer that you use, check now to make sure that the name of the printer you intend to use appears in the Name field at the top of the dialog box. If not, click the down arrow for the Name field's drop-down list and choose the correct printer.

5. **For multiple copies, click the Number Of Copies box (in the Print dialog box) and type the number of copies that you want (but don't press the Enter key).**

   Or you can click the up or down arrows next to that box to change the copy count.

6. **To print a specific group of pages, click Pages (in the Print dialog box) and enter the starting and ending page numbers.**

7. **Click the OK button (or press the Enter key).**

   If all goes well, you can now just close your eyes and wait for your document to be printed. If you change your mind about printing — quick, read the next section, "Terminating Printing."

Terminating Printing

Stopping a document before it gets to the printer is like trying to catch a bus that has just left the bus stop. If you're really fast, you can flag the bus down. Otherwise, you have to run to the next bus stop. Sometimes you simply get flattened by the bus.

Except as a last resort, don't just turn off the printer. Your paper may get stuck halfway and need to be carefully extracted; your PC will get confused and start tossing complaints on your screen; and when you start the printer up again, your first page may be a mess.

The printing route has three bus stops. To stop printing, you can interrupt the process at any point.

Stop 1. If you move really, really fast, you can click the Cancel button in the Printing dialog box. This box disappears so quickly that most people never see it unless they are printing a large document or one with many pictures.

Stop 2. If you miss the opportunity to cancel printing in Works, you can still catch the bus at the next stop.

Certain types of printers bring up their own bus stop — a dialog box in which you can stop or pause printing. Check your printer manual for instructions.

If your printer doesn't come with its own bus stop, use the Windows Print Manager. At the end of the taskbar opposite the Start button (near the time-of-day display), a printer icon appears. Double-click it to open a Print Manager window. Click the name of your document in the list shown there and then click the Delete button. After a pause, the document name no longer appears. Click the X button at the top right of the dialog box to exit. Your printer should stop printing after a few pages — more, if your pages have large blank areas.

Your printer may keep on printing for a while because your PC has already transferred part of your document to the printer's memory. Nothing short of taking your printer offline or turning it off will stop the printer at this point.

Stop 3. If your printer has an online/offline button, press that button. Otherwise, turn your printer off. Your printer software or the Print Manager eventually discovers your action and displays a box complaining that `The printer on LPT1 is offline or not selected` or some such stuff. Click the Cancel button in this box. Next, follow the directions for Stop 2. Finally, press the online/offline button or the On switch on your printer again.

Selecting or Installing a Printer

Chances are that Works already knows what printer you have and how you want that printer to work. No, Works hasn't been snooping in your credit card records. When you (or your friendly local software guru) installed Windows, you installed the printer there, too: You told Windows what printer or printers you would be using, and you loaded some software. If you said that you may use more than one printer, you may also have specified one printer as the standard (or *default*) printer. Unless you tell Works otherwise, it uses this default printer.

Here are the main circumstances under which you may need to tell Works or Windows something about a printer:

✔ If you just installed a new printer (or a fax modem), you need to tell Windows about it.

✔ If you are switching to another printer, or if you want to send a fax with your fax modem and fax software (which makes Works think that the fax modem is a printer), you need to tell Works about these actions.

Selecting a printer or fax modem in Works

After a printer has been installed (both physically and in software), Works can use it. If you have more than one printer installed and you want to switch to another printer, you have to choose the other printer from Works. Although you probably don't have more than one real printer, you may have a fax modem that transmits faxes; usually the fax modem and its program work like a printer. To send a fax in that case, you have to choose the fax selection in place of a printer, and then print.

Here's how to select an installed printer or fax modem:

1. **Choose File⇨Print in the menu bar or press Ctrl+P.**

   The Print dialog box winks into existence on your screen.

2. **In the Print dialog box, click the down arrow on the Name box.**

   This action displays the list of installed printers or fax modem software.

3. **Click the printer or fax software of your choice in the list.**

   After a brief delay, you're done. Now proceed to print.

 Before you print, you may want to check the document's appearance with Print Preview (refer to "Previewing Coming Attractiveness," earlier in this chapter). Choosing a different printer or selecting fax software can affect the document's appearance because of different limitations (like minimum allowable margins) or other properties of these devices.

When you print to a fax modem, your document is automatically handed off to special fax modem software where you enter the fax number, perhaps create a cover sheet, and do other fax-specific tasks before the document is actually transmitted over the phone line.

Installing a new printer or fax software

Here's how to go about installing a new printer and telling Windows about it. You may need to have your Windows installation disks or CD handy; or if your printer came with a disk containing *printer drivers,* you may need that disk. If you are installing fax software, you need to follow the directions that came with it. To install a printer, do the following:

1. **Shut down Windows and turn off your PC.**

2. **Physically unpack and set up the printer.**

   Remove all the tabs, Styrofoam chunks, and rubber bands that the manufacturer tells you about. Read the instruction manual and do your best to follow the instructions. In the process, you'll plug the printer's cable into a *parallel (printer) port, serial port,* or *Universal Serial Bus (USB) port* on your PC.

3. **Turn on your PC.**

4. **Choose Start⇨Settings⇨Printers from the Windows taskbar.**

5. **In the Printers dialog box that appears, double-click the Add Printer icon.**

   An Add Printer wizard appears.

6. **Click the Next button and follow the directions to install the printer.**

Part II
Doing Anything Instantly (Or Almost)

The 5th Wave   By Rich Tennant

BOB'S DECISION NOT TO BE CONNECTED TO THE COMPUTER NETWORK CAUSED SOME SUSPICION ON THE PART OF THOSE WHO WERE.

In this part . . .

A big part of survival is doing what you need fast *and* well. If you're in a hurry for a good-looking, professionally laid-out, or well-designed result, this part is the place to turn.

Much of this part is about a big convenience feature of Works: its *tasks,* which are automations that build specific kinds of documents, spreadsheets, and databases for you. Unlike instant foods, these convenience items deliver not only fast, but also well. You still have to write your newsletter or enter your own data, but Works takes care of appearances, spreadsheet calculations, chart design, and database reports.

Other convenient Works features covered in this part include creating address and other labels, printing envelopes, sending letters with individualized information (for example, dollars pledged) to large groups, and using predesigned artwork (called *clip art*) and other graphics to make your point and brighten up your results.

If you are being pressured by deadlines, or pursued by colleagues, friends, editors, or others to deliver that document *"now,* for cryin' out loud!" try this part for almost anything, almost instantly.

"Exit, pursued by a bear."

—*The Winter's Tale,* William Shakespeare

Chapter 5

Timesaving Tasks and Templates

In This Chapter

▶ Launching tasks

▶ Using task wizards and templates

▶ Creating, modifying, and using your own templates

*W*orks is a task master. Fortunately, it takes *itself,* not you, to task. You reap the benefit: You save time and you get professional-looking results. Even more importantly, you get cool stuff that, otherwise, you might not attempt to create in the first place! Print your own business cards? No problem. Put out a newsletter for your neighborhood? Why not? A nice, printed grocery list organized by aisle? Sure.

In Works, *task* is a general name for automated helpers. Works comes with a lot of tasks, but you can also create your own. Some of these tasks create documents for you in the Works word processor, spreadsheet, or database program. Others may launch Internet Explorer, or start an e-mail in Outlook Express, or open an appointment screen in Works Calendar.

In this chapter, I focus mainly on the tasks that create documents for you. The other tasks are nice, but the document builders are the real timesavers.

Launching Tasks from the Task Launcher

Not surprisingly, the Task Launcher is the place to turn to launch tasks. See Chapter 1 for all the details on the Task Launcher, but, in a nutshell, here's what you do to launch a task:

1. **Start the Microsoft Works Task Launcher by double-clicking the Microsoft Works icon on your PC screen, or by choosing File⇨New from the menu bar of your Works spreadsheet, database, or word processor program.**

2. **On the Task Launcher that appears, click Tasks.**

   The Tasks page appears in the Task Launcher window.

3. **Click any category of Task that appears down the left side of the Tasks page.**

   A list of tasks in that category appears on the right. Pause your mouse cursor over any task or category to see its full name. You can also find the same tasks listed on the Programs page, categorized by the Works program that the task uses.

4. **Click the task you want.**

   A description of the task appears on the right.

5. **Click the blue, underlined text (called a *link*), <u>Start This Task</u>.**

At this point, Works opens whatever program is appropriate for that task. If the task is one that creates documents, a document appears in the word processor, spreadsheet, or database program. Otherwise, you are taken to a particular page, screen, or dialog box in one of the other programs that Works links to, such as a page on the Web in Internet Explorer.

A quick way to find a task related to some subject is to type a word or words related to that subject (a *keyword*) into the text box next to the Search button (on the Task Launcher). Then click the Search button or press the Enter key on your keyboard, and the Task Launcher lists a series of related tasks on the right side of the screen. For instance, searching for the keyword car lists all tasks related to automobiles.

Working with Tasks

Tasks that create documents come in two types:

✔ **Wizards** present you screens with different options you choose to build a document to your specifications. For instance, the letterhead-designing task lets you choose different type and layout styles. Most of the tasks that come with Works are of this type (even if they call themselves templates).

✔ **Templates** don't present you with any options. If you create your own tasks, templates are the type of tasks you create. For instance, you might create a template for your newsletter. It would be all prepared with a banner, with dummy or placeholder text laid out and set in your chosen font, ready for you to substitute the actual text each time you create an issue. Templates save time and create a uniform appearance for each issue.

The following two sections discuss wizards and templates in more detail.

Note: You can't determine by looking at the Task Launcher whether a task is a wizard or template. You have to try the task (or read about it in this book).

Using the Works wizards

If the task is of the wizard type (and most of them are), a wizard screen appears on top of the Works program's screen. (The screen says Something Something Wizard at the top.) For example, Figure 5-1 shows the Works Brochures wizard.

Click your choice. . .

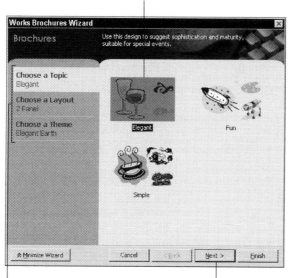

Figure 5-1:
A typical wizard screen that appears when you choose a task.

. . .or click any of the Wizard screens here.

Click Next to move to the next screen.

Here's how to use a Works wizard:

- ✔ **Making choices:** Click one of the design or layout choices that the wizard shows on the right. The wizard then shows you how your choice changes the document appearance in the program window.

- ✔ **Shrinking the wizard:** To see the document better, temporarily shrink the wizard. Look for a Minimize Wizard button at the bottom left of the wizard screen. If you find one (and not all wizards have them), click it. The wizard becomes a thin bar with a single working button — Maximize Wizard — that you click to restore the wizard screen.

✓ **Navigating between screens:** Wizards give you two ways to go from screen to screen. If a Next button appears on the wizard screen, as shown in Figure 5-1, click that button. You proceed to another screen to make yet more choices. (That screen also has a Back button that you can click to return to earlier screens.) Each screen is also represented in a short list down the left side of the screen, as shown in Figure 5-1. Rather than using the Next and Back buttons, you can click any screen you want in the list on the left.

✓ **Filling out screens:** Screens contain option buttons to click, and text boxes to fill out. When you need to enter a name and address, the wizard often provides a way to get that address from the Address Book. See the section, "Grabbing an address from the Address Book," later in this chapter. One screen, the Choose a Theme page, has sliders to drag. See the section, "Choosing themes in the wizard," later in this chapter.

✓ **Removing text that you don't want:** Often, the document contains instructions to you, such as `Enter your own text here`. Some documents include lots of instructions, such as descriptions of the different ways to format entries in a bibliography. You need to delete the instructions, and replace these placeholder prompts with your own text.

✓ **Finishing up:** When you see a Finish button, click it to finalize your choice and make the wizard go away. Now you have the beginnings of a nice, professionally designed document. All you have to do is fill the document out!

Grabbing an address from the Address Book

When screens appear that require names and addresses, Works' wizards almost always let you grab an address from the Address Book instead of making you have to type it into a text box. A button with an Address Book icon, shown here in the margin, appears to the right of the text box.

 Click the Address Book button. In the Select Name dialog box that appears, click any of the contact names listed. (If you have added folders to the Address Book, you may first need to click the drop-down list currently labeled `Main Identity's Contacts` and choose the correct folder for the person you want.)

To (optionally) check the address data on the person you select, click the Properties button to see the Properties dialog box I discuss in Chapter 6. Click OK in the Select Name dialog box when you're done, and the contact you choose is inserted into the text box.

 If you recently used a person's address from the address book, click the down arrow next to the Address Book button. Recently used names appear there. Click that name to use it again.

Choosing themes in the wizard

Themes are, well . . . a recurring theme in wizards that use the word processor program. A *theme* is a combination of colors and fonts, with a name like *Engraved Winter.* (The first word of the name indicates a font choice, and the second word indicates a particular set of colors.) When you choose a layout or design on the first screen of a wizard, Works initially chooses a theme for you. On the Choose a Theme page, however, you can make your own choices. Here's how:

- ✔ Drag the Font Set slider left or right to change fonts. Fonts are simpler to the left, and jazzier to the right.

- ✔ Drag the Color Set slider left or right to change colors. Colors are more drab (conservative) to the left, and jazzier to the right.

- ✔ On each slider, a subtle mark that looks like an indentation shows Works' original setting, so you can return to those settings if you like.

To change themes after the wizard is done, use the word processor's Format Gallery. Choose Format⇨Format Gallery. I discuss this feature in more detail in Chapter 15, but basically it works like the preceding bullets describe. On the Format All tab, adjust the sliders, and then click the Apply All button at the bottom.

Using the Works templates

A few of the Works tasks are templates, not wizards. In general, these tasks simply create a standard document in one of the Works programs and then leave you alone with it: No additional screens with suggestions or choices appear.

A few templates also launch standard features of a program, leaving you answering dialog boxes without step-by-step instructions. For instance, the Mail-Merge Documents task starts you on a process of opening files and inserting fields. This is the process that the word processor program begins when you use its mail-merge tool.

For additional help with tasks, check out the other chapters in Part II of this book to see whether I cover the task you're using. Or, look in the chapters for the Works program that's being used for a description of the feature.

Saving Time with Your Own Templates

Templates you create yourself are prototypes for documents you need to use frequently, such as your own letterhead, a design for a monthly newsletter, or a seasonal game schedule for sports teams. By using a template, you can create a document customized for each occasion. For instance, you might use a newsletter template every month to create a new newsletter document. You can even use one of Works' pre-built Tasks to start a document; then you can modify the document and save it as a personalized template.

Creating your own template

To create a template, begin by creating a document that contains all the text and graphics that don't change (such as your address or logo). Format the document and set up the page layout. If you want the text that will be added later to have a particular format, insert dummy (placeholder) text and format that. To later replace the dummy text, don't just delete it. Select the dummy text, type replacement text, and the new text takes on the same format.

To save the document as a template, follow these steps:

1. **Choose File➪Save As.**

    The Save As dialog box appears. Don't bother opening a folder or typing a name here. Works saves templates in a special folder.

2. **Click the Template button in the lower-right corner of the Save As dialog box.**

    A Save As Template dialog box appears, requesting a name.

3. **Enter a name for the template in the Save As Template dialog box.**

4. **Make this template the default, if you like.**

    If this template represents a document that you frequently use (say, a blank letterhead), click the Use This Template For New *Whatever* Documents check box (with *Whatever* being Word Processing, Database, and so on). This action turns your template into a default template. Now, whenever you start a new document of that type — a word processing document, for instance — your document automatically takes the form of that template.

    To restore the original default that Works uses, click the Default button. The Save As Template dialog box expands. Click the Reset button that appears.

5. **Click the OK button.**

Works stores your template in a special folder. Word processor templates are stored as a special type of file that ends in `.wpt`; spreadsheet templates are regular `.wks` (spreadsheet) files; and database templates are regular `.wdb` (database) files.

Works stores the templates in the folder C:\Windows\Profiles\[your login name]\Application Data\Template. By [your login name], I mean the name you use to log on to your PC when Windows starts.

Modifying your template

If you need to modify a template in any way, simply replace the template with a new template, using the same name. To do so, follow these steps:

1. **Open the Task Launcher and click the Tasks tab.**

   At the bottom of the Tasks list, you see the entry Personal Templates. (If the Personal Templates entry doesn't appear after you create your first template, close the Task Launcher and reopen it.) Your templates also appear in the list of Tasks for each program. You see them when you choose the appropriate program on the Task Launcher's Program tab.

2. **Click Personal Templates to see a list of templates that you can use.**

3. **Click the template you want to modify and then click the Start button that appears.**

   Works creates a document that looks exactly like your template.

4. **Modify this template as you like and then save it as a template.**

   Follow the preceding numbered steps for saving a template, and use the name of the original template in Step 3.

5. **Click Yes in the dialog box that warns you,** The template [your template] already exists. Do you want to replace the existing template?

   The modified template replaces the old template.

Using your template

When you use a template, Works creates a new document that reproduces an exact copy of that template. To use a template you have created, do the following:

1. **Open the Task Launcher and click the Tasks tab.**

   At the bottom of the Tasks list, you see the Personal Templates entry. (If the Personal Templates entry doesn't appear after you create your first template, close the Task Launcher and reopen it.) Your templates also appear in the list of Tasks for each program. You see them when you choose the appropriate program on the Task Launcher's Program tab.

2. **Click Personal Templates to see a list of templates that you can use.**

3. **Click your template and then click the Start button that appears.**

   Works creates a document that looks exactly like your template.

4. **Modify this new document as you like and save it as you would any document.**

   When you save your document, Works saves it as a document and not as a template.

If you have dummy text that has been formatted, don't just delete it! Instead, select it and type your replacement text so that your new text takes on the old format.

Chapter 6

Creating an Address Book

The Address Book is a small program that plays a central role in lots of different things you might want to do, such as sending e-mail, addressing letters, or remembering birthdays with the Works Calendar. The Address Book can store all of the following information:

✔ People's names, mailing addresses, nicknames, and titles

✔ Birthdays and anniversaries

✔ Spouses's and children's names

✔ Business information: titles, phone, fax, and pager numbers, and the like

The Address Book also lets you organize people (contacts) into groups, in case you want to send all those people the same letter or e-mail. You may want to create several groups in your Address Book — one for friends, another for clients, and another for members of some organization that you run.

You can search for people in the Address Book by name, by address (both mail and e-mail), by phone (both home and business), or by any other kind of data stored in the Address Book. You can also sort by common data — such as zip code.

This chapter explains how to set up, organize, and view information in the Address Book.

Use a Works database instead of the Address Book if you need to include a wide variety of information about each person, such as his or her shoe size, team position, or payment status. See Part V of this book for more about databases.

Using the Address Book with Other Programs

One of the good reasons for using the Address Book is that it doesn't just stand alone, as a paper address book does. It helps you enter address information automatically in programs that require address information. Many types of software, especially Works and other Microsoft software, work this way. For instance, the Address Book does the following:

- ✔ Supplies name and address information for letters and envelopes created in the Works word processor.

- ✔ Provides e-mail addresses for Outlook Express.

- ✔ Exports birthdays and anniversaries to the Works Calendar for automatic reminders.

- ✔ Provides mailing addresses and other information so you can send out your own junk mail or newsletters by using Works' mail merge feature (described in Chapter 8).

- ✔ Finds you a map to someone's address, obtaining the map from the Web by using Internet Explorer.

- ✔ Supplies phone or fax numbers for dialing or fax software.

- ✔ Stores information for and initiates a NetMeeting session if your PC is equipped with Microsoft's NetMeeting software. (NetMeeting comes with Windows 2000.)

With NetMeeting, you can chat (in text or audio), see video, or doodle with several people, using the Internet to link everyone up. A discussion about this complex software is beyond the scope of this book. Once you have Internet Explorer running (see Chapter 24) go to Microsoft's Web site, www.microsoft.com/windows/netmeeting, for more information.

In previous editions of Works, Address Books were Works databases. In the new millennium, Microsoft wants everyone — Works users or not — to use the same Address Book. Microsoft now makes its special Address Book part of Windows and uses it in various Microsoft products, as outlined in the preceding list. By way of apology to old users, Works regularly offers to import old Works Address Books into the new one. You, of course, can continue to use a Works database to store your addresses, but databases are not as compatible with programs that use those addresses, such as Outlook Express.

Viruses and your address book

The one big risk of using Microsoft's Address Book for e-mail addresses is that it's a target for viruses because of its widespread use and its interconnectedness to other programs! The most virulent viruses in recent history obtained e-mail addresses from individual Address Books and used Outlook Express and Internet Explorer to e-mail the virus to those addresses. The risk is highest for people using all-Microsoft e-mail and Web software — namely you, if you use Works' programs. The best defense is to observe safe e-mail practices — *never* open an e-mail attachment that you're not expecting. Obtain a good book on e-mail, such as IDG Books Worldwide's *E-Mail For Dummies,* to learn more about how to avoid problems.

Opening the Address Book

You can open the Address Book by using one of the Tasks that Works supplies. Here's how:

1. **Click the Programs tab in the Task Launcher.**

   If you'd rather skip the Works Task Launcher, you can choose Start➪Programs➪Accessories➪Address Book, and then skip to Step 4.

2. **On the left side of the window, click Address Book. Then select Address Book from the list that appears on the right.**

3. **Click the <u>Start This Task</u> link.**

4. **Depending on whether you created an Address Book previously, Works may ask whether you want to import that Address Book. If you don't want to import anything, click the Cancel button. If you click OK, Works leads you through an importing process.**

   To get rid of this query about importing, click the check box labeled `Don't Display This Message in the Future.`

   The Address Book is now ready to receive information on all your friends and business associates. When you're done with your Address Book, choose File➪Exit.

Refer to Figure 6-1 for how the Address Book normally appears and a few of the basic controls. The panel (or column) on the left shows the folders and groups into which your Address Book is organized. Whatever folder you open on the left (by clicking it) is displayed on the right. Most people just use the Main Identity's Contacts folder, which is what the Address Book initially displays.

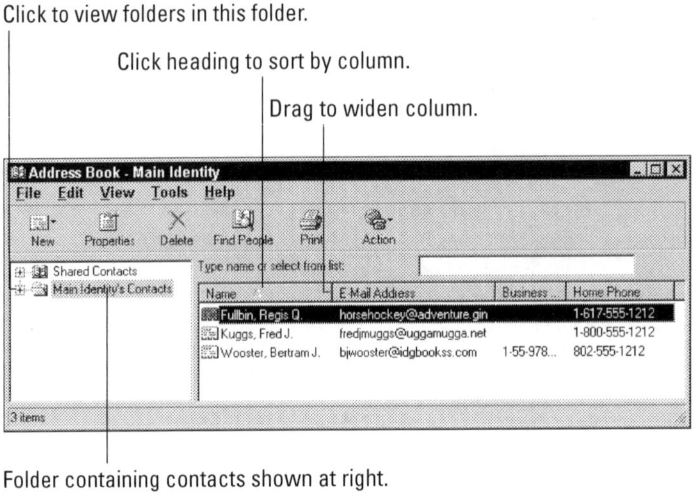

Click to view folders in this folder.

Click heading to sort by column.

Drag to widen column.

Figure 6-1:
Address
Book
basics.

Folder containing contacts shown at right.

Keep things simple. If you don't intend to organize your addresses into several different folders, you don't even need to view the panel on the left. All your information should go into the Main Identity's Contacts folder. That folder needs to be highlighted to make sure that all your addresses go there, so click it if it is not already highlighted. You can remove the left panel from view by choosing View➪Folders and Groups. You can restore the panel by repeating the same command.

Adding or Editing a Person (Contact)

To add a person (contact) or business to the Address Book, take the following steps. (If you created folders in addition to the Main Identity's Contacts folder, first click the folder where this information should go. If you are adding a person to a group, click that group.)

1. **Click the New button (at the top left) and choose New Contact from the menu that appears.**

   You now see the Properties dialog box.

2. **Click any of the seven tabs in the Properties dialog box and then enter any appropriate information about your contact.**

   At the very least, enter a name on the Name tab, as shown in Figure 6-2. (Don't bother with the Display field on the Name tab. Microsoft chooses a display name automatically from the name fields you use.)

   You can enter addresses for both home and business. In instances when Works consults the Address Book for address information, Works uses the home address unless you specify otherwise. To tell Works (and other programs) to use the business address, click the Default check box under the address fields on the Business tab.

A couple of areas of the Properties dialog box are tricky. See the section, "Coping with e-mail addresses, sex, and kids," later in this chapter, for more information.

3. Click OK to add this contact to the Address Book.

The Properties dialog box goes away.

Editing contact information

To edit information for a contact, click the contact's name in the Address Book window and then click the Properties button (or just double-click the contact's name). You then see the Summary tab of the Properties dialog box. You can click any of the tabs in this dialog box to edit the information there.

Coping with e-mail addresses, sex, and kids

I wouldn't want to imply that e-mail has anything to do with sex, or that either one has anything to do with having kids, but I will acknowledge that all three subjects do share something in common: They can all be confusing. As in life itself, the answer lies in knowing exactly what buttons to push.

The Shared Contacts and Main Identity's Contacts folders

What are those Shared Contacts and Main Identity's Contacts folders all about? The Address Book is initially set up to let you put contacts into either of two folders: Shared Contacts or Main Identity's Contacts. *Identities* are people who share the same Address Book — like you, your family, or co-workers who also use your PC or share a networked disk drive. You are the Main Identity, and each user has an identity that he or she can switch to in Outlook Express and in the Address Book (by choosing File⇨Switch Identity). Any contacts you want to share with

other identities go in the Shared Contacts folder, which you access by clicking that folder.

In this book, however, I'm trying to keep things simple, so I assume you don't plan on using Microsoft's identities scheme. If you are the only user of your PC and you don't plan on having other people with different e-mail addresses use Outlook Express for e-mail, you don't need to worry about identities. Put everyone in the Main Identity's (your) Contacts group. This is what the Address Book normally does anyway.

Adding e-mail addresses

Here's what to do to add a contact's e-mail address in the Properties dialog box:

1. **Select the Name tab (refer to Figure 6-1).**

2. **Type an e-mail address into the E-Mail Addresses text box.**

3. **Click the Add button to add that address to the list of addresses.**

4. **Repeat Steps 1 through 3 to enter additional e-mail addresses.**

Figure 6-2 shows the process.

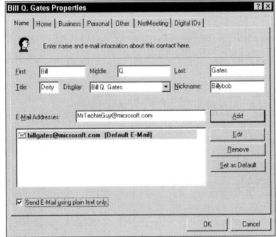

Figure 6-2:
Type an e-mail address; then click Add. Then you can add more, if necessary.

The first address you add is the default address – the one that is normally used by various programs. To make another address the default address, click that address in the list, and then click the Set as Default button. To remove an address from the list, click it, and then click the Remove button. To edit an address, click it, and then click the Edit button.

E-mail can have fancy formatting, such as font styles, colors, and sizes, but many people who receive it (like me) find such formatting annoying. More importantly, not all e-mail programs can handle special formatting. Such special effects can make replying messy, and using that formatting just puts unnecessary bits on the Internet, slowing it down. Give everyone a break by selecting the check box marked Send E-Mail Using Plain Text and sending plain text messages.

Choosing sex

The Personal tab of the Properties dialog box has a Gender choice. Most people find gender choice a bit confusing. The confusion here is that Gender does not refer to the spouse or kids who all appear on that same page. Gender refers to the sex of the main contact — him/her/it. Click the Gender drop-down list and choose Male, Female, or Unspecified (Unspecified being a good choice for a business name).

Adding kids

What about adding a person's kids to the Address Book? The process is similar to adding e-mail addresses, but not identical. Just follow these steps:

1. **Select the parent's entry in the Address Book.**

   The Properties dialog box appears.

2. **Select the Personal tab in the Properties dialog box.**

3. **Click the Add button.**

   A space opens up in the Children text box where you type in the child's name.

4. **Type the child's name where the words Child Name appear highlighted.**

To add another kid, click the Add button again. (See, adding kids is simpler than you thought.) To edit a kid, click him or her and then click the Edit button. To remove a kid (don't get excited, parents), click the kid and then click the Remove button.

Adding contacts without typing

If someone has sent you an e-mail message, adding that sender's e-mail address — and possibly other information — to the Address Book is very easy. To add someone's name and e-mail address, within Outlook Express, click the message from a sender you want to record. Then choose Tools⇨Add Sender to Address book.

If you already have an address book in some other program, such as Eudora, you may be able to import those addresses. Choose File⇨Import⇨Other Address Book. Choose the type of address book you wish to import in the Address Book Import Tool dialog box that appears, and then click the Import button. The import feature doesn't always do a very neat job of properly handing the information in foreign address books (for instance, people with multiple e-mail addresses in Eudora may end up as groups), but at least the e-mail addresses are imported.

Getting Contact Info from the Address Book

The Address Book gives you several ways to get the information you need. A simple way is to view the list of contacts, which shows you a few things about each person. Or, you can print out the Address Book, either entirely or by folder or group.

Viewing and sorting contacts

The most informative view of the Address Book — and the view that the Address Book normally shows you — is the Details view. (Other views — List, Large Icon, and Small Icon view — are available choices in the View menu. These views show more contacts at once, but fewer details.) Initially, the Details view shows you columns (called fields) for the contact's name, e-mail address, and phone numbers (see Figure 6-3), but you can change which fields appear (more on that in a second).

If you organize your addresses into folders or create groups (see "Organizing and Simplifying with Groups and Folders," later in this chapter), you can limit your view to just the people in a specific folder or group. Just click the folder or group in the left panel of the Address Book.

Clicks cycle between up/down, first/last name.

Indicates sorting column, direction.

Right-click to change display.

Figure 6-3:
Clicking column headings in various ways lets you change sorting or what data is displayed. Here, birthdays replace work phone numbers.

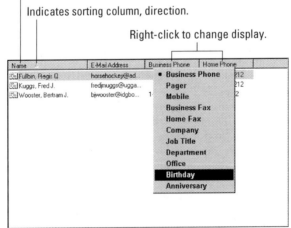

As I mention, you can change which fields appear. To display a different data field, such as a column of Birthdays, right-click a column heading for data you do not need at the moment (such as Business Phone — but not Name or E-Mail Address, which are always present). In the menu that appears, as shown in Figure 6-3, choose any kind of information you want displayed in that column.

Initially, contacts are sorted alphabetically by surname. To list the contacts in order of a different field, such as by phone number (in numerical order), click that field's column heading. An up or down arrow in the column heading indicates which heading is currently being sorted and in which order. Click the arrow in that column heading to sort in reverse order, such as names from Z–A instead of A–Z.

You can sort by last or first names. In the Names column, if you continue clicking the column heading, sorting changes in the following way: your first click sorts by last name, in reverse order; your second click switches you from sorting by last names to sorting by first names; your third click sorts first names in reverse; your fourth click takes you back where you started.

Locating contact information

Here are a few ways to locate the people or information you need in the Address Book:

✔ **To see the information about a contact:** Double-click that contact. The Properties dialog box in which you entered all of that contact's information appears.

✔ **To find people by name or any other information:** Choose Edit➪Find People. In the Find People dialog box that appears, type whatever information you have. (Type a full or partial name in the Name box, for instance, or just a few letters of either name.) Then click the Find Now button.

For instance, you can find everyone in the Acme Corporation by typing **Acm** in the Other text box. If your search is successful, the Find People dialog box expands to display a name or list of names. Double-click any of those names to see the details.

✔ **If the person you're looking for is not in your address book:** You can look for that person on the Web by using Internet Explorer. In the Address Book, choose Edit➪Find People, click the Look In box, and select any of the Web services listed there. Click the Find Now button. To go to the Web site you choose, click the Web Site button.

Printing contacts

You can print your Address Book, but only rarely will you want to print the whole thing — it simply holds much more information than most people need at one time. To help you trim down the print job, the Address Book lets you select certain records for printing, and also gives you three choices of what information to print. Follow these steps to print just what you want:

1. **To print less than the entire book, first select the contacts you want to print.**

   To select a single contact, click it.

   To select several contacts, hold down the Ctrl key and click them.

   To select a series of contacts, click the first one, and then hold down the Shift key and click the last one. You can add individuals to the series by holding down the Ctrl key and clicking.

   To select a folder or group, click it in the left panel of the Address Book window.

2. **Click the Print button near the top of the Address Book window.**

   The Print dialog box appears.

3. **Choose one of the three selections in the Print Style area:**
   - **Memo:** Prints a bulleted list of contacts with all the information you have entered about each contact. Blanks — any fields that you haven't filled in (say, fax number) — aren't printed.
   - **Business card:** Prints a list of contact names, with their companies, business numbers, and e-mail addresses.
   - **Phone list:** Prints a list of contacts, with all the phone numbers you have entered for that contact.

4. **Enter the number of copies you want printed in the Number of Copies box.**

5. **Click the Print button.**

Organizing and Simplifying with Groups and Folders

After you get a few dozen people in your Address Book, you may want to get organized. You have two tools to help you clean things up:

✔ **Folders:** *Folders* are collections of contacts that make finding certain contacts easier. For instance, you might have a folder for the contacts in each business you sell to. To create a new folder, choose File⇨New Folder, type a folder name in the Properties dialog box that appears, and click OK. Open that folder by clicking it. Add contacts to it as you would to the Main Identity's Contacts folder. You can also drag contacts from other folders into the new folder, just as you would with Windows Explorer.

✔ **Groups:** A *group* is a single name that refers to a bunch of people to whom you want to send the same e-mail messages or printed documents. A group is often more useful than a folder for e-mail or bulk printed mail.

If you have a group of people — your family, for instance — to whom you regularly send the same e-mail or printed document, you can make life easier by creating a group alias for these people. An *alias* is a nickname for a list of contacts in your address book — like *family* for your family, *golf buddies* for your golf buddies, or *fellow idiots* for your nude bungee-jumping group.

When you send e-mail with Outlook Express, you can type that single group alias instead of typing a half-dozen different addresses. When you send bulk mail (say, print a bunch of labels for your newsletter), you can tell Works what group to use.

To create a group, take the following steps. (If you have created additional folders besides the Main Identity's Contacts folder, first click the folder in which you want this alias stored.)

1. **Click the New button on the Address Book's toolbar, and choose Group from the drop-down menu that appears.**

   A Properties dialog box appears, with two tabs: Group and Group Details. Click the Group tab if it's not already selected.

2. **Type a name for the group in the Group Name text box.**

3. **Add group members.**

   You can add group members in either of two ways:

   • If they're not already in your Address Book, type their name in the Name text box, type their e-mail address in the E-Mail text box, and then click the Add button. Repeat for each member.

   • If the group members are already in your Address Book, click the Select Members button. In the Select Members dialog box that appears, click a person or group on the left, and then click the Select button to add that person or group to your Members list (on the right).

• To remove someone's name, click that person's name in the Members list and then press the Delete key on your keyboard. To add someone's name from another folder, choose that folder from the drop-down list just above the list of names on the left side of the dialog box, click the person's name, and then click the Select button.

4. After you add all the members of your group, click OK.

5. When you're done adding members to the group, click the OK button.

To return to that same Properties dialog box and make changes, double-click the group in the left panel of the Address Book. To remove a member, click that member's name in the Group Members list box, and then click the Remove button. You can also add or remove group members by using the right panel of the Address Book, just as you would in a folder. See the section, "Adding or Editing a Person (Contact)," earlier in this chapter.

If someone has more than one e-mail address, Outlook Express uses the default address. For information about default addresses, see the discussion of adding e-mail addresses in the section, "Coping with e-mail addresses, sex, and kids," earlier in this chapter.

Chapter 7

Almost Instant Letters and Envelopes

A s cool as electronic communications are — e-mail, paging, instant messaging, and the rest of it — the day will arrive when you want or need to send a letter on paper. Works has a word-processor task to help you create a good-looking letter in practically no time: the Letters task. The envelopes tool can give you a professional-looking envelope to send your letter in. If only Works could lick stamps. . . .

Creating a Letter

T he Letters task on the Works Task Launcher is, not surprisingly, a good way to launch a letter. On the Tasks page of the Works Task Launcher, choose the Letters & Labels task category, and launch the Letters task that is then listed. (See Chapter 5 for help on launching tasks.)

The Works' Word Processor window appears, maximized to fill your screen. On top of that is the magical, mystical Works Letter wizard ("the wiz" to its friends). The wiz provides up to five different screens to fill out. The screens are listed down the left side of the wizard screen, as Figure 7-1 shows, and as discussed below.

You don't need to fill out all the screens. As soon as you like what you see in the word processor window, you can click the wiz's Finish button.

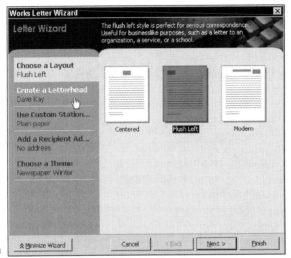

Figure 7-1:
Choosing a
layout on
the first
screen. You
can move to
any other
screen
(listed on
the left side)
by clicking
it, as the
cursor
shown here
indicates.

To proceed in order from screen to screen, just click the Next button on each screen. To go directly to a screen, click its name; refer to Figure 7-1. Here are the screens, in order:

- ✔ **Choose a Layout:** On this screen, click Centered, Flush Left, or Modern. Use this screen to position your name and address, and to indent the text. The wiz also makes an initial choice of font and colors for you, but you can change that on the Choose a Theme page.

- ✔ **Create a Letterhead:** Here's where you put in your own name, address, and other information about yourself. Click in each text box and type the requested information — unless you intend to use pre-printed stationery that already provides such information. In that event, leave these text boxes blank. Return to the Choose a Layout screen to see how your letterhead looks now.

- ✔ **Use Custom Stationery:** If you have preprinted stationery, here's the place to tell the wizard: Click the option box labeled `Leave Room For Custom Stationery`. If you don't have pre-printed stationery, click the option box marked `I Have Plain Paper`.

  If you are using pre-printed stationery, tell the wiz how much room to reserve for the printed area of your stationery. Enter distances in the Top, Bottom, Left, and Right value boxes. For instance, if your letterhead's printable area begins 2.5 inches down from the top, type **2.5** in the Top value box.

✔ **Add a Recipient Address:** If you want the recipient's address on your letter, this is the place to enter it. For a personal letter, which usually doesn't use such an internal address, click the option labeled `Do not include a recipient address`. Otherwise, click the option labeled `Type Or Select A Single Individual From The Address Book`. Then, either type the address in the space provided, or click the Address Book button to grab the address from the Address Book. See the discussion of grabbing an address from the Address Book in Chapter 5.

Works uses a person's home address (the address on the Home tab of the Address Book) unless you have selected the Default check box under the business address (on the Business tab).

✔ **Choose a Theme:** Drag the sliders left or right to change the font and color set. See the section on choosing a theme in Chapter 5 for more details.

You can get rid of the Help panel by clicking the X at the top-left corner. The end result of using the Letter task gives you . . . by George . . . a letter! Well, maybe not a letter you would care to send. For one thing, the text that appears:

```
Dear Friend,

Replace this text with the contents of your letter.
```

is rather imperious, demanding that your friend write you a letter. Not nice. You also might take issue with the way it's designed. The following sections detail how to customize this letter to your needs.

Replacing text with your own words

All the text in your letter can be changed. You just type new stuff in its place. In general, I find the best way to replace text is to highlight the existing text (drag across it, as Figure 7-2 shows), and then begin typing the replacement text. That way, you're reasonably sure of not losing any special text formatting that the wizard has created for you. Another alternative is to click just before the existing text, type your stuff, and then delete the rest.

If you delete everything that appears in a particular style (say, the entire return address) before you type in new text, you run the risk of losing the formatting (font, color, style, alignment, spacing) that the text had. Leave some of the to-be-replaced text with the format you want to retain. Then, when you type in your replacement text, Works knows how to format your text.

Works picks up its text format either from the character before the blinking cursor where you're typing, or (if no such character remains in the paragraph) from the formatting of the hidden paragraph mark. (See Chapter 13 for more about cursors and paragraph marks and other invisible characters.)

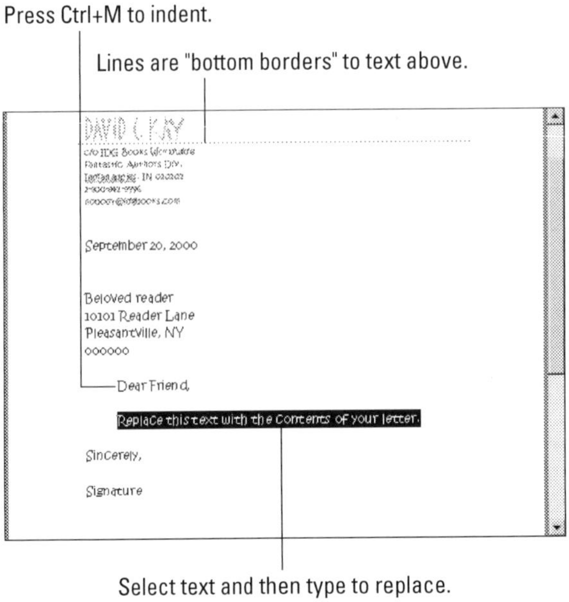

Press Ctrl+M to indent.

Lines are "bottom borders" to text above.

DAVID C KAY

c/o IDG Books Worldwide
Fantastic Authors Div.
Indianapolis, IN 032202
7-800-762-2974
nobody@idgbooks.com

September 20, 2000

Beloved reader
10101 Reader Lane
Pleasantville, NY
000000

Dear Friend,

Replace this text with the Contents of your letter.

Sincerely,

Signature

Figure 7-2:
A few
changes
you could
make.

Select text and then type to replace.

If you make a mistake, you can always undo it by pressing Ctrl+Z. Press it repeatedly to undo multiple actions.

Fooling with formatting

Works uses a number of tricks to get text to appear in various ways. For detailed help with text formatting, see Chapters 15 and 16. Here are some tips for specific formatting issues:

- **Text size or color:** The wizard uses mainly 10-point type for the body text when it creates letters. You may find that size a bit squinty. To enlarge text, select all the body text and choose Format➪Font. In the Size list box (in the Font dialog box that appears), choose a bigger number for larger text. For a different color, choose from the Color drop-down list box.

- **Date:** The wiz automatically puts today's date on your letter. How thoughtful! Or is it? If you save this letter to reopen it later, guess what? The date is automatically updated to *that* day's date! (The wiz is using the word processor's Insert➪Date and Time feature.)

  If you don't like this auto-date-update feature, you can change this setting. Type in a date yourself — either today's (if you don't want the date to change during later edits) or some other day's.

Note: When you try to change the date, however, Works doesn't let you edit it. That's because the date is actually a special code, so you can't edit the text that makes it up. Instead, delete it entirely and type an entire new date. If you type in a new date, it will not change automatically when you later reopen the letter file.

✔ **Name in all capitals:** When you use certain layouts or themes, your name appears in all capitals. Two settings can make this happen: Either your font doesn't offer lowercase letters, or you've selected the All Caps option.

If you don't want this appearance, changing it is easy. Choose Format⫐Font, and in the Font dialog box that appears, see if the All Caps check box has a check mark. If so, click the check mark to clear it. If not, choose a different font in the Font list box. The Sample area shows the result of your choices so that you can choose a font that offers both uppercase and lowercase letters.

✔ **Horizontal lines:** Certain layouts or themes place a line under certain text. The line comes from border formatting of that paragraph. To change the line, click anywhere in the text above the line and choose Format⫐Borders and Shading. In the Borders and Shading dialog box that appears, click to select the Bottom box. Then choose a new line style in the Line Style drop-down list (or None, at the top of the list). You can also choose a line color in the Line Color drop-down list box.

Note: Paragraph indentation affects the length of the line. To indent text without indenting the line, click before the text and press the Tab key, or increase the first-line indentation. (See Chapter 13.)

✔ **Indenting:** The Letters task sometimes indents paragraphs by using paragraph formatting, not tabs. You can increase indentation by half-inch increments by selecting text and pressing Ctrl+M. To decrease indentation, press Ctrl+Shift+M. In some layouts, lines that are initially blank (used for spacing) are not indented, whereas others are indented. If you place text on these blank lines, you need to indent them so they match the others.

✔ **Center/left/right alignment:** You choose the alignment of your letterhead in the first wizard screen. If you now want to change alignment of any line or paragraph, click anywhere in the line or paragraph and press Ctrl+L for left-alignment, Ctrl+R for right-alignment, or Ctrl+E for centering.

✔ **Letterhead for subsequent pages:** Professionally designed stationery has a larger letterhead on the first page than on subsequent pages. Not so for Works letterheads. If you want that effect, use a header for subsequent letterheads. Check out Chapter 16, in which I describe how to create headers and turn off the header on Page 1 of your document.

✔ **Margins:** Margins are the responsibility of the Page Setup command that lives in the File menu. Read more about setting up the page in Chapter 4.

Unless your letter is just a quick note to a friend, you probably want to save it on your PC's hard drive. I discuss saving files and creating folders in Chapter 2.

Turning your letter into a reusable letterhead

If you want to keep the letterhead portion of your letter for future use, turn your letter into a template. Later, you can use that template whenever you want to create a letter. Delete all text except the letterhead and any other text that you want to keep. Scoot over to Chapter 5 for instructions on saving your file as a template, and later using it.

If you're not happy with the letterhead you can create with the Letters task, you have an

alternative. The Stationery task, while very similar to the Letters task, is even simpler because it has fewer screens. Check it out for semi-cute graphic clip art to adorn your letterhead. Most of the letterheads are for personal letters, however, and not business. As with the Letters task, go to the Tasks page of Works' Task Launcher, and choose Letters & Labels. Instead of choosing the Letters task, however, choose the Stationery task.

Creating and Printing an Envelope

May we have the envelope, please? And the winner is . . . you! You win because creating and printing envelopes is one of the dirty little jobs that Works makes easier than it used to be. In the dark ages of word processing (six or seven years ago), printing an envelope was a job that took a squadron of software engineers, five phone calls to the printer and software vendors, four Tylenol tablets, and ultimately, a ballpoint pen. (Another tale I can bore younger people with when I get old.)

Creating the envelope

The best way to create a single envelope depends on whether you already have a letter written to the addressee. If you have such a letter, open it (if it's not open already) and copy the addressee's name and address from your letter to the Windows clipboard. (Select the text by dragging across it, and then press Ctrl+C or choose Edit⇨Copy.)

Then follow these steps to create an envelope:

1. **If you're already using the word processor (say, you're looking at a letter), choose Tools⇨Envelopes from the word processor menu bar. If you're not already using the word processor, launch the Envelopes task in the Works Task Launcher.**

   You can launch the Envelopes task by choosing Tasks, clicking Letters & Labels on the left side of the window, choosing Letters in the task list that appears, and then clicking Start This Task (on the far right).

Whichever way you start, an Envelopes dialog box appears, asking whether you want to print a single envelope or print mail-merge envelopes. `Single envelope` is already chosen for you, and that's the choice you want.

2. **Click OK.**

   The Envelopes Settings dialog box appears.

3. **Choose the size of your envelope in the Envelope Size list box.**

   Sizes are given both by number (as in a *number 10 envelope*) and by dimensions. Standard business envelopes are #10, and that's what Works initially chooses for you.

4. **Click the New Document button.**

   The Envelopes Settings dialog box disappears, and a new word processor window opens, containing a blank envelope document. As shown in Figure 7-3, the envelope has two boxed areas — one for the addressee and one for your return address. Your blinking typing cursor is already placed in the addressee box.

Figure 7-3: The envelope document appears in its own word processor window. You add the text.

David C. Kay
c/o IDG Books Worldwide
Fantastic Authors Div.
Indianapolis, IN 010101

Beloved reader
10101 Reader Lane
Pleasantville, NY
000000

5. **Add the addressee information.**

   The typing cursor is already present and blinking in the addressee box. If you started out by copying addressee information from an existing letter, press Ctrl+V (or choose Edit⇨Paste from the menu bar) to paste the addressee information in the main box.

   If you started this envelope from scratch, you need to type the addressee information.

6. **Make any formatting or alignment changes you want to the text.**

   If you pasted text from your letter, it's in the same style and color as it was in the letter. You may or may not want that on the envelope. If you desire, select all the text and then change font or paragraph formatting.

7. **Move or change the addressee box, if you want.**

   You can move the box by dragging its outline. Drag it by any point on the outline except the black squares. To resize the box, drag any black square to move a side or a corner. Your cursor turns into a two-headed arrow showing the directions you can drag.

8. **Click inside the return address box and type your return address.**

9. **Save the envelope document with File⇨Save (see Chapter 2) if you want to send other mail to this person in the future.**

By deleting the addressee information and saving the file as a template (read more about this in Chapter 5), you can avoid typing the return address on new envelopes in the future. Just open your envelope template (which now contains your return address), type the addressee information, and print. Or, you can copy and paste the addressee information from any letter that's open in another window.

Printing the envelope

The procedure for printing your envelope is like for any other document: Choose File⇨Print. One possible confusion, however, is the number of different ways you can put an envelope into your printer. Follow these steps to avoid this problem:

1. **Choose File⇨Page Setup.**

2. **Click the Envelope Feed tab in the Page Setup dialog box that appears.**

   A set of icons labeled Feed Method shows different orientations of the envelope in the feed tray. An arrow indicates the direction that paper moves from the tray toward the printer.

3. **Position your envelope according to the picture you choose — the lightest one. Or click the icon that represents how you will be placing your envelope in the tray.**

4. **Click OK when you're done, and then go ahead and print the envelope.**

Don't neglect any special instructions about mechanical issues that are in your printer manual. On some printers, for instance, you need to set a paper-thickness control to handle the envelope thickness. On others, envelopes need to be fed by hand into a special slot.

Chapter 8

Almost Instant Labels and Junk Mail

"*D*on't miss this amazing offer, *Mr./Ms. Resident* of *Anywhere, Some Country.* Now you, too, can create junk mail for all those groups we know you belong to, like *Your Club, Your Religious Organization,* or *Your Favorite Charity.*"

Junk-mail paragraphs like the above are made possible by the wizardry of something called mail merge: the ability to extract specific data (say, addresses) from a collection of data and place (merge) this into a letter, on a label, or on an envelope. Works offers you mail-merge power, too — although I'm sure you have legitimate, non-junk uses for this power, such as:

⮞ Labels for mailing bulletins to a group or organization

⮞ Letters to people in your religious organization who have children

⮞ Bills to your customers

⮞ Confirmation letters for registrants to a conference

⮞ Announcements or advertisements to your customers

⮞ Invitations to a party

Of course, you have to have the data (such as names, addresses, amounts due, shoe size, number of children, and so on) in order to use it to create your own non-junk mail. For instance, you would need my address in order to invite me to a party. (Author Dave Kay, c/o IDG Books Worldwide, Indianapolis, IN 46256-3917. Serve chocolate, offer airfare, and I'm yours.) That collection of data is called your database. If you're sending a letter, you also have to write that letter, leaving special holes for the data to be inserted, like the words that I've italicized in the first paragraph. In this chapter, I point out the easiest way to do your own junk . . . er, bulk mailing, create a database, write customized letters, and print letters, labels, or envelopes.

You may have simpler labeling tasks to do, too. File folders, cassette tapes, and jars of fruit jam may all need labels. Or, you may need labels or cards that all have the same printing on them. You don't need a database for these simple tasks; you just type in the information. To find out more about these types of tasks, read the sidebar elsewhere in this chapter, "Creating other labels or business cards."

Obtaining a Database of Addresses and Other Information

The first step in being able to send bulk mail is to create or otherwise obtain a list of addresses in some electronic form. For plain old mailing labels or envelopes, you only need names and addresses. For anything else, like dunning letters telling people how much they owe, your list must also include that additional information.

Using the Address Book

If you only need people's names and addresses, one database of addresses that Works can use is your Microsoft Address Book. What? You don't have a Microsoft Address Book? Heavens. Quick, page back to Chapter 6 before your friends find out.

Is the Address Book the best database for your needs? The advantage of using the Address Book is that you'll probably fill out parts of the Address Book anyway, for e-mail. For bulk mailing, one disadvantage is that the Address Book is designed to hold only addresses and certain specific other data, like birthdays and spouses' names. If you need to print out letters containing non-standard data, such as dues paid by the addressee, the Address Book won't suffice. (You could dedicate the Notes field on the Other tab of the Address Book to such a purpose, or use the Pager Number field on the Business tab for dues paid, but that gets rather messy.)

If you plan to use your Address Book but don't want to send mail to everyone in it, you can use the Groups feature. With this feature, you can separate out friends from co-religionists from fellow nude bungee-jumpers. Sending a letter about the next jump meet to your church members will probably complicate your life. Assigning contacts to groups enables you to send mail to exactly the right people. Even if someone is both a church member and fellow jumper, you will send him the right mail at the right time.

Using other sources

Works can also import addresses and other information from a wide variety of files. This is a handy feature because often the information comes to you as a file from someone else who uses a different program. What's more, if you need to print more than just names and addresses, the Address Book may not do the job. Works can import data from the following types of files:

- Microsoft Works Database
- Microsoft Access
- Microsoft Excel
- Paradox
- Text files of various types (files ending in `.txt`, `.csv`, `.tab`, or `.asc`)
- dBASE III, IV, and 5

Most programs that store data can save it as one of these file types.

If you want to input your own data in a Works file, one option is to create a Works Database containing the names, addresses, and other information that you need. (See Part V of this book for more on databases.) Another option is to write a document in the word processor that has this form:

```
Lastname, Firstname, Street, City, State, ZIP
Kay, David, 10101 Dummies Rd., Boston, MA, 01210
Cooper, D.B., 101 Nowhere Rd., Noplace, ND, 01234
```

And so on. The first line (called field headings) gives names for each type of information on the following lines (the data). Everything on a line is separated by commas or some other character that is not used in your data, such as an asterisk. (Spaces after the comma are allowable.)

Save the word processor document as a text file. Choose File⇨Save As to open the Save As dialog box. Then choose Text File in the Save As Type list box, enter a file name in the File Name text box, and click Save.

Creating Address Labels for Bulk Mailings

The Works mailing labels feature is designed to print addresses on labels (or cards) made by Avery and other label companies. Before you begin, get to know the different kinds of labels available to you. Take a trip to your local office supply store or visit a vendor's Web site, such as www.avery.com. Ink-jet printers and laser printers need different types of paper, so be sure you get the right kind of labels for your printer. If you're not certain what type of printer you're using, take your printer's manufacturer and model number to the store with you.

If you want to send out form letters, you can avoid printing labels altogether. Just use envelopes with windows in them. Insert the addressee field in the form letter, positioned so that it shows through the window!

To print address labels, you can either launch the Mailing Labels Task from the Task Launcher or use the labels function in the word processor program. Follow these steps to create address labels:

1. **Click <u>T</u>asks on the Works Task Launcher menu bar. Or if you're already using the word processor, choose <u>T</u>ools⇨<u>L</u>abels and skip ahead to Step 5.**

   The Tasks page appears, as shown in Figure 8-1.

2. **Click Letters & Labels in the list of tasks on the left side of the window.**

   The right side of the window lists the letters, labels, and envelopes for which tasks exist.

3. **Click Mailing Labels in the list on the right side of the window.**

4. **Click the <u>Start This Task</u> link on the far right.**

   Works splats a Labels dialog box on your screen, asking what kind of labels you want to print.

5. **In the Labels dialog box, choose Mailing Labels and click the OK button.**

   You see the Label Settings dialog box. It initially shows Avery labels. (For a different manufacturer, click the Label Products box and choose a new vendor.)

6. **Click the product number of the labels you are using.**

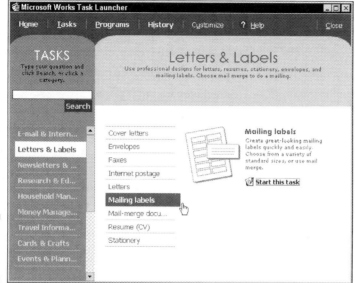

Figure 8-1:
Launching
labels.

7. **Click the New Document button.**

   Works creates a new document and sets up the page size, layout, and printer settings to print on your chosen labels.

   If you started from the Task Launcher, Works now displays the Open Data Source dialog box on top of the blank document. If you started from the word processor program, you have to open this dialog box yourself by choosing Tools⟶Mail Merge⟶Open Data Source.

8. **In the Open Data Source dialog box, choose your data source.**

   In other words, where are your names and addresses (and possibly other data) coming from? Choose Merge From the Address Book, if that's where your names and addresses are. If not, choose Merge Information From Another Type of Database.

9. **If you chose Merge From the Address Book in Step 8, the Insert Fields dialog box appears; skip ahead to Step 11.**

   If you chose Merge Information From Another Type of Database, a new dialog box (also named Open Data Source) appears.

   The Open Data Source dialog box works like any other file-opening dialog box. (For help, read through my discussion in Chapter 1 of opening documents when you're using a program.) Here, however, you must pay attention to the Files of Type drop-down list at the bottom. Click that list and choose the type of file that your address (and possibly other) information is in. If you create your database file manually, as described in the preceding section, choose Text Files. Then open the folder where your file is stored on your PC's hard drive and choose your file.

10. **If your database file is a text type file, follow these steps:**

    1. Reply to the query dialog box that appears: Do you want to use the entries in the first row of your data as field names? Click Yes if the first line of data in the file consists of field names (as in the example in the preceding section); click No if your data file begins with data (someone's name and address).

    2. In the Select Separator Character dialog box that appears, choose the character that separates the data in your text file, and click OK. (That would be a comma in the example of the preceding section.)

    The Insert Fields dialog box appears.

11. **Insert fields into your document using the Insert Fields dialog box.**

    The basic idea is to create a label by inserting the appropriate field names (such as "Surname") from your database file in the order you want them on the label. View this process in Figure 8-2. If the blinking cursor is not already positioned where you want data to appear, click in that location in the document.

    In the Insert Fields dialog box, click the name of field you want to insert first (for example, First Name) and then click the Insert button. The field appears in your document in funny brackets, like this: «Firstname». (If you're using a text file for your database, and it doesn't have field names, the fields are named F1, F2, and so forth.)

    Repeat this action for each field you want on the label. As you insert fields, you can click in the document to position where the field goes to add line breaks, spaces between fields and other text, or to alter formatting. For instance, to create a new line after the person's last name, click at the end of that line after «Surname» (or whatever the field is called), and press the Enter key.

At this point, you could print your labels. But before you print, thumb through the section, "Viewing Real Data in Your Label, Form Letter, or Envelope," later in this chapter. Also, you may want to save your work first (as you would any document). When you are ready to print, also peruse the section later in this chapter, "Printing bulk mail letters, envelopes, and labels."

You can remove the Insert Fields dialog box at any time by clicking the X in its upper-right corner.

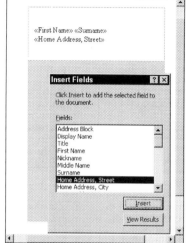

Figure 8-2:
Inserting
fields
into your
document.

Creating Envelopes for Bulk Mailings

To print a stack of envelopes addressed to a list of people, you can either launch the Envelopes Task from the Task Launcher or use the envelopes function in the word processor program. Here's the process:

1. **Click Tasks on the Works Task Launcher menu bar. Or if you're using the word processor, choose Tools⇨Envelopes and skip ahead to Step 5.**

   The Tasks page appears.

2. **Click Letters & Labels in the list of tasks on the left side of the window.**

   The right side of the window lists the letters, labels, and envelopes for which tasks exist.

3. **Click Envelopes in the list on the right side of the window.**

4. **Click the Start This Task link on the far right.**

   Works deposits an Envelopes dialog box on your screen.

5. **In the Envelopes dialog box, choose Mail Merge Envelopes and then click OK.**

6. **Choose the size of your envelope in the Envelope Size list box.**

   Sizes appear both in number form (as in a *number 10 envelope*) and in their dimensions. Standard business envelopes are #10, and that's what Works initially chooses.

If you can't find your envelope listed, click the Custom Size button. Enter your envelope's dimensions in the Envelope Size dialog box that appears.

7. **Click the New Document button.**

   A word processor window opens, containing an envelope. The envelope has two boxed areas, one for the addressee and one for the return address. On top of that window is the Open Data Source dialog box.

8. **At this point, creating an envelope is just like creating a label, so follow the steps in the preceding section, starting with Step 8.**

Creating Form Letters

To write a form letter, begin by writing your letter in the word processor program, leaving out any information that will come from a database. For instance, your letter might begin with your name and address, as usual, and then the salutation, Dear _____: — which omits the person's name (you add that later). If you were writing to tell them which hotel room they're assigned to (and that information is in your database), you might write, You have been assigned to Room _____ in the hotel, omitting the room number (which will be added later).

After you write your letter, link it to your database and insert data by using the following steps:

1. **Choose Tools⇨Mail Merge⇨Open Data Source.**

   Or choose Insert⇨Database Field. Either way, Works displays the Open Data Source dialog box.

2. **Tell Works where to find the data your letter is going to use.**

   If you use names, addresses, and other data from Microsoft's official Address Book, choose Merge From The Address Book. If you use names, addresses, and other data stored in a Works database or other type of file, choose Merge Information From Another Type of File. In the dialog box that appears, locate and double-click your chosen database.

   The Insert Fields dialog box appears (refer to Figure 8-2).

3. **Select and insert the fields that contain the data you need.**

   Data is stored in fields in your database or Address Book. The fields have names like Title or First Name. The task at this point is to choose fields from the Insert Fields dialog box and insert them into the appropriate places in the form letter. The procedure goes like this:

   1. Click in your document at the point where you omitted something that will come from the database. For instance, click just before the colon in Dear _____: to insert data there.

2. In the Insert Fields dialog box, find the field containing the data you want (for instance, Title); click that field name, and then click the Insert button to copy it to your document.

   Works inserts the field name in « » symbols in your document. For instance, your salutation may now read Dear «Title»:.

3. Repeat the preceding two steps until you have inserted all the fields you need in your document. See the tips following these steps.

   For instance, the complete salutation may read Dear «Title» «Surname»:.

When you're done inserting fields into your letter, your form letter is done! You can save the form letter as a file by pressing Ctrl+S.

See Figure 8-3 for an example of what you see when you're done. To check out your letter and see how it looks with actual data, check out the section later in this chapter,"Viewing Real Data in Your Label, Form Letter, or Envelope."

At this point, you can close the Insert Fields dialog box (click the X in its upper-right corner) or leave it on the screen to help you view your letter with real data.

Figure 8-3:
Your letter
with the
fields
inserted
into it.

```
«Title» «First·Name» «Surname»¶
«Home·Address,·Street»¶
«Home·Address,·City»,·«Home·Address,·State·or·Province»·«Home·Address,·Postal·
Code»¶
¶
Dear·«Nickname»:¶
¶
Start·typing·your·letter·here.¶
¶
```

You may want to clean up your letter a bit. Here are a few tips for the final cleanup:

- ✔ You can click in the document at any time — even while the Insert Fields dialog box is on your screen — and type new text or edit existing text.

- ✔ You can format the text of fields just as you would any other text — make it bold, for instance.

- ✔ If you make a mistake, highlight the field name in your document and press the Delete key.

- ✔ Add or remove spaces as necessary. For punctuation and spacing purposes, treat the field name as if it were the actual word. Leave no space between «Surname» and the colon in the salutation, for instance, but do put a space before and after any field that appears in mid-sentence. Press the spacebar to leave a space between the fields you insert, and press the comma key to type a comma — for example, to separate city from state.

Mail merge central

If you decide you want to change the database you use, add fields, view your work using real data, or do darned near anything related to the mail-merge feature described in this chapter, Works provides a central place to go.

Choose Tools➪Mail Merge, and you find a menu of various functions mentioned in various

places in this chapter. Note that if you choose to change databases (the Open Data Source option on the menu), Works prompts you to make sure you want to do that. If your document has fields that don't match the new database's fields, it won't print properly.

Viewing Real Data in Your Label, Form Letter, or Envelope

When you're done inserting the fields you need in your document, you're basically ready to print. However, I suggest reviewing the document first — looking at real data from the database, and not just field names. Unexpectedly long, short, or missing data in the database can create surprising results and make your document look weird. A letter to a person without a title in the database (Mr., Ms., or Dr.), for instance, sounds a bit rude: Dear Jones:.

To view your form letter, envelope, or envelope with real data in it, follow these steps:

1. **If the Insert Fields dialog box is still on your screen, click the View Results button. Otherwise, choose Tools➪Mail Merge➪View Results from the menu bar.**

   The tiny View Results dialog box appears. Some real data (someone's name and address) from your database appears in your document. View Figure 8-4 to see this effect.

2. **Check a few long names and addresses in the document by using the buttons in the View Results dialog box.**

   Click the ▶ button to advance to the next person, or the ◀ button to go back. Click the ▶▶ button to go to the top of the list, or ▶▶ to go to the end. Make sure that even long names and addresses fit on the label! If not, you need to change to a smaller font. (See Chapter 15 for details.)

   You can still edit the document or insert fields; just click either in the document window while the View Results dialog box is on the screen or in the Insert Fields dialog box. (You see results, not field names, if you insert fields now.)

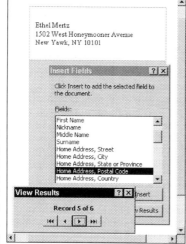

Figure 8-4:
Viewing real
data with
the View
Results
dialog box.

3. **When you're finished viewing your letter with a variety of records, click the X in the upper-right corner of the View Results dialog box to clear it from your screen.**

You can also see the results of your work by using Print Preview. Choose File⇨Print Preview from the menu bar and enjoy the view. Just click the Next button to see the next letter.

Continue editing the document if necessary; print for real when the document is ready. If you need to add fields, choose Tools⇨Mail Merge⇨Insert Fields to return to the Insert Fields dialog box. If the data is wrong or missing, you need to edit your database. To filter your data (select only certain records in your database), move on to the next section, "Mailing to Only a Select Few."

Mailing to Only a Select Few

You may not want to send your mailing to everyone in your database, especially if the database you're using is your Address Book. The Address Book contains a wide range of people from Aunt Mathilda to your boss. Sending your boss a family reunion invitation may not be a good career move, depending upon your family.

Unless you use a special database that contains only the people you want to mail, you need to select, filter, or mark certain records (people). Exactly what tools are available to do this depends on whether you use the Address Book or some other database file.

Selecting names from the Address Book

If the database linked to your document is your Address Book, you can use the Select Names option. (Select Names does not work with any other database.) This option enables you to select individuals or groups.

With your envelope, label, or form letter open in the word processor, here's how to specify exactly what records you want to select from the Address Book:

1. **Choose Tools➪Mail Merge➪Select Names.**

   The Select Names dialog box appears, showing you your list of contacts. If you want to see a list of contacts from a different folder than the one displayed, click the down arrow in the box just above the list of contacts and choose the name of the folder you want.

2. **Select the people who will get your letter.**

   To select people individually, click a name in the contacts list (on the left) and then click the Select button to add the name to the Merge Recipients list (on the right). To select names from a specific folder, click the drop-down list under the Find button and choose a folder by name.

   Rather than select people individually, however, this is a good time to make use of groups you have set up in the Address Book. (Go back to the earlier section of this chapter, "Using the Address Book.") Groups are listed on the left side, and you can select a group just as you would an individual's name.

3. **After you have chosen all your recipients, click the OK button.**

   You are now ready to print a letter for each person you selected.

Selecting records based on criteria

If you are using any database other than Microsoft's Address Book, the Filter and Sort option of the Works word processor enables you to select certain records (people) by using criteria. For instance, you can mail your letter to everyone with a zip code of 01920.

If you use a Works database file, you can limit your mailing to certain people. You mark records by using the database program, and then include only marked records. For more detailed information about filtering and marking, hop over to Chapter 22.

To select certain records, follow these steps:

1. **Choose Tools➪Mail Merge➪Filter and Sort.**

   The Filtering and Sorting dialog box of Figure 8-5 appears.

2. **In the Filtering and Sorting dialog box, apply criteria to various fields in your database.**

   For example, the Comparison and Compare To boxes let you create a filter, such as the `Serial number` field `is greater than 1000`, as you can see in Figure 8-5. Read through Chapter 22 for a discussion of filters for the full details.

3. **If you have already marked the records in your Works database to be included in this mailing, click the Use Marked Records button.**

   Only the marked records are now used. Any filtering criteria you set up in this dialog box apply to the marked records. If you want to remove filtering, click the Clear Filter button.

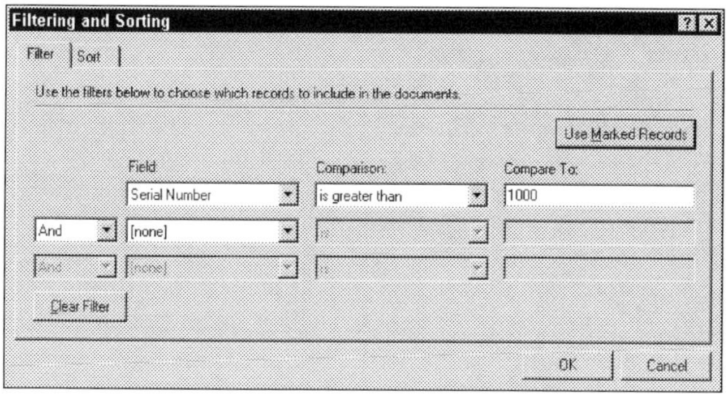

Figure 8-5: Controlling who gets your mailing by choosing criteria.

4. **Click the OK button when you are done.**

   The View Results dialog box pops up. You can step through your marked (or filtered) records and see the results as they will appear in your letter. If no records match your criteria, you return to the Filtering and Sorting dialog box. To turn off criteria in that dialog box, choose None in the Field drop-down list box.

Printing bulk mail letters, envelopes, and labels

Before you print anything that uses data from a database, check it out in Print Preview. (Choose File⇨Print Preview; read through Chapter 4 for details.) When you're ready to put ink on paper, don't click the Print button in the Print Preview window, however. Instead, choose File⇨Print, which displays the Print dialog box.

In the Print dialog box, you can control your printing so that you don't waste a lot of paper. Here are some of your options:

- ✔ You may print a single, test document before printing everything. Click the Test button. Use blank paper instead of your expensive label sheets to test. Put the test sheet under the label sheet and hold both up to a light to check alignment.

- ✔ You may specify which records (from your database) that you print. In the Print Range area of the Print dialog box, click Record and enter a starting and ending record number in the From and To boxes provided there.

- ✔ You may compile the entire set of letters, envelopes, and labels into a single document, and then (after reviewing and editing it) print that. Click the Send Merge Result to A New Document checkbox.

- ✔ You may skip lines that have no data in them. Click the Don't Print Lines With Empty Fields check box.

After you click the OK button in the Print dialog box, Works prints one letter, envelope, or label for each record in your database that you have allowed it to print. This could be a very large number! Make sure that you are ready to feed paper, envelopes, or blank labels into the printer.

Make sure that you use Avery (or other) labels that are designed for your type of printer. For laser printers, make sure that the labels are designed for laser printers, or you may end up with a gummy mess! Using laser printer labels in ink-jet printers sometimes works, but sometimes causes smears or paper misfeeds.

Chapter 9

Almost Instant Ads and Newsletters

*I*n the movie *Field of Dreams,* the advice, "If you build it, they will come," (given to a prospective builder of a baseball field) was astounding. And not just because the advice was given by a disembodied voice from the sky — we accept that in movies. No, the advice was astounding because it didn't suggest any marketing effort was necessary to get people to come! As anyone who has opened a business or a ballpark, run a fair, or tried to sell a car knows, "they" don't come unless you get the word out with a brochure, newsletter, poster, or flyer.

Works can help you turn out decent-looking promotional documents and newsletters with very little effort on your part. Just turn to your hard-working friends, the Works tasks.

Making a Newsletter

Newsletters come in as many different varieties as plant life, varying similarly in both content and appearance. Fortunately, Works has a newsletter task that can help you avoid vegetating and quickly create good-looking versions of the most popular types.

Designing a newsletter with the Newsletter wizard

To design a newsletter, go to the Tasks page of the Works Task Launcher, choose the Newsletters & Flyers category, and launch the Newsletters task. (Check out Chapter 5 for help with launching tasks.) The Works word processor window appears, maximized to fill your screen. On top of that window is the newsworthy, Newsletter wizard (alias, the wiz).

The wiz provides three different screens to fill out. The screens are listed on the left side of the wizard screen, as I discuss in the following list.

You don't need to fill out all the screens. After you like what you see in the word processor window, click the wiz's Finish button and be done with it all. To go from screen to screen, just click the Next button on each screen; to go directly to a screen, click its name.

Here are the screens, in order:

- ✔ **Choose a Topic:** On this screen, click Club, Family, Volunteer, or Winter. (Winter? Why Winter?) This screen is mainly about choosing a graphical image, not a topic. The wizard also makes an initial choice of font and text colors for you, which you can change on the Choose a Theme screen.

- ✔ **Choose a Layout:** This screen provides you a choice of one, two, or three columns, and wide or tall layout. All are designed to print on 8½ x 11-inch paper.

  The word processor window, underneath the wizard, shows the result of whatever choices you make, as you make them. Read Chapter 5 for help getting the wiz screen out of your way.

- ✔ **Choose a Theme:** Drag the sliders left or right to change the font and color set. For more details, see Chapter 5.

Pouf! You have a newsletter. Of course, it reads something like `Lorem Ipsum Dolor Sit Amet`, which may not be precisely the message you intend to convey. One reader recently wrote, "Why is this Spanish newsletter on the screen?" Well, it's not Spanish, but it's probably Greek to you, as it is to me. This is placeholder text, provided so that you can see how the newsletter looks, and so that when you replace it with your own text, it takes on the same appearance.

You can remove the Works Help panel by clicking the X in its upper-right corner.

Adding text and graphics to the newsletter

After designing your newsletter with the Newsletter wizard, you're ready to replace the placeholder text with your own. In general, the best way to replace text is to highlight some existing text (say, a heading, paragraph, or multiple paragraphs), and then type your own text. Your text immediately replaces the old text but retains the same character and paragraph formatting. With newsletters, however, Works bolds the first letter of each newsletter section. To keep that formatting, highlight the initial letter separately and type your own initial letter. Then highlight the rest of the text and type the rest of your text. To omit bolding, press Ctrl+B to turn off bold style immediately after selecting a bolded line or paragraph in each section.

For other general tips about making changes to text, peruse Chapter 7 for more about working with the results of the Letter task. In that chapter, I discuss font, alignment, and indentation changes, as well as replacing text.

Here are some specific insights into features of the newsletters that you might want to fool with, and references to finding help in this book:

✔ **The headline banner:** In the Family style, as shown in Figure 9-1, the banner across the top is contained in a text box, a word processor feature I discuss in this chapter's sidebar, "Text boxes for labels and sidebars." The line in Family style is done by using Microsoft Draw. The text "Publisher . . . Volume . . ." and so on is separated by tabs, so text may jump a bit as you insert it. (Flip over to Chapter 15 for help with tabs.) In other styles, the banner is simply center-aligned text. If you use a multi-column layout, you may want to use a text box like the Family style banner to get something that stretches across the entire top of the page.

In all cases, the illustration that Works provides is a piece of clip art. You can delete the illustration and insert a different one (clip art or your own creation); see Chapter 12 for help on this.

In newsletters, the publisher is your organization, the volume refers to the year of operation of the newsletter (3, if this is the third year, for instance), and the issue is the number of newsletters so far this year (2, if this is the second newsletter).

✔ **The headers:** The headers are in larger, colored type; they are all center-aligned except in the Family style. You can left-align headers by clicking in them and pressing Ctrl+L, or right-align them with Ctrl+R; Ctrl+E center-aligns them. In single-column layout, many headers have a line under them. You can create this line by applying a bottom border to the header paragraph, as I discuss in Chapter 16.

✔ **Column breaks:** The columns run text continuously, automatically beginning at the top of the next column when one column is full. If you need to force a column to end at some point, click there and choose Insert➪Break➪Column Break.

✔ **Adding illustrations to the text:** When you insert pictures (read through Chapter 12 for more on this), they initially go within the column borders. Some newsletters look cooler, however, if the pictures are kind of free-floating, crossing over the column borders as the text art in Figure 9-1 does (check out the circular text `Stop The Plague`). For that effect, format the picture as square or tight. Here's how: Click the picture, choose Format➪Object, and on the Wrapping tab of the Format Object dialog box, choose Square or Tight.

The Brochure wizard, like the Flyers wizard I describe earlier in this chapter in the "Making a Newsletter" section, provides three screens of choices, as follows:

✔ The Choose a Topic screen mainly chooses a graphical image for you, but also makes an initial choice of font and colors for you.

✔ The Choose a Layout screen provides a choice of a one-, two-, or three-panel brochure.

✔ The Choose a Theme screen is the same font and color choice tool used in many other wizards. Thumb through Chapter 5 for details.

When you click the Finish button on the wizard screen, you get a prototype brochure, ready for you to fill with your own text and figures. (Remember, you can click the X in the upper-right of the Help panel to remove the panel and see your brochure better.) As with nearly all word-processor documents created by tasks, the prototype brochure has placeholder text in Latin. All brochures are designed to print on a single piece of folded 8½ x 11-inch paper.

Clip art you can replace

Text box

Figure 9-1:
A three-column newsletter in the Family style.

Your own illustration

Adding mailing addresses to newsletters

To mail a newsletter, leave a space for the address. The address space for most newsletters is usually one third of the back page — the bottom third for a tall (portrait-oriented) newsletter, and the right or left third for a landscape-oriented newsletter. The address fits in these locations because the paper is folded in thirds to mail it. To create this space for a portrait newsletter, you either insert a column break two-thirds of the way down on the back page on all columns *but* the last column, or else place a text box to occupy that third. For a wide (landscape)

newsletter, you need to set your text box rotation to 90 (degrees). Read the sidebar later in this chapter, "Text boxes for labels and sidebars."

After you have the space set, you either hand-address the newsletter, place an address label in that space, or have Works print each address for you. Check out Chapter 8 for help with creating address labels. If you want Works to print the addresses, treat the newsletter as a bulk mail letter, as I describe in Chapter 8. Insert the address fields in the space you create.

For other general tips about making changes to text, read my discussion in Chapter 7 about working with the result of the letter task. That discusses font, alignment, and indentation changes as well as replacing text.

As I point out in Chapter 5, you can change your chosen theme even after the wizard is finished: Use the Works Format Gallery.

Understanding which page is which

To see the brochure better, choose View➪Zoom, and then click Page Width in the Zoom dialog box. Or, use Print Preview (go to Chapter 4 for more on this feature), and click the Multiple Pages button on the toolbar so that you can see both sides (both pages) of the brochure. Look at the three-panel brochure of Figure 9-2: You're seeing it in the Print Preview window, where you can get a better idea of how the pages work out.

The brochure document has two pages. The first page is the back side (as you see in Figure 9-2), and the second page is the front side. You print on both sides of a piece of paper; read the section, "Two-Sided Printing of Newsletters and Brochures," later in this chapter, for the scoop on two-sided printing.

Make sure you're clear about which panel you're working on, or you end up with text on the wrong panel! On a three-panel brochure, from left to right on the first page, you're seeing the gate panel (which folds into the brochure), the back panel, and the cover. The second page contains the three panels that appear when you unfold the brochure, from left to right. As readers unfold a three-panel brochure, they see, in order: the cover, the gate, and then the inside three panels.

Outside   Inside

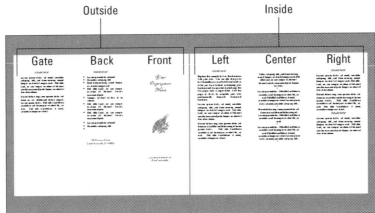

Figure 9-2:
The pages
of a three-
panel
brochure. A
two-panel
brochure
does not
have gate
and center
panels.

Print out the brochure that Works creates with placeholder text and fold it. That way, you have a physical model to work from when you're substituting your own text.

For self-mailing brochures, the back panel is used for the address. Because the address is then printed sideways relative to the rest of the brochure, if you want Works to use its mail-merge feature to address a stack of brochures, you need to use a text box rotated 90 degrees. (Read the sidebar later in this chapter, "Text boxes for labels and sidebars," for help with text boxes. Look through Chapter 8 for help with mail merging.) Treat the brochure as a junk-mail letter, and insert the fields in the text box.

Making a Poster (Flyer)

Whether you're selling a car or launching a theatrical performance, Works has tasks that can create the poster you need. On the Tasks page of the Task Launcher, choose the Newsletters & Flyers category, and then launch either the Flyers or Event Flyers task. (Flyers are posters for selling things; Event Flyers are for events.)

Each of these very simple wizards gives you two screens of choice. The Choose a Topic screen chooses the initial text, graphical image, font, and colors for you. The Choose a Theme screen works as it does in other wizards (check out Chapter 5 for details).

Two-Sided Printing of Newsletters and Brochures

To save paper and postage, and for the best appearances, most newsletters and brochures are printed on two sides. On most printers, the easiest way to print on both sides is to print a stack of paper one side first, and then turn the stack over and print the blank side. When you flip the stack, make sure the correct end of the paper goes into the printer first (usually the top of the page).

Text boxes for labels and sidebars

When your word processor documents need a label or a sidebar, try a text box. A text box is a rectangular area that can be any size or located anywhere in your document, around which your regular document text wraps. Do the following to create a text box:

1. Choose Insert⇨Text Box.

   A gray rectangle (the text box) appears, with tiny squares (called handles) around its edge. Document text appears on either side of the box.

2. Type the text that you want to appear in the box. You can format the text as you would any other text.

3. To change box dimensions, drag the handles. As you do, the mouse cursor displays a two-headed arrow that shows you which way you can drag.

4. To move the box, drag anywhere along the box's edge where your mouse cursor displays a four-headed arrow.

To add a border or shading, choose Format⇨Borders and Shading. In the Borders and Shading dialog box that appears, choose a border style from the Border Art list box. Adjust the Border Art Width value box downward for a thinner border, or up for a thicker one. Choose shading from the Fill Style list box, and optionally choose a shading color from the Color 1 list box. Click OK.

To size or position the box precisely, to rotate the text (as in a mailing label that runs sideways to the document text), or to control how document text wraps, choose Format⇨Text Box. The Format Text Box dialog box appears, in which you can make the following changes:

✔ To alter text box size or text rotation, click the Size tab. Enter new values in the Height or Width value box to set size precisely. Enter a rotation in degrees in the Rotation value box; enter 90 or 270, for instance, to run text sideways.

✔ To control text wrapping, click the Wrapping tab. To avoid having document text on the left or right of the text box, click to place a check mark in either the No Text On Left or No Text On Right check box, respectively.

✔ To adjust the space between the text in the box and the box edge, click the Text Box tab. Enter values in any or all of the four Internal Margin value boxes — Left, Right, Top, or Bottom — to set spacing on those four sides of the text.

Click OK when the text box is exactly as you want it. To return to working on document text, click anywhere outside the box. To make any changes to the text box, first click it; a typing cursor appears in the box so you can edit text, and the rectangle and its handles reappear.

To avoid confusion, the best procedure is usually to print one page at a time, in page-number order. For instance, print 100 copies of Page 1; flip the stack upside-down and put it back in the paper feed, and then print 100 copies of Page 2. Print a few more copies than you need and experiment by printing single test copies to make sure the orientation is correct.

If you are in a particularly well-equipped office, you might have a two-sided printer. Check the printer manual to see how to tell the printer to print two sides.

Chapter 10

Almost Instant Databases

* *

In This Chapter

▶ Creating a recipe or inventory database

▶ Putting data in the database

▶ Getting the information you need from your database

* *

Databases are simply collections of information. Your address book (whether on paper or on your PC) is a database. A card file of recipes is a database. A list of the CDs or books you own is a database. In business, a database might record thousands of people, their addresses, and what products they are interested in.

Computer databases are cool because they can hold lots of information, and you can get useful information out of them quickly. For instance, if you are a radio DJ with 3,000 music CDs and you want to do a Peter Frampton retrospective, your CD database could list all the Frampton recordings.

Part V of this book goes into detail about how to set up and use a database in Works. In this chapter, I show you how to whip up some of the popular, pre-designed databases Works offers, using Works tasks, and how to use them.

Creating Recipe or Inventory Databases

Microsoft gives you a choice of two kinds of database: recipes and inventories. The inventories are for various objects: books, CDs, videotapes, wine, and home possessions. All the databases work basically the same way.

On the Programs page of the Task Launcher, choose Works Database, and then launch any of the tasks listed on the right side of the page. (The same database tasks appear on the Tasks page, but they are simply easier to find on the Programs page.)

Now what? Works opens a window in the database program, with a database displayed in that window. You may or may not have a wizard screen over that window, depending on what task you chose:

- **Home Inventory Worksheets:** A Home Inventory wizard screen appears. Click Books, CDs and Tapes, Home Inventory, Videos, or Wine Inventory; then click the Finish button, and your database is ready!

- **CD and Tape Inventory:** This is a template-style task, so no wizard screen appears over the database window. You're ready to start adding data to this database.

- **Recipe Book:** A Recipe Book wizard appears with a single screen in which you choose the style of recipe book page you want. The recipe book that this task creates is designed for printing either on 4 x 6-inch recipe cards (index cards) or 8½ x 11-inch paper.

  - For 8½ x 11-inch paper, choose either Full Page Recipe or Heirloom Recipe. The Heirloom Recipe style provides spaces for you to record who created this recipe and when, and what family tradition it's associated with.

  - To print cards, choose 4 x 6 Recipe Cards. You'll need to purchase Avery Laser Index & Postcard #5389. These cards are intended for laser printers; they may work okay in ink-jet printers or they may not — I haven't tried them. A cheesy alternative is to print the 4 x 6 recipes on plain paper, cut them out, and then glue them to cards!

Entering Information in Your Database

It's time to play Fill in the Blanks — like tax time, but even more fun. Imagine you're looking at the top of a stack of forms, one form for each item (each recipe, book, CD, or whatever) you're recording. Each form is called a record. To move up or down in the stack, use the controls shown in Figure 10-1, which are located at the lower-left corner of the window.

Figure 10-1: Controls for moving among the records.

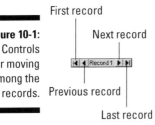

First record

Next record

Previous record

Last record

The idea is to type information about every item into the blanks provided. (You don't have to fill out every blank, however.) Each piece of information that you supply about that item (say, the purchase date) is called a field. The field has a name (such as Purchase Date) and a blank in which to enter data.

To enter data into the blank area, click in it and type. (Any existing text is replaced by what you type.) After typing, press the Enter key on your keyboard. To move on to another field, simply click in the blank area for that other field. Check out Figure 10-2 to see one of the Works databases, with data entered into the fields.

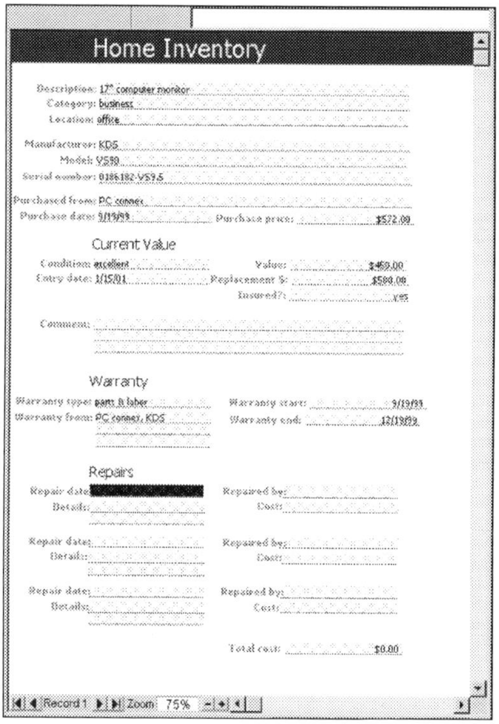

Home Inventory

Description: 17" computer monitor
Category: business
Location: office

Manufacturer: KDS
Model: VS50
Serial number: 0186182-VS75

Purchased from: PC connex
Purchase date: 9/19/98   Purchase price: $572.00

Current Value

Condition: excellent   Value: $450.00
Entry date: 1/15/01   Replacement $: $580.00
                                Insured?:   Yes

Comment:

Warranty

Warranty type: parts & labor   Warranty start: 9/19/98
Warranty from: PC connex, KDS   Warranty end: 12/19/99

Repairs

Repair date: Repaired by:
    Details: Cost:

Repair date: Repaired by:
    Details: Cost:

Repair date: Repaired by:
    Details: Cost:

                                Total cost: $0.00

Record 1   Zoom: 75%

Figure 10-2:
Entering
data into
the Home
Inventory
database.

Save your database as a file, as you would any Works document. (Go to Chapter 2 for more on saving files.)

Here are some additional tips to keep in mind when working with your database:

> ✔ **You can add records to, or delete records from, your database.** When you open the database file later to add more data, you can go to the next blank record in the stack by clicking the last record button, as shown in Figure 10-1. To delete the record that you're viewing, choose Record↪ Delete Record from the menu bar. To change the content of a field, just click in that field and type replacement text. For additional help with navigating or editing the contents of your database, read through Chapters 20 and 21.

✓ **The order in which you enter items into your database doesn't matter much.** You can sort those items into any order later: alphabetically, for instance, by description or category or any other field. Sorting forces similar items to be grouped together; for example, all the recipes that have Appetizer entered in the Category field are listed together if you sort on Category. For instructions on sorting, see Chapter 23.

✓ **Use exactly the same words to describe similar objects, wherever possible.** For instance, if you type **Appetizer** in the Category field as an identifier for some appetizer recipes, don't type **Hors d'oeuvres** for other appetizer recipes. Likewise, don't type **Jimmy Buffet** in the Featured Artist field in some of his records and **Buffet, Jimmy** in others. Using identical text helps you group similar items together later. Otherwise your appetizers and hors d'oeuvres are listed separately when you use the database's sort feature. (However, you could still use the database's more powerful filtering feature to locate both appetizers and hors d'oeuvres. Go to Chapter 22 for help with that.)

Getting Information from Your Database

One simple way to get information from your database is to browse through it. Click the previous record and next record buttons of Figure 10-1 to navigate around.

Additional ways to get the information you need are:

✓ **Print your information on paper.** To print a record, navigate to it so you see it on your screen, and then choose File➪Print. Notice that the Current Record option is selected in the What to Print area of the Print dialog box — meaning that you're about to print the record you're looking at. Click OK, and that record is printed. (If you want all the records, you click the All Records option before clicking OK.)

✓ **Search for particular records.** To find the next record in the stack containing a particular word/name or words/names, choose Edit➪Find (or press Ctrl+F). In the Find dialog box that appears, type the word in the Find What text box and click the OK button.

To find all the records containing your search text, press Ctrl+F, type your search text in the Find What text box, and then click the All Records option button in the Find dialog box. When you click OK, the database program hides all records that don't contain your search word(s). As you browse through, the records containing that text are all you see.

The unwanted records remain hidden until you reveal all the records again by choosing Record➪Show➪1 All Records.

✔ **Print or view just records of a very particular type.** For example, say you want to print or view records of CDs featuring Peter Frampton performing with the Mormon Tabernacle Choir. You need to create and apply a filter, which I describe in detail in Chapter 22. You also need to choose your pharmaceuticals with more care.

✔ **Put your information in a particular order (for instance, by date).** Choose Record➪Sort Records. In the Sort dialog box that appears, click the Sort By drop-down list and choose what field you want to sort by (Date, for instance, if your database has a Date field). Click OK. Scope out Chapter 23 for details on more complex sorting.

✔ **Generate a report (an organized summary).** For example, you may want a summary of all your CDs sorted by artist. Reports are intended only for printing, but you can see them in Print Preview, too. Each database created by the Works tasks has one or two built-in reports that you might find useful. Or maybe not, but hey . . . they're free.

You can find these reports by choosing View➪Report. In the View Report dialog box that appears, click one of the report names listed, and then click the Preview button. You are now using Print Preview, which I discuss in Chapter 4. Here, you can zoom in, zoom out, navigate through the pages of the report, or print the report on paper.

To exit from print preview, click the Cancel button. Whoa! Suddenly you're looking at some very weird stuff. Don't panic: Press the F9 key or choose View➪Form. Whew! Back to normal. (You were briefly in the Report view.)

Speaking of views, the Works Database program offers several views of your data. Read about selecting a view in Chapter 22. The view you normally use (the view in Figure 10-2) is the Form view. You can always return to Form view by pressing the F9 key on your keyboard.

You can modify your task-created database to your heart's content: add fields, change existing ones, redesign the form that you fill out, create new reports, create different filters, add pictures of your dog to the form . . . all kinds of stuff. Thumb through Part V of this book for details on databases.

Chapter 11

Almost Instant Graphs and Charts

In This Chapter

▷ Creating a chart with the Graphs and Charts task

▷ Creating a chart from a spreadsheet

▷ Changing chart types and variations

▷ Adding data, titles, and labels

▷ Changing appearances in a chart

*F*or a multitool package with plenty of other things on its mind, Works offers a rather nice selection of charts, and makes the job of charting a breeze. Or is it a snap? Whatever. A snapping breeze, perhaps. Very easy, in any event.

In this chapter, explore the mysterious link between spreadsheets and charts, learn how to exploit this connection to your advantage, and create graphical eye candy to delight the soul and satisfy the intellect.

Works is very loose about using the words *chart* and *graph*. In its menus, Works refers only to *charts,* and by that it means the graphical things with bars, lines, or circles. In its Graphs and Charts task wizard, Works occasionally uses the word *graph* to mean the same thing. Whatever. I use both terms interchangeably.

You can create your chart in one of two ways:

✔ By modifying an example, created by a task

✔ By charting your own data

In this chapter, I cover both ways.

Creating a Chart from a Task

Works has tasks that give you graphs and charts. You can adapt them to your use by changing text, replacing the numbers with your own numbers, and inserting rows or columns of additional data.

To try one of Works predesigned graphics or charts, follow these steps:

1. **Click Programs on the menu bar to go to the Programs page of the Task Launcher (as shown in Figure 11-1).**

2. **On the Programs page, click Works Spreadsheet, click the Graphs and Charts task, and then click the Start This Task link.**

Figure 11-1:
On the Programs page, choose Works Spreadsheet, then the Graphs and Charts task, and then click Start This Task.

The Works Spreadsheet program launches and opens a window, and the Graphs and Charts wizard appears on top of that window, offering you a wide array of choices.

3. **In the Graphs and Charts wizard, click any choice, and the spreadsheet for that graph or chart appears in the spreadsheet window.**

4. **Click the Finish button in the wizard to finalize your selection.**

The wizard departs.

Viewing the chart

If you choose a task that promises a bar graph, line graph, or pie chart (or in other words, a picture), you may wonder, "Where's the picture?" All you can see is a spreadsheet (a table) of data. The answer is that the graph appears in another window. To open that window, choose View⇨Chart.

A gaggle of graphs and charts

Works offers a veritable optical smorgasbord of graphs (charts). Here are the basic types:

✔ **Bar:** In a bar chart, each number in a row or column results in a bar. The value of that number determines the height of the bar. For multiple rows or columns of data, bars are differently colored and can be positioned side by side or stacked to show the sum.

✔ **Pie:** In a pie chart, each number in a row or column determines the size of a slice of a pie.

✔ **Line:** Each number you chart in a row or column determines the height of a point along a line. Line charts can appear with dots (the data points), dots alone, or high/low/close (for stock values).

✔ **Stacked Line:** Stacked line charts are for multiple sets (series) of data that you want to display summed together in a way that reveals what portion of the total comes from each set of data. For instance, a stacked line chart could show how sales from your Eastern, Western, Northern, and Southern sales divisions contribute to your total sales. The divisional sales stack on top of each other to show the total. In the chart, the bottom line is for data in the first column (or row), the second line is for the sum of data in the first and second column (or row), and so forth.

✔ **Area:** An area chart is like a stacked line chart, but filled in with color underneath the lines.

✔ **Scatter:** A scatter plot puts lotsa dots on an X/Y plot. For instance, if your data is in columns, the first column is for X (horizontal) values, and the second is for Y (vertical) values. Therefore, each row in this pair of columns specifies a dot's location in X and Y. Scatter plots are used for showing correlation between two types of measured phenomena, such as degree of baldness and IQ in men (strongly correlated; the dots form a nice, straight line).

✔ **Radar:** A radar chart is kind of like a line chart going around in a circle: Instead of the line's height varying, its distance from the center varies. Radar plots are useful for showing variations in cyclical events — for example, popularity over several months of different flavors of ice cream by phase of the moon.

✔ **Combination:** This choice enables you to mix lines and bars in a single chart.

Works offers even more chart types, but I don't have room to get into all of them. But after you learn the basic chart types, you can pick up the others pretty easily.

The data in the spreadsheet is what drives the graph: The column and row headings appear in the graph, and the numbers determine the height or size of whatever elements (bars, lines, or pie slices) make up your graph.

To see both the data and the graph, choose Window⇨Tile. The two windows appear side by side, as shown in Figure 11-2. This way, you can see the effect of your changes to the data as you make them. Or, to switch between windows, choose View⇨Chart or View⇨Spreadsheet.

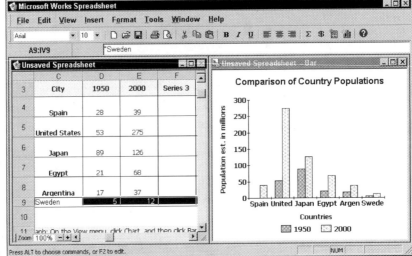

Figure 11-2:
Data and
the graph
it creates,
side by side.

Customizing the chart

After creating a chart from a task, get a feel for how the numbers and text
affect the graph. In the spreadsheet window, click a number (not a heading),
and type a new number to see changes in the lines, bars, or pie wedges of the
graph. (Microsoft uses bold to indicate row and column headings.) To see
changes in labels, click a row or column heading and type new text.

After you see how the numbers and headings affect the graph, you can change
them to meet your needs. Part IV of this book is the best place to turn if you
need to do more than change numbers and text in the spreadsheet. If you need
to add data to your spreadsheet and graph, read the section in this chapter,
"Adding Data to Your Chart." If you need to change the graph appearance,
look over the last several sections of this chapter.

Starting from a Spreadsheet

If you want to make a chart from an existing spreadsheet, arranging the data
and headings on the spreadsheet to simplify your chartwork is a good idea.
Works is pretty good at dealing with various kinds of spreadsheet layouts,
but a little care can make your life easier and give you better results.

Here is a checklist for preparing your spreadsheet:

  ✔ **Use row and column headings, if possible.** They'll turn into labels on
    your chart. Ideally, your top row should be column headings and your
    leftmost column should be row headings.

✔ **Don't use blank rows or columns between headings and data.** When headings immediately adjoin data, Works can use them to label your chart automatically. Having blank rows or columns between headings and data means you have to add labels to the chart manually.

✔ **Keep sets of numbers together if you want to chart them together.** For instance, to chart a column of costs and a column of revenues by month in the same chart, make those columns adjacent to each other. If practical, put your column or row of data adjacent to the column or row headings. If you want to plot a row or column of data that is not adjacent to the heading row or column, select the row or column of data and drag to put the data next to the headings.

✔ **Use number formatting (more about this in Chapter 21) to make the numbers appear the way you want them on the chart.** For currency, for example, use currency formatting.

Creating a Chart from a Spreadsheet

To create a new chart, start with a spreadsheet — preferably one laid out with row and column headings, but any spreadsheet can be charted. Then follow these steps:

1. **Select a range (a group of cells) with the data you want to chart, including headings if they are in an adjacent row or column.**

   Select a range by dragging across cells. For a pie chart, select just the one column (or row) containing the numbers to be charted, and any headings in an adjacent column (or row) that identify each of the numbers. If headings aren't adjacent, leave them out; you can add them later.

2. **Choose Tools⇨Create New Chart, or click the New Chart button (which looks like a tiny bar chart) on the toolbar.**

   The New Chart dialog box shown in Figure 11-3 swings into action. Showing you a sample of a bar chart based on the data you selected, it also tries to figure out whether you included line and column headings — if so, they become labels in the chart.

3. **Choose a chart type from the graphical, Chart Type picture gallery.**

   The sample area on the right shows you what your chart will look like. Works always starts out by showing you a bar chart. To review your other choices, refer to the sidebar elsewhere in this chapter, "A gaggle of graphs and charts."

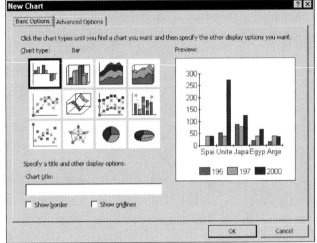

Figure 11-3:
The New
Chart dialog
box initially
suggests a
bar chart.

4. **If your data is plotted incorrectly in the chart in the sample area, click the Advanced Options tab in the New Chart dialog box. Otherwise, skip to Step 8.**

   Works possibly misinterpreted your spreadsheet data and is reading your data series across instead of down, or vice versa.

5. **If necessary, change the first option, labeled** `The series data in the spreadsheet is organized:`.

   A *series* is a column or row of data that you want to chart in a single color. If the chart looks wrong, choose the opposite of the currently chosen option, either Across in Rows or Down in Columns.

6. **If necessary, change the check box settings that begin** `Use text in the first...`.

   If you have numbers in the first row or column of your selection and you actually intend them to be labels used in the legend (the thing that relates colors to data) — and not as data to be charted — make sure the option labeled `Use text in the first row` (or `column`) `as legend text` has a check mark. Click it if it doesn't.

   If you have dates or times in the first row or column, Works may think you want them to be labels for the horizontal axis. If you actually intend them to be data and not labels, clear the check box labeled `Use text in the first column` (or `row`) `of your selection as the horizontal (X) axis label`.

7. **When you're finished using the Advanced Options tab, click the Basic Options tab.**

8. **Enter a title for the chart in the Chart Title text box.**

   Click the text box marked Chart Title, and type in something descriptive, such as **Sales by Quarter**. The sample chart in the dialog box reflects your choice.

9. **If you want a border around the whole chart, select the Show Border check box; if you want gridlines, select the Show Gridlines check box.**

   The sample chart shows you what you'll get.

10. **Click the OK button.**

    A chart window appears with your lovely work of numeric art in spunky primary colors.

To see how your chart will really look on your printer, choose View➪ Display As Printed from the menu bar. (Repeat the command to go back to the original view.)

Changing Chart Types and Variations

Just because you initially chose, say, a bar chart, that choice doesn't prevent you from switching to another type: a line chart, for instance. Or, within a given type, by using Works *variations,* you can radically customize your work. For instance, you can display your pie charts whole, with one slice partially removed (a common pie condition in our house), or exploded into its separate slices (which is what happens if you microwave the pie).

You can change the chart's type or variation by following these steps:

1. **While viewing your chart, choose Format➪Chart Type.**

   In the Chart Type dialog box that appears, you get a lovely graphical display of various ways to display your data that looks just like the one in Figure 11-3. (To review the available chart types and variations, read the sidebar, "A gaggle of graphs and charts," elsewhere in this chapter.)

2. **If you want to choose a different type of chart, click the Basic Types tab and then choose a different type by clicking one of the pictures.**

   This tab shows you the basic types of charts available, such as bar, line, or 3-D bar.

3. **If you want to choose a variation of a chart, click the Variations tab and then click the chart variation of your choice.**

   This tab shows you different versions of the basic type. Some look a lot alike; to see the differences, watch the example chart closely as you switch between the variations.

4. **When you're finished, click the OK button.**

Adding Data to Your Chart

Chances are that at some point, you want to add more data to your chart. To add new data to your graph, you need to do two, or possibly three, things:

✔ Add the data to the spreadsheet.

✔ Tell the graph to include the data.

✔ If you need a label for the new data, add the label.

To add data to your spreadsheet, either fill in the next available row or column, or insert rows or columns (check out Chapter 19 for more on this). After the data is in your spreadsheet, pasting is the fastest way to add it. Follow these steps to paste a data series into your chart:

1. **In your spreadsheet window, highlight a range of data (exclude headings).**

2. **Press Ctrl+C (the more-or-less universal Copy command).**

3. **Switch to the chart window (choose View⇨Chart and select the chart you want); then press Ctrl+V.**

   Zap! Your chart has expanded to include the new data.

When you paste the data, the data (bars or stacked lines) may not be in the order that you want — especially if you insert rows or columns in between existing rows or columns. For instance, if you insert a column of data for the year 1975 between 1950 and 2000, that bar in a bar chart may follow the year 2000 data. You may need to resort to a less automatic approach that allows you to change the order or to add data in any order you want; here's how:

1. **Choose Edit⇨Series.**

   The Series dialog box that appears lists the range of cells in the spreadsheet (say, D5 through D9, written D5:D9) for each range (1st, 2nd, and so on.)

2. **To change the order or to add a new series of data, edit the content of the text boxes (first, second, and so on).**

   For instance, if your second range is to be E5 through E9, type the range expression E5:E9 in the second text box. If you copied a range of data, as in Steps 1 and 2 of the preceding numbered steps, you can click in a text box and then click the Paste button to paste that range expression. Click OK when you're done.

Editing or Adding Titles in a Chart

To create or edit chart or axis titles, follow these steps:

1. **Click the title bar of the chart window (if it's not already active) and choose Edit⬧Titles.**

   The Titles dialog box appears.

2. **Just click the appropriate text box and type.**

   Here are a few pointers for using this dialog box:

   - You can enter two lines of title for the chart: Chart Title and Chart Subtitle.

   - Optionally type text in the text box for Horizontal (X) Axis Title or Vertical (Y) Axis Title.

   - Type in the Right Vertical Axis Title only if you have added a second Y axis.

3. **Click OK when you're done.**

Editing or Adding Labels in a Chart

Each series of data in your chart has (or can have) a label in the legend — the little box that relates data to a particular color. To change the series labels, click the title bar of the chart window (if it's not already active) and perform the following steps:

1. **Choose Edit⬧Legend/Series Labels.**

   Works displays the Edit Legend/Series dialog box. If you don't want a legend at all, deselect the Show A Legend check box and click OK (you're done).

2. **If you have boring labels of the *Series 1, 2, 3 . . .* variety, click the option box labeled** Use values in spreadsheet for series labels.

   The dialog box displays one text box for each series (each color or pattern), labeled 1st Value Series, 2nd Value Series, and so on.

3. **To type the labels, just click the appropriate box and type.**

   You may see that for some existing labels (taken from the spreadsheet), text is preceded with quote marks; you don't need to type any quote marks, however.

4. **To obtain label text from a cell in the spreadsheet, click the appropriate text box and type the label's cell address.**

   For instance, type **D5** to use the text in the spreadsheet cell at row 5, column D.

5. **Click OK when you're done.**

Changing Appearances in a Chart

Works has a whole slew of appearance-changing features available to you when you're working in a chart window. Click the title bar of the chart window (if it's not already active) and choose Format. The Format menu appears, offering numerous possibilites: changing fonts, shading and colors, the appearances of the X and Y axes, and more. I'm not going to go into these details, as most people don't care to fool around with them much.

I will, however, point you to a shortcut. Rather than use the Format menu, do this:

1. **Double-click the feature you want to change: a bar of a particular color (series), a title, an axis, a value along an axis, or text in a legend.**

   A dialog box opens up with all the controls for the appearance of that object!

2. **Change the items you want in that dialog box, and then click the OK button.**

   (If you're in the Shading and Color dialog box, however, you won't see an OK button. Click the Format button instead to format your chosen bar, line, or pie slice, or click the Format All button to format all the bars, lines, or pie slices the same way.)

Chapter 12

Almost Instant Art

As my friend Art says, "Expose yourself to Art." Or, in this case, expose your art to your readers. Scary thought? Don't fret. Works' art tools can help you make quick work of artsy stuff, whether the artwork is functional, decorative, or just to show off. You can add art to any word processor document (or, if the art is ClipArt, WordArt, or a drawing, to a database form in Form Design view); however, you can't add art to a spreadsheet or place it in a database as data.

Inserting Your Own Images

Let's face it, the real fun is seeing your own pictures in a document. If you're currently able to see the image on your PC screen, in any program, here's a simple procedure for inserting it into a Works Word Processor document. With that document open on your screen, and your image also visible on your screen (yes, you can have more than one program running at once on your PC), follow these steps:

1. **Select the image.**

   Depending upon the program you're viewing the image in, you typically either drag your mouse cursor across the image (in which case the image changes color slightly), or click on the image (in which case a frame of some sort appears around the image).

2. **Drag the image into the Works Word Processor document.**

   As you drag, the image itself doesn't move, but your cursor should depict two tiny rectangles and a + sign if this process is going to work. When you release the mouse button, the image should then appear in the Works document.

The preceding steps may not work in some instances. You can tell they're not going to work if the cursor depicts a circle with a slash through it as you drag. In that event, release the mouse button and do this instead:

1. **In the program window where the picture appears, choose Edit⇨Copy or press Ctrl+C. (You may now close that program window, if it's in the way.)**

2. **Click in the Works Word Processor window and press Ctrl+V.**

If you have your own images, photographs, or other forms of art in the form of files (and know where to find those files on your PC), you can insert them into a Works Word Processor document with the following procedure:

1. **Click in your document wherever you want the object to appear.**

2. **Choose Insert⇨Picture⇨From File.**

   The Insert Picture dialog box appears.

3. **Click the file that you want to insert.**

   You may have to open folders or look on other disk drives, just as you do when opening a file using the Open dialog box in any program (see Chapter 1). If the object is on a floppy or other removable disk, tape, or CD, click the Look In drop-down list and look for that disk in the list ($3^1/_2$ `floppy`, for instance, or `D:` or `E:`).

   When you click on a file, a preview of the image appears on the right side of the Insert Picture dialog box. (If no preview appears, click the Enable Preview check box.)

4. **Click the Insert button.**

   Works displays your image in the document, and you can now mess around with it. To move, resize, or otherwise fool around with the object as a whole, skip down to the final section in this chapter, "Messing Around with Art in Your Document."

To edit the image, double-click it, and Windows launches whatever program is associated with that image on your PC. After you make changes, exit the program.

Collecting and Using Art from the Works Portfolio

If you're a highly organized person, and if you have lots of images on your PC, you may appreciate the new Works Portfolio. Not being highly organized myself, I don't find much value for it.

Works Portfolio enables you to create collections of images and other things (such as documents, sounds, animations, and videos) and view the images easily. You can give these collections a name and save them in certain locations on your PC. When the portfolio window is open, you can copy, drag and drop, or send items from the portfolio into other documents, including Works Word Processor documents. You can also print images stored in a collection.

Launching the Portfolio

The Portfolio launches automatically when you first start Works, and hovers — in the form of a silvery rectangular panel — near the top right of your screen. (I suggest you remove the Portfolio panel from your screen.)

To launch the Portfolio manually from the Task Launcher, click Programs in the menu bar to go to the Programs page. Choose Works Portfolio from the list of programs, and then click Start Works Portfolio, on the right of the Programs page.

Choosing views

The Portfolio can take any of three shapes: Compact view (a small rectangle), Gallery view (a window), and Docked view (a strip along one edge of your screen). In Compact view, the Portfolio is rolled up; to unroll it, click it. To keep it open, click the push-pin icon; otherwise the Portfolio rolls up when you begin to work in another window.

To change views, click one of the three view buttons near the four-colored-rectangles icon of the Portfolio. (Unroll Compact view to see these three buttons.) A tag identifies each button when you pause your mouse cursor over the button.

Using collections

The Portfolio can contain many collections; however, it contains only the Sample collection when you first use it. To create your own collection, choose Tasks⇨New Collection. Enter a name in the New Collection dialog box and click OK.

Pictures added to the Portfolio go in whatever collection is open at the time. In Gallery view, you can open a collection by clicking its name on the left side of the window. In Compact or Docked view, the currently open collection is displayed on a button near the top of the window. To change collections, click that button and choose another collection from the drop-down list that appears.

One good way to add a picture or something else to a collection is to copy and paste it from another window into the Portfolio. For instance, double-click the My Computer icon on your PC desktop and browse to a place where you store image files. Then click your file, press Ctrl+C, click in the Portfolio window, and press Ctrl+V. If you can view the image — say, in Outlook Express — select the image, copy it with Ctrl+C, and paste it into the portfolio with Ctrl+V.

A straightforward way to add a file to a collection is to choose Tasks⇨Insert File. Choose the file from the Insert File Into collection name dialog box, just as you would choose a file in an Open dialog box (flip back to Chapter 1 for more on this). Click the Insert button when your file is chosen.

Here are a few additional pointers for using the Portfolio:

- **To annotate a picture with comments,** a comment field is provided for each picture. You can type your notes there. In Gallery view, the comment field is visible. In Compact or Docked view, click the Actions button under a picture to access the comment field.

- **To use a picture from the Portfolio,** try dragging it from the Portfolio window to the destination window. If that fails, click the picture, press Ctrl+C to copy it, click in the destination window, and press Ctrl+V to paste it.

- **To delete or rename a collection,** click Tasks and then click <u>D</u>elete Current Collection or Rena<u>m</u>e Current Collection. Other choices in the Tasks menu, in particular the Send Item To choices, I find either don't work very well or aren't particularly useful.

- **To close the Portfolio,** choose Tasks⇨<u>C</u>lose, or press Ctrl+F4.

Using Works' Clip Art

When your document needs a little pizzazz, use some clip art. *Clip art* is nothing more than a bunch of Microsoft-provided illustrations that you can use in your documents. Works comes with a batch of drawings installed on your PC's internal hard drive; depending upon how Works was installed, you may also need to re-insert the Works CD into your PC. (Works will tell you, if so.)

If someone gives or sends you something called "clip art," don't try to use the Works clip art feature. Treat it like your own artwork and see the first section of this chapter, "Inserting Your Own Images."

If you're replacing clip art that was placed in your document by a Works task, double-click that artwork. You'll probably be transported directly to the Insert Clip Art dialog box, from which you can choose replacement art. If so, you can skip the upcoming two steps. In a few instances, you'll be transported to Microsoft Draw, described later in this chapter.

However, if you're inserting fresh clip art into your document, begin with these two steps:

1. **Click in your document where you want the art to appear.**

   If you're inserting a clip into a database, you must be in Form Design view.

2. **In the word processor, choose Insert⇨Picture⇨ClipArt. (In the database's Form Design view, choose Insert⇨ClipArt.)**

   You may have to wait, staring at a cursor-turned-hourglass, while Works quietly builds its museum of masterpieces.

   Eventually, the Insert Clip Art dialog box appears, as shown in Figure 12-1.

Figure 12-1:
Where clip art lives in Works. The Browse and Find tabs give you two ways to locate the art you need.

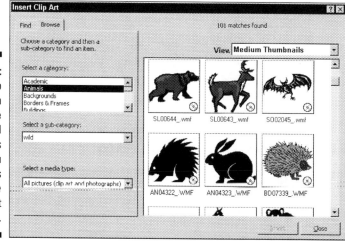

3. **Click the Browse tab, if it's not already selected.**

   The Browse tab enables you to look for clip art in various categories (such as Animals) and subcategories (such as Wild).

4. **Choose a category in the Select A Category list box.**

   The clips for that category appear on the right.

5. **To narrow down the field of choices, choose a sub-category in the Select a Sub-Category drop-down list box.**

   The clips are narrowed down considerably. *Note:* Unless you have fooled with it, the Select A Media Type list box displays All Pictures. This is the widest possible selection. You can choose narrower categories from this list box, if you like.

6. **Click the picture you want on the right side of the dialog box.**

   Scroll the gallery window on the right to see more clips in any category.

7. **Click the Insert button.**

After the art is inserted into your document, you can size it the same way you do for your own drawings. See the final section of this chapter, "Messing Around with Art in Your Document," for more information.

If you choose the Find tab, do this:

1. **Type one or more descriptive words (keywords) into the Type A Keyword text box.**

   To re-use a previously used keyword, click the down arrow for this text box to choose from a list. Adding words (like wildlife tiger) narrows down the list.

2. **Click the Search button.**

   All pictures that are associated with your keyword(s) appear on the right.

3. **Click the Insert button.**

You can replace clip art by double-clicking the illustration in your document. Works reopens the Insert Clip Art dialog box, from which you can choose a new figure.

Using Draw to Do Basic Blob Art

Blob art is my name for putting together a bunch of simple shapes with lines and text. Microsoft's Draw tool is great for blob art, which is why Microsoft stuffs Draw into various programs that it makes.

Starting up Draw (inserting a drawing)

To start up Draw (that is, to create and insert a drawing into your word processing or into a database document in Form Design view), click at the point in the document where you want the drawing and then choose Insert⇨ Picture⇨New Drawing.

The Microsoft Draw tool springs into action in a window of its own. The Draw tool window looks like Figure 12-2 (without the stuff I have drawn in Figure 12-2).

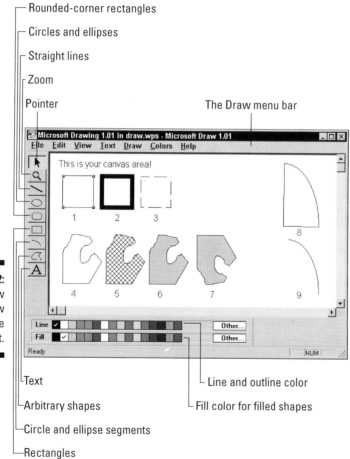

Rounded-corner rectangles

Circles and ellipses

Straight lines

Zoom

Pointer

The Draw menu bar

Figure 12-2:
The Draw
window
and some
blob art.

Text

Arbitrary shapes

Circle and ellipse segments

Rectangles

Line and outline color

Fill color for filled shapes

Here's what you have to work with in creating your work of art:

- ✓ **Drawing tools:** Tools along the left edge of the window help you create blobs in your drawing.

- ✓ **Line and Fill Colors:** Two strips (palettes) at the bottom of the window enable you to choose colors as you draw. The Line palette specifies the color of a line or outline. The Fill palette determines what color fills the shape. A check mark indicates the current color — the one Works uses when you next make a shape. Clicking a color applies it to any currently selected object and to the next objects you create.

  To control whether a shape has a line (frame), a fill, or both, choose Draw from the menu bar. A check mark next to Framed or Filled indicates that the feature is turned on. To toggle either feature between on or off, choose it in the menu. Your choice applies to any currently selected objects and to the next objects you create.

- ✓ **Menu bar:** Menu commands change or improve the way the tools and palettes work — such as using different line width, changing font, or aligning shapes — and also help copy and arrange shapes.

Making shapes and text

Objects you create in Draw are separate and movable objects, like cutouts on a piece of paper. These objects can have fills, or solid centers, in which case they can cover up underlying objects. You can fiddle with them in many ways — check out the upcoming section, "Modifying objects."

To use a tool, click the tool and then click at various points in the drawing — or, for certain results, drag. Holding down the Shift key while drawing (referred to as Shift+click) creates more regular objects, such as circles and squares, from the more general ellipse and rectangle tools. Here's the lowdown on specific tools:

- ✓ **Line:** Click to begin a line; then click to end. Shift+click creates horizontal, vertical, or 45-degree angle lines.

- ✓ **Ellipse or circle:** Click and then drag in any direction to create an ellipse. For a circle, use Shift+click.

- ✓ **Rectangle or rounded-corner rectangle:** Drag diagonally. For a square, use Shift+click.

- ✓ **Ellipse or circle segment:** Drag diagonally for quarter-ellipse segments. (Refer to shape 8 in Figure 12-2.) Turn Fill on for a closed shape; turn it off for a line. Shift+drag creates a quarter-circle. If the curve bends the wrong way, press the Delete key to delete the shape and then try again starting at the other end of the curve.

- ✔ **Arbitrary shapes:** Click at a starting point. For a straight line segment, click somewhere else; continue clicking around and you'll get a bunch of line segments. To draw as you would with a pencil, just drag. To make a closed shape, click the original starting point. To end the line without closing the shape, double-click when you make the last point.

- ✔ **Text:** Choose Text➪Font, Bold, Italic, Underline, or Plain (no bold, italic, or underline) to set fonts and styles. Check marks next to styles indicate the current settings. To use the text tool, just click anywhere in your drawing and type. Press Enter when you're done.

- ✔ **Zooming in or out:** Choose View, then any percentage in the drop-down menu. Alternatively, click the magnifying glass tool in the toolbar, and then click on the drawing to zoom in. Shift+click to zoom out.

In the shape-drawing tools, holding down the Ctrl key while you click means that your click marks the center of the object. As you drag, the object expands in all directions around that center.

Modifying objects

To select an object for modification, click the arrow (selection) tool at the top of the toolbar, and then click the object. A frame of four square dots appears around the object to tell you that it's selected.

To select a bunch of objects to modify at once, drag the selection tool diagonally across the shapes you want. A dashed rectangle encloses the selected shapes. To select objects scattered all over the drawing, hold down both the Ctrl and Shift keys, and click each object individually.

After you have selected an object or objects, you can do the following:

- ✔ **Move:** Click anywhere within the object and drag. Use Shift+drag to move the object horizontally or vertically.

- ✔ **Copy:** Press Ctrl+C and then Ctrl+V. A copy appears nearby; drag it where you want it.

- ✔ **Stretch or shrink shapes:** Click any of the squares around the shape and drag. Use Shift+drag to stretch a shape straight, horizontal, vertical, or at 45 degrees. To avoid distortion, Shift+drag a corner handle diagonally.

- ✔ **Line thickness and style:** Choose Draw➪Line Style. In the list that appears, click any line style (such as dashed) or any line width (in increments of one seventy-second [$\frac{1}{72}$] of an inch). Shapes 2 and 3 in Figure 12-2 show line variations.

- ✔ **Color:** To change the line or outline color, click a color in the Line palette at the bottom of the window. To change the fill color, use the Fill palette instead. To remove fill, choose Draw➪Filled.

- ✔ **Text:** To change font, size, style, or alignment, choose Text and then click commands in the drop-down menu. The common keyboard short-cuts, such as Ctrl+B for bold, also work for text in Draw.

- ✔ **Fill:** To switch between filled and unfilled, choose Draw➪Filled from the menu bar. Unfilled shapes are transparent, showing objects underneath them.

- ✔ **Fill pattern:** To use a fill pattern instead of, or in addition to, a color, choose Draw➪Pattern and click a pattern in the box that appears. (The Line and Fill colors must be different for the pattern to show up.)

- ✔ **Outlining:** To remove an outline from a filled shape, choose Draw➪Framed. (To restore the outline, repeat the command.)

- ✔ **On top/underneath:** Objects cover up each other in Draw; to change an object's position in the pile, click Edit in the menu bar, and then click either Bring To Front or Send To Back.

- ✔ **Rotate or flip:** Choose Draw➪Rotate/Flip from the menu bar. Click Rotate Left or Rotate Right to turn the object 90 degrees. Click Flip Horizontal for a mirror image or Flip Vertical for upside down.

If you immediately realize that you made a mistake (maybe you moved some-thing that took you a long time to get in exactly the right place), you can undo it. Ctrl+Z works here just as it does everywhere else.

If you get a few objects positioned just perfectly relative to each other, you can freeze them in their relative positions by selecting them all and choosing Draw➪Group. Now Works considers the collection to be one single object, and anything that is done to one is done to all. If you decide later that you want to modify the objects individually, select the grouped object (by click-ing any of its pieces) and choose Draw➪Ungroup.

Leaving and restarting Draw

When you exit the Draw program, choose File➪Exit And Return. In the query box that appears, click either Yes to save your drawing (in your document) or No to discard your work.

When you return to your document, the drawing appears in a box with squares around it. See the section "Messing Around with Art in Your Document" at the end of this chapter to do further work on your drawing.

WordArt

Oh, those madcap Microsoft engineers! First blob art, then clip art, and now word art. What's next, punctuation art? WordArt is fun, and great for getting someone's attention (see Figure 12-3).

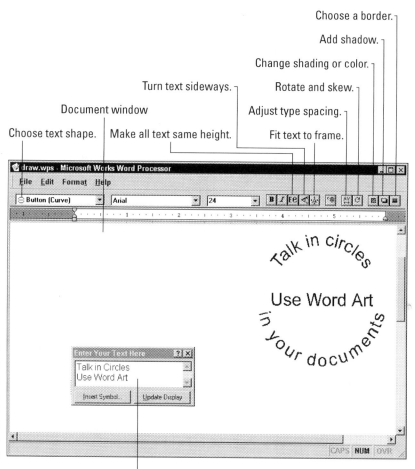

Choose a border.

Add shadow.

Change shading or color.

Turn text sideways.   Rotate and skew.

Document window   Adjust type spacing.

Choose text shape.   Make all text same height.   Fit text to frame.

Figure 12-3:
Playing with
WordArt.
Curved text
can turn
heads.

Type text here.

Paint

In addition to Works' Draw tool, you can also use Windows' Paint tool in a Works word processor document. Painting is a lot like drawing, but you can't easily edit the shapes you create. When you draw, you create individual objects that can be moved or changed. When you paint, you're just applying color to areas of one continuous surface. The Paint tool does, however, allow you to cut images apart or apply "spray" paint, which you cannot do by drawing. You can also open image files of the popular BMP, JPEG, or GIF type and edit them. For most of your document illustration needs, Draw works just fine.

To try Paint, choose Insert⇨Picture⇨New Painting. Paint puts a Paint box in your document, and the menu and toolbars change to reflect the Paint tools. To find your way around Paint, choose Help⇨Help Topics and review the topics. To return to your document text, click outside the Paint box.

Here's the basic procedure for getting swoopy, loopy text in your word processing or database document:

1. **Click at the place you want your text art.**

2. **Choose Insert⇨Picture⇨WordArt in the word processor, or choose Insert⇨WordArt in the database.**

3. **Type one or more lines of text in the Enter Your Text Here dialog box that appears.**

   Click the Insert Symbol button if you need a special symbol, such as a copyright mark. In the Insert Symbol dialog box that appears, click whatever symbol you would like, and then click OK.

4. **Click the list box in the toolbar (where it currently reads** Plain Text**) to choose from a gallery of weird shapes for your text. (Shapes with multiple lines are intended for multiple lines of text.)**

5. **Click the down-arrow button where the words** Best Fit **appear in the toolbar, and choose a type size in the drop-down list.**

   Works may display a Size Change dialog box babbling about enlarging a frame and asking the question, Resize WordArt object? Click Yes.

6. **Choose special effects, such as adding a shadow, by clicking buttons on the toolbar as Figure 12-3 indicates.**

   The **B** and *I* buttons change your text to bold or italic. The text alignment button (which has lines on it and a tiny C) gives you a menu with text alignment choices (centered, left, right, and justified).

Here's what the rest of the buttons do. I refer to them by their descriptions in Figure 12-3:

- The Make all text same height button (displaying Ee) makes capital and lowercase letters the same height.

- The Turn text sideways button (displaying a sideways A) *doesn't* turn your letters sideways as the icon suggests. Letters remain vertical, but the line of text runs like the column of a crossword puzzle.

- The Adjust type spacing button (displaying AV) adjusts the space between letters of your text.

- The Rotate and skew button (displaying an arrow going in a circle) turns your text at any angle.

- The Change shading or color button (displaying diagonal lines) controls the fill color and pattern of letters. (You need big letters to show these effects; otherwise, the fill is too small to see.)

- The Add shadow button (displaying a box with a shadow) makes your text cast a shadow on the page. You get to choose the direction and angle of the light source.

- The Choose a border button (displaying three lines of different thickness) puts a border around your letters.

7. **Click the Update Display button to see the results.**

8. **When you're done, click in the document anywhere outside of the gray-shaded frame.**

To edit your WordArt, double-click it. Double-clicking is how you edit any graphical object in a Works document, such as clip art, drawings, or charts.

Messing Around with Art in Your Document

When you return to your document from Draw, the clip art gallery, Paint, or WordArt, the illustration you create appears in a nominal size that Works thinks is best, with no frame or text wrapping around it — nothing. What a way to treat a great work of art!

First, click the illustration to select it. (In the database, you must be in Form Design view.) The illustration then appears in a box with tiny black squares around it. (If the box with squares does not appear, click anywhere outside the illustration, and then click the illustration again.)

✔ **To delete the illustration,** press the Delete key on your keyboard.

✔ **To resize the illustration,** click and drag any of the squares around the illustration.

✔ **To modify the illustration,** double-click the illustration, and you launch the program on your PC (a Works feature or otherwise) that is capable of making changes to that kind of artwork.

✔ **To put a frame around your illustration,** choose Format⇨Borders and Shading from the menu bar. Click a line width and, if you like, a color.

✔ **To change the illustration's dimensions,** choose Format⇨Object from the menu bar (or click the illustration with your right mouse button, and choose Format⇨Object from the menu that appears). In the Format Object dialog box that appears, click the Size tab and enter new values for the width and height of the picture.

✔ **To make text wrap around the illustration in the word-processor tool,** choose Format⇨Object, and choose one of the Style options on the Wrapping tab. To better understand what each option does, right-click the example image shown and click the What's This? text that appears.

✔ **To position an illustration,** drag it. What you actually drag is a cursor or a dashed-line rectangle, which shows you where the illustration goes when you release the mouse button.

Part III
Pursuing the Wily Word Processor

The 5th Wave   By Rich Tennant

"WELL, RIGHT OFF, THE RESPONSE TIME SEEMS A BIT SLOW."

In this part . . .

So, you're ready to dash off that important report or write that long-awaited letter in the Works Word Processor? Well, Works makes it pretty easy — but as with all word-processing software, it's still a bit wild. Don't expect to just walk right up and pounce on it. It's a good idea to sidle up to it, nice and easy, and know what sort of interesting behavior to expect when you finally lasso it and put it to use.

This part covers everything from basics, such as typing and deleting, to subtle and elusive facts, such as where paragraph formatting hides. Discover the word-processing habitat: why it's important to replace your old typing habits with new word-processing habits. Finally, discover how to teach your newly tamed word processor advanced tricks, such as page numbers, tables, borders, lines, headers, footers, and footnotes.

> ". . . let me bring thee where crabs grow;
> And I with my long nails will dig thee pig nuts;
> Show thee a jay's nest and instruct thee how
> To snare the nimble marmoset"

> —*The Tempest*, William Shakespeare

Chapter 13

In Search of the Wily Word Processor

So, you're ready to hunt down the wily word processor? Well, pack up your safari gear and get to know the wiles and ways of this wacky word-ivorous wonder. Soon, you, too, will be able to write such annoying alliterative allegories as this one — and then avoid embarrassment by quickly deleting them again, as I should have — without the trials of typewriter ribbons and correction fluid.

What's the Big Deal about Word Processing?

Three being a magical number, there are, of course, three big deals about word processing:

Big Deal 1. You can make documents that you would never even attempt to create with a typewriter, such as two-column newsletters or presentation transparency foils (those see-through thingies that you put on an overhead projector) using big type.

Big Deal 2. Your documents look better and fancier, without pain and strain, when you use nice typefaces (fonts) of different size and style, centered or indented text, borders, and graphics.

Third and Final Big Deal. Playing around with things until you like the results — changing words or sentences, moving paragraphs, or changing margins and page breaks — is really easy in word processing.

In addition to the three big deals, word processing has some tiny little deals, such as copying text from one place to another, spell-checking automatically, sending documents via e-mail, and being able to add word processing to your résumé. So word processing is a good deal all around.

How it's different from using a typewriter

You can do lots of things with a word processor that you can't do with a type-writer. (Word processors don't make that cool clickety-clack sound, but what the heck?) But even for doing things that you're accustomed to doing on a typewriter, watch out for these few differences:

- ✔ Do not, *absolutely* do NOT, use the Enter key like you're accustomed to using the carriage return key — you know, pressing it at the end of every line of text. This habit, a carry-over from the old typewriter days, all but guarantees a bitter, contentious relationship with your word processor. A person who buys a word processor and then presses Enter after every line is like an old farmer who buys his first car and then hooks up his horse to pull it. (He then spends his days cursing this newfangled means of transportation because his miles-per-bale-of-hay went down.)

- ✔ Think twice before using the Tab key and the spacebar to position text. Get to know some of the cool automatic formatting features, like automatic centering or justifying a line of text. Strange things can appear on the page when your tab-and-space formatting starts to interact with the automatic formatting. Works provides better ways to do the indentations and positioning that you want, as I describe in Chapter 15.

- ✔ Some keys, such as the Backspace key and the Caps Lock key, work a bit differently. See the section, "Keyboard tips and peculiarities," later in this chapter.

- ✔ Text flows around on your screen like spilled coffee on a desktop. (At least the text doesn't soak through to other documents.) When you add something or remove it, the remaining text moves away or flows in to fill the gap. For example, if you remove the special marks that keep paragraphs separate, the paragraphs merge together. Paragraphs are supposed to behave this way. You just have to go with the flow.

- ✔ Your screen doesn't always show you exactly what your document will look like if you print it. Using Print Preview, as I describe in Chapter 4, is the best way to see what your final printed output will look like.

✔ Do not use dashes and other symbols to make lines. Heavens, no — this way of making lines is far too tacky. Works offers lots of other, cleaner ways to do lines and borders.

What you can do with a word processor

Use the Works word-processing program to create all kinds of documents, including simple letters and memos, newsletters, scholarly reports, or even things that need big letters, such as signs or transparency foils for presentations. Check out some of the things that this program lets you do with documents:

✔ Move text and graphics, or copy them, from one place (or one document) to another.

✔ Use any of a wide variety of typefaces, in sizes from barely legible to utterly humongous — even in color, if you have a color printer.

✔ Automatically indent, center, left-justify, or right-justify your text.

✔ Quickly set or change line spacing or spacing between paragraphs.

✔ Automatically add bullets to lists (such as this one).

✔ Automatically insert page breaks in the right places.

✔ Automatically floss your teeth.

✔ Put your socks in the correct drawer.

✔ Use charts, tables, and illustrations.

✔ Automatically number footnotes and keep them on the correct page as you move text around.

✔ Automatically search for certain words or phrases — and even replace them with other text, if you want. (For example, you may want to find all occurrences of "you pompous old windbag" and replace them with "Mr. Wiggins.")

✔ Automatically check your spelling.

✔ Find synonyms for words using a built-in thesaurus.

✔ Walk your dog.

✔ Print envelopes.

✔ Automatically put headers or footers on each page (as in this book, where each page has a header identifying the chapter number or part).

Just kidding about the teeth, the socks, and the dog, but the rest is true (unless your name is Wiggins). And this is just the beginning.

Starting a Word Processor Document

Enough preamble. Time to gird your loins and stroll onto the word-processing wrestling mat.

From the Task Launcher, you can start a new word processor document, if you like, or open or find an existing document. (Flip back to Chapter 1 for more details about the Task Launcher.)

To start a new word processor document from a Task, click Programs on the Task Launcher, and then click Works Word Processor (at the top of the left-hand column) to display a list of word-processing Tasks. Choose a Task for the type of document you want to create, click Start, and a wizard builds a document for you in the word processor window. The wizard doesn't go away, though, but leaves its window on top of the word processor window so you can choose alternative forms of the document. Click the form you like, and then click the Finish button.

If you want to start with a simple blank word processor document without the aid of a wizard, click Start a Blank Word Processor Document right above the column of Task names.

You are now gazing at the word-processing window, its toolbar, and other assorted paraphernalia. If you got here by way of a Task, that window has a filled-out document in it. Check out Part II for more about dealing with wizard-built documents. If you got here by just starting the word processor program, you have a blank document.

The Word Processor Window and Toolbar

Look at Figure 13-1 to see what's what in the Works Word Processor window. You see a document with one of the dweeby sort of startup names that Works gives new documents — like *Untitled Document* — is on the screen. (You would think they would baptize these documents or something, so that they would be saved.) Then there's the usual Works menu bar (with all the commands) near the top of the Works window, and the Standard and Formatting toolbars are underneath that.

You may also find a Help panel occupying the right-hand side of your Works window. If you find this panel helpful, leave it there. Otherwise, click the X button in its upper-right corner. For more on Help, see Chapter 2.

Don't try to memorize all the names in Figure 13-1. Stick a pencil here (or turn back the corner of the page) and come back whenever you need to refresh your memory.

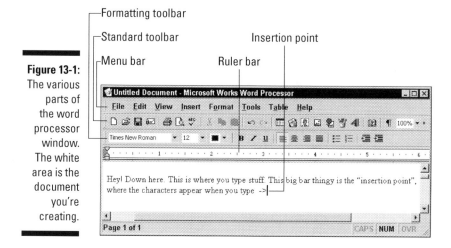

Formatting toolbar

Standard toolbar

Menu bar

Insertion point

Ruler bar

Figure 13-1:
The various parts of the word processor window. The white area is the document you're creating.

The Standard and Formatting toolbars are optional. You can turn them off or on. To turn them off, choose View⇨Toolbars in the menu bar, and then click Standard or Formatting in the menu that pops out — click whichever one of these bars you want to turn off. To turn that bar back on, do the same thing again. The Ruler is also optional and can be turned on and off by choosing View⇨Ruler. Everything else is pretty permanent.

The word processing Standard and Formatting toolbars are similar to the toolbars in other Works programs. For more on the Works toolbars, read through Chapter 2. To learn the name (and get a hint at the purpose) of a button, pause your mouse cursor over the button. A tiny tag pops up with the button's name.

Most of the toolbar buttons are the usual suspects mentioned in Chapter 2 for starting, saving, printing, doing basic cut-and-paste edits, changing fonts, and getting help. The remaining toolbar buttons are more specific to word processing and are discussed in the following chapters of this book:

- ✔ **Align Left/Align Right, Center, Justify:** Read through Chapter 15.
- ✔ **Bullets for lists:** Check out Chapter 16.
- ✔ **Make a table:** Go to Chapter 16.
- ✔ **Check spelling:** Peruse Chapter 14.
- ✔ **Address Book:** Thumb through Chapter 6.

Typing and Deleting in a Document

Typing and deleting are the existential underpinnings of word processing — existence and nonexistence: calling into creation and returning to the void. All else is illusion (or maybe illustration).

Typing

If you're now looking at a word-processing window, away you go. Just start typing. All the regular keys on the keyboard — the letters, numbers, and punctuation — put characters on the screen when you press them.

Keep on typing and do *not* press the Enter (or Return) key when you get to the end of the line. The text you type automatically starts on the next line; this phenomenon is called line wrap. When you get to the bottom of the document window, the document scrolls up, like paper in your typewriter. Press the Enter key when you get to the end of a paragraph — *not before!!!*

If you want space between your paragraphs, you can press the Enter key twice at the end of the paragraph, but there's a better way — called paragraph formatting — that I discuss in Chapter 15. For now, try this technique: If you want a line's worth of space above the paragraph that you're currently typing (and a line's worth of space above subsequent paragraphs), press Ctrl+0 (that's the numeral zero, not the letter *O*). If you want that space to go away, press Ctrl+0 again.

The insertion point

As you type, you start pushing around that big vertical bar, known as the insertion point. The insertion point's main function in life is to mark where the next character appears when you type or where a character disappears when you delete.

You can nudge the insertion point up, down, or sideways by pressing the arrow and other navigation keys on your keyboard. Or you can teleport the insertion point: Just click the mouse pointer at the place in your document where you want to start typing. (See the section, "Getting Around in Your Document," later in this chapter.)

Notice what happens to your mouse pointer when you move it into the white area where you type. The mouse pointer changes into a mouse cursor — an I-beam shape — that's a little easier to fit in between characters than the pointer is.

Beware the insidious Insert key

Works provides two ways for you to type with your keyboard: insert mode and overtype mode. (A third mode, *à la mode*, is when your ice cream cone drops onto the keyboard.)

Normally, you are in the insert mode, which means that if you move the insertion point into the middle of text and type, the existing text scoots to the right to make room. If, however, you should accidentally press the Insert key (which lives over by your navigation keys, just waiting to be pressed accidentally), you find

yourself transported to the parallel dimension of overtype mode. (The text OVR appears in a small box near the bottom-right corner of your word processing window.)

Now, if you move the insertion point into the middle of text and type, the existing text vanishes as you type over it. If you find you are typing over existing text, you probably pressed Insert. Press the Insert key again to return to your home dimension.

Don't confuse your mouse cursor (where you're pointing) with the insertion point (where you're typing). The mouse cursor is the symbol that you move with your mouse. Clicking the mouse brings the insertion point to where the mouse cursor is.

Deleting

You can delete stuff with either the Backspace key or the Delete key. To delete a character you just typed, press the Backspace key (usually on the upper-right corner of the typewriter keys). Technically speaking (geek-speak), the Backspace key deletes the character before the insertion point, and the Delete key deletes the character after the insertion point.

To delete a character in the middle of a line of text, you can use either the Backspace key or the Delete key — your preference. If you click just after the character, you can use the Backspace key. If you click just before the character, you can use the Delete key (which hangs out near your navigation keys).

To delete a block of text, select the text by clicking and dragging your mouse cursor across it; then press either the Backspace key or the Delete key. The selected area can span as many words, lines, paragraphs, or even pages as you want. For more on selecting text, read through Chapter 3.

To undelete (that's *un-delete*, not *un-dulate* — don't get excited) something that you deleted by accident, press Ctrl+Z. You have to do this immediately, like cardiopulmonary resuscitation, or you lose the patient. To untype something you just typed, you can also press Ctrl+Z.

Rapping about wrapping

If you've never used a word processor before, here's something about line wrapping that may catch you by surprise: Lines unwrap when you delete, just like they wrap when you type. Try it. Type a couple of lines; then move the insertion point to somewhere in the second line and start deleting by pressing the Backspace key. When the insertion point gets back to the beginning of the line, don't let up. The insertion point jumps back up to the end of the first line and starts gobbling characters there. (The Backspace key on your typewriter definitely doesn't work this way.)

The same thing happens when you move the insertion point with the arrow keys. If you're at the end of a line and go right, you wrap down to the beginning of the next line. If you're at the beginning of a line and go left, you wrap up to the end of the preceding line.

Typing spaces, tabs, and other invisible characters

You've probably already suspected that your document is haunted by powerful invisible beings. What you probably didn't know is that you're the one who puts them there. Yes, indeedy. You pressed the keys that brought them into existence.

Some of these characters, such as the space character, are familiar and fairly innocuous. Other characters, such as the tab mark that you get when you press the Tab key, are somewhat more mysterious. These characters include the following.

- ✔ The **spacebar** puts a space mark (character) in your text. Unlike the space on a typewriter, the word processor's spacebar gives you a very skinny space (much thinner than most other characters you type). The space mark's width depends on the font (typeface and size) that you're currently using.

- ✔ When you press the **Tab key,** you insert a tab mark. The tab mark creates space in your text starting from where the insertion point is and ending where the next *tab stop* is. See Chapter 15 for more on tabs.

- ✔ The elite of these invisible beings — the **paragraph mark** that you get when you press the Enter key — is so powerful that it gets its own section in this chapter, "Paragraphs and paragraph marks," coming up soon.

"What tab mark? What paragraph mark?" you say. Well, these marks are *invisible,* of course, which is why they don't stand out in a crowd. They're easy to overlook when you format or delete. But they do affect the way your document looks and can cause weird, spooky, inexplicable things to appear. Be on the lookout for: big gaps in your text (because of a tab mark or a series of spaces you didn't know was there); or a paragraph merging with another (when a paragraph mark gets deleted); or a font for your text that you didn't expect (when the insertion point gets plunked down next to an invisible character that has a different font attached to it).

For all these reasons, you need to be able to see these invisible characters, at least occasionally. Read on.

Seeing invisible characters

I discuss the why and how-not-to of these mysteries later, but for now, just choose one of the two following ways to see these creepy invisible guys:

 ✔ Choose View➪All Characters.
 ✔ Click the ¶ button on the toolbar.

AAAaaggghh! Your document is filled with nasty dots and funny marks! In fact, it looks almost as bad as the document shown in Figure 13-2! What a mess! Aren't you glad that these characters are normally invisible? Those dots between your words are spaces. The little backwards-P-looking thing is a paragraph mark (look back at the preceding bulleted list), and it hangs out with the text that precedes it. Tab marks look like arrows with a deodorant-failure problem (lots of space around them).

Now, if any of these invisible dudes are giving you trouble, just revoke their existence (delete them). Put the insertion point in front of them and press the Delete key. The visible text moves around to fill the gap.

To make these characters invisible again, choose View➪All Characters again. Frankly, however, until you get used to having these characters lurking around, your life may be easier if you leave the characters visible.

Paragraphs and paragraph marks

Your English teacher told you what a paragraph is, right? Topic sentence? Two or more related sentences? Well, Works has its own idea about para graphs. When you press the Enter key, you create a Works paragraph and you also create one of those secret, invisible paragraph marks that I talk about in "Typing spaces, tabs, and other invisible characters," earlier in this chapter.

relieve·its·internal·pressure ·In·the·next·section,·we·will·explore·some·of·the·basic·
pressure-releases·for·different·types·of·motion.¶

Section·3¶
Pressure·against·the·side·of·the·track¶
Varying·pressures·against·the·side·of·the·track·result·in·the·pressure·releases·of·Table·3-1,·
below.¶

Table·3-1·Lateral·pressures·and·their·indications¶

Pressure → **Indications**↵
Light → crest↵
Moderate → cave↵

That paragraph mark is very powerful, as invisible beings tend to be. Here are three extremely important and utterly critical things to know about the paragraph mark:

✓ **A paragraph mark tells Works, "Do not line wrap beyond this point; start a new line."**

A paragraph mark is the thing that keeps paragraphs apart.

✓ **The paragraph mark controls paragraph formatting for its paragraph.**

In other words, the mark affects all the text preceding it (up to the preceding paragraph mark).

Paragraph formatting is indentation, spacing between paragraphs, tab stops, alignment, justification, and other stuff that I talk about in Chapter 15. When you format a paragraph, all this formatting information is owned by the paragraph mark and applies to the text preceding it. The paragraph mark does not, however, specify the typeface (font) or any aspect of it, such as style or size. Therefore, if you copy a paragraph mark and paste it somewhere else, it brings its paragraph formatting with it!

✓ **Every time that you press the Enter key (creating a new paragraph mark), the new paragraph mark inherits all the paragraph formatting of the paragraph you were just in.**

The indentation, the spacing, the tab stops, and all the other paragraph stuff are the same. In other words, just type, and new paragraphs look just like the first one. To change appearances of new paragraphs, adjust the final paragraph's formatting. Any new paragraphs you create from it inherit its appearance.

What these points mean for you is the following:

- ✔ Don't press the Enter key at the end of every line; press it only at the end of your paragraph. Otherwise, your paragraph is actually a bunch of Works paragraphs. If you try to accomplish something paragraph-y — such as indenting everything but the first line — the format won't work properly because (as far as Works is concerned) every line is the first line!

- ✔ Do press the Enter key at the end of short lines in a list, such as this one.

- ✔ To split one paragraph into two, put the insertion point where you want the split and press the Enter key. The two new paragraphs have identical paragraph formatting.

- ✔ To create a new paragraph in front of the one that you're currently in, move your insertion point to the beginning of the current paragraph and press Enter.

- ✔ To create a new paragraph to follow the one that you're currently in, move your insertion point to the end of the current paragraph (click within the last line and press the End key to be sure) and press Enter.

- ✔ If you delete text that includes a paragraph mark (for example, if you select and delete text crossing two paragraphs), the two paragraphs merge. The remaining single paragraph takes on the paragraph formatting of the bottom of the original pair. Try pressing Ctrl+Z to undo whatever you did. You can also take a look at Chapter 15 for more on formatting changes.

Keyboard tips and peculiarities

Check out these tips and peculiarities of the keyboard that are important to word processing:

- ✔ The two Shift keys work just as they do on a typewriter.

- ✔ The Caps Lock key does *not* work as it does on a typewriter (by changing to the upper character set) — it only makes letters uppercase.

- ✔ If you hold down a key long enough, it autorepeats — that is, it repeatedly and rapidly types the character.

- ✔ The Backspace key doesn't just backspace; it deletes at the same time.

- ✔ The Tab key inserts an invisible character that pushes your text around. (Flip on over to Chapter 15 for more on tabs.)

Getting Around in Your Document

Sometimes you just want to look around in your document and check things out. Other times you want to move the insertion point to do some work on your document.

Looking around

You can scroll around to look at one part of the document, maybe to review something you wrote earlier (which I never do, personally), while leaving your insertion point (that vertical bar) where you're typing. Leaving your insertion point in place is convenient because while you look around, you don't lose your place. To perform this trick, scroll the document with the scroll bar on the right side or bottom of the document window. (See Chapter 2 for information on the scroll bar.)

If you type a word or if you press Delete, however, your view suddenly returns to the insertion point because that's where you just typed. Works figures that if you're working somewhere, you ought to be looking at what you're doing.

Moving around

To work someplace different, move your insertion point. To move your insertion point by using the mouse, just click somewhere in your document.

To move your insertion point by using the keyboard, press the arrow or other navigation keys, such as Page Up and Page Down. Review Table 13-1 to see how to move the insertion point by using the keyboard. Read through the section, "Rapping about wrapping," earlier in this chapter, for more on how the insertion point moves from one line to another.

Table 13-1	Navigating with Keys
Navigation Key	*Where It Moves the Insertion Point*
←/→	One character's worth left or right
Ctrl+←/→	One word's worth left or right
↑/↓	One line's worth up or down
Page Up/Page Down	One window's worth up or down

Navigation Key	Where It Moves the Insertion Point
Home	Beginning of the line
End	End of the line
Ctrl+Home	Beginning of the document
Ctrl+End	End of the document

Going to a page, or someplace else specific

If you've got a big document to edit — especially if you're working from a printed copy — the fastest way to get around may be to go to a specific page, footnote, or other feature. For that, Works gives you the "Go To" feature. Choose Edit➪Go To or press Ctrl+G.

The Find and Replace dialog box appears with the Go To tab displayed. Select your destination from the Go To What list on that tab: a page, footnote, end-note, database field (for form letters), or a table. Type the number of the page, footnote, or whatever in the text box on that tab. Then click the Go To button and you're on your way.

For pages, tables, and fields, Works simply counts to get to the right number. It doesn't know about any captions you may have used, such as *Table 13-1.*

Seeing What Your Document Really Looks Like

One of the weird things about word processors is that they're all a little reluctant to show you exactly what your document looks like. In the Works word processor, you have two ways of looking at your document (apart from printing it).

While you are working on your document, you see it in a view often called Page Layout. In this view, you can see your page breaks and margins realistically. Also, if you use page numbers, headers, or footers, you can see them, too.

Your other choice, the Print Preview feature, enables you to see something that's as close to the paper printout as Works can manage. You can't work on the document while looking at it in Print Preview, however. For more on this feature, check out Chapter 4.

Printing Your Document

Ahh, printing. Where the ink meets the paper. So visceral, so satisfying, so . . . confusing! At least it is sometimes. When everything works well, printing is fun. But getting everything to work the way that you want it to work can be a bit exasperating.

Fortunately, printing is pretty much the same for all the programs of Works. That's why the place to read all about printing is Chapter 4, not here. Here, I just give a quick executive summary and point out what's different about printing a word-processing document.

The executive summary goes like this:

- ✔ You can print your whole document or any set of pages in it.
- ✔ The easiest way to print a single copy of the whole document is to click the Print button on the toolbar.
- ✔ To print a portion of your document, choose File➪Print, or press Ctrl+P, and specify (in the Print dialog box) the pages that you want to print.

The main peculiarity of printing using the word processor is the envelope tool (or Envelopes wizard). For information on creating envelopes, see Chapter 7.

Saving Your Document

Saving your word-processing document is just like saving any other Works document: Click the Save button on the toolbar (the one with the diskette icon), or choose File➪Save from the menu bar, or press Ctrl+S. See Chapter 2 for detailed information about saving documents.

Exiting the Word Processor

To exit the word processor, all you have to do is close your word-processing document. Click the X at the top right corner of the document window. (This will not close the Works Task Launcher.) If you prefer using menus, choose File➪Close; or if you like using the keyboard, press Alt+F4.

If your current document is still unsaved, or if it has changed since the last time you saved it as a file on a disk, Works puts up a dialog box to ask you whether you want to save changes to your document. Click the Yes button, unless you really want to throw away what you've done since the last time you saved your work. If that's the case, click No.

Chapter 14

Hacking through the Jungle of Your Text

*H*as your document become a tangle of misplaced paragraphs, wrong-headed words, and excessively long, lengthy, redundant, and duplicate descriptions? Time to sharpen up the old machete and cut an editorial swath through the underbrush.

In this chapter, I show you how to find and target such text and then move it, copy it, delete it, or replace it. Gird your loins (if not already girded from Chapter 13), buckle your swash, and have at it.

Selecting Your Target Text

In order to do anything to the text you've typed, such as move it or copy it, you have to be able to tell Works exactly which text you're talking about. This process is called selecting or highlighting text, and it works pretty much the same in all the Works tools. See Chapter 3 for details on the following two methods of selection:

> ✔ **Mouse method:** Click and drag the mouse cursor across the text you want to select. Release the mouse button when all the text you want to select is highlighted (you see white text on a black background).

✔ **Keyboard method:** Position the insertion point at one end of the text, hold down the Shift key, and then press an arrow key or another navigation key to expand the highlight. Release the keys when all the text you want to select is highlighted. For example, to select big gobs of text, press Shift+Page Up or Shift+Page Down; then switch to Shift+arrow keys for precision. Or to select forward from the insertion point to the end of the line, press Shift+End. (Again, you see highlighted text as white text on a black background.)

The word processor offers some additional selection options not found in the other tools:

✔ When you use the mouse, you can select one individual character at a time within the first word, but after you have selected more than one word, you get one word at a time. Why? Go figure.

✔ To select a line, click in the white area to the left of that line; to select several lines, hold down the mouse button and drag.

✔ To select a paragraph, double-click anywhere in the white area to the left of the paragraph. To select several paragraphs, hold down the mouse button when you make the second click and drag up or down.

✔ Finally, to select the whole document, choose Edit⇨Select All.

Chopping Up Your Text — Moving, Copying, and Deleting

Remember the machete that you strapped on at the start of this chapter? Time to unbuckle it. And put on your pith helmet, too, because now's the time to cut that editorial swath through your pithy prose.

To aid you in this worthwhile endeavor, the Works Word Processor provides a variety of features that let you move text around, delete blocks of text, and copy text that is too tedious to retype every time it needs to appear.

These features are pretty much the same in every tool in Works. So rather than repeat them here, I just give you the executive summary of how to edit text. (For a more thorough discussion, check out Chapter 3.)

✔ To delete a block of text, select it and then press the Delete or Backspace key.

✔ To move text, select it; then click it again and, keeping the mouse button down, drag it. (The text doesn't actually move until you release the mouse button after dragging.)

   ✔ To copy text, do the same thing as for moving text, but hold the Ctrl key down while you drag.

   ✔ To make multiple copies, select text and then press Ctrl+C; click wherever you want a copy of that something to appear, and press Ctrl+V.

   ✔ To remove text and put a copy of it elsewhere, select it and then press Ctrl+X; then click wherever you want a copy to appear and press Ctrl+V.

You can use the buttons on the toolbar in place of the key combinations:

   ✔ Ctrl+C is Copy, the button that shows two documents overlapping.

   ✔ Ctrl+V is Paste, the button that shows a clipboard.

   ✔ Ctrl+X is Cut, the button with the scissors.

Or you can find Copy, Paste, and Cut on the drop-down menu that appears when you click Edit on the menu bar.

Finding Elusive Fauna (Or, Where's That Word?)

In the jungle of words that is the typical document, you can easily lose track of important words and phrases. Perhaps way back somewhere in a 70-page tome, you had a discussion of the fauna of temperate transition zones (like the Chicago suburbs). You want to cross-reference that discussion at this point, but you can't remember quite where it is.

Finding a word or phrase is no problem for your efficient and jungle-wise guide, the Find tab of the Find and Replace dialog box. Here's how to give this trusty companion its marching orders:

1. **Press Ctrl+Home.**

   This action moves the insertion point to the beginning of the document. Because the Find feature starts looking at the insertion point, pressing Ctrl+Home ensures that Works searches the entire document.

   Or if you know that what you seek is in a certain area, you can highlight (select) that area instead of pressing Ctrl+Home. The Find feature then restricts its search to the selected area.

2. **Choose Edit⇨Find or press Ctrl+F.**

   The Find tab of the Find and Replace dialog box springs into action and presents itself for duty, as shown in Figure 14-1.

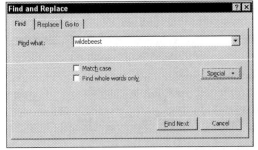

Figure 14-1:
Tell Find to
go forward
and seek a
word or
phrase.

3. **Type the word or phrase that you want to look for in the Find What box.**

   If you know that the word or phrase you want includes certain uppercase or lowercase letters, type them exactly that way here and turn on the Match Case feature. (Select the Match Case check box to enable the feature.) If, for example, you know that you are looking for a section of your document entitled *Wildebeest,* use the capital letter *W* and enable the Match Case feature.

4. **Click the Find Next button or press Enter.**

   Find scurries forward into the underbrush, looking for *wildebeests* or *Wildebeests* or whatever. When Find finds a match, it highlights (selects) the *wildebeest* so that you can do stuff to it if you want to: delete it, format it, copy it, or just observe it in its native habitat.

   If Find can't find your requested word or phrase, it runs smack into the end of your document (or into the end of the text you selected for the search). Rubbing its forehead, Find puts up a little box to ask whether it should continue searching from the beginning of your document. Click Yes if you think that the *wildebeest* may be lurking behind you (located prior to where you began your search). Otherwise, click No to return to the Find and Replace dialog box so that you can revise your marching orders.

   If Find searches the entire document (or all of the text that you select) without success, it puts up a box that reads `The search item was not found`, which is Work-speak for "Back to the drawing board." Click OK in this box to return to the Find dialog box.

5. **To find another instance of the word or phrase, click the Find Next button or press the Enter key again.**

   Remember that your document may be swarming with *wildebeests*. Keep searching until you find the right one.

6. **To find something different, edit your search word or phrase in the Find What box.**

7. **Click the Cancel button in the Find dialog box when you're done with your searching.**

Whole wildebeests or pieces?

Is it *wildebeest* or *wildebeast?* If you're not sure how to spell what you're searching for (or not sure that you spelled it correctly when you used it before), try typing in just the portion of the word or phrase that you are sure of. You can just type **wilde** and be pretty certain of finding wilde-whatevers. This trick also works if you're simply lazy and don't want to type the beest/beast part. Sloth is not a sin in finding words. (Although when you're finding sloths — well, never mind.) This method also works if you want both singular and plural *wildebeest(s):* Just leave off the ending *s.*

> *Q: What did one wildebeest say to the other when they met in the jungle?*
>
> *A: What's gnu with you?*

(Oh, sorry. You say you gnu that one?) For any of these find-the-partial-word tricks to work, however, you have to make sure that the Find Whole Words Only check box (in the Find dialog box) does *not* have a check mark in it. Click that check box to clear the check mark if it's present.

Searching for wildebeests and finding Oscar Wilde

Sometimes, searching for pieces of a word is not such a good idea. The Find feature may return from the hunt with *Oscar Wilde* instead of a *wildebeest.* Very embarrassing. Alas, Find offers no way to tell it, "Do not find dead playwrights."

So if your document may include both the fragment (Wilde) and the whole word (wildebeest), tell Find to search for whole words only. (A *whole word* is a bunch of characters set off by spaces or punctuation.) This whole-word option is very useful for short words, such as *an,* that crop up now *an*d again as fragments of other words.

To tell Find to search for whole words only, make sure that the Find Whole Words Only check box has a check mark in it. Click that check box if it does not.

Replacing Words and Phrases (Wildebeests with Whelks)

If you're typing along about wildebeests and suddenly realize that you want whelks, and not wildebeests, you have some personal problems that go beyond software, and I will not attempt to deal with them here. I can, however, tell you how to replace *wildebeest* with *whelk.*

Your companion on this environmentally dubious quest of replacing mammals with shellfish is not Find, but Find's not-quite-identical twin, Replace. To use the Replace tab of the Find and Replace dialog box, you do exactly as you do with the Find tab. Enter a word or phrase to look for, but you also give Replace something new to replace that word or phrase with. When Replace finds instances of the original word, you have the option of replacing each instance. You can also replace all instances.

Here's how to replace some text with other text:

1. **Narrow the area for your search and replace, if you can.**

   Like Find, the Replace command starts searching from your insertion point and goes forward. Click just before the area in which you want to replace text. If you know what you seek is in a certain area, highlight (select) that area. Replace restricts its search to the selected area.

2. **Choose Edit⊷Replace or press Ctrl+H.**

   The Replace tab of the Find and Replace dialog box springs into action and presents itself for duty, as shown in Figure 14-2.

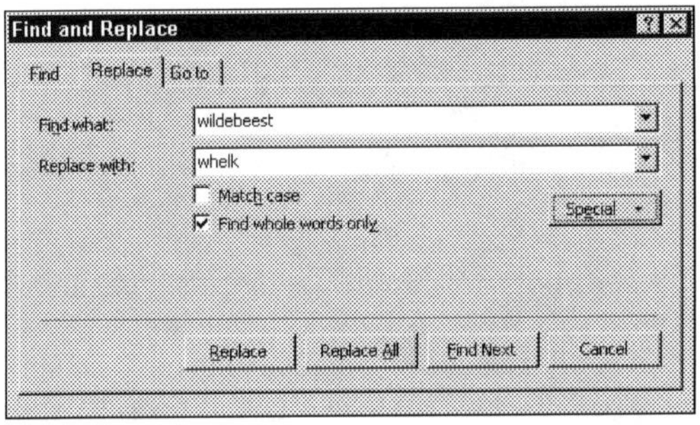

Figure 14-2:
Wantonly
replacing
wildebeests
with whelks.

3. **Type the word or phrase that you want to find in the Find What box.**

   Read through the section, "Finding Elusive Fauna (Or, Where's That Word?)," earlier in this chapter.

4. **Type the replacement word or phrase in the Replace With text box.**

   Unless you specifically want the replacement word to always be capitalized, using all lowercase letters is best. If the original text is capitalized, Replace cleverly capitalizes the new text.

5. **Click the F̲ind Next button or press Enter.**

   Replace scurries forward into the underbrush, looking for *wildebeest*s to replace. When Replace finds one, it highlights (selects) the *wildebeest* so that you can see whether this particular *wildebeest* is one that you want to replace.

   If Replace can't find your word or phrase, it runs into the end of your document and, like its sibling, Find, asks whether you want it to search from the start of the document. If you like this idea, click Yes. If Replace searches the entire document without success, it displays a No Match Found box. Click OK in this box.

6. **To replace the highlighted text, click the R̲eplace button.**

   Poof! Your wildebeest is now a whelk and as happy as a clam.

   Or, to replace all instances of the search text, click the Replace All button. Replace All doesn't pause for each instance to ask your permission; it just does the replacement. If you selected a region of text back in Step 1, only that region is affected.

   If you don't want to replace the particular instance that's currently highlighted, move on to Step 7.

7. **To find another instance of the word or phrase, click the F̲ind Next button or press Enter again.**

   Remember that your document may be swarming with *wildebeest*s. Keep searching until you find all the ones that you want to replace.

   Replace lets you know when it has finished searching the whole document (or whatever text you selected).

8. **When you're done with your replacing, click the Cancel button or the X in the upper-right corner of the Replace dialog box.**

Sticky boxes and words

The check boxes in the Find dialog box, such as Match Case, are *sticky*. No matter which way you leave them when you quit Find (checked or not checked), that's how they appear when you use Find again later. Always look to be sure that the check box is marked correctly before you begin searching. The word that you type is also sticky (as are the words that you type when using the Replace dialog box).

Here are a few tips and tricks for replacing:

- To replace a noun throughout your document, use the singular form (say, *wildebeest* or *whelk*) and make sure that the Find Whole Words Only check box does *not* have a check mark in it. (Click the check box, if it does.) Where you once had *wildebeests,* you now have *whelks.* (This trick doesn't work if you're changing *wildebeests* to *octopi,* however.)

- The Replace All button can be dangerous. Use it carefully and make sure that you are replacing only what you want to replace. If you want to change *days* to *weeks,* make sure that you're not changing Sun*days* to Sun*weeks.*

Finding and Replacing White-Space Characters

Many documents are teeming with invisible, microscopic life — tabs and paragraph marks, in particular — inserted by their authors to control the spaces within and between paragraphs. (Read more about these invisible characters in Chapter 15.)

Finding and replacing these so-called white-space characters can sometimes be useful. For example, you may have long lists of items separated by commas (as in apples, oranges, bananas, whale uvulas) and want to put the items on separate lines instead. If you replace the two separating characters — a comma and a space — with a paragraph mark, each item appears on its own line.

An even more common task is to replace multiple tabs or paragraph marks with single ones. Newcomers to word processing often press the Tab key several times to indent (rather than using a single tab and setting the tab stop), or they press the Enter key multiple times to add space between paragraphs instead of changing the paragraph format. As newcomers grow more familiar with word-processor formatting, they often want to change or get rid of some of these characters because the overabundant characters create more work.

In the Find and Replace dialog box (described earlier in the chapter), you can't simply press the Tab key to enter a tab character or press the Enter key to enter a paragraph mark. Works requires you to enter special codes to represent these characters. Because the tab and paragraph marks are so commonly used, Works provides the Special button for entering their special codes in the Find and Replace tabs. Click Special and then choose Paragraph Mark or Tab Character from the list that drops down. The Special list also lets you choose several other kinds of white-space characters.

Meeting the Mighty Thesaurus

Among the various critters roaming around in the word processor is the thesaurus. Although not quite as mighty as the brontosaurus, the thesaurus is, perhaps, superior in intelligence. Use it to help you find alternative words. (Note, *Star Trek* fans, that I said alternative *words,* not alternative *worlds.* Stay with me here.) Although your word processor thesaurus is nice and convenient, it can't really hold a candle to a printed thesaurus (which is good, because those are generally flammable). Still, when you're stuck for a word, the Works thesaurus is a good saurus to have around.

The basic idea is to select (highlight) a word and then let the thesaurus look up alternatives. You can even select compound words, such as blow up. If the word can have several very different meanings (like balloon, for example), the thesaurus lists those and also lists alternative words within each meaning. You can explore alternatives for any of these words if you like. At any point, you can choose a word to replace the selected one.

Here's the click-by-click description of how to use the thesaurus:

1. **Select (highlight) the word you want to look up.**

2. **Choose Tools⇨Thesaurus (or press Shift+F7).**

   The Thesaurus dialog box, as shown in Figure 14-3, lumbers out of the wilderness and wants to be your friend.

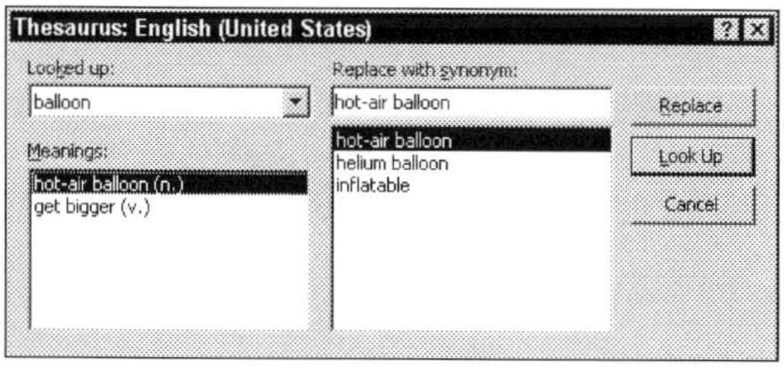

Figure 14-3:
The baby thesaurus in Works is not purple, like Barney, but it still wants to be your friend.

3. **Click any likely looking word or phrase either in the Meanings box or in the list of synonyms just below the Replace With Synonym box.**

   Your substitute word can come from either list. If you click a meaning, you get a new list of synonyms to play with.

4. **To look for synonyms to your synonyms, click anything in either list and then click the Look Up button.**

   You can keep up like this all day. From *balloon,* you can eventually float to almost anywhere. What fun! (If at any point you think, "How the heck did I get here?", click the down arrow next to the Looked Up box, and the whole list of what you looked up so far drops down.)

5. **When, in either list, you see a good substitute word or phrase, click it and then click the <u>R</u>eplace button.**

   Your original word or phrase in the document is replaced.

Your new word or phrase may not be any better than your old one, but what a good time you had. Beats working!

Snaring Your Misspellings

Typos and misspellings can sneak up unnoticed into the undergrowth of any document. You may be amazed at how many errors you make that the Works' Spelling Checker can discover and help you correct. This helpful feature is available for several tools; you can find the details of using it in Chapter 3. But here's the executive summary.

The Works' Spelling Checker runs automatically (unless you tell Works otherwise), and underlines all words it thinks are suspect with a red, wavy line. Right-click on any such word, and Works presents a short list of possible, correctly spelled alternatives that it thinks you *really* mean. Click any of those to replace the underlined word.

For slightly more sophisticated spell checking, run the spelling checker yourself manually. Press F7, or choose <u>T</u>ools⇨<u>S</u>pelling and Grammar from the menu bar, or click the Spelling Checker button (the check mark with ABC) on the toolbar.

Automatically (Or Annoyingly) Fixing Typos

The Works' Word Processor has adopted an automatic feature of its big brother, Microsoft Word: AutoCorrect. This feature is either a wonderful innovation or a royal pain in the anatomy, depending upon what you are trying to do.

If you mis-type or misspell a word in a way that is fairly common, the word processor will probably repair the word. The repair takes place as soon as you complete the word by pressing the spacebar or typing a punctuation mark. Type **teh,** for instance, and Works replaces it with *the.* If you misspell *occurred* as *occured,* Works adds the missing *r.*

This correction even applies to special symbols, punctuation, capitalization, and superscript or subscript letters or numerals. Straight quotes (" ") turn into smart (curly) quotes (" "); the trademark symbol notation (TM) turns into ™ ; the fraction 1/2 turns into ½; and so on. Fantastic!

This feature becomes a problem when you really want to type things like 1/2, not ½. Also, with Microsoft bent on making everything work on or for the Internet, Internet addresses turn into hyperlinks (text you click in a Web page) and appear underlined and blue.

One way to negate AutoCorrect's auto-assumptions is to press Ctrl+Z immediately after Works makes its correction. The change is undone. A better solution to getting the most out of AutoCorrect is to keep AutoCorrect under your own control. Choose Tools⇔AutoCorrect to open the AutoCorrect dialog box, as shown in Figure 14-4.

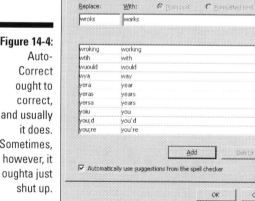

Figure 14-4:
Auto-
Correct
ought to
correct,
and usually
it does.
Sometimes,
however, it
oughta just
shut up.

To turn AutoCorrect off altogether, click the Turn AutoCorrect On to Replace Text As You Type check box at the top of the AutoCorrect tab. (Click this check box again later, if you want to turn AutoCorrect back on.)

To see what AutoCorrect does, examine the two-column list of words. Each word in the left column (Replace) is paired with a correction in the right (With) column. When you type a word that appears in the left column, Works replaces it with the word on the right. To remove one of these word pairs, click it and then click the Delete button. To change either word, click the pair and then edit the words in the Replace or With text boxes.

In addition to words on that list, any words unrecognized by the Works' spelling checker are replaced by the spelling checker's guess as to the most likely correction. To turn off that feature, clear the check box labeled Automatically Use Suggestions from the Spell-Checker.

To add your own correction to that list, click in the Replace text box and type the erroneous word. Then click within the With text box and type the correct spelling. Finally, click the Add button.

You can use the AutoCorrect feature to create useful shorthand terms. For instance, make it easier to write your company name — Dingelhausen-Schnitzenbaum Furniture Prefabrication Co. — by simply entering a shortcut. Type **DSF** (or **dsf**) in the Replace text box; type **Dingelhausen-Schnitzenbaum Furniture Prefabrication Co.** in the With text box; and click Add.

You can find the AutoCorrect feature on the Options tab of the AutoCorrect dialog box. This tab lists errors and their corrections, with a check box for each. Simply click to clear the check box for any correction that causes you problems.

Chapter 15

Keeping Up Appearances

. . . .

In This Chapter

▶ Formatting text

▶ Using and creating styles

▶ Indenting and aligning paragraphs

▶ Adjusting the spacing between lines and paragraphs

▶ Setting tab stops

▶ Using the ruler

▶ Setting page margins

▶ Printing sideways

▶ Using different sizes of paper

▶ Inserting page breaks

. . . .

*E*ven when on safari in the world of word processing, one must keep up appearances. You have no excuse for frumpy fonts, untidy indentation, improper alignment, unkempt tab stops, and mismanaged margins. Indeed, those who format fastidiously can even print sideways and control page breaks.

In this chapter, I show you how to attain all those niceties of civilization — first-line indentation, line spacing, paragraph spacing, and more — automatically, without typing a bunch of tabs and blank lines. I work from the small to the large — from characters to paragraphs to documents — and explore how Works can help give your document a civilized and smart look.

Charming Characters

When your characters are losing their charm, it's time to look for a prettier face — typeface, that is (or *font,* as it is misnamed in the geeky world of computers). Works can put your type in any face (just what the world needs, more in-your-face typing) that you happen to have lying around on your PC, from stodgy Times New Roman to swirly Script. Not only that, but Works can make the type large enough to see from across the room or small enough to be mistaken for flyspecks on your contracts. But wait! There's more! You can also easily change your font's style, making it **boldface,** *italic,* underlined, ^{superscript} _{subscript} or ~~strikethrough~~!

Sometimes called *character formatting,* you have three different kinds of formatting to play with: font, size, and style.

Changing the font, size, and style of your characters is one of those things that functions the same way for all the Works tools. So for full details, turn to Chapter 3.

The executive summary goes like this. Works offers you four alternative techniques to change character formatting. To change the appearance of a particular chunk of text, first select (highlight) that text and then do one of the following:

- ✔ **Alternative 1.** Use the toolbar. The Font Name box is at the far left end of the Formatting toolbar, and the Font Size box is right next to it. The Bold, Italic, and Underline buttons (**B,** *I,* and U, respectively) are just left of the center of the toolbar. For the other styles, you have to use Alternative 2.

- ✔ **Alternative 2.** Choose font, size, and style from the Font dialog box. To open this dialog box, choose Format⇨Font.

- ✔ **Alternative 3.** To change style only, press Ctrl+B for bold, Ctrl+I for italic, and Ctrl+U for underline.

To change the appearance of the text you're currently typing, use one of these alternatives with no text selected. When you do this, you change the formatting of the insertion point, and any new characters that you type have the same formatting that the insertion point has. (To find out what the current formatting of the insertion point is, just look up at the toolbar.)

What about Alternative 4? The Works' Word Processor offers a new feature in Works 6: the Format Gallery. Read through the following section, "A Gallery of Stylish Characters," for details.

A Gallery of Stylish Characters

If you're concerned about appearances — and who isn't? — you want to coordinate the fonts and colors of your document to communicate a certain overall impression. Such concerns are particularly appropriate for public communications like newsletters or brochures. If you're selling hydraulic pumps, for instance, you want something that communicates power, reliability, and speed; if you're selling flower arrangements, you want something a bit more delicate.

Creating a fashion statement is a laudable end, and to this end, Microsoft puts its design professionals to work for you in the Works' Word Processor's Format Gallery. At your disposal are specially teamed fonts and colors in a variety of named sets of styles that you can use to format your text. You have two ways with which to put these preset schemes to work:

✔ Apply a named set of styles (such as Bistro Spice) to the document as a whole; headings and body text are all formatted at once. This all-at-once way is a real timesaver, but it doesn't always succeed in formatting everything.

✔ Apply individual, coordinated styles from a set (a particular font, size, and color in, say, the Bistro Spice set) to whatever text you select: one style for top-level headings, another for second-level headings, and yet another for body text, for instance. You'll find that this is the most reliable way to apply styles, but you must do it manually, one selection at a time.

Applying a named set of styles to the document as a whole works best when the document is originally created by using a task. Tasks make use of formatting from the gallery to begin with, which makes the gallery's job of recognizing headings and body text easier. Imagine its thought process: "Ah! I've seen this 48-point pink French Script before; it's a large heading in the Bistro Spice set. The closest fit in the Elegant Summer set that the user has now selected is 48-point red Blackadder ITC."

Take these steps to format the document as a whole:

1. **Choose Format⬦Format Gallery.**

   The Format Gallery appears.

2. **On the Format All tab, adjust the two sliders as follows to choose a named set of styles:**

   • Drag the Font Set slider left or right to change fonts. Fonts are more drab to the left, and jazzier to the right.

   • Drag the Color Set slider left or right to change colors. Colors are more uniform and conservative to the left, and brighter and more varied to the right.

3. **Click the Apply All button at the bottom.**

   For reasons best known to Microsoft, only some of your text may be changed while other text may not. Text that originally used styles from the Format Gallery is the most likely to be reformatted. If some of your text remains unchanged (or is not changed to your liking), follow the next set of steps to fix that text.

To format text individually (a heading, for instance, or plain text in the body of your document) in a style-coordinated way, do this:

1. **Choose Format⇨Format Gallery.**

   The Format Gallery appears, as shown in Figure 15-1.

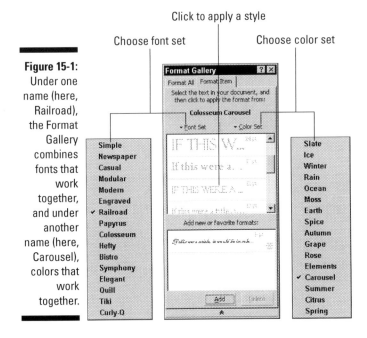

Figure 15-1:
Under one
name (here,
Railroad),
the Format
Gallery
combines
fonts that
work
together,
and under
another
name (here,
Carousel),
colors that
work
together.

2. **Click the Format Item tab.**

3. **Click the Font Set button and choose a named font set from the list that appears.**

   The names are fairly descriptive of the fonts in this set. Colosseum, for instance, contains fonts you might use on a Greek fraternity or sorority newsletter.

4. **Click the Color Set button and choose a named color set.**

   Again, the names are descriptive and intended to remind you of colors you find in a certain scene. Ice, for instance, uses various shades of light blue and gray.

5. **Select (highlight) the text in your document that you want to change.**

   For instance, select a heading by clicking in the left margin next to that heading.

6. **Click the style you want to apply.**

   Under the Font Set and Color Set buttons, a list of styles appears with the different colors, fonts, and text sizes. Microsoft combines these colors and fonts to look good together. When you click a style, the gallery applies the style to your selected text.

7. If you want to format additional text, repeat Steps 5 and 6.

You can leave the Format Gallery on screen as you stylize your entire document. Be consistent, and always use the same style for similar text — headings of a given level, or figure captions, for instance, should all look the same.

8. When you're done applying styles, close the Gallery by clicking the X in the upper-right corner.

The Gallery always lists more styles than you're likely to use in any given document. You probably won't have seven levels of headings and four styles of body text, for instance. To avoid mistakes, copy only the styles you intend to use into a list of favorites at the bottom of the Gallery. To do so, click any style in the list immediately under the Font Set and Color Set buttons, and then click the Add button at the bottom of the Gallery. Apply styles from the favorites list as you would any style (select text in your document and then click the style).

You can also create and add your own styles to the list of favorites in the Gallery, if you like. Format some text in the font, size, color, and style you want. Apply any paragraph formatting you like (see the next section, "Pretty Paragraphs," for details). That formatting is also recorded as part of the style when you create your own. (Microsoft's own built-in styles include no paragraph formatting.) Select (highlight) the text, and then click the Add button in the Gallery. To remove a style from the list of favorites, click it and then click the Delete button.

Pretty Paragraphs

There's no accounting for taste. (In fact, there's no Personnel, Purchasing, or any other department for taste.) Some folks like the first line of their paragraphs indented. Others, perhaps plumbing professionals, like their paragraphs flush right. Some folks like their lines double-spaced, and maybe they like bigger spaces between paragraphs, too. All this stuff is called paragraph formatting, which boils down to a few things you can fool with:

- **Indentations:** Adjust this to set how far the paragraph's margins should be from the page's margins, and also to set how far the first line of the paragraph should be from the left page margin.

- **Alignments:** Play with this to set how the paragraph's text lines up with the margins.

- **Spacing:** Amend this to change how many blank lines (if any) appear before or after each paragraph, and whether your lines are single-, double-, or otherwise-spaced.

You can record paragraph formatting — all your carefully chosen indentations, alignment, and spacing — as part of a style, and then apply that style to following paragraphs. That way, all similar text (say, figure captions) is formatted alike. Jump back to the preceding section, "A Gallery of Stylish Characters," for the lowdown on adding your own styles to the Format Gallery.

The big deal about using Works' paragraph formatting is that you need to set your formatting only once if you want all your paragraphs to be the same. As you type — spawning new paragraphs from the original whenever you press the Enter key — the same paragraph formatting applies to those descendants.

Alignments: Making your lines line up

Alignments are the simplest kind of paragraph formatting, so I get them out of the way first. Works has four kinds of alignment.

Left, left.

Center, center, center, center, center, center, center, center, center, center, center, center, center.

Right, right, right, right, right, right, right, right, right, right, right, right, right, right, right, right, right, right, right, right.

Justify, justify.

You have two really easy ways to change alignment. First, select the paragraphs you want to realign (or, for a single paragraph, simply click to place your insertion point anywhere within it), and then do one of the following:

✔ Click one of the four alignment toolbar buttons.

Toolbar buttons are above the ruler, each showing a bunch of horizontal lines representing the lines of text in your paragraph. These buttons appear next to this paragraph and are (from left to right) Align Left, Center, Align Right, and Justify.

✔ Or press the appropriate keys on the keyboard.

- Ctrl+L for align left

- Ctrl+ R for align right

- Ctrl+E for centered

- Ctrl+J for justified

If you happen to find yourself using the Format Paragraph dialog box for some other reason, you can alternatively click one of the four alignment buttons there. The Format Paragraph dialog box is explained later in this chapter and is shown in Figures 15-4 and 15-5.

Spaced-out paragraphs

Space is the final frontier of paragraph formatting. If you need a little air in your text, you can always ventilate your paragraph by double-spacing or adding space between paragraphs. But don't add spaces the way you did on your old Dumbrowski-Stanowitz steam-powered typing machine:

- Don't press the Enter key twice at the end of every line to double-space. (Don't even press it once.)
- Don't press the Enter key twice at the end of every paragraph to get spaces between your paragraphs.

The quick way to get space between paragraphs is by pressing Ctrl+0. (That's the numeral zero, not the letter *O*.) Doing this inserts one line of space before the current paragraph if that space isn't there already. If one line of space is already there, this action takes it away. You can also use keyboard commands to set the line spacing within a paragraph:

- Ctrl+1 single-spaces the current paragraph (where your insertion point is) or selected paragraphs.
- Ctrl+2 double-spaces the current or selected paragraphs.
- Ctrl+5 imposes one-and-a-half-line spacing on the paragraph(s). Why use 5? Well, in the strange math of Works, 5 = 1.5. Or at least it does here.

You can also set line spacing (and lots more) with the Format Paragraph dialog box. Check out the section, "Having it your way: The Format Paragraph dialog box," later in this chapter.

Quick indenting and outdenting

If you're used to typing on a typewriter, you're probably accustomed to using the Tab key to indent stuff. In Works, the Tab key makes your text begin at the next tab stop. Unless you set things up differently, tab stops occur at every half inch, starting at the left margin.

Using the Tab key is okay for the first line of a paragraph, but if you have to indent a whole paragraph or a series of paragraphs, tabbing gets pretty tedious. Here's a better way:

Select the paragraphs you want to indent (or, for a single paragraph, click anywhere in it), and then use Ctrl key combinations as follows:

- ✔ **To indent the left side:** Press Ctrl+M; the paragraph indents to the first built-in (so-called default) tab stop (normally at one half inch). Press Ctrl+M again, and your paragraph indents another half inch, and so on. (The *default* is the setting that Works uses until you tell it otherwise.)

- ✔ **To undo any left-side indentation:** Press Ctrl+Shift+M; this action outdents (reverses indentation) by one tab (moves the left edge of the paragraph left one default tab stop).

You can also use the Decrease Indent and Increase Indent buttons at the right end of the Formatting toolbar.

The tab stops here

You know all about tab stops, right? Those things that you used to set on your Smith-Corona that, when you pressed the Tab key, moved to the next stop? Nice and simple. Well, tabs in a word processor are a tad (or a tab) more complex than they were on the old Smith-Corona, but they also do nice, new things.

Using the Tab key

Using the Tab key is a good way to do certain, um . . . tabular stuff, such as creating neatly lined-up columns of text or numbers. (It's far better than using multiple spaces, which cause lots of problems during editing.) Don't use the Tab key to indent anything that runs longer than one line, however. For instance, tabs are a terrible way to indent every line of a paragraph because you create a document that is very awkward to edit later. To avoid problems, learn to align paragraphs, indent them, and set tab stops rather than pressing the Tab key repeatedly.

Most of the time, the Tab key works much like it does on your typewriter: When you press the Tab key, your text jumps to the next tab stop. In Works, unless you change the tab stops yourself, stops are at every half-inch point from the left margin.

The big difference between tabs in Works and tabs on a typewriter is that the Tab key in Works does its job by inserting a special tab character (normally invisible), which creates a space between the preceding character and the next tab stop. (To see the tab character in your document, choose View⇨All Characters.) Here are four examples of how that tab character behaves:

- ✔ If you begin a line by pressing the Tab key, you insert one tab character, and your text begins at the half-inch point (assuming the standard Works half-inch tab stops).

- ✔ If you begin a line by pressing the Tab key twice, you insert two tab characters, and your text begins at the 1-inch point. (A better solution, however, is to set your tab stop to 1 inch and insert one tab character. Setting tab stops often makes editing easier.)

- ✔ If you're typing and your insertion point is currently at the 2-inch point, pressing the Tab key inserts a tab character, and that character forces subsequent text to begin at the next tab stop: the 2½-inch point (again assuming standard Works half-inch tab stops).

- ✔ If you add a half-inch worth of text at the beginning of that same line, the text following the tab character jumps to the 3-inch point (which is the next tab stop).

Newfangled tab stops

Your old, manual Smith-Corona had only one kind of tab stop. Works (like most word processors) has four kinds of tab stops:

- ✔ **Left tab stop:** The conventional tabs that you're accustomed to are called left tabs in a word processor because after you press the Tab key, what you type begins after the stop. Therefore, the text has its left edge at that point. Works uses left tab stops unless you tell it otherwise, and it presets them every half inch, starting at the left margin.

- ✔ **Decimal tab stop:** For columns of numbers, you may want to use the decimal tab stop, which aligns every number at the decimal point. You set the tab stop in the position where you want the decimal point to be (or at the end of a number without a decimal point). When you type a number (having first set up the tab stop and then pressing the Tab key to move to this stop), Works types — oddly enough — to the left of this stop. Works continues to type to the left of the stop until you type a decimal point; then it types to the right of the stop.

- ✔ **Right tab stop:** Unsurprisingly, the right tab stop is the opposite of the traditional left tab stop. Instead of the left edge of text aligning with this stop, the right edge does. When you type (having first set up the tab and then pressing the Tab key to move to this stop), Works shifts text over to the left, keeping the right edge of the text aligned with the tab stop.

- ✔ **Center tab stop:** After you set up one of these guys, press the Tab key to move to it and then start to type. Works spreads your characters to the left and right as you go, in order to keep your text centered on the tab position. Whatever you type ends up centered at the tab stop.

To see the four kinds of tab stops in action, check out the examples in Figure 15-2. How do you set these tab stops? You can set all four types of stops with the help of the Tabs dialog box, which I discuss next.

Setting, clearing, and changing tab stops with a dialog box

If you want something other than the conventional tab stops of a left tab every half inch, the time has come to have a little dialog — a little dialog box, that is — that helps you set the position and alignment of your tab stops. (Check out Figure 15-2.) You, too, can get one of these lovely dialog boxes by choosing Format➪Tabs; but first, read the following discussion about how the Tabs dialog box works.

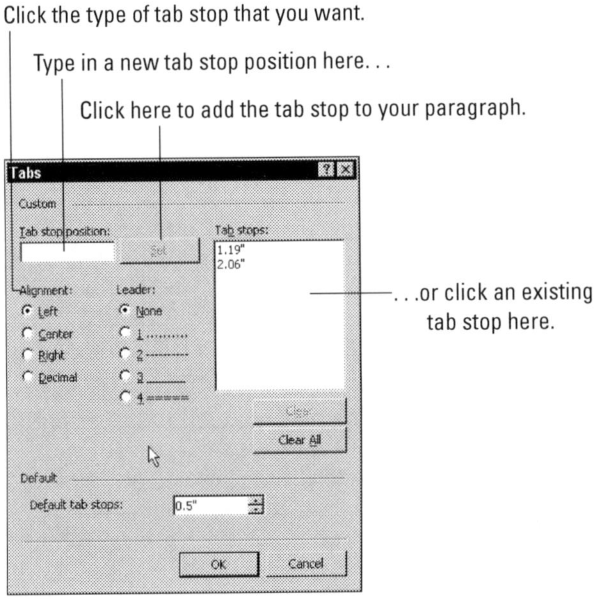

Click the type of tab stop that you want.

Type in a new tab stop position here. . .

Click here to add the tab stop to your paragraph.

. . .or click an existing tab stop here.

Figure 15-2:
Having a
dialog about
your tab.

You may find that setting, clearing, and moving conventional left tab stops is easiest by using Works' ruler. (Hop down to the section, "The ruler — a benevolent monarch," later in this chapter.) However, to set tab stops very precisely (say, at 1.37 inches), or to set right, center, or decimal tab stops, use the Tabs dialog box.

The executive summary of how to use the Tabs dialog box goes like this: Work on one tab stop at a time (identified by its position), specify its alignment or leader (the character that fills the space that the tab creates — usually none), and then click the Set button. As you create new stops, they are listed in the Tab Stops box on the right. You can delete a tab stop or change its alignment by first clicking it in that box and then using the controls in the dialog box.

The blow-by-blow instructions for using the Tab dialog box to add, remove, or modify a tab stop are as follows:

1. **Select the paragraphs whose stops you want to set or change.**

   If you don't select anything, Works assumes that you want to format the paragraph where the insertion point is. Select multiple paragraphs to give them all the same tab stops.

2. **Open the Tabs dialog box (as shown in Figure 15-2) one of two ways:**

   - Choose Format⇨Tabs.

   - Double-click the bottom of the ruler bar (where the numbers are).

   Any tab positions already set in the selected paragraph are listed in the Tab Stops box on the right side of the dialog box. The Works default tab stops are listed in the Default Tab Stops box at the bottom of the dialog box.

3. **To add a new tab stop, type its position in the box labeled Tab Stop Position.**

   Click the box immediately under the Tab Stop Position label and type the position you want the tab stop to take (measured from the left margin). Whatever you do in the dialog box — changing alignment and so on — now applies to that tab stop position.

   Or

   To modify or clear an existing tab stop, click that tab in the Tab Stops box on the right side of the Tabs dialog box.

   That tab stop position now appears in the box labeled Tab Stop Position. Any settings you make in the dialog box now apply to that tab stop position.

4. **Click an alignment for this tab stop in the Alignment area.**

   Flip back to the preceding section, "Newfangled tab stops," for a discussion of the different types of alignment.

5. **Click the Set button to add this tab stop to your paragraph.**

   When you add your own tab stops, Works removes any default tab stops between the left margin and your new tab stop.

6. **To remove this tab stop, click Clear.**

7. **To clear out all the tab stops in this paragraph, click Clear All.**

8. **Repeat Steps 3 through 5 with additional tab stops until you have just the tab stops you want in the Tab Stops list box.**

   To review the tabs' alignments, just click them in the list box.

9. **When you're finished, click the OK button.**

The Tabs dialog box also says something about a leader. No, the tabs have not formed a political system. Normally, when you type on a typewriter and press the Tab key, you get a blank area up to the position of the tab stop. That's not necessarily true in Works. A *leader* is what Works puts in this area. For example, in a table of contents, you may want a line of dots or something between the topic and the page number (like the one in this book). To have a leader associated with a tab stop, click 1, 2, 3, or 4 to choose one of the four styles shown in the Leader area; otherwise, click None.

Finally, if you really don't want to set a bunch of individual tab stops but you do want to change the spacing of the tab stops that Works provides (the default tab stops), just type a new spacing in the Default Tab Stops text box. These tab stops are important because Works uses them for indenting paragraphs, as I discuss in the upcoming sections.

The ruler — a benevolent monarch

Nothing keeps order like a good ruler, so the Works word processor comes equipped with a royal one. Sometimes Works is a royal something else, but this ruler is a benevolent monarch.

If your ruler is missing, choose <u>V</u>iew⇨<u>R</u>uler. Don't be shy; if a cat can look at a king, you can View your Ruler.

The ruler reigns over indentations, alignments, and tab stops. A modest kingdom, perhaps, but an important one. You can see how the ruler rules the indentations, alignments, and tab stops in Figure 15-3.

Notice how the left side of the paragraph in Figure 15-3 aligns with the paragraph indent mark. Also, the first line aligns with the first line indent mark. (Pretty reasonable, huh?) The author of the document in Figure 15-3 entered tabs to position things. Dates in the table align along their left edges because this clever author used a particular kind of tab stop (the left tab stop). Using a decimal tab stop causes the numbers to align along their decimal points. The locations align along their right sides because of (together now, everyone — yes, that's right) the right tab stop. Finally, the whole line comes to a stop at the right paragraph indent mark. And now this paragraph comes to a stop, and not a minute too soon.

The ruler shows you what's going on in the paragraph where your insertion point currently resides: Look for the blinking cursor. Or, if you select a paragraph, the ruler tells about the paragraph you selected. The ruler, however, can describe only one paragraph at a time — if you select a bunch of paragraphs, it shows you the first one.

The totally, utterly cool thing about the ruler is that it not only shows you the paragraph stuff, it also lets you control the paragraph stuff. I know; this news is pretty exciting, right? Read on.

Reading the ruler

As any good subject knows, you should understand your ruler. In particular, with this ruler, understanding what the tick marks and numbers correspond to is vital. Looking at the zero-inch mark, for example, you may well ask, "Zero inches to what?" Well, zero is where the left margin of your page is. All points on the ruler are measured from this left margin.

The tick marks are at one-eighth-inch intervals if you're using inches. (You're not limited to one-eighth-inch precision, however. You can set your indentations and tab stops at even more precisely measured intervals than one eighth of an inch.) To use units other than inches, read through Chapter 4 for details.

The tiny little tick marks that are barely visible in the thin gray line below the ruler are the built-in tab settings. You can put in your own tab marks, too, where you want them, but the tab marks you insert look like little black Ls, not tiny gray lines. More on tabs in a minute.

Left page margin equals zero

Paragraph indent from left margin

First line indent

Right indent

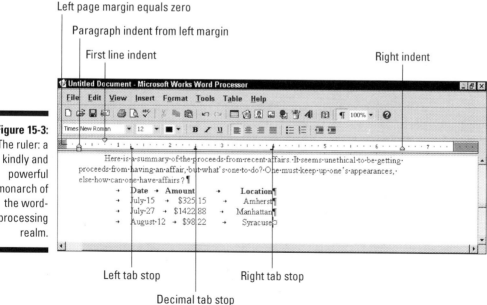

Figure 15-3: The ruler: a kindly and powerful monarch of the word-processing realm.

Left tab stop

Right tab stop

Decimal tab stop

Indenting with the ruler

The cool thing about using the ruler for indents is that the ruler lets you adjust them graphically. Just click the left or right indentation mark and drag it. You change the edges of the paragraph that your insertion point is currently on. To set the edges of a bunch of paragraphs, select the paragraphs before you drag the marks. These edges are technically called the left and right paragraph indentations, not paragraph margins.

The tricky thing about the three indentation marks on the left side is that they are related, like triplets. These marks are like an enhanced version of the right indent mark. The top triangle of this set controls only the first line of the paragraph. The bottom triangle controls hanging indents, and the box below the bottom triangle controls the left side of the entire paragraph.

So having said all that, here's the blow-by-blow on changing paragraph indentations with the ruler (refer to Figure 15-3 for the various gizmos I mention):

1. **Select the paragraphs you want to indent.**

   If you don't select anything, Works assumes that you want to format the paragraph where the insertion point is.

2. **To indent the first line, drag the top triangle on the left of the ruler bar.**

   If you pause your mouse cursor over that triangle, a tiny tag appears, reading `First Line Indent`.

3. **To create a hanging indent (where the first line sticks out to the left of the rest of the paragraph), drag the bottom triangle.**

   If you pause your mouse cursor over that triangle, a tiny tag appears, reading `Hanging Indent`. Drag that bottom triangle farther to the right than the top triangle.

4. **To indent the whole paragraph, drag the little box below the bottom triangle of the pair.**

   Pausing your mouse cursor over that box makes a tiny tag appear, reading `Left Indent`. The whole set of symbols, including both triangles, move at the same time.

5. **To indent the right side of the paragraph, drag the triangle on the right side of the ruler bar.**

You can also change indentations by using a dialog-box approach. Although it's not as cool and graphical as the ruler, the dialog box is easier to use for those of us who are riding in a car across Connecticut at the moment with a mouse that keeps falling off our knees while trying to move those tiny triangles around. See the section, "Having it your way: The Format Paragraph dialog box," later in this chapter, for details.

Tab stops on the ruler

For setting nice, normal tab stops of the conventional sort that you would approve marrying into your family (left tab stops, I mean), the ruler is ideal. For anything newfangled and outlandish, such as decimal or right tab stops, read through the section, "The tab stops here," earlier in this chapter. The ruler bar shows you these crazy newfangled tabs, but it quite stodgily refuses to have anything else to do with them (other than remove them, that is).

Works already provides a nice set of built-in tab stops, spaced about every half inch (if you're using inches). (The built-in tab stops are the little tick marks in the thin gray line below the ruler.) If you want more tab stops, just follow this complicated instruction:

Click in the bottom half of the ruler where you want your tab.

That's all.

Your (left) tab marks look like tiny black Ls. (An upside down T is a center tab stop; if the T has a decimal point next to it, the tab is a decimal tab. If the L is reversed, the tab is a right tab.) Here's what to do with the tabs when you've got them:

- ✔ To move your tab marks around, drag 'em. The built-in default marks that fall before or between your marks are conveniently removed.

- ✔ To remove one of your tab marks, drag it off the ruler and into the document, where it evaporates in the rarefied atmosphere of your prose.

- ✔ To go for an exotic right, center, or decimal tab mark, double-click the ruler bar and see the section, "The tab stops here," earlier in this chapter.

Having it your way: The Format Paragraph dialog box

For one-stop shopping in the world of paragraph formatting, use the Format Paragraph dialog box, as shown in Figures 15-4 and 15-5. This dialog box supplies nearly all your paragraph formatting needs. Indentations, alignments, breaks, mufflers — you name it; everything paragraph-ish and even a button for tab stops.

Begin by placing your insertion point in a paragraph to be formatted or selecting several paragraphs. Then open the Format Paragraph dialog box in either of two ways:

- ✔ Choose Format⇨Paragraph. (Or press Alt+O and then press P on the keyboard.)
- ✔ Double-click the left or right indent marks on the ruler bar.

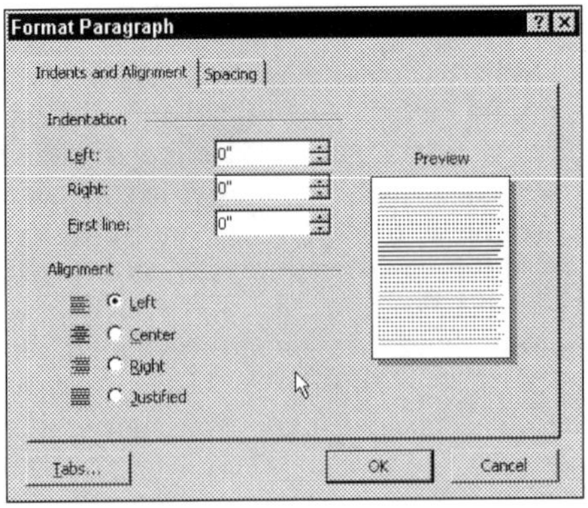

Figure 15-4:
The
Indents and
Alignment
tab of the
Format
Paragraph
dialog box.

The box looks like two index cards — one named Indents and Alignment, and the other named Spacing. These cards are called tabs. You can switch between them by clicking the top tab of the hidden card. Both tabs have a Preview box that shows you what the reformatted paragraph may look like on a page.

You use the Format Paragraph dialog box by making whatever changes you want on the two tabs and then clicking the OK button. Nothing is changed in your document until you click OK. If at any time you click the Cancel button, you return to your paragraph unchanged.

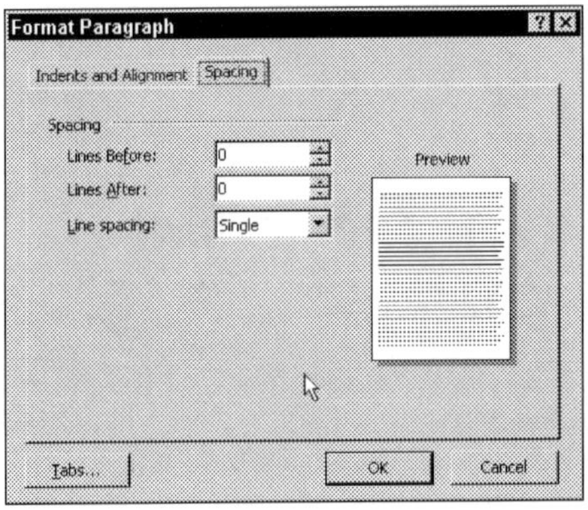

Figure 15-5:
The Spacing
tab of the
Format
Paragraph
dialog box.

Indents and alignments

The Indents and Alignment tab has an Indentation area, an Alignment area, and a Preview area. The Indentation area (refer to Figure 15-4) contains three boxes that work as follows:

✔ **Left:** Sets the distance between the left paragraph margin and the left page margin.

✔ **Right:** Sets the distance between the right paragraph margin and the right page margin.

✔ **First line:** Sets the distance between the left page margin and the beginning of the first line.

You can type a number into any of the three boxes and get that many inches of indentation. Or you can click the up or down arrows beside the boxes to raise or lower the number inside. By using these controls, you can indent paragraphs without having to type tabs. You can also control indentation with the ruler bar, as I discuss earlier in this chapter.

In the Alignment area, click the white dot next to your chosen alignment's name. You can get any of the four basic alignments (Left, Center, Right, and Justified). (If you've forgotten what these terms mean, go back and read the section, "Alignments: Making your lines line up," earlier in this chapter.)

Spacing between paragraphs and between lines

When you make choices on the Spacing tab of the Format Paragraph dialog box (refer to Figure 15-5), you tell Works how this paragraph should get along with its neighbors and how much space to put between its own lines. Here's how to use the Spacing tab:

✔ To tell Works how many lines to skip before or after the paragraph, type numbers into (or click the up and down arrows next to) the Lines Before and Lines After boxes.

✔ To tell Works how many lines to skip between lines of the paragraph, use the Line Spacing drop-down list box. Setting Line Spacing to 2, for example, double-spaces the paragraph. You can use fractional lines greater than 1, such as 2.5, as well.

Pages, Margins, and Sideways Documents

All this stuff about letters and paragraphs and stuff is just dandy, but what about the document? How big is a page, what's on what page, and what are the margins? How do you print sideways? Good questions.

Works begins (as usual) by assuming a bunch of stuff about the page — namely, the page defaults:

- ✔ You're using 8½ x 11-inch paper, oriented the normal way for a letter (portrait).
- ✔ Top and bottom margins are 1 inch. Left and right margins are 1¼ inches. If you're using headers and footers, they are a half inch from the top and three-quarters of an inch from the bottom, respectively.

The places where Works puts page breaks are determined by these settings, and are also determined by how big and airy you want to format your characters and paragraphs. You can change these page breaks if you like.

Most of this formatting-of-the-overall-document stuff is tucked away inside the Page Setup dialog box. To open this dialog box, choose File⇨Page Setup.

When you first use this Page Setup command, the top tab is the Margins tab, as shown in Figure 15-6. The tabs in this dialog box all deal with different aspects of page setup and printing. Click a tab to choose it. (If you change to another tab before quitting the Page Setup dialog box, that tab is on top the next time that you use this dialog box.)

Each tab in the dialog box also shows you a Preview to give you a rough idea of what your document can look like using the changes you make. One thing to notice is that if you type something into a box, the Preview automatically shows you the effect of your change.

Figure 15-6:
Page Setup
stuff looks
like Mom's
recipe card
file, but
without the
blueberry
pie stains.
This tab
contains the
recipe for
margins.

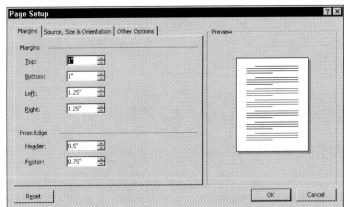

Margins

Using the Page Setup dialog box (refer to Figure 15-6), click the tab marked Margins. If you don't see the Page Setup dialog box, choose File⇨Page Setup. To change one of the margins listed on this tab, click the box for a margin and edit the margin setting or type in a new number.

The default unit is inches, so if you want inches, just type the number. If you want to use another unit, type the number and then one of the following abbreviations for the unit: **cm** for centimeters, **mm** for millimeters, **pi** for picas, and **pt** for points. If you live in a sensible country that uses metric units, you can change the default. Flip over to Chapter 4 for more on metrics.

To go back to using the default margin values, click the Reset button.

Click OK when you're all done setting up the page.

Sideways documents

If you want to print sideways, most PC printers these days let you do that. Because you can't normally put paper sideways into your printer, it has to be able to print sideways — which your printer can probably do, unless it uses type-wheels like some typewriters use. You just have to let Works know that sideways printing is what you want. Use the Page Setup dialog box (choose File⇨Page Setup if the box is not already up) and then follow these steps:

1. **In the Page Setup dialog box, click the Source, Size & Orientation tab.**

2. **Click Landscape to print sideways.**

   (Portrait is the usual orientation, like the *Mona Lisa.*) The page icon, with the letter A, illustrates how type will be printed on the page. The Preview also changes to show you how the lines of text run.

3. **Click OK unless you need to set up something else, such as the paper size.**

Differently sized documents

If you're using anything other than 8½ x 11-inch paper (or if you're using an envelope), you need to tell Works about it. (Works has special features for envelopes; thumb through Chapter 7 for details.) Use the Page Setup dialog box (to open it up, press Alt+F, and then press U) and follow these steps.

1. **In the Page Setup dialog box, click the tab marked Source, Size & Orientation.**

2. **On the Source, Size & Orientation tab, click the box marked Size.**

3. **Click one of the standard paper or envelope sizes in the box that drops down.**

   If you're using a paper size that's not shown here, click the box marked Width and type in a new value; then do the same for Height. (Width always refers to the direction that a line of text runs.) Preview shows you the appearance of your page.

4. **Click the Reset button if you want to return to the default paper size.**

5. **Click OK when you're done setting up the page.**

Page Breaks

When you fill one page, Works begins another page automatically as you're typing. If you want the page to break at an earlier location, you can put in a page break yourself. If you want the page to break later, forget it. Works can't squeeze any more on a page unless you change some formatting.

Most of the time, Works' automatic page breaks are just fine because Works counts lines and measures spaces much better than you can (it being a computer program and all). But occasionally you know something that Works doesn't, such as the fact that this particular line is the start of a new chapter and really needs to come at the top of a page. Then you want to be able to put in a page break by hand. (Well, by typing on the keyboard or something.) This is what has happened in Figure 15-7.

Here's how to put in your own page break:

1. **Click exactly where you want the page break to occur.**

   If the page break is to occur between paragraphs, click at the beginning of the first line of the paragraph that's going on the next page. Clicking at the beginning of the first line avoids problems with invisible paragraph marks.

2. **Press Ctrl+Enter or choose Insert➪Break➪Page Break.**

   A dotted line appears; this is your page break symbol, as shown in Figure 15-7. You can delete, cut, paste, or drag the page break symbol just like any other symbol on the page. To select the page break by itself, click in the left margin next to the symbol.

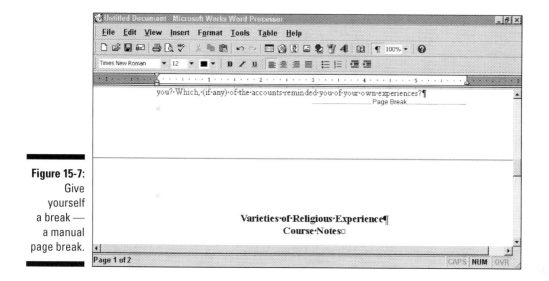

Figure 15-7:
Give
yourself
a break —
a manual
page break.

Your manual page break appears on the screen as a faint dotted line labeled Page Break, followed by a solid dark line. After your page break, Works continues to do its own normal, automatic page-breaking thing. (For more information on what your document really looks like, go to Chapter 4 and read about Print Preview.)

Chapter 16

Fancier Word Processing Documents

*I*t's payoff time! You paid your dues. You editorially slashed your way through the jungles of text and stood your ground in the face of pouncing paragraphs, rampaging thesauruses, and terrible tab stops. Now's the time to have a little fun. (Fun in the highly abstract, metaphoric sense of the word, that is. If you really find yourself eagerly looking forward to adding footnotes to a document, you may want to consider enlisting the aid of some competent professional.)

One way to make a fancier document is to add graphics of various kinds, such as charts or pictures. This chapter discusses charts (among other things), but if you want to add pictures, check out Chapter 12.

Creating Bulleted Lists

It's a jungle out there, and a few bullets may come in handy — bulleted lists, that is. Bulleted lists are made up of indented paragraphs, each with a little dot next to its first line. The paragraphs may be a single line, or regular multi-line paragraphs; Works doesn't care.

Shooting from the toolbar

 If you want simple, big-black-dot-style bullets, you can get them easily from the Bullets button on the toolbar. (The icon on the Bullets button looks like a bulleted list.) All you have to do is type your paragraphs in the usual way, select the ones you want to add a bullet before, and then click the Bullets button shown here in the margin.

 Likewise, if you want your paragraphs numbered with basic Arabic numerals, select the paragraphs you want numbered and click the Numbering button on the toolbar. (It's right next to the Bullets button, and looks like a numbered list, as you see in the button in the margin.)

The Bullets and Numbering buttons indent your paragraph to the first default tab stop — the stops marked with little gray tick marks right below the ruler — not the tab stops that you create. To change these tab stops, read through Chapter 15. You can also adjust indentation from the keyboard. Each time you press Ctrl+M, the indentation increases by one tab stop. Pressing Ctrl+Shift+ M does the opposite — it reduces the indentation by one tab stop.

You can remove bullets without an anesthetic. Just select the bulleted paragraphs and click the Bullets button again. (Likewise with numbering: Select the numbered paragraphs and click the Numbering button.)

 Bullets are a paragraph-formatting kind of thing. So you can get a new, already-bulleted paragraph by pressing Enter within any bullet-formatted paragraph. This feature lets you type with bulleting on so you can spawn new bulleted paragraphs as you go.

Using the Format Bullets and Numbering dialog box

Bullets of any make and caliber and numbers (or letters) of several styles are available in the Format Bullets and Numbering dialog box, as shown in Figure 16-1. To use this dialog box, follow these steps:

1. **Click in the paragraph to be bulleted or numbered (or select several paragraphs by dragging across them); then choose Format↷Bullets and Numbering.**

   The Bullets and Numbering dialog box appears.

Click a symbol.

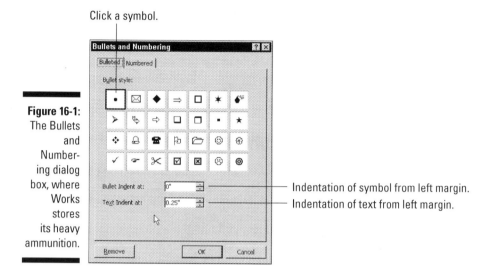

Figure 16-1:
The Bullets
and
Number-
ing dialog
box, where
Works
stores
its heavy
ammunition.

Indentation of symbol from left margin.
Indentation of text from left margin.

2. **For bullets, click the Bulleted tab and then click the bullet of your choice in the Bullet Style area. Likewise, for numbers, click the Numbered tab and then choose a numbering style.**

   You can choose Arabic or Roman numerals, letters, or other standard outline numberings.

3. **If you want to adjust how much the bullet or number is indented from the paragraph left margin, click the Bullet Indent At (or Number Indent At) box; then type a value, or click the up or down arrows there.**

4. **To adjust how much farther (beyond the bullet or number) the text is indented, you can set the value in the Text Indent At box.**

5. **Click OK when you have the format you want.**

   If you would rather disarm your paragraph, click the Remove button in the Bullets and Numbering dialog box. The box closes, and the bullet (or number) disappears.

You can set the starting number of your numbered list. Click in the Starting Number text box and type a number. This comes in handy if you start a list, insert some unnumbered text, and then need to continue the list where you left off.

Headers, Footers, and Page Numbers

You probably don't need to be told what page numbers are, but headers and footers may be unfamiliar to you. *Headers* and *footers* are optional chunks of text that you can insert in every page of a document in a special location at the top (for headers) or at the bottom (for footers). Headers and footers are typically used for chapter or section titles or to remind everyone who the author is.

How do page numbers fit into this discussion of headers and footers? Page numbers in Works are a special feature that you add to a footer (or a header).

Creating headers and footers

You don't create a header or footer for each page individually. You create a single header or footer, and Works makes it appear on every page of the document. Usually, the text of a header or footer is exactly the same on every page, except for these special cases.

- ✔ Page numbers change on each page! (Every page having the same number is kind of useless.) Still, you don't have to enter a different number on each page — just a single, special page-number code does the job.

- ✔ Another special case is the first page of a document. You can, if you like, have a header and a footer on every page *except* the first one. This arrangement is common for documents where the first page is a title page. A special setting in Page Setup does this trick.

To put a header or footer into your document, just follow these instructions:

1. **Choose View↪Header and Footer.**

   You see both a header and a footer box on your page. Note that the insertion point is now in the header box on the current page. Scroll down to the bottom of the page to see the footer.

2. **Type the text that you want to appear on each page.**

   Anything that you can format in ordinary text can be formatted in a header or footer. Bold, italic, giant fonts, alignments — anything goes.

3. **If you want page numbers and/or the date or time to appear in your header or footer, move the insertion point to the place in the header or footer where you want your choice to appear. Click Insert on the menu bar, and make a selection from the drop-down menu.**

   Clicking the Date and Time option takes you to a list of many, many possible date and time formats. Click the format you like, and Works inserts it into the header or footer. The outcome may look like something you could easily type yourself, such as "4:15 Wednesday." But every time you print or view your document in Print Preview, the date and time are updated.

   If you don't want a number on your first page, or if you want your first page to be some number other than 1, you now need to use the Page

Setup dialog box. Move on to Step 4. Otherwise, skip to Step 5.

4. **If you want to prevent header or footer text from appearing on the first page, choose File⇨Page Setup.**

   The Page Setup dialog box appears. (See Figure 15-6, in Chapter 15.) The Page Setup dialog box has three tabs on it; click the Other Options tab. On this tab are two check boxes: No Header On First Page and No Footer On First Page. Select the one(s) that you want.

   The Other Options tab of the Page Setup dialog box also enables you to select whatever number you want to appear on your first page. (All right, all right, the number has to be an integer. You can't choose a number like π. Good grief!) Type a number into the Starting Page Number box at the top of the tab, or click the up- or down-arrow keys.

5. **To return to your document text, choose View⇨Header and Footer again (which clears the check mark next to it), or double-click in your document text, outside the header or footer box.**

The header and footer boxes have their own special tab stops: a center tab in the center and a right tab in the right margin. These tabs make life easy if you just want a one-line header (or footer) that has something on the left, something in the center, and something on the right. First type (or insert, from the Insert menu) the text you want on the left (for example, the document name). Press Tab, and type (or insert) what you want in the center (for example, the page number). Press Tab again, and type or insert what you want on the right (the date, for instance).

High-quality books (like this one) have different headers on the left and right pages. Microsoft Word can do that, but don't even try to do that in Works; you're likely to sprain your head (or foot). If Microsoft puts every possible feature into Works, how will it sell its higher-priced word processor?

Adjusting header and footer margins

Anybody who has ever slept in a short bed is sensitive to having suitable margins for their headers and footers. To change your header or footer margin, choose File⇨Page Setup to get the Page Setup dialog box. Click the tab marked Margins and type in a new margin value for your header or footer.

Headers are supposed to appear within the top and bottom page margins. So in the Page Setup dialog box, you must make sure that the header margin is less than the top page margin, and that the footer margin is less than the bottom page margin. Otherwise, you're back to the short-bed situation, and nobody's happy — least of all Works. (What actually happens is that Works simply ignores you and resets the margins while you're not looking.)

Footnote Fundamentals

When I get old (which should be by next Friday, at the very latest), I won't bore younger people with tales of how I trudged miles to school in the deep snow. Oh, no — I plan to bore younger people by telling them how we used to do footnotes before the dawn of word processors. But if you want to be bored, you don't need me; you can just read the manual. (Besides, how can I tell whether you're younger than I am?)

Here's how to do automatically numbered footnotes:

1. **Put the insertion point just after the text you want to footnote.**

2. **Choose Insert⇨Footnote.**

   The footnote footman (in the form of the Footnote and Endnote dialog box) comes to your aid.

3. **Click the OK button in the Footnote and Endnote dialog box.**

   The Works footman transports you to a mysterious region: the footnote area at the bottom of your current page. The insertion point is waiting, right after an automatic reference number that Works provides.

4. **Type in your footnote text, beginning with a space (for appearances).**

5. **Press the Page Up key or scroll up to get back to where you were typing.**

If you don't like numbers and would rather use asterisks or something else, all you need to do is to change Step 3 in the preceding steps. Click Custom Mark in the Insert Footnote and Endnote dialog box. Then type the mark that you want (usually * or **) in the Custom Mark box and click the OK button. If you later change your mind and decide to return to numbers, choose Insert⇨Footnote and then choose Autonumber instead of Custom Mark.

To delete any footnote, just delete its reference mark in the text. The mark and the footnote go away, and the remaining footnotes are renumbered.

If you would rather group all your footnotes at the end of your document, choose Endnote in the Footnote and Endnote dialog box.

If you find yourself doing really heavy-duty footnotes — as you would if you were writing a scholarly thesis of some sort — you should check out a few of the Tasks on the Task Launcher. (Choose File⇨New to get the Task Launcher.) Works provides you with a School Reports Task and a Bibliography Task.

Doing It by the Numbers: Tables, Spreadsheets, and Charts

When you want your word-processing document to display a bunch of numbers in an attractive, comprehensible way (or at least in as attractive and comprehensible a way as numbers allow), you need a table, spreadsheet, or chart in your document. Works lets you use any of these three ways of displaying numbers, depending on your needs.

To take full advantage of all the cool features Works provides for tables and charts, you need to know how to use the spreadsheet and charting tools. Check out Part IV for spreadsheet information, and Chapter 11 for charts. On the other hand, you may be saying, "Just let me get this table into my report, and I promise I'll never, ever go near a number again." In that case, this section is for you.

Works provides three ways to create a table:

- ✔ The unofficial way, using the Tab key, provides simple tables with little formatting.

- ✔ The official way, using Table➪Insert Table, provides nice formatting.

- ✔ The spreadsheet way, using Insert➪Spreadsheet, offers nice formatting and charts, too.

If you need to chart some data in your document, you must do it the spreadsheet way. Otherwise, the choice is yours.

Typing a table without a license

If you want only a very simple table, with no gridlines and no easy way to chart its numbers, then Works doesn't need to know what you're up to. You can make an unofficial table like you would on a typewriter. Each line of the table is just a funny-looking paragraph, as far as Works is concerned. You can see an example of such a table in Figure 15-3 in Chapter 15.

To create such an unofficial table, start a new paragraph; you can use it for the first row, including your column headings. Format your paragraph with tab stops where you want your columns. Use left or center tab stops for this header text. (For more information on tab stops, check out Chapter 15.) Type the column headers in this paragraph, separating them by pressing the Tab key; you may want to use bold text for the column headers throughout. Make sure to keep your lines short enough so that Works doesn't wrap them onto the next line. (Remember that Works doesn't know what you're doing, so it can't help you.)

Press the End key to go to the end of this first line; then press the Enter key to make a new paragraph that has exactly the same tab stops as your first paragraph. Use this new paragraph for your first line of data in the table. If some columns have numbers, you may consider changing the tabs for those columns to decimal tabs.

Press the End key to go to the end of this second line; then press the Enter key to make a new paragraph that has exactly the same tab stops as the paragraph that preceded it. (A pattern emerges, no?) This third paragraph is for your second line of data. Continue on like this until your table is done.

To dress up your table with horizontal lines, you can apply a bottom border to each of the row paragraphs (and maybe even a heavier border across the column-headings row). See the section, "Lines, Borders, and Shade," later in this chapter, for details.

Creating a table the official way

A table in Works is a spreadsheet's younger brother — affable and good-looking, but not nearly so hard working. When you make a table, you're actually using the spreadsheet tool, but Works does its best to hide the ugly details from you. Sounds lovely, but Works' habit of hiding details can lead to problems if you need to do a lot of updating or if you want to make a chart of the data later on.

Here's the shortcut rundown on making tables:

1. **Make a blank line for your table.**

   Click the last line of the paragraph that you want the table to appear after, press the End key to move the insertion point to the very end of that paragraph, and then press the Enter key. (You don't have to make a blank line for your table; you can put it in the middle of a sentence, if you like. Tables are inserted wherever the insertion point is.)

2. **Click the Insert Table button on the toolbar.**

   The Insert Table button is the one that looks like a tiny, illegible calendar. (Or you can choose Table⇨Insert Table.) The Insert Table dialog box appears on the scene, as shown in Figure 16-2.

3. **Size and format your table.**

   Type the number of rows and columns that you need into the two boxes at the upper right of the Insert Table dialog box (or click the up arrow or down arrow alongside the boxes to increase or decrease the number already in a box). Don't forget to add a row for your column heads and a column for your row heads. The Example in the dialog box always shows five rows and five columns — its function is to show off the formats, not the sizes.

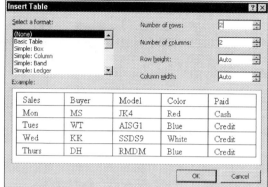

If you leave your Row Height and Column Width set to Auto, the table automatically resizes itself to accommodate your data. If you type a specific row height and column width into these boxes (or click the tiny up arrow attached to the box to increase the value), your data entries may line-wrap (continue on a new line within a cell) if they exceed the size you chose.

Choose a format (appearance) for your table in the Select a Format list box on the upper-left side of the dialog box. Each time you click a name, the Example box changes to show you how that format looks.

4. Click OK.

You now see a table, similar to Figure 16-3.

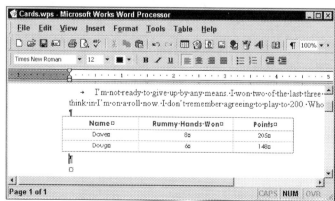

5. **Type in the contents of your table.**

   The square (the cell) where your insertion point is located and where you're currently typing is the *active cell*. To move to another cell, press any of the arrow keys on the keyboard, click another cell with your mouse, or press the Tab key.

Pressing the Tab key moves your cursor to the next cell in the table; it doesn't produce an invisible tab character as it does normally. You can enter a Tab character by copying and pasting one from someplace outside the table.

Editing and formatting the table

The format that you choose in Step 3 of the preceding steps takes care of all the picky details, such as what gets centered and what font and style to use in any given cell. You can change these details with all the usual editing and formatting commands and buttons, but if you choose a good format, you probably won't want to do much. Here are some fundamental changes you might make:

✔ **Selecting:** If you do need to formatting stuff in your table, you first have to select it; just as you do any other text, drag your mouse across it. You can also select a row, column, cell, or the entire table by first clicking in it, and then choosing Table⇨Select Cell, Select Row, Select Column, *or* Select Table from the menu that appears. Once you select a row or column, you can format everything in it at once — make all of your selection bold, for instance, by clicking the Bold button (**B**) on the Formatting toolbar.

✔ **Formatting:** You can indent, align, shade, or apply a border to a cell, row, column, or an entire table by selecting it and then using the same menu commands or toolbar buttons you would use for paragraph formatting. Format text in a cell as you would text anywhere.

✔ **Deleting:** To delete any contents of the table, select the contents and press the Delete key. But, to remove rows or columns, or to delete the entire table itself, first select the row(s), column(s), or table, and then click Table on the menu bar. You find a Delete Columns, Delete Rows, or Delete Table command in the menu bar, depending upon what you select.

✔ **Adding rows or columns:** To add columns or rows to the table, you have to click inside one of the cells and then choose Table⇨Insert Row or Table⇨Insert Column. You can choose to insert a row or column before or after the row or column where you put your insertion point (where you click).

✔ **Adjusting sizes:** If you discover that your rows, columns, or the entire table are the wrong size, you can adjust them. Move your mouse cursor around the table until it changes to a two-headed arrow at a row or column boundary. Then click and drag to make the row or column larger or smaller. To change the overall height, drag the table's bottom edge; to change width, drag the table's right edge. You then have to adjust all the other boundaries to even out the cells.

✔ **Cutting, pasting, or copying:** To cut, paste, or copy the contents of a cell in a table, select it and then use the usual editing tools, such as pressing Ctrl+X to cut or Ctrl+V to paste. Dragging the cell contents works nicely, too; especially for moving things from cell to cell. Note that any formatting follows the contents when you move something.

Creating a spreadsheet

Spreadsheets may look like tables, but they're actually smarter than your average table. Spreadsheets do all kinds of calculations automatically for you, such as totaling up the figures in a column. Quite often, people create spreadsheets for the sake of illustrating a document — for instance, a report on quarterly sales — and they want to pop it into the document when it's done. For more details about spreadsheets, read Part IV. Meanwhile, here's how you insert a spreadsheet into a word-processing document.

1. **Make a blank line for your spreadsheet.**

   Click the last line of the paragraph that you want the table or chart to appear after, press the End key to move the insertion point to the very end of that paragraph, and then press the Enter key.

2. **Choose Insert⇨Spreadsheet, or click the Insert Spreadsheet button on the toolbar.**

   A blank spreadsheet appears, displaying three columns and five rows.

   "Whoa! What's all this?! And why does it have its fat little edges splotted all over my text?" you ask. "All this" is a tiny window on a spreadsheet. This tiny window looks sort of like a table if you ignore all the letters and numbers around the outside edges. Naturally, the letters and numbers mean something, but if you're getting that deeply into creating a spreadsheet, you ought to read about spreadsheets in Part IV of this book.

3. **Expand the spreadsheet window to the size you need.**

   The spreadsheet window has little handles (those white dots on the black borders). With spreadsheets, the handles adjust the number of rows and columns. The spreadsheet's cells stay the same size, but you get more or fewer of them. For more columns, click the tiny black handle in the center of the right edge and drag it to the right. For more rows, click the handle in the center of the bottom edge and drag it down.

4. **Type in the contents of your spreadsheet.**

   The square (the cell) that you're currently typing in is the one outlined in black. To move to another cell, either press any of the arrow keys on the keyboard or click another cell with your mouse. In this window, your mouse cursor is a big fat + symbol.

Numbers may change appearance when you change cells. Controlling the appearance of numbers is a bit tricky. The easiest way to pretty up your table is to use the AutoFormat command in the Format menu; you can read about formatting spreadsheets in Chapter 21.

As long as those big, fat edges are displayed, Works is actually using its spreadsheet program. (The spreadsheet is said to be open.) If you use the menu bar, you notice that it's now the spreadsheet menu bar, not the word processor menu bar any more.

5. **Click anywhere in your document outside of the table window.**

   Check it out. All those letters and numbers around the outside go away, and you're left with something that looks an awful lot like a table.

To cut, paste, or copy the spreadsheet as a whole, first select it by clicking it once. Black dots (handles) appear around the edge. The dots tell you that your spreadsheet, while no longer open for internal changes, is still selected. Because it's selected, you can make changes to the spreadsheet as a whole, such as cutting, pasting, or dragging its edges to reveal more rows or columns. After it's selected, use the usual editing tools, such as Ctrl+X to cut or Ctrl+V to paste.

To do anything inside the spreadsheet, first double-click it to open it. After it's open, you can change the contents.

Inserting spreadsheet data from a file

If the spreadsheet already exists as a Works file, getting all or part of it into a word-processing document is easier than if you have to create the spreadsheet on the fly. (Creating anything on a fly is tough — they're just too small.)

Begin with your word processor document open. Then, open the spreadsheet in its own window. (Choose File➪New to open the Task Launcher so that you can open a spreadsheet-type document file. See Chapter 1 for more about opening a file within a tool.) Now both documents are open in their own separate windows.

In the spreadsheet window, select the range of cells you want to copy (or press Ctrl+A to select all) and then press Ctrl+C. Switch to the word-processing document window (click anywhere in that window), click where you want the spreadsheet, and press Ctrl+V.

Creating charts

To create charts in Works, you have to start with a spreadsheet in your document. (If you don't have one, go back to the section, "Creating a spreadsheet," earlier in this chapter.) Creating a basic bar chart from data in a spreadsheet is pretty easy; just follow these steps. (For anything more than that, though, you really need to read about charting in Chapter 11.)

1. **Double-click the spreadsheet in your document.**

2. **Highlight one or more rows or columns in your table.**

   Click the first (leftmost) cell of the first row that you want to chart; hold down the mouse button and drag to the last (rightmost) cell of the last row that you want to chart. Release the mouse button.

   If you include a first row or column of words, they become labels for the chart. If you want them to be used differently or if you don't like the way they look, check out Chapter 11 for further information.

3. **Click the tiny, squinty bar chart icon in the lower-left corner of the spreadsheet, to the left of the words** Choose Spreadsheet or Chart.

   Wow! The New Chart dialog box appears. Go to Chapter 11 for more about this dialog box. To get your chart into your document, just click OK.

4. **Click anywhere on your document outside of the chart area.**

   You should end up with nice bars and a legend. (If not, I know of some nice bars with legends in Key West — drop me a line. Or a lime.)

Here are a few additional points about charts:

- ✔ To change the size of the chart, click the chart to select it and then click one of the handles (little black squares) around the periphery and drag it. (Drag the handles along the sides sideways and the handles along the top and bottom vertically.)

- ✔ To deselect the chart and see the final effect, click somewhere in the text of your document.

- ✔ To change the chart data, double-click the chart; then click the tiny icon that looks like an illegible calendar in the lower-left corner of the chart window. This move turns the chart back to a spreadsheet, which you can edit.

Lines, Borders, and Shade

Nothing like a few good lines to liven up the party! Works has got 'em, in the form of borders around paragraphs. You want a horizontal line? A *horizontal line* is a bottom or top border on a paragraph. A vertical line? A *vertical line* is a left or right border alongside your paragraph. If you want to box in your paragraph or box in a set of paragraphs, you use an *outline* border. You can even draw a border around your whole page. Want to give your paragraph some shade? (It can get awfully hot down there by the border.) No problemo.

How far do these border lines go? Horizontal borders run from the left to the right indent of the paragraph (which, for normal paragraphs, is from the left to the right page margin). Vertical borders run the height of the paragraph for as many lines as are in the paragraph.

What about a line by itself? To get a stand-alone horizontal line, like the rule across a letterhead, use a blank line (single-line paragraph) with a top or bottom border. Do this to set the line width independently of the width of your surrounding paragraphs. Unfortunately, you won't find a stand-alone vertical line like you may want to have for a typing-style table (go back to the section, "Typing a table without a license," earlier in this chapter). You can get a vertical line between columns, however; hop down to the "Columns" section, coming up soon.

If you press the Enter key while working in a bordered paragraph, the new paragraph is bordered, too. (By working, I mean where you have your insertion point, but saying "insertion point" all the time sounds so nerdy.) Borders are actually a part of paragraph formatting, and paragraph formatting gets passed along when you create a new paragraph.

Marking your borders

Here's how you, too, can create borderline documents, just like the pros:

1. **For a horizontal line by itself, create a new paragraph.**

   Click the last line of your current paragraph, press the End key, and then press the Enter key. If you want the line to be shorter than the space between the page margins, drag the left and right indent marks (the inward-pointing triangles) on the ruler to mark the length of the line you want to insert.

   Or

   For a border around a group of paragraphs, select the group.

   For this technique to work, the selected paragraphs should all have the same left and right indents. After selecting the paragraphs, drag the left and right indent marks (the tiny squares) on the ruler to change indents.

   Or

   For a border on a single paragraph, click anywhere within the paragraph.

2. **Choose Format⇨Borders and Shading.**

   The Border patrol arrives on the scene in its four-wheel-drive dialog box. Have your passport ready.

3. **Click as many borders as you want in the Border dialog box.**

   Click the boxes on the right of the dialog box: Left, Right, Top, Bottom, or all the way around (Outline) — whatever. A line indicates which borders you select. Click a box again to deselect it.

   If you select a bunch of paragraphs in Step 1 and want an outline around the bunch, click Outline.

4. **Click the line style you want in the Line Style drop-down list.**

   You can also click the box labeled Line Color and then choose a color from the list that drops down.

5. **Click the OK button in the dialog box.**

To remove a border, repeat Steps 1 and 2 to get the Borders tab back. Any border that is selected has a line in its box. Click the selection box of any border that you want to get rid of. Click OK in that dialog box when you're done.

Making shady paragraphs

If you have a really red-hot paragraph, you can draw the reader's attention to it by making it shady (filling it with a color, shade, and/or pattern). Here's how:

1. **Repeat Steps 1 and 2 in the preceding section, "Marking your borders."**

   You should now be looking at the Borders and Shading dialog box.

2. **Click the Fill Style box to choose a shading pattern (on the bottom left side of the tab).**

   The fill styles listed in this box use two colors: Color 1 and Color 2. You get less of Color 1 and more of Color 2 as you proceed to the bottom of the list.

3. **Choose colors by clicking the Color 1 and/or Color 2 box, and then choosing a color from the list that appears.**

   The Fill Style box shows the result of your choices. You may want to return to Step 2 and choose a different pattern.

4. **Click the OK button in the dialog box.**

If the result is truly ugly, press Ctrl+Z to undo it. Start again with Step 1.

To put a border around an entire page, choose Page in the Apply To list box at the top left of the Borders and Shading dialog box. Then choose border art-work from the Border Art list box, and set a width for the border in the Border Art Width value box.

Columns

Works lets you put your text in columns, although it doesn't give you a lot of help in formatting a page that uses columns.

To make all the text in your document wrap in columns, do the following:

1. **Choose Format⇨Columns.**

   The very straightforward Format Columns dialog box appears.

2. **Enter how many columns you want in the Number Of Columns box.**

3. **Enter how much space you want between the columns in the Space Between box.**

4. **Click the Line Between Columns check box to add a vertical line between your columns.**

5. **Click the OK button.**

Here are a few tips for working with columns:

- If you're using columns to make a newsletter, you probably want a banner at the top of the newsletter, spanning all columns. You can type such a banner into the Header space if you don't mind it appearing on all pages. (Refer to the section, "Headers, Footers, and Page Numbers," earlier in this chapter.)

- Text flows automatically through the columns. To force a particular piece of text to wrap to the top of a column, click just before that text and then choose Insert⇨Break⇨Column Break. Works inserts a special invisible column break character. Click the ¶ button on the toolbar to see it.

Part IV
Setting Sail with Spreadsheets

The 5th Wave   By Rich Tennant

"These kidnappers are clever, Lieutenant. Look at this ransom note, the way they got the text to wrap around the victim's photograph. And the fonts! They must be creating their own— must be over 35 typefaces here...."

In this part . . .

*E*ver since the invention of the spreadsheet, PC users have been able to circumnavigate the world of calculations with ever-increasing ease. If you've been left standing at the dock, looking wistfully out to sea, Part IV is your ticket to adventure on the high seas.

Here are the fundamentals of entering data and doing calculations with the Works spreadsheet tool, with tips for making the job faster and easier. Whether you're planning your finances or just making lists, the spreadsheet tool can save you a lot of tedious hours on the calculator.

Heigh, my hearts! cheerly, cheerly, my hearts!
yare, yare! Take in the topsail. Tend to the
master's whistle. Blow, till thou burst thy wind,
if room enough!

—*The Tempest,* William Shakespeare

Chapter 17

Spreading Your First Sheets

* *

In This Chapter

▶ Understanding spreadsheets

▶ Using and abusing spreadsheets

▶ Creating a new spreadsheet

▶ Examining the spreadsheet window and toolbar

▶ Using cells and ranges

▶ Typing text and numbers

▶ Changing column widths and row heights

▶ Inserting and deleting rows and columns

▶ Entering sequential headings and data automatically

▶ Saving your spreadsheets

* *

So, you're ready to set sail into the uncharted seas of calculation? Well, batten down the hatches, hoist the anchor, strop the strmf'r'sq's'l, and add a few other such nautical allusions. With the Works spreadsheet hoisted squarely to the wind (hold the book open to this page, which is about as windy as they get), you can reach exotic lands where budgets, business plans, alphabetized lists, expense analyses, profit-and-loss statements, surveys, scientific experiments, and sales forecasts live. After you get the general idea of spreadsheets, you discover all kinds of exciting things to do with them — most of them legal, moral, and nonfattening (but still rather nice).

If you've never used spreadsheets before, however, you need to know a few basics first, which is where this chapter comes in. Here you find out what you can do with a spreadsheet, what's what in the spreadsheet window, how to navigate around in spreadsheets, and how to enter text and numbers. To do calculations and the more exciting stuff, skip over to Chapter 18.

If You've Never Used a Spreadsheet Before

If you've never used a spreadsheet before, try to think of it as a table of numbers and formulas in which all the calculations are done for you, or as a calculator that shows you all the numbers that you're adding or multiplying. Or you may think of it as gnomes sitting on a chess board with calculators, where the pawns are numbers and the rooks add rows and columns, and the queen is actually a copy machine, and, um, well . . . hmmm. This isn't helping, is it?

Truth to tell, you can't fully appreciate a spreadsheet until you've used one (sort of like an electric toothbrush, but even more fun — if that can be imagined). The best concept to start with is to imagine something that can automatically add up rows and columns of numbers in a table. Spreadsheets do that familiar task quite easily.

So what's the big deal?

Spreadsheets are a big deal — compared with, say, a calculator — for several reasons. Here are a few:

- **See all your numbers at once:** Because spreadsheets are tables, you can see and change all the numbers at any time.

- **Change one number and see the result:** Few calculators let you back up and change a number and then recalculate. This ability to change a number in a spreadsheet and then immediately see the result enables you to do "what-if" analyses. For example, what if inflation goes to eight percent? When can I afford to retire? Or, what if I switch to no-tillage corn farming? Do the labor savings offset the herbicide cost? What if I sell this computer? Can I then afford to pay someone else to do all this stuff?

- **Fancy calculations:** Use spreadsheets for all kinds of fancy calculations on the numbers they contain: sums, averages, net present values, sines, cosines — all kinds of stuff. They can even do calculations based on the results of other calculations, or calculations based on time — 30-day running-average annualized yield from an investment, for example. If you know how to do a certain calculation on a calculator, you can make a spreadsheet do the calculation, too.

- **Rows and columns:** Spreadsheets visually organize your data into rows and columns. You can even have several different tables of rows and columns. The Works spreadsheet enables you to dress up your tables with borders, colors, lines, and text formatting so that you can easily see what's going on.

✔ **Business forms:** Because spreadsheets are laid out on a grid, you can use them to create business forms of various kinds. You can even fill in those forms right in Works, do calculations on the data you've filled in, and print out the results.

✔ **Short lists:** Use spreadsheets for simple lists and collections of data — the names of students in your class and their grades, inventories of equipment and their dollar values, and so on. Spreadsheets kind of overlap with databases in this sense; spreadsheets are more useful for smaller projects or projects involving more calculation, and databases are more useful when lots of data and summary reports are needed.

✔ **Charts:** The final big deal is that after you have data in a spreadsheet, you can turn that data into a chart in minutes. I look at this in more detail in Chapter 11.

What can you do with a spreadsheet?

People use spreadsheets for all kinds of stuff. Here are some examples:

✔ Doing budgets

✔ Recording and plotting your daily weight and calorie count

✔ Recording lists of people and how much they owe or have paid

✔ Creating invoices, bills of sale, and other business forms

✔ Recording, totaling, and forecasting sales

✔ Tracking and computing expenses

✔ Planning finances

✔ Analyzing statistics

✔ Recording experiments

✔ Convincing your spouse that you're working when you're really playing Minesweeper

Nearly anything you can do with a calculator works better on a spreadsheet. Some of the things you can do in a Works spreadsheet are the following:

✔ Adding columns of numbers

✔ Adding rows of numbers

✔ Computing the average, standard deviation, and other statistics on rows or columns of numbers

✔ Computing depreciation, net present value, and other financial results

✔ Finding the minimum or maximum value in a set of values

✔ Computing the number of days between two dates

✔ Computing the number of dates that you've eaten in two days

✔ Sorting lists alphabetically or numerically

✔ Finding specific items in a list

In general, you should use spreadsheets for anything that involves creating tables, making charts, doing calculations, or keeping short lists of things.

What shouldn't you do with a spreadsheet?

You should not plot to overthrow the world or cheat on your taxes; it reflects badly on the software industry. (Like you care, right?) But mostly, you should not do anything that can be done better with another Works program. For example:

✔ If you're writing a report that includes spreadsheets, don't write the report using the spreadsheet program. That's as bad as using the knife blade in your Swiss Army Knife for a screwdriver. Write the report in the word processor and copy the spreadsheets into the word-processing document.

✔ If you're making long lists of things that you may want summarized — say, an inventory — use the Works database program.

✔ If you're making a list of names and addresses to use for mailings, use the Address Book or database program.

Getting Started with the Works Spreadsheet Program

Enough wool gathering. Time to collect our crew, spread our spreadsheets to the wind, and set forth into the Sargasso Sea of making calculations. Start Works, and the Task Launcher appears. (If you're already using another Works program, choose File➪New.)

To get a nice, shiny, untrammeled, new spreadsheet document from the Task Launcher, do this:

1. **Click Programs on the menu bar.**

   The Works Programs page appears.

2. **Click Works Spreadsheet in the column on the left.**

   A list of various ways to start a spreadsheet appears.

3. **Click Start a Blank Spreadsheet above the column of spreadsheet Tasks.**

   You're now gazing at the spreadsheet window, its toolbar, and other assorted paraphernalia.

But wait! Maybe you don't want a nice, shiny, untrammeled, new spreadsheet document. Maybe you want a pre-designed, pre-trammeled spreadsheet, such as an invoice or a spreadsheet for recording your students' grades. Well, okay. You can get those by starting with a Task. (See Chapter 1 for the basics of starting with a Task, and check out Chapter 10 for more specifics about spreadsheet tasks.) But until you know a bit more about spreadsheets, you may find Tasks a bit tricky to use. The folks who designed them did a lot of fancy formatting and other tricks that you find out about in this part of the book.

What's what in the spreadsheet window

Look at Figure 17-1 to see what's what in your spreadsheet window. It also gives examples of the various kinds of entries you can make in a spreadsheet. Works has given the spreadsheet document the forlorn name of Unsaved Spreadsheet — one of the nerdy sort of startup names Works gives new documents that haven't yet been saved as a file. Near the top of the Works window is the usual Works menu bar with all the commands, and underneath that is the spreadsheet toolbar with all its buttons and icons.

Don't try to memorize all this stuff unless it's 3 a.m. and you really, really need to get back to sleep. Stick a pencil or small inanimate object of your choice here and come back whenever you need to refresh your memory.

The spreadsheet menu

As in fine restaurants and programs everywhere, one way you can give commands to the Works spreadsheet program is by using a menu. You click the item that you want. Works menus are like the menus at franchised fast-food joints: They look pretty much the same no matter what joint — or program, in this case — you're in.

In fact, the first line of the menu bar (the line with File and all the other command words on it; refer to Figure 17-1) for the spreadsheet program is nearly identical to the one for the word processor program. The differences appear when you go to use the menu bar: The little menus that drop down when you click on these command words are somewhat different. Rather than cram a bunch of menu descriptions here, I explain the spreadsheet menu differences as I go along in this book.

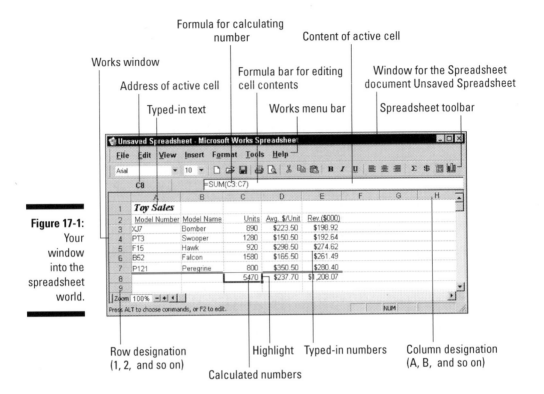

Figure 17-1:
Your
window
into the
spreadsheet
world.

Formula for calculating number

Content of active cell

Works window

Formula bar for editing cell contents

Window for the Spreadsheet document Unsaved Spreadsheet

Address of active cell

Typed-in text

Works menu bar

Spreadsheet toolbar

Row designation (1, 2, and so on)

Highlight   Typed-in numbers

Column designation (A, B, and so on)

Calculated numbers

The command menus that drop down when you choose File or Edit are much the same as for the other Works programs. The File and Edit menus include commands for starting a new document, opening an existing document file, closing a document, saving a document to a file, and making basic edits. Even the spreadsheet's Edit⇨Find command is practically the same as in the word processor.

I discuss most of the commands for the File and Edit menus in detail in Part I of this book. In Chapter 4, I discuss basic printing.

The spreadsheet toolbar

The other popular way to give commands to Works (other than traditional shouting methods) is with the toolbar — the thing with all the picture-laden buttons under the menu bar (see Figure 17-2). The toolbar is just a faster way than the menu bar to do some of the same things. You click a button and stuff happens.

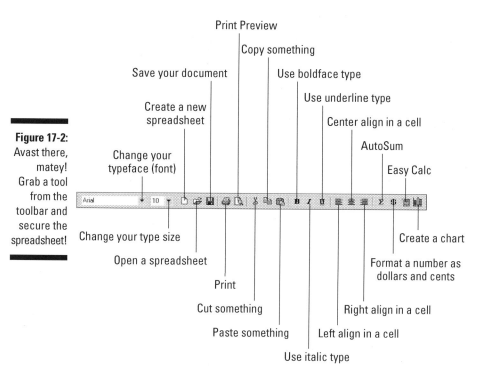

Figure 17-2:
Avast there,
matey!
Grab a tool
from the
toolbar and
secure the
spreadsheet!

That's toolbar, not crowbar. No matter how much you're tempted, do not use a crowbar to give commands to Works.

Most of the spreadsheet toolbar is similar to the toolbar in other Works programs. All the buttons but four (the AutoSum, Currency, Easy Calc, and New Chart buttons), for example, are the same as the ones in the word processor. (For more on Works toolbars, thumb through Chapter 2.)

I don't go into detail about these buttons here, but I bring them up as I go along. Here's where to go to read about the buttons that are particularly interesting for spreadsheets:

✔ **Left, Center, and Right Align:** Read more about changing alignment in a cell in Chapter 21.

✔ **Format a number as dollars and cents:** Find more on formatting numbers in Chapter 21.

✔ **AutoSum:** Discover how to create formulas with the point-and-shoot method in Chapter 18.

✔ **Create a chart:** Read how to create charts in Chapter 11.

The spreadsheet document

The spreadsheet document (the window with the title bar Unsaved Spreadsheet in Figure 17-1) looks like a big table, which is correct because that's what a spreadsheet is. Each row in this table has a number, which appears at the far left of the table, in tasteful battleship gray. Each column has a letter, at the top, also in gray.

A spreadsheet has no pages; it's one vast table. The size of your spreadsheet — in theory only — can be more than 16,000 rows by more than 250 columns. In reality, you'll run out of memory (and so will your PC) long before you can make a spreadsheet that big.

As is usually the case with Windows programs, you can look at only a small piece of the document at a time. (This is good. Imagine how illegible a long document would be if it were squooshed to fit entirely on your PC screen!) To see more of the document, scroll the document up or down or left or right by using the gray scroll bars along the right and bottom sides (read the instructions in Chapter 2 on how to get around in your document).

Cells and their addresses

A *cell* is one of those little boxes on the spreadsheet; it's the intersection of a row and a column. Everything you type goes into a cell.

Each cell has an address so that you can talk to Works about it in your calculations, graphs, and other activities: "Hey, Works! Multiply the number at this address by 18," to paraphrase. A cell address is made up of the column letter and row number, smushed together like this: B12 (which is the cell at the intersection of column B and row 12).

Cell addresses figure prominently in everything you do in a spreadsheet. For instance, Works displays the address of a cell you click (the active cell) to the left of its formula bar. In Figure 17-1, I've clicked on the cell in column C, row 8, so C8 appears in the space labeled `Address of active cell`.

Entering and Editing Data in Cells

If you have a rough idea in your head for your spreadsheet, it's time to start entering data. Working in a spreadsheet is not quite like typing on a typewriter, however, so first read in this section about how you can move around and enter different types of stuff into the spreadsheet.

Choosing a cell to type into

The easiest way to choose a cell is to move your mouse so that the mouse cursor (a big, fat plus sign: +) hovers over the cell, and then click. The newly clicked-upon cell is then surrounded by a rectangular halo that Microsoft calls the highlight. (In computer heaven, the halos are rectangular.) This highlight indicates which cell you're about to type in, edit, or otherwise muck around with. Microsoft calls this the active cell.

Notice that the address of the cell that you've currently selected appears near the upper-left of the Works window, under the font window of the toolbar. (Of course, you can't click what you can't see. To view various areas of your spreadsheet, use the scroll bars on the right side and bottom of the document window.)

You can also move the highlight with the navigation keys on your keyboard. Those are the arrow keys: the Page Up and Page Down keys, and the Home and End keys. And, as a special added bonus in the spreadsheet program, you can also use the Tab key. These keys move the highlight in the ways that I list in Table 17-1.

Table 17-1	Navigating Spreadsheets with Keys
Navigation Key	*Where It Moves the Highlight*
←/→	One column's worth left or right
↑/↓	One row's worth up or down
Tab	One cell to the right
Shift+Tab	One cell to the left
Page Up/Page Down	One window's worth up or down
Ctrl+Page Up/Ctrl+Page Down	One window's worth left or right, respectively
Home	To column A of the row you're currently in
End	To the last column you used, in the row you're currently in
Ctrl+Home	To cell A1
Ctrl+End	To the last row and column you used

If you know the cell address that you want to go to and it's nowhere nearby, here's a faster way to get there: Press the F5 key. The Find and Replace dialog box appears, with the Go To tab displayed on top. Type the cell address (in the Go To text box where your typing cursor already sits) — **Q200**, for example — and click the OK button.

Typing stuff in cells

How do the cell-dwellers get into their cells? You put them there, of course, either by typing or by copying and pasting. The first cells, naturally, have to get there by typing because there isn't anything to copy yet. So I start there, with the first cells. In this chapter, I explain typing text and numbers into a cell. In Chapter 18, I cover calculations.

Typing something into a cell involves the following simple procedure:

1. **Click a cell.**

   Or move your highlight to the cell with the arrow or other navigation keys.

2. **Type.**

   Use the Backspace key to delete any mistakes.

3. **After you have the text, number, or formula the way you want it, press the Enter key or move to another cell with a mouse click or a navigation key.**

If, while typing, you get a change of heart and decide not to type anything at all into the cell, press the Esc key.

You can type more stuff than fits into a cell's width. If the cell or cells to the right are empty, Works displays the excess on top of those empty neighboring cells. (It doesn't actually put the excess in those cells, however.) After those neighboring cells are filled, the excess no longer appears on-screen. Everything you typed is still in the cell where you typed it, but you need to expand the column width to see it all on-screen at once or on the printed page.

If you type more text than a cell can display, or if you type a number that turns into a bunch of ##### characters, your column is too skinny. To discover how to change this, see the next section, "Changing column widths and row heights."

Changing column widths and row heights

One of the big juggling acts with spreadsheets is getting the column widths just right. (While I'm at it, I also cover row heights because you adjust them more or less the same way.)

There you are, traipsing along, making, say, a list of the students in your class: Smith, Jones, Yu, and then . . . Okiniewskiwitz! If nothing's in the cell to the right of Ms. Okiniewskiwitz's name, the text just slops over into that cell. If something is in the cell to the right, Ms. O's name looks like it's been chopped off. (The full name is still in the cell — Works hasn't forgotten it or anything — but it just looks truncated.) You need a wider column.

Why would you need to increase the height of a row? The most common reason is to allow two or more lines of text in a single cell. A column heading that reads, for example, "Assumed Rate of Inflation," is rather wide. By increasing the row height, the line can wrap to two lines. (Read the discussion following the upcoming numbered steps.) You can also accommodate larger type by increasing row height.

The simple way to change the width of a column (or the height of a row) is to do the following:

1. **Position your mouse cursor over the gray area around the top or left edge of the spreadsheet that has the column letter (or row number) in it.**

2. **Slowly move the cursor toward the right-hand edge of the column (or the bottom edge of the row); the cursor changes to a double-headed arrow labeled Adjust.**

3. **Click and drag to the right, and the column gets wider. Drag to the left, and it gets smaller. (For rows, dragging up makes a row shorter and dragging down makes it taller.)**

To automatically set a column's width, double-click the column letter at the top of the column. The column is sized to fit the largest entry. To automatically set a row's height, double-click the row letter at the left of the column. The height adjusts to the font size you choose. To adjust height to display multiple lines, skip down to the text that follows the next list of numbered steps.

A more precise way to change the width of a column or the height of a row is with the Format Column Width or Format Row Height dialog boxes:

1. **Click in, or otherwise highlight, any cell or cells in the column (or row).**

   To set a group of columns to the same width (or a group of rows to the same height), drag across them to select them.

2. **Choose Format➪Column Width (or Row Height).**

   The Format Column Width (or Format Row Height) dialog box springs into action.

3. **Type a new width number into the box marked Column Width (or Row Height).**

   (Press the Delete key to delete the current digits.) If you're setting the column width, the width number equals roughly how many characters wide the column is, assuming you use 10-point type. To set the column width to include all the characters in your selected cell(s), click the option box labeled `Set column width to fit the widest text`.

   To set the width (or height) back to the Works default, original value, click the Use Default button.

If you're setting the row height, the height number is in points (as in a 12-point font). You need 20 percent more height than the height of your characters. A 12-point font, for instance, needs 14.4 points. To avoid doing the math and automatically adjust row height to your text, click the option button labeled Set row height to fit the tallest text in the row instead of entering a height value.

4. **Click the OK button.**

To display multiple lines of text in a cell (line wrapping), you must increase the row height (as I describe in Step 3 in the preceding steps) and also make sure that line wrapping is enabled. To enable line wrapping, choose Format⇒ Alignment. On the Alignment tab of the Format Cells dialog box that appears, click to put a check mark in the Wrap Text Within a Cell check box. Text now wraps automatically to a second line when the length exceeds the column width. To force the text to break at a particular place, add extra spaces between the words where you want the break to occur.

Entering different kinds of cell content

Cell content can take three different forms in the spreadsheet world, and Works treats each of them differently. A cell can contain only one kind of content. The three kinds of cell content are as follows:

- ✓ **Text** (in Figure 17-3, the model names are text)

- ✓ **A typed-in number** (in Figure 17-3, the revenues)

- ✓ **A number (or, sometimes, text) that results from a calculation or other kind of formula** (in Figure 17-3, the totals in the last row)

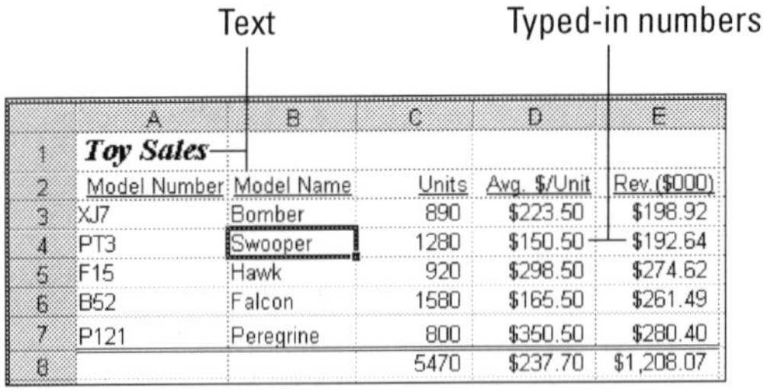

Text   Typed-in numbers

Figure 17-3:
Contents
of a few
example
cells in the
Toy Sales
spreadsheet.

	A	B	C	D	E
1	*Toy Sales*				
2	Model Number	Model Name	Units	Avg. $/Unit	Rev. ($000)
3	XJ7	Bomber	890	$223.50	$198.92
4	PT3	Swooper	1280	$150.50	$192.64
5	F15	Hawk	920	$298.50	$274.62
6	B52	Falcon	1580	$165.50	$261.49
7	P121	Peregrine	800	$350.50	$280.40
8			5470	$237.70	$1,208.07

The following two sections explain how to enter the first two kinds of cell content: text and typed-in numbers. I explain calculations and formulas in Chapter 18.

Typing text

To simply enter some text, such as a column heading or title — something that isn't used in a calculation — just click the cell and type the text. Press the Enter key when you're done. Works recognizes any entry containing letters as a text entry.

After you type your text and press the Enter key, you may notice that up in the formula bar, Works sticks a quotation mark (") in front of what you typed. The quotation mark doesn't appear in the cell, just in the bar. This character is Works' subtle way of saying that it interprets the contents of this cell as text, not as a number or calculation.

Sometimes you have to enter that quotation mark yourself. Keep an eye peeled for the following situations:

✔ You type a numeric entry that you intend to use as text (a serial number or zip code, for example), but it happens to consist of all numerals. The zip code 07920, for instance, ends up as the number 7920 if you don't begin it with a quotation mark. (You can also use a special number format called leading zeros. In Chapter 21, I discuss number formats.)

✔ You type something that you intend to use as text, but it begins with the symbol =, +, or –. Typing +/–10% as, say, a column heading, causes Works to display an error message because it thinks you tried to type a formula (and did it badly).

✔ You want your text entry to begin with a visible quotation mark ("), such as "Junior's" monthly allowance.

In any of these situations, type a quote (") character before you type anything else. This rule means, for instance, typing ""**Junior's**" to make "Junior's" appear in the cell. If you find it hard to keep your eyes peeled for the preceding three situations, you can simply acquire the habit of entering a quotation mark at the beginning of every entry that you intend to be text.

Text entries require only a single, opening quotation mark. Don't add one at the end of the entry.

Typing numbers

Entering numbers into a cell is as simple as entering text into a cell. Just click a cell and type the numbers in. Here are a few options you have for entering numbers:

✔ You can precede a number with a minus sign (–) if it's negative, or you can use a dollar sign ($) if it's money. If the number represents negative money, you can begin the number with –$ or enclose the number in parentheses. Works displays negative dollar amounts in parentheses: Negative five dollars is displayed in a cell as ($5). Use as many decimal places as you need, but Works rounds off the number to two decimal places if you use the dollar sign or parentheses.

✔ You can put commas at the thousandth point, but Works throws them out (unless you tell it differently — read more about formatting numbers in Chapter 21).

✔ For percentages, follow the number with the percent sign (%). Remember that 100% is the same as 1.00.

✔ If you're a scientific type, you can use scientific notation: 1,253,000,000 can be typed 1.253e9, or 1.253E+09, for example. In fact, if you type in a big number, Works automatically shows it in this format. (You can tell Works to use a different format by changing number formatting, as I discuss in Chapter 21.)

Don't follow a number with units in the same cell, as in *36 fathoms.* If you put *fathoms* in the same cell as *36,* Works thinks the entire entry is supposed to be text (not a number), and it isn't able to do calculations with the entry at all. If you want to display units in your spreadsheet, you have to type them in as text in another cell, but don't expect Works to recognize them as units. For instance, in the real world, dividing 12 inches by 3 feet should result in .333; but because Works doesn't see or care about your units, it divides 12 by 3 and gives you an answer of 4. The simplest way to avoid such problems with units is to use the same units throughout your data (meaning don't mix inches and feet, for example).

After you finish typing the number and press the Enter key (or move the highlight), notice that the number is smushed against the right side of the cell (or right-aligned, in dweeb-speak). If you've previously typed any text, notice that the text is smushed against the left side of the cell. This is how Works aligns numbers and text unless you tell it differently. I get into "telling it differently" in the section on cell alignment in Chapter 19.

Editing inside a cell

You may have noticed something a bit odd as you typed things into cells. Works is normally set up so that when you type things into cells, you're actually typing in two places at once: in the cell you've selected and in the formula bar. If you observe this phenomenon, your copy of Works is set up to enable you to do either of the following whenever you edit:

✔ Edit the contents of a cell by working in the formula bar.

✔ Edit the contents of a cell by working in the cell itself.

Personally, I like this editing flexibility. If you prefer to always edit in one place, you can change Works' setup. Skip down the sidebar later in this chapter, "Specifying where to edit," for information on how to make the change.

$!@($?)&$!!! What's all this ######### ?

If you're typing a number that's too wide for the column, you often get a distressing result. You get a bunch of pound (or score) symbols (####) in the cell, which is a message from Works saying, "I can't print this here; make the column wider, will ya?" Sometimes this situation occurs because the cell in question has the wrong number format — some formats are wider than others. If you use Works' default format for numbers, called General format, Works simply switches to nice, compact scientific notation when a number gets too large. You may or may not approve of this switch. For details on number formats, read more about formatting numbers in Chapter 21.

Here's how to edit the contents of a cell, either in the formula bar or in a cell:

1. **Click the cell that you want to edit.**

   The cell shows its little rectangular halo and displays the contents of the cell in the formula bar.

2. **Click in the formula bar to edit in the formula bar, or double-click the cell to edit in the cell. (Or, press F2 and let Works decide where you edit.)**

   Wherever you choose to edit, a vertical line — an insertion point like the one in the Works word processor — appears, to help you in your editing task.

3. **Move the insertion point to the place you want to edit.**

   To do this, move your mouse pointer over your data; the mouse pointer changes to an I-beam shape. Position that I-beam where you want to type or delete something, and then click. The insertion point jumps to that position.

4. **Use the Backspace or Delete key to get rid of the old stuff you don't want.**

   To change or delete a bunch of characters at once, drag the I-beam cursor across those characters to highlight them, and then type replacement characters or press the Delete key. (To select an entire word or formula, double-click it.)

5. **Type in the new stuff.**

   As usual in Works, if you type over text that you've highlighted, you replace that text.

6. **Continue clicking and editing until you're done; then press the Enter key.**

If you prefer, you can use the arrow keys instead of the mouse to position the insertion point in the formula bar.

Three buttons are located next to the formula bar: one with an X, one with a check mark, and one with a question mark. Here's how to use them:

- ✔ **Click the X to cancel your edit and return the cell to its original condition.** (This works just like pressing the Esc key.)

- ✔ **Click the check mark to enter the contents of the formula bar into the cell.** (This works just like pressing the Enter key. If you're entering a formula, Works also checks for errors.)

- ✔ **Click the question mark if you want to open the Works Help window and read about formulas.**

Working with Ranges: Groups of Cells

One big deal about spreadsheets is that you can do calculations and other operations on groups of numbers. For instance, you can sum a column of numbers, or average all the data in your spreadsheet without having to add one number at a time. Any block (rectangular block, that is) of cells is called a range. A range can be a large, small, skinny, or wide rectangle of cells anywhere in your spreadsheet. A range can be just two adjacent cells, a column, a row — even the entire spreadsheet. Read on for how to work with ranges.

Selecting a range of cells

The easiest way to point out a range of cells to Works, either because you're about to format them all in some way or because you're referring to them in a calculation, is to select them. (The other way is to refer to them by their range address, as I describe in the following section.) The mouse or keyboard technique for selecting a bunch of cells is pretty much the same as the technique for selecting bunches of stuff in all the Works programs, as the following list shows.

For spreadsheets, you have three methods of selecting multiple cells:

- ✔ Click and drag the mouse cursor across the cells that you want to select. You can move across or up and down, highlighting any row, column, or rectangular area. Release the mouse button when you're done.

- ✔ Click one end or corner of the range of cells that you want to select. Then press the Shift key together with an arrow key or another navigation key to expand the highlight. Release the keys when you're done.

✔ To select an entire row or column, click the column letter or row number (in the gray area of the spreadsheet). To select the entire spreadsheet, click the unmarked button where the row-number and column-letter areas intersect (the upper-left corner).

To select a group of filled cells in a column (stopping at any empty cells), click the top filled cell and then press Ctrl+Shift+↓. To select a block of filled cells in a row, click on the leftmost filled cell and then press Ctrl+Shift+→. The selection stops at the first blank cell in the column or row. (Or, if you start with a blank cell, the selection stops at the first cell with data.)

I actually prefer using navigation keys to using the mouse when I select ranges in spreadsheets. Navigation keys simplify expanding the highlight to include exactly the cells you want. When you press an arrow key, the highlight's edge moves by precisely one row or column. With the mouse, I tend to slop around too much. Of course, if I weren't riding New Hampshire's Kancamagus Highway with my mouse pad on my knee, I might do better. (Hey, that could be a catchy little tune, ". . . for I come from Kancamagus with my mouse pad on my knee. Oh, Susannah! . . .")

Referring to a range by its address

The way Works describes a range in its formulas (calculations) and in various dialog boxes is by using the range's address. You need to understand range addresses in order to use these formulas and dialog boxes. A range's address combines the addresses of the two cells in opposite corners of the range, with a colon (:) in between. Which cell address comes first doesn't matter.

Here are the addresses of a few of the ranges shown previously in Figure 17-3:

All the model names	B3:B7 or B7:B3
Everything concerning the XJ7	A3:E3 or E3:A3
All the column sums	C8:E8 or E8:C8
All cells representing amounts of money	D3:E8 or E8:D3

Specifying where to edit

To set up Works to perform editing in the formula bar, the cell itself, or both places, choose Tools➪ Options from the Works menu bar. In the Options dialog box that appears, click the Data Entry tab.

Choose one of the three options in the box labeled Cell Data Entry Modes and then click the OK button.

Trying out an example spreadsheet

Here's an example of a spreadsheet. In Figure 17-4 you see the first week of a diet plan for an anonymous, but very earnest, calorie-counting person.

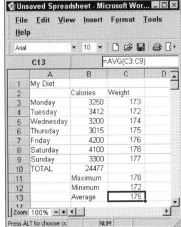

Figure 17-4:
A typical first-week diet, with typical first-week results.

Follow these steps to duplicate this spreadsheet (18 quick steps to weight control!):

1. **To get a fresh spreadsheet, click the Programs tab on the Task Launcher, click Works Spreadsheet, and then click Start a Blank Spreadsheet.**

   (Or, if you're already using the spreadsheet program, click the New button on the toolbar. It looks like a blank document with a corner folded.)

2. **The current active cell (where the highlight is) is A1. Type** MyDiet **and press the Enter key.**

3. **Click on cell B2 (column B, row 2). Type** Calories.

4. **Press the right-arrow key to move to cell C2. Type** Weight **and press the Enter key.**

5. **Click on cell A3 and type** Monday.

6. **Press the down-arrow key and type** Tuesday. **Keep pressing the down-arrow key and entering days of the week through Sunday. After the seventh day, rest.**

   To avoid manually typing the days of the week, you can try out Autofill here, instead. Check out the section, "Entering Sequential Headings and Data Automatically with Autofill," later in this chapter.

7. **Click on cell B3 and type** 3250.

8. **Press the down-arrow key and type** 3412. **Refer to Figure 17-4 for the other calories and keep on like this through Sunday.**

9. **Click on cell C3 and type** 173. **Refer to Figure 17-4 for the other weights and keep on like this through Sunday.**

10. **Wake up; it's about to get interesting.**

11. **Click cell A10 and type** TOTAL.

12. **Press the right-arrow key to move to cell B10 and type** =SUM(B3:B9). **Press the Enter key.**

    Wow! Magic! The total calories for the week.

13. **Press the down-arrow key to move to cell B11 and type** Maximum.

14. **Press the down-arrow key to move to cell B12 and type** Minimum.

15. **Press the down-arrow key to move to cell B13 and type** Average.

    Now make it interesting by typing in the formulas, as I describe in the remaining steps. Don't worry if you don't understand them right now; just type them in. I explain formulas in Chapter 18.

16. **Click cell C11 and type** =MAX(C3:C9).

17. **Press the down-arrow key to move to cell C12 and type** =MIN(C3:C9).

18. **Press the down-arrow key to move to cell C13 and type** =AVG(C3:C9). **Press the Enter key.**

    With any luck, you're now looking at an exact duplicate of Figure 17-4.

Notice that you save some effort by not pressing Enter every time you type something (although you can press Enter, if you like). All you need to do is highlight a new cell to enter whatever you've typed in the previous cell.

Try changing some of the calorie or weight values (click on them and type new values) and see what happens to the calculated values at the bottom.

Copying, Moving, and Deleting

Works provides a variety of features with which you can copy, move, and delete chunks of your spreadsheet. These features work pretty much the same way in every program in Works. For the general picture, take a look at Chapter 3.

Here's how these things work in your spreadsheet (note that copying and moving are a little different in spreadsheets than they are in the word processor):

✔ To delete the contents of a cell or range, select it and then press the Delete or Backspace key.

- ✔ To move the contents of a cell or range, select it and then slowly move your mouse cursor across the thickish frame that appears around the selected area until the cursor changes to an arrow labeled Drag. At that point, click with the mouse button and drag a copy of the frame that appears to the new location. Release the mouse button, and the cells are moved.

- ✔ To copy, do the same thing as for moving, but hold down the Ctrl key while you drag.

- ✔ Another way to copy is to select the cell or range to be copied and then press Ctrl+C to copy it to the Windows Clipboard. Click the cell where you want the copy, and press Ctrl+V to paste. If you're pasting a range of cells, click where you want the upper-left corner to go.

- ✔ To make multiple copies of the contents of a cell, click the cell to copy and then press Ctrl+C. Then highlight (select) a range and press Ctrl+V. All the cells in the highlighted range are filled with a copy.

- ✔ To cut contents out of a cell or range and paste it elsewhere, select the something to be cut and then press Ctrl+X; then click wherever you want a copy and press Ctrl+V to paste. If you're copying a range, just click where you want the upper-left corner to go, and then paste.

You can use the buttons on the toolbar in place of the key combinations:

- ✔ Ctrl+C is Copy, the button with two documents overlapping.

- ✔ Ctrl+V is Paste, the button with the clipboard.

- ✔ Ctrl+X is Cut, the button with the scissors.

Here are a few things to remember when moving and copying things around:

- ✔ When you move or copy something to already-occupied cells, the original contents are replaced by what you moved or copied.

- ✔ Formatting (font and alignment) goes along with whatever you copy.

- ✔ When you move the contents of a cell (say, you move the contents from A1 to B5), and the original cell address (A1) is used in a formula (say, =A1/3), the formula changes to use the new address (in this example, B5/3). Peruse Chapter 18 if you're not familiar with formulas.

- ✔ When you copy a formula, the addresses in it change. Explore the mysteries of copying formulas in Chapter 18.

Inserting and Deleting Rows and Columns

There you are, a high-priced lifestyle consultant, typing up your monthly invoice for September. You've got a row for each day that you worked. You've made it to September 30, and suddenly you remember that you taught your client country-and-western line dancing on Saturday the 18th. Swell — what do you do now?

Well, you can select everything after the 18th and move it down a row, but how tedious and pedestrian! No, no, — a with-it, turn-of-the-millennium kind of person like you should be inserting rows. Or columns, or whatever. Here's how:

1. **To insert a row, click anywhere in the row under where your new row is to appear.**

   For example, to insert a row above row 5, click row 5.

2. **To insert a column, click anywhere in the column to the right of where you want your new column.**

   For example, to insert a column to the left of D, click column D.

3. **Choose Insert⊃Insert Row or Insert Column.**

Deleting a row or column (as opposed to just deleting its contents and leaving the row or column blank) is a similar procedure: Click anywhere in the row or column you want to delete; choose Insert⊃Delete Row *or* Delete Column. Clicking Insert in order to delete may seem odd, but that's the way it is.

When you insert a row or a column — say, a new row 5 — and a formula anywhere in your spreadsheet includes a range that spans that row or column — say, =SUM(A1:A10) — the new row or column is included in the formula. However, if you insert a new row or column on the edge of a range of numbers (a new row 1 or a row 11), the new row or column is not included in the formula. So if you have an alphabetical list and add an Aaron or Zykowski, you may want to check to see that your totals are defined correctly.

Entering Sequential Headings and Data Automatically with Autofill

Sometimes the entries in a row or column — especially row and column headings — follow some predictable sequence. That sequence may be 1, 3, 5; or January, February, March; or Monday, Tuesday, Wednesday; where there is an equal interval between each entry. Unfortunately, typing in these predictable sequences can be really boring. After awhile, you find yourself thinking, "This sequence is so predictable. This thing I'm typing on is a computer. Couldn't the computer, like, predict or something?"

The answer is yes. In general, you need to type in only the first two items from one of these sequences, and Works can take it from there. To try this, follow these instructions:

1. **Type the first item from the sequence in adjacent cells.**

   In the example in Figure 17-4, for instance, type **Monday** in A3 and **Tuesday** in A4. In your spreadsheet, you can type **1** and then **3**.

2. **Select the two cells that you just typed in.**

   The cursor changes to a big plus sign.

3. **Move your mouse cursor to the lower-right corner of the two-cell block that you just selected, until the word _Fill_ appears under your cursor.**

4. **Click and drag over all the cells that you want to be filled automatically.**

   In the example in Figure 17-4, drag until the highlighted area includes the two cells that you typed, plus the next five in the same column.

5. **Release the mouse button.**

Presto! Works extends the sequence to fill the selected cells. Was it worth figuring this out just to avoid typing the names of five days? Maybe, maybe not. But if you ever need to type all the days of a year into a row or column, you may come to think very fondly of Autofill.

This Autofill trick is actually a special use of the Fill Series command in the Edit menu. You can read more about the use of Fill Series in the section on filling cells with numbers in Chapter 19.

Saving Your Work

As the banking industry says, "Save regularly, and watch your interest grow," or some such avuncular aphorism. (Bankers are, or used to be, fond of avuncular aphorisms and kept hothouses full of them at their country estates.) Likewise, you should regularly save your spreadsheet document as a file. Doing so doesn't make your interest grow — unless the electricity fails, in which case your interest grows immeasurably.

Saving your spreadsheet document is like saving any other Works document: Choose File⇨Save, or press Ctrl+S, or click the button with the diskette icon on the toolbar. If you need a refresher on saving files, browse through Chapter 2. For basic information on files and disks, check out Chapter 1. Note that if you're working in some distant corner of the spreadsheet when you save it, you're returned to that distant corner when you reopen the spreadsheet.

Chapter 18

Making Calculations

*W*orks gives you the means to create darn near any calculation that you may need. You have two fundamental ways to approach doing calculations in Works spreadsheets:

✔ Works' Easy Calc, an automated take-you-by-the-hand approach to doing calculations

✔ The traditional write-it-yourself approach (aided, if you like, by a special point-and-shoot feature)

Easy Calc is a great feature for doing simple calculations, and it's a useful teaching tool for learning how calculations are done. Easy Calc is less helpful for more complex calculations and doesn't help you at all if you have to edit a calculation. To do those jobs, you need to know how formulas are written and what the formula gibberish means. In this chapter, I introduce you to both Easy Calc and the write-it-yourself method, showing you how formulas are written and explaining a few tricks that can make the job easier.

The General Idea of Spreadsheet Calculations

In spreadsheets, which are essentially big tables, you do calculations by putting formulas in cells; those formulas refer to various other cells in the spreadsheet. For instance, to sum up a column of numbers, you can put a summing formula in the cell at the bottom of the column. That formula refers to all the cells containing the numbers you want to sum. After you enter a formula in a cell, that cell displays the result of the calculation (not the formula itself). The nice thing about the way spreadsheets do calculations is that any time you change the data (one of those numbers being summed, for instance), the formula cell immediately displays the new result.

Spreadsheets can display many different calculations at once, such as calculating the sums of several columns of data or displaying the sum, average, and minimum and maximum values of a single block of data. To help you do multiple calculations, spreadsheets come with another important feature: the ability to copy formulas. After you write a formula, you can reuse that formula by copying it. For instance, if you have many columns to sum up, and they all have the same number of data cells (say, 20 cells in the column), you can simply copy your summing formula from the bottom of one column to another similar column (or columns). See the section, "The Joys and Mysteries of Copying Formulas," later in this chapter, for the tantalizing details of this process.

Using Works' Easy Calc

The Works engineers knew that many people aren't fond of writing formulas or anything that looks like math, so they created a special tool called *Easy Calc.* Easy Calc asks you questions about where your data is and where you want the result of the calculation, and then it builds a formula for you. Of course, you need to know what sort of data the calculation you're doing requires. If you're computing Net Present Value, for instance, Works expects you to give it a value for the Rate of Return.

View Figure 18-1 to see an example of a spreadsheet ready and waiting for formulas. In the figure, the spreadsheet is helping me determine an average cost per night for lodging during a Canadian vacation. I enter data, including an exchange rate for how many Canadian dollars I get for my American dollars. I'm now ready to enter my calculations.

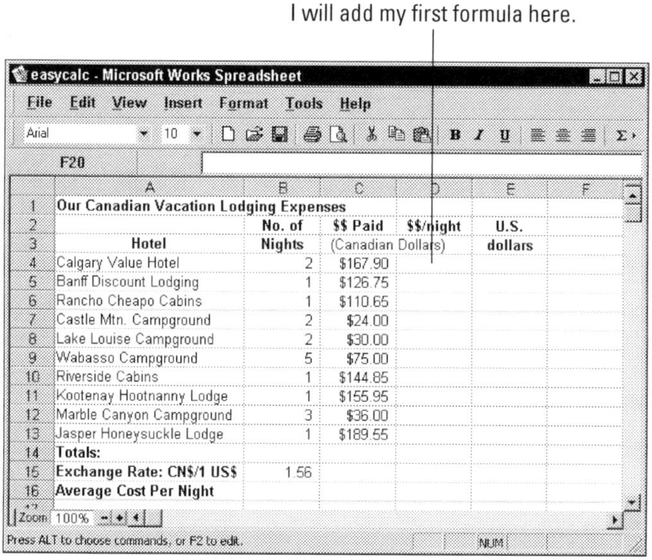

I will add my first formula here.

Figure 18-1:
A spread-
sheet with
data in place,
ready to add
formulas.

Here's how to use Easy Calc to perform basic calculations on data that you've entered in your spreadsheet:

1. **Choose Tools⇨Easy Calc from the spreadsheet menu bar.**

   The Easy Calc dialog box appears, listing a few of the most popular calculations, such as sums and averages, plus an Other button, which takes you to the vast range of other calculations that Works can do.

2. **Click the name of the kind of calculation you want to do, such as Multiply.**

   If you don't see the calculation that you want, click the Other button. (Read the sidebar "Doing 'other' calculations in Easy Calc," elsewhere in this chapter.)

   In the example of Figure 18-1, I first want to compute the dollars per night for each lodging place, which means that I click the Divide button to divide the total dollars in column C by the number of nights in column B.

   A different Easy Calc dialog box now appears.

3. **Enter the numbers or the cell addresses that the Easy Calc dialog box prompts you to enter.**

   You can type numbers into the white boxes if the number doesn't already appear in your spreadsheet. If the number does appear in your spread-sheet, either type its cell address (such as B12 for column B, row 12) or click that cell. (To click a cell, you may have to drag the Easy Calc dialog box to one side, or use the vertical or horizontal scroll boxes on the right or bottom side of your spreadsheet window to see the portion of the spreadsheet that you need.)

If Easy Calc prompts you for a range, you can either type in the range (such as B1:D20) or drag your mouse cursor across the range to highlight it. Thumb through Chapter 17 if you don't understand cell addresses or ranges.

If you make a mistake, click in the white box containing the mistake and try again. If you've made a mistake in a previous step, click the Back button.

An example helps make this step clear: If I were adding formulas to the example spreadsheet of Figure 18-1, at this step I'd now be looking at the Easy Calc dialog box (as shown in Figure 18-2). I first click cell C4 and then cell B4 to enter the numbers that Works requires.

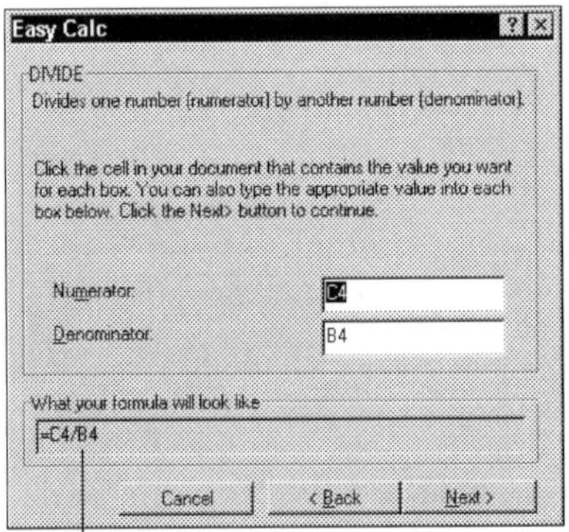

Figure 18-2:
Dividing the
contents
of one
cell by the
contents of
another cell.

The formula Easy Calc is preparing for you

At the bottom of the Easy Calc dialog box, Works shows you the formula it has constructed for you. This display is a good way to figure out how formulas are written.

4. **Click the Next button, and enter additional numbers, text, ranges, or cell addresses, as prompted by the Easy Calc dialog box.**

   Depending on the sort of calculation you ask for, Easy Calc needs additional information. You may need to go through one or two more dialog boxes, clicking Next each time to proceed.

5. **The final piece of information that Easy Calc asks for is the cell address where you want the result to appear. You can type the cell address or click that cell; then click the Finish button.**

   In the example of Figure 18-1, I choose cell D4 for my result, and then click the Finish button.

Here are some of the other calculations I can do for the spreadsheet of Figure 18-1:

✔ Computing American dollars from Canadian. This calculation involves dividing the Canadian dollars in column D (beginning with D4) by the currency exchange rate in cell B15 and putting the results in column E (beginning with E4).

✔ Computing the total number of nights, just as a check to make sure that I didn't miss any. This calculation involves summing the range B4:B13 and putting the result in cell B14.

✔ Computing the total cost by summing C4:C13, with the result in cell C14 (for Canadian dollars) and then doing the same for the American dollars in column D.

✔ Computing the average cost per night for lodging in American dollars. You can do this calculation by dividing the total cost in cell D14 by the total number of nights in cell B14.

Some of this calculation work can be made easier by copying formulas. For example, I can copy the formula that summed Canadian dollars (from cell C14), and I can paste it in cell E14, where it sums American dollars.

Doing "other" calculations in Easy Calc

If basic arithmetic and averaging doesn't do the job that you have in mind, Works is capable of doing lots of other calculations, called functions, which you can access by clicking the Other button in the initial Easy Calc dialog box. (Skip down to the section, "You're Invited to a Function," later in this chapter, for more details about these mathematical marvels.) Here are the steps for doing "other" calculations in Easy Calc:

1. **Choose Tools➪Easy Calc and click the Other button.**

   The Insert Function dialog box swings into action. In this dialog box, the Choose a Function list box shows all the functions that Works offers.

2. **Scroll down the Choose a Function list to find the function that you want.**

If you don't see what you want on the main list, click a category in the Category area to reduce the display of functions to a specific type. For example, to see only mathematical and trigonometric functions in the Choose a Function box, click Math and Trigonometry. (Oddly, the SUM function is in the Statistical collection.)

3. **Click a function in the Choose a Function area.**

   You can see a brief description of what the selected function does at the bottom of the Insert Function dialog box.

4. **Finally, click the Insert button.**

   Easy Calc resumes its helpful dialog, as in Step 3 of the instructions in the earlier section, "Using Works' Easy Calc."

The same trick does not, however, work well for copying the formula for computing American dollars in cell E4 to the other cells in column E. The copied formulas fail to refer to the exchange rate in cell B15. As the formula was copied for each of the nine rows, the copies refer instead to cells B16, B17, and so on, through B24. To understand why this error occurs and how to prevent it, read the section, "The Joys and Mysteries of Copying Formulas," later in this chapter.

Writing Formulas: Beyond Easy Calc

Writing your own formulas (as opposed to using Easy Calc to write them for you; see the preceding section, "Using Works' Easy Calc") enables you to do more powerful calculations in a single cell. To do a calculation, you type a formula into a cell. You can design a formula to do a lot of work all at once, such as the following:

```
=(SUM(B1:B8))/(SUM(C9:C17))*A17-3.7
```

Believe it or not, this formula is not a random collection of symbols. It means something, or at least it does to Works. This section helps you write formulas like that one (or simpler ones).

Works doesn't care whether you write formulas, cell addresses, or ranges in uppercase or lowercase letters. Works may convert some of the lowercase letters to uppercase letters, but that's its business.

Entering a formula

As you type a formula into a cell, the formula appears in both the cell itself and the formula bar. You can do your typing and editing in either location. To use the other location, just click there. Read through Chapter 17 for more information on typing things into a cell.

You'll find a disconcerting result of entering a formula, whether you type it yourself or let Easy Calc do the job. After you've enter the formula, the formula itself doesn't appear in the cell; the result of that formula (the answer) appears there! Disconcerting, perhaps, but very tidy. After all, you're interested in the answer, not the formula. Your calculator shows you only answers, right? A calculator doesn't show which buttons you pushed to get an answer. Neither does Works. So you pick where on your spreadsheet you want the result to appear, and that cell is where you type in the formula.

To enter a formula into a cell (whether you type directly into the cell or into the formula bar), do this:

1. **Click the cell where you want the formula.**

   Or use the navigation keys to move the highlight to that cell. Use a blank cell; don't try to put the formula in the same cell that holds the numbers that you're using in the calculation.

2. **Type an equal sign (=) and then a mathematical expression.**

   Spreadsheet formulas are mathematical expressions, which look something like this: =5.24+3.93. (Look through Table 18-1 for other mathematical operators besides the + symbol.)

   Starting Works formulas with an = sign is usually necessary so that Works knows that you're doing a calculation and not entering text or a number. Sometimes Works can figure that out for itself, based on what you type, but why trust luck?

3. **Press the Enter key.**

   Or click the check mark button on the formula bar, or move the highlight by clicking in another cell, or press a navigation key.

   These actions enter the formula into the cell, which then displays the result. *The formula remains in the cell,* but Works only displays the result.

If you're doing a calculation, type in only the right side of the equation, (=**5.24+3.93**, for example). Don't type in the left side. Some folks try to assign the value to a cell by typing **A1=5.24+3.93**, for example. If you type such an equation, however, the equation ends up as text, not as a calculation.

If you typed =**5.24+3.93** into a cell and pressed the Enter key, the cell shows the answer: 9.17. Isn't that exciting! This is why people spend thousands of dollars on computers and software. Well, maybe not; you may have been able to do that more easily on a five-dollar calculator. What you can't do on a five-dollar calculator, though, is type something like this: =**5.24+B1**.

Hmmm. Shades of algebra. What this formula really means is, "Show me the sum of 5.24 and whatever is in cell B1." If B1 has the number 3.93 in it, you get 9.17. If B1 has the number 6 in it, you get 11.24. You can keep plugging new numbers into cell B1 and watch the answer change in the cell that has this formula in it.

Okay, this is amusing, but wait! There's more! What if you want a formula to add up a bunch of cells? You can type =**B1+B2+B3+B4+B5+B6+B7+B8**.

Pretty boring. You can see where this may drive you back to your calculator. So to avoid losing your business, the software folks came up with a better idea. Rather than type all these cells and + signs, how about saying to Works, in effect, "Sum up the range B1 through B8." You say this by entering =**SUM(B1:B8)**.

Because B1 through B8 are all neighboring cells covering a rectangular area — a column, in fact — you can express them as a range. (Read more about describing groups of cells in Chapter 17 for information on ranges.) If you want to include cells or additional ranges that aren't within that range, you can add them to the formula individually, like this: =SUM(B1:B8, F15:B52, X15).

"Which means *what?*" you may ask. Well (aside from being a way to string together the names of a bunch of great airplanes), B1:B8 is a column; F15:B52 is a rectangular block of cells; and X15 is a single cell. If those cells contained numbers, the preceding formula would add them up.

SUM and other built-in calculations are called functions. And, used correctly, they do — function, that is. Works has a whole passel of other functions for doing all kinds of things. (More about those in the section, "You're Invited to a Function," later in this chapter.) You don't even have to remember the functions, as you see in the section, "Point and shoot for functions," also later in this chapter.

All calculations, no matter how complex, are done this way in the spreadsheet: by mixing numbers, mathematical operations (such as addition and subtraction), and functions together to make formulas.

Seeing and editing formulas

The spreadsheet displays only the result of a formula, even though the formula actually remains in the cell. "So," you may well ask, "how can I see my formula?"

You can see an individual formula at any time by clicking its cell (or using the navigation keys to place your highlight on the cell) and looking in the formula bar. Figure 17-4, back in Chapter 17, shows a formula in the formula bar.

You edit a formula the same way that you edit any other contents of a cell: To edit using the formula bar, click the cell, and then click the formula bar. To edit directly in the cell, double-click the cell. (Find out more about editing inside a cell in Chapter 17.)

To see all the formulas in your spreadsheet, choose View➪Formulas from the menu bar. This turns on a Formula view that's pretty ugly but does show all your formulas. You can work using this view, if you like. To turn off the Formula view, do the same thing you did to turn it on.

Hello, operator?: Mathematical operations

In a previous section, I employ the + symbol to represent addition in a formula. In Table 18-1 you see some of the other common operators (math actions) and other symbols that you can use to create your mathematical formulas.

This table also shows the order in which Works performs the operation, if two or more operations are in the cell.

Table 18-1	Math Operators	
Symbol	*Action*	*Order of Evaluation*
^	Raised to the power of	First
*	Times (multiplied by)	After ^
/	Divided by	After ^
−	Minus	After ^, *, and /
+	Plus	After ^, *, and /

The order in which you use operators in your expressions can be important. Following the basic rules of math, Works (just like calculators) calculates the formula in groups, performing exponential (that's the ^ symbol) calculations first and the addition calculations last.

View Table 18-2 for examples of mathematical expressions and what they do. Pretend for the moment that you're typing the function in cell B4.

Table 18-2	How Mathematical Expressions Work
Function in Cell B4	*What It Does*
=A2+A3	Adds the number in A2 to the number in A3 and shows the result in B4.
=10+A3/D8	Divides the number in A3 by the number in D8, adds 10 to the first result, and shows the final result in B4.
=A2*A3+B12	Multiplies the number in A2 by the number in A3, adds to that the number in B12, and shows the final result in B4.
=A2+A3*3.14+B12^3	Cubes the number in B12, multiplies the number in A3 by 3.14, adds those two results together with the number in A2, and shows the result of the whole mess in B4.

By putting an expression in parentheses, you force Works to evaluate that expression first. For example, Works evaluates the expression (2+3)*4 as 5*4, giving 20 as the result. Without the parentheses, the expression is 2+3*4. In that case, Works does the multiplication first, creating 2+12; then it does the addition, giving 14 as the result. When you use parentheses within parentheses, the expression in the innermost pair is evaluated first. When you use too many parentheses, you may end up being dragged off to be "evaluated" yourself.

You're Invited to a Function

Works has quite a few of those convenient built-in functions, such as SUM, which are very inviting. Functions produce some sort of value as a result, which you can in turn use within a formula, as in SUM(A2:A22)/B4. Here are some functions, in addition to SUM, that people tend to use often:

AVG(cells)	The average of the values in the cells
MAX(cells)	The maximum value among the cells
MIN(cells)	The minimum value among the cells
SQRT(cell)	The square root of the value in the cell
ROUND(cell, # of digits)	The value in the cell rounded off to some number of digits

The word *cell* in the preceding list means that you type in a single cell address, such as B1, not the word *cell*. And the word *cells* means that you type in a range, such as B1:B8. For *cells,* you can also type in a bunch of ranges and individual cell addresses, all separated by commas. For example, you can use =MAX(B1:B8, D5:D13, F256) to give a result equal to the maximum value among all those cells. (Microsoft uses the term *range reference* instead of *cells.*)

When I write *# of digits,* I mean a number, such as 2 or 3. (Oh, all right. Instead of a number, *# of digits* may also be a cell that contains the number of digits or another function that produces a number of digits, but that's getting complicated.)

In formulas, as in résumés, it's against the rules to be your own reference. If one of the cells that a function refers to is the cell that your function is in, you're in trouble. You're also in trouble if the formula in your cell makes reference to another cell, which in turn makes reference back to your cell. And so on. In short, if Works needs to know what *is* in C4 in order to calculate what ought to be in C4, there's a problem. If you're lucky, Works tells you that you've got a circular reference and refuses to go on until you fix the problem. If you're not lucky, Works just merrily calculates something bizarre and doesn't tell you why.

Getting Information about Functions

Because there are so many functions, even a short list is more than this book can handle. How many functions are there? To be precise: many — maybe even a gaggle of them. These functions are described in two places: in the spreadsheet program itself and in the Works Help feature. I discuss the spreadsheet program's listing in the section, "Creating Formulas the Point-and-Shoot Way," later in this chapter.

To read about functions by using the Help feature, do this:

1. **Press F1.**

   This step opens the Works Help window.

2. **Type** functions **in the question box (where it says, "Type a question here, . . .") and click the Search button.**

   You can see a number of folders having to do with functions.

3. **Click Use Spreadsheet Functions.**

   You see a list of functions arranged by type — date functions, financial functions, mathematical functions, statistical functions, and so forth.

4. **Click the subject line for the type of function that you're looking for.**

   If you want a function that does averages, for example, click Use Statistical Functions, which gives you a list of documents describing all the functions of this type. The list appears at the bottom of the Help panel, underlined.

5. **Click the document (which all begin "Use . . .") describing any likely looking function.**

   In the document that appears, the numbered steps are great, but not particularly helpful in understanding how the function works. For a general overview of that function, click the line of text that says, "What Is The *whatever* Function?" (*whatever* being the function you're inquiring about.) Click the Back arrow at the top left of the Help panel to return to the step-by-step instructions, or any earlier screen of help.

6. **When you're done typing your function, click the X in the Works Help window to remove it from your document.**

Creating Formulas the Point-and-Shoot Way

Typing formulas is okay until you get to the part where you have to enter a range. In order to type in the range address, you have to leave your formula behind and go find out where your data is. Or, you have to go look up the way the formula is supposed to be written. What a pain. Fortunately, Works provides a far more convenient way to enter ranges and other things in your formulas. I call it the point-and-shoot approach, and you can use it while you're creating formulas in the formula bar.

You can point and shoot cell addresses and ranges, and you can point and shoot functions. You can do a whole summation just by pointing and shooting. The details are in the sections following this list, but here's the big picture:

- ✔ **Cell addresses and ranges:** As you're typing a formula, if you need to enter a cell address (such as A1 — you know, the steak sauce) or a range (such as B4:A1, which is what people used B4 steak sauce), just go click the cell or highlight the range while you're typing.

- ✔ **Functions (SUM and so on):** Whenever you're typing in a formula and you need a function, you can insert one by just choosing it from a nice list. Pause in your typing of the formula and choose Insert➪Function in the menu bar to get a dialog box with the nice list in it.

- ✔ **AutoSum:** Whenever you have a column (or row) of numbers that you want to add up, just select the empty cell at the bottom of the column (or at the end of the row) and click the AutoSum button on the toolbar. The sum formula then appears in the empty cell, with the column or row automatically entered.

Point and shoot for cell addresses and ranges

Here's the blow-by-blow for entering cell addresses in a formula that you're creating:

1. **Click a cell and start creating your formula.**

   Type an = sign, for example. Or you can click in the white area of the formula bar and type an equal sign there. Type your formula right up to the point where you need a cell address or range. If you're using the SUM function, for example, type the following (including the left parenthesis): =SUM(.

2. **When your formula needs a cell or range address, select (highlight) whatever cell or range you want to use.**

   Click a cell or drag the mouse pointer to select an area. (Or use the navigation keys.) The cell address or range you select is automatically entered in your formula in the formula bar. How about that?! The address or range is highlighted to show off the fact that you didn't actually type it in but are pointing at it. If you selected the wrong address or range by mistake, just select a different one.

Do not press the Enter key at this point! If you press Enter prematurely, Works thinks that you're done typing the formula.

3. **Complete your formula.**

   Type the closing parenthesis, if it's not already there, or enter whatever the next math symbol is. The next character you type appears right after the cell or range address in the formula. For example, if you started with =SUM(and selected the range B5:B15, the formula reads =SUM(B5:B15, so type the final parenthesis: **)**.

   If you have additional addresses to enter, do them the same way. To multiply the sum in the example by the contents of cell D5, continue by typing the multiplication symbol (*****) and then pointing to cell D5.

4. **Press Enter when you're done.**

Point and shoot for functions

Here are the details on how to pick a function from a list instead of typing it in:

1. **Click a cell and start creating your formula.**

   Type an = sign or click the formula bar. Type your formula right up to the point where you need a function. For instance, to enter the formula =A1*SUM(B1:B10), you would type **=A1*** and then move on to Step 2.

2. **Choose Insert⟹Function.**

   The Insert Function dialog box swings into action. At this point, the big list box labeled Choose a Function shows all the functions that Works offers. Scroll down the list to find the function that you want.

3. **If you don't see what you want on the main list, click a category in the Category area to reduce the display of functions to a specific type.**

   For example, to see only mathematical and trigonometric functions in the Choose a Function box, click Math and Trigonometry. (Oddly, the SUM function is in the Statistical collection.)

4. **Click a function in the Choose a Function area.**

   You can see a brief description of what the selected function does at the bottom of the Insert Function dialog box.

5. **Click the Insert button.**

   The dialog box goes away, leaving you with your chosen function typed into the formula bar. Works doesn't know yet what cell or cells you want the function to apply to, however, so it leaves text as a placeholder in the places where cell addresses go.

6. **Edit the formula to put in cell addresses.**

   You have two ways to go. If you like, you can type in the cell addresses you need and delete any extraneous text. Or you can highlight some of the placeholder text and then use the point-and-shoot method for addresses and ranges (which I previously describe) to replace it.

7. **Press Enter when you're done.**

Point and shoot for summing columns or rows

Thanks to Works' Autosum feature, summing a row or column of numbers is a piece of cake. Here's exactly how to do it:

1. **To sum up a column of numbers, place your highlight on the cell beneath the last number.**

   Or

   To sum up a row of numbers, place your highlight on the cell to the right of the last number.

2. **Click the Autosum button on the toolbar — the button with the Greek letter sigma on it (Σ).**

3. **Press the Enter key.**

If you use AutoSum on a cell that is both at the bottom of a column *and* at the end of a row, AutoSum sums the column, not the row.

The Joys and Mysteries of Copying Formulas

Copying is not what most folks think of as an exciting activity, unless they're confused by the sign over their employer's copy department, which often reads "Reproduction." But rest assured that copying can be a far more interesting activity than you suppose when it comes to spreadsheet formulas.

Where copying formulas works well

In a spreadsheet, you often have a column or row in which essentially the same formula is used over and over again — when you're summing a set of columns, for example. The only difference from column to column is the range being summed. You can save a great deal of effort by copying such a formula rather than retyping it. Works automatically takes care of giving the formula the correct, new range.

For formula copying to work easily, one condition must be true: The location of a formula relative to its data must be the same for all copies as for the original. Okay, that sentence was pretty mind-boggling, so here's an example: If the original formula is immediately under a column of 20 data cells, each copy must also be immediately under its own column of 20 data cells. In Figure 18-1, for instance, I can easily copy the formula that appears in cell C14 to cell C15. If the original formula uses a cell that's three columns over and one row down from its address, each copy must be provided with a number three columns over and one row down from *its* address.

Here's how to copy a formula across a row or down a column. The procedure for copying is really just the same as copying a number or text or anything else (although the result is unique):

1. **Enter (or click) the formula you want to copy.**

   If you intend to copy the formula down a column, entering the formula in the top cell is traditional. If you intend to copy your formula across a row, the traditional place to enter the initial formula is the leftmost cell of the row. But any old place will do.

2. **With the formula selected, press Ctrl+C or click the Copy button on the toolbar.**

   This copies the formula to the Windows Clipboard.

3. **Select the rest of the row or column where you want the copies to appear.**

   You may include the original formula cell in your selection, if you feel it makes life easier. It doesn't matter.

4. **Press Ctrl+V or click the Paste button on the toolbar.**

   Bingo, you're done.

The best way to explain what happens when you copy a formula is with an example. In Figure 18-3 you see part of a spreadsheet. Three columns of numbers are shown: C, D, and E. The top five numbers in C and E are typed in; the last number in each column is the sum. The D column is calculated from the C and E columns. So the figure contains ten typed-in numbers and eight formulas.

	A	B	C	D	E
1	*Toy Sales*				
2	Model Number	Model Name	Units	Avg. $/Unit	Rev. ($000)
3	XJ7	Bomber	890	$223.50	$198.92
4	PT3	Swooper	1280	$150.50	$192.64
5	F15	Hawk	920	$298.50	$274.62
6	B52	Falcon	1580	$165.50	$261.49
7	P121	Peregrine	800	$350.50	$280.40
8			5470	$237.70	$1,208.07

Rather than write eight formulas, I had to write only one. Here's how I did it:

1. **I summed column C by selecting C8 and clicking the Autosum button on the toolbar.**

2. **I summed column E by selecting E8 and clicking the Autosum button on the toolbar.**

3. **I entered the formula =1000*E8/C8 into cell D8 and pressed Enter.**

   In case you're curious, the 1000 is there because the revenues in column E are expressed in terms of thousands of dollars. (Multiplying by 1000 expresses them in terms of dollars.)

4. **I clicked the Copy button on the toolbar to copy the formula in D8.**

5. **I selected the range D3:D7, as Figure 18-3 shows.**

6. **I clicked the Paste button on the toolbar to paste in copies of the formula.**

Each copy of the formula uses cells in a different row, which you see in the formula bar when you click those cells. The formula in cell D5, for example, is =1000*E5/C5; in cell D6, it's =1000*E6/C6; and so on. Pretty neat, huh?

Here's what happens to cell addresses when you copy formulas:

✓ **When you copy a formula to a new column, the letters change.**

   That is, the column portions of any cell addresses in your formula change. They change by exactly the number of columns that you move: If you copy something three columns to the right and you have an address of A1 in your formula, it changes to D1, Q17 changes to T17, and so on.

✓ **When you copy a formula to a new row, the numbers change.**

   That is, the row portions of any cell addresses in that formula change. They change by exactly the number of rows that you move: If you copy something three rows down and you have an address of A1 in your formula, A1 changes to A4, Q17 changes to Q20, and so on.

If you copy a formula to a new row and column, both the row and column change in any cell addresses in that formula.

When you *move* a formula (by dragging it), or cut and paste the formula, the addresses in the formula do not change. Addresses change only when you copy something — either by dragging or by using the Copy and Paste commands (Ctrl+C and Ctrl+V).

When formulas don't copy right

Sometimes copying doesn't work the way you want it to. Commonly, this situation occurs when you've got a single value somewhere that you want to use in a row or column of calculations. Back in Figure 18-1, the formula in cell E4 (American dollars) depends on the exchange rate in cell B15. If you copy that formula to the other rows (E5, E6, and so on), the reference to B15 changes rows — to B16, B17, and so on — and is wrong.

To avoid this problem, you can enter each formula separately instead of copying. But if you prefer to copy, there's a trick that lets you copy properly. To keep a cell reference from changing when you copy, put a dollar sign in front of the column letter and/or row number in the formula. For example, in cell E4 of Figure 18-1, type **=D4/B15** instead of **=D4/B15**. When that formula is copied to the next row, the E4 changes to E5, but B15 remains the same. This copying trick is called absolute addressing.

If you use the point-and-shoot method of entering addresses, when you "point," press the F4 key to create an absolute address like B15. Press it again to get B$15, and again to get $B15. This trick also works when you enter cell addresses in Easy Calc. What this all boils down to is: *Put a dollar sign in front of any portion of a cell address that you want to keep from changing when the formula is copied.* For example, a formula using A$8, copied down one row, still reads A$8. If A$8 is copied one column to the right instead, A$8 changes to B$8. The part with the dollar sign does not change; the rest does.

Note: The dollar sign, here, has absolutely nothing to do with dollars (U.S. or Canadian) *or* currency formatting; use of the dollar sign is just an ancient convention in spreadsheets, probably started by Dan Bricklin when he did VisiCalc, or by one of the other spreadsheet pioneers.

Recalculating Large, Slow Spreadsheets

Works recalculates all its formulas whenever you change any cell's contents. As a result, a really big spreadsheet can slow you down; you have to wait for Works to recalculate every time you enter something.

If your spreadsheet seems to take a long time to recalculate, you can switch to manual calculation, which makes Works put off recalculating formulas until you press the F9 key. To switch from automatic to manual calculation (and vice versa), choose Tools⇨Options from the menu bar. The Options dialog box is a collection of tabs, one of which is named Data Entry. Click that tab. Then select the Use Manual Calculation check box. Click OK.

Chapter 19

Tidying Up and Printing Your Spreadsheets

*M*aking a spreadsheet is one thing. Getting the spreadsheet ready for prime time — formatting its numbers and dates properly, giving it a face lift, and finally, printing it — is another.

Are your spreadsheets looking kind of clunky, industrial, and bland? In this chapter, I examine how to use the AutoFormat feature and borders to add beauty and grace and also how to use alignment and other formatting to add style and deep, philosophical significance. (Didn't know it was that easy, did you?)

Are your dates always late? Or do your dates seem to last forever? This chapter helps with those date dilemmas by describing how to deal with dates, time, and basic date-and-time arithmetic. (The chapter helps because you can read it while you're waiting for your date to begin or end. Reading this chapter also gives you that air of elevated intellectual capacity that always attends someone seen reading a *For Dummies* book, thereby impressing the heck out of your date. Unless, as my technical editor points out, you're reading *Dating For Dummies.*)

Are your lists feeling out of sorts? In this chapter, I show you how to bring alphabetical or numerical order to your lists of people, places, or things, and how to safely include calculations in your sordid — oops, I mean *sorted* — lists.

Finally, I delve into the unique opportunities that spreadsheets present for really messing things up when you print. Why, I even provide some solutions in this chapter.

Formatting in One Swell Foop!

Back when disco ruled and quiche was the trendy food of the day, spreadsheets were dull, boring grids. No more! Today's spreadsheet sports designer colors, shadings, lines, borders, 3D shading, and fancy fonts in different sizes and styles.

Works is no slouch when it comes to formatting; you can apply all of these fancy formats as you like, where you like. But Works has also combined a bunch of formatting into various stylish ensembles, which Works refers to as automatic formatting. Automatic formatting — *autoformatting* — is truly a great idea.

Autoformatting your entire spreadsheet

Take a look at Figure 19-1 to see what happens to the toy sales spreadsheet (refer to Chapter 18) when it's decked out in an automatic format called 3-D Effects 2. All kinds of stuff have changed here, even the formats of some of the numbers. Zowie! All these changes resulted from a few mouse clicks.

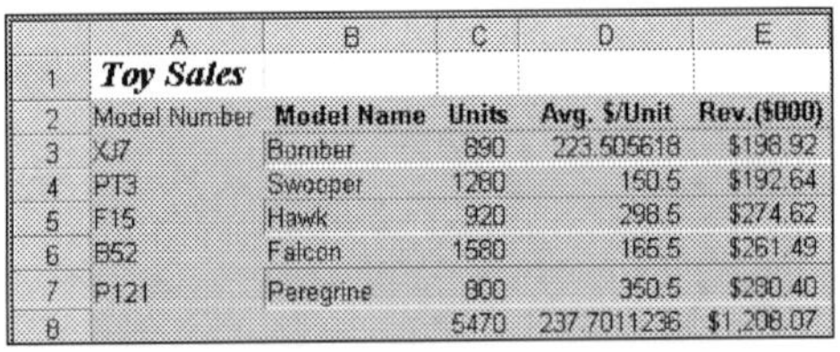

Figure 19-1:
Auto-
formatting:
Just a few
clicks can
get you
a whole
new look.

	A	B	C	D	E
1	Toy Sales				
2	Model Number	Model Name	Units	Avg. $/Unit	Rev.($000)
3	XJ7	Bomber	890	223.505618	$198.92
4	PT3	Swooper	1280	150.5	$192.64
5	F15	Hawk	920	298.5	$274.62
6	B52	Falcon	1580	165.5	$261.49
7	P121	Peregrine	800	350.5	$280.40
8			5470	237.7011236	$1,208.07

The AutoFormat feature presumes that you have a fairly classic table structure: rows, columns, and maybe (though not necessarily) totals. If you meet these standards, AutoFormat away by following these steps:

1. **Make sure that you have column and row headings.**

   Or, if you don't have 'em, at least have a blank row above and a blank column to the left of your table. (Use these blank rows for your title row and column in Step 2.)

2. **Select all the rows and columns, including the title row and column and the total row and/or column.**

   If you have a title for the whole spreadsheet, you can include or exclude it, as you like. I excluded the "Toy Sales" line in Figure 19-1.

3. **Choose Format⇨AutoFormat.**

   The AutoFormat dialog box, as shown in Figure 19-2, leaps into action.

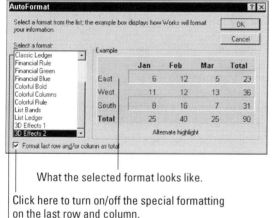

Figure 19-2:
The Auto-
Format
dialog box.

What the selected format looks like.

Click here to turn on/off the special formatting
on the last row and column.

Click a format here.

4. **Click any interesting-sounding format in the Select a Format list box.**

   The Example area shows you what the format looks like. If you don't like this format, click another format. If you don't like any of 'em, press the Esc key to exit the AutoFormat dialog box.

5. **Look at the Format Last Row and/or Column As Total check box.**

   If you haven't used a total row or column, or if you have your total some-where other than at the end of the range, make sure that this check box is blank. If you do have a total row or column, click in the check box to place a check in it, but look at the example to see whether this particular format puts the total in the same place you did.

   In the toy sales example, I chose to leave the check box blank because cell D8 is an average, not a total.

6. **Click the OK button.**

   Foop! There's a brief flurry of activity, and suddenly your table looks like the inside pages of a quarterly report. If you don't like the results, press Ctrl+Z immediately to undo the formatting — before you make any other changes to the spreadsheet — and try again.

7. **Throw in some finishing touches if you want.**

   In Figure 19-1, I'd probably do something to get rid of the long decimal expansions in D3 and D8, either by using the ROUND function (read more about the point-and-shoot method for functions in Chapter18) or by selecting column D and changing to currency format (see the section, "Formatting numbers," later in this chapter).

Formatting the appearance of characters

One of the ways that you can fool with the appearance of the text, numbers, and formulas in your spreadsheet is to change the font, size, style, or color. Appearance formatting is one of those things that works the same way for all the Works programs.

For the full details on formatting characters, refer to Chapter 3. The executive summary goes like this. You have three ways to change how your type looks as you enter it:

✔ **Alternative 1.** Choose the font, size, and style from the toolbar.

✔ **Alternative 2.** Choose font, size, style, or color from the Font tab of the Format Cells dialog box. To get this dialog box, choose Format⇨Font and Style.

✔ **Alternative 3.** (To change style only.) Press Ctrl+B for bold, Ctrl+I for italic, and Ctrl+U for underline.

To change the appearance of characters that you've already typed, just select them first and then use one of the previous three alternatives.

Formatting numbers

Numbers? You want numbers? Works has got your number. In fact, you've probably never realized how many ways there are to display numbers.

Formatting numbers is not quite like formatting text. After all, when you change the formatting of text, the characters themselves don't change — just their font and style change. But when you format numbers, the actual characters and punctuation change to different characters and punctuation — adding dollar signs or parentheses, for example. The number itself doesn't change, but it puts on a radically different face. Sometimes it doesn't even look like a number any more.

For example, if you put the number 3284.2515 in a cell and use your formatting options (which I list in Table 19-1), you can make that number look like any of the stuff in the How It Looks column of Table 19-1.

Table 19-1	Different Formatting for the Number 3284.2515	
How It Looks	**Format Name**	**About That Format & Options You Can Specify**
3284.25	General	As precise as possible for the column width; this is how Works formats numbers unless you tell it otherwise.
3284.251	Fixed	Specifies decimal places (in this example, three).
$3,284.25	Currency	Dollar sign, comma, specifies decimal places; negative numbers appear in parentheses. Optional: negative numbers also in red.
3,284.25	Comma	Like Currency, but no dollar sign.
328425.15 %	Percent	Displays number multiplied by 100, adds percent symbol; specify your decimal places.
3.28 E+03	Exponential	Single digit number with power of ten; specify your decimal places (in this example, two).
03284	Leading Zeros	No fraction; displays as many digits as you specify (in this example, five); adds zeros or trims leading digits to do so. Good for zip (postal) codes.
3248 3/10	Fraction	Expresses fractional part as fraction: Choose halves, thirds, quarters, eighths, tenths, and so on (in this example, tenths).
TRUE	True/False	If zero, displays FALSE; if not zero, TRUE.

(continued)

Table 19-1 (continued)

How It Looks	Format Name	About That Format & Options You Can Specify
November 21, 1908	Date	Interprets number as number of days since 12/31/1899; Works uses this format when you enter a date.
6:02 AM	Time	Interprets fractional part of number (only) as fraction of one day; displays fraction as hour of that day. Works uses this format when you enter a time.
3284.2515	Text	If format applied before number is entered, turns number into text. Useful for serial numbers or other numeric codes.

Date and time formats are among the weirder ones in this list because they make numbers look like text. For more on using them, read the section, "Formatting dates and times," later in this chapter.

Currency format is the easiest to apply: Select the cell or cells to format and click the toolbar button with the $ icon on it.

You don't actually format numbers in the spreadsheet program; you format cells. The cell can be empty when you format it, and when you type a number in that cell, the number takes on that format. If you type text in that cell, the text is not affected. If you delete an entry from a cell, the number format remains.

Works starts by applying the General format to every cell. The way to change the format of specific cells is as follows:

1. **Select a cell or bunch of cells.**

   Click the cell or highlight the bunch of cells.

2. **Choose Format➪Number.**

   The Number tab of the Format Cells dialog box presents itself for duty.

3. **Click any format in the Format area of the dialog box.**

   A sample appears in the Sample area near the bottom of the dialog box. If a number is already in the cell, that number is used in the sample. If you don't like what you see, click another format. Refer to Table 19-1 for notes about these formats.

Some formats enable you to specify how many digits are to the right (or left, in the case of the Leading Zeros format) of the decimal point. Normally, Works uses two digits here. To change this situation, just type a number to go into the Decimal Places box.

The Currency and the Comma formats give you the option to put negative numbers in red; just click the Negative Numbers in Red check box.

The Fractions format normally reduces fractions. For example, if you choose one thirty-second (1/32), and your number ends in the decimal .125, this format converts your number to one eighth (1/8). If you really want one thirty-second or whatever fraction you choose, click the Do Not Reduce check box.

4. **Click the OK button when you're done.**

Changing Alignment in a Cell

Another way to change the appearance of something in a cell is to change its alignment: Smushed left, smushed right, or smack dab in the center of a cell are the basic choices. Normally, Works aligns text to the left and numbers (including dates) to the right, but you don't have to live with that.

Alignment is another one of those things that works pretty much the same (at least for the basics) in all the Works programs:

✔ Select a cell or cells and then click the Left, Center, or Right Align button in the toolbar. (These buttons are the ones with the lines on them.)

When you specify an alignment, the alignment sticks to the cell, not to what's in the cell. If you specify alignment for a blank cell, whatever you type later gets aligned accordingly. If you delete what's in a cell, the alignment remains in the cell.

✔ You can tell how any cell is aligned by clicking it and observing the alignment buttons on the toolbar. If one of them is depressed, the cell is aligned in that way.

✔ To remove an alignment, click the alignment button that is depressed. (The Alignment reverts to left alignment for text, right for numbers.)

You can find these basic alignments, plus some other fancier alignments, on the Alignment tab of the Format Cells dialog box. I don't get into those things here, but if you want to experiment with that dialog box, choose Format⇨ Alignment.

The clockwork behind dates and times

Here's what's behind the scenes: Works computes dates by giving every day a number. Works starts the sequence at January 1, 1900, which is represented as 1. Days are whole numbers. Hours and minutes in that day are represented by a fractional portion. So the number that represents 8 a.m. on January 1, 1900, is 1.333333333. Works runs out of dates on June 3, 2079, so don't make any 100-year plans. (Works is Y2K-compliant, but apparently not Y2079-compliant!)

If you type in a date or a time, Works shows it to you as a date or a time, which is nice. But Works secretly changes the entry to a number. If you type **8 AM**, for example, Works enters 0.333333333 and chooses a time format for the number. If you type in a date, Works enters the number for that date and applies a date format that resembles the format in which you typed the number.

Making Dates

You've probably made your share of bad dates; now try good dates. Works provides date arithmetic, formatting, and functions so that you can calculate things based on time without having to recite to yourself, "Thirty days hath September, April, June, and December . . . or was it November?"

Entering dates

If you're North American, you can enter a date into a cell in most of the ways that you probably consider normal (such as August 28, 1945). If you're European, you have to use the weird, backward American way. Look at Table 19-2 to see good and bad ways to enter the date of August 28, 1945. The bad dates aren't really bad; Works just interprets them as text because they're in the wrong format, so you aren't able to do any calculations with them. If you want them simply for labels, though, feel free to type them the "bad" way.

Table 19-2	Good and Bad Dates
Good	**Bad**
August 28, 1945	August 28 1945
8/28/45	28/8/45
8/28/1945	8-28-1945
Aug 28, 1945	Aug. 28,1945

Note that if you leave the century off the year (45 instead of 1945), Works assumes the century past (the 1900s).

To enter a date in the current year, just enter the day and month part (8/28, for example). To enter today's date, press Ctrl+; (that's Ctrl and the semicolon key). Amazing!

To enter a date that's current all the time, as on a day/date watch, type in the formula =**NOW( )** and format the cell with a date format (see the section, "Formatting dates and times," later in this chapter). The date is updated every time you change a cell, press the F9 (recalculate) key, open the spreadsheet, or print it.

Entering times

Just like entering dates, Works understands the "good" ways to enter times; any other ("bad") way causes Works to interpret the entry as text. But, as they say, you gotta (everyone together now . . .) "take the good times with the bad." Sorry. Had to do that. In Table 19-3 you see good and bad ways to enter times.

Table 19-3	Good and Bad Times
Good	*Bad*
2:30PM	230PM
14:30	1430
8:00	0800
8 AM	8 AM EST
8am	eight o'clock

To enter the current time, press Ctrl+Shift+; (that's Ctrl+Shift+semicolon).

To enter a time that's always current, as the time on a clock, type in the formula =**NOW( )** and format the cell with a time format (see "Formatting dates and times," later in this chapter). The time is updated every time you change a cell, press the F9 (recalculate) key, open the spreadsheet, or print it. (Again, if you're using manual recalculation rather than the normal automatic recalculation, you have to press the F9 key.)

Doing basic date and time arithmetic

The Works spreadsheet program enables you to do calculations based on time, but you have to be a little careful. Works secretly uses numbers to represent dates and makes them look date-ish by using a date format. If you do calculations, the results may come out as funny numbers instead of the date, number of days, or number of hours that you want. The following instructions can generally keep things working well.

Subtracting dates; adding days to dates

Subtract the difference between two dates to easily calculate exactly how much time has elapsed between them.

Calculating intervals between dates can be depressing if you're single and your social life is less than satisfactory.

You subtract dates just as you subtract regular numbers, except that each date either has to be in its own cell or, if you're using the dates in a formula, in single quotation marks (apostrophes) and in the slash-date format, as in '9/15/94'. Here are the rules of date subtraction:

- ✔ To use dates in a formula, type the dates in single quotation marks and in the slash format: ='9/15/95' – '4/14/95'.

- ✔ To write a formula using dates that are in separate cells, type something like =B4–B8, where cell B4 has one date and B8 has the other. You can enter dates in cells B4 and B8 in any acceptable format.

- ✔ The first date in a subtraction should be the later of the two if you want a positive number.

- ✔ The result that you get is the number of days between the dates.

After you read the section, "Formatting dates and times," later in this chapter, you may be tempted to format the result of date subtraction with a date format, just on general principles. Do *not* do it! Such an action has confusing results. For example, the answer to the sentence '9/15/95' - '4/14/95' is 154 days. If you now put that into date format, Works gives you June 2, 1900 — day 154 for Works. (Check out the sidebar, "The clockwork behind dates and times," elsewhere in this chapter.) Unless the space-time continuum is more complicated than we think, this information is useless. Leave the result as a number of days, with a regular old number format.

Adding dates sounds like the logical complement to subtracting them but, in fact, is complete nonsense. (Christmas plus the Fourth of July equals . . . what?) You can, however, add *days* to dates by using a formula. Just as in subtraction, to put the date right into the formula, use single quotation marks around the date and use the date-slash format. For example, ='9/15/94' + 35 adds 35 days to September 15.

If you're adding days to a date to compute another date, such as adding 35 days to September 15, 1994, *do* use a date format; otherwise, you just see a weird number. (See the section, "Formatting dates and times," later in this chapter.)

Subtracting and adding times

You subtract time in much the same way as you subtract dates. You can use times either in cells by themselves or as parts of a formula:

- ✔ If you're going to enter a time directly in a formula, put single quotation marks around it ('10:00 PM' or '22:00', for example). For minutes, the hour is zero, as in '0:30' for 30 minutes.

- ✔ If the times are in cells of their own, you can omit the single quotation marks.

The only trouble with subtracting times is that the result may need a little fixing up because Works uses units of days for time, not hours or minutes. Here's a quick example.

If you're a hotshot lawyer making, oh, $450 an hour, you, of course, want to bill your clients precisely for your time. So perhaps you keep three columns for each client: one (say, column B) for starting time, another (column C) for ending time, and the third (column D) for the difference between the two. You make the following entries in row 3:

```
Cell B3 Cell C3  Cell D3
10 AM   10:15 AM =C3-B3
```

The only problem is that the result in column D is 0.010416667. That number represents the fraction of a day that equals 15 minutes. Two problems with this result are as follows:

- ✔ **The number doesn't look like minutes or hours.**

  To fix this appearance problem, use a time format (see "Formatting dates and times," a bit later in this chapter, and "Formatting numbers," earlier in this chapter); the best time format to use is one of the 24-hour formats — the ones without AM or PM after them.

- ✔ **Even if you fix the format, if you use this number to calculate your fee, you'll go broke!**

  If you multiply your time in column D (0.0104) by your rate of $450, you earn only $4.65 — a pittance to a high-priced person such as yourself. You spend more than that for a cup of cappuccino in the lobby coffee shop.

Your problem is that Works keeps track of hours as fractions of a day. One hour is one twenty-fourth of a day. So to fix the problem in this example, multiply by 24. The "fix" rules go like this:

- **To convert the result of time subtraction to hours, multiply by 24.** The formula in column D of the example is (C3-B3)*24.

- **To convert the result of time subtraction to minutes, multiply by 24*60.** For instance, the formula in column D of the example is (C3-B3) *24*60. (Or, if writing successive multiplications confuses you, you can multiply by 1440, which is what 24*60 equals.)

Now for time addition. Adding *hours of the day* together is just as nonsensical as adding dates together. (What is 2 p.m. plus 3 p.m.?) But you can certainly add *times* together or sum up a bunch of times. (Two hours plus three hours is five hours. No problem.) If you bill by the hour, adding up time is useful — it allows you to eat, for one thing.

To add or sum times, enter your times by using time format as you type (for example, 1:36 for one hour and 36 minutes); time format is easier on your brain. Also, format the formula cell that sums the times up with a 24-hour time format (without the AM or PM). If you're going to enter the times right into the formula, make sure that you put the times in single quotation marks: '1:36'.

Formatting dates and times

Every now and then, while you're doing some date arithmetic, instead of seeing a nice, date-looking result, you get a weird number, such as 16679. No problem. What you've got there is the date serial number that Works actually uses when it handles dates. (Quick, how many puns can you make out of "date serial"?) Most of the time, Works manages to hide how it really handles dates from you. When Works fails, you need to format the number as a date. (Unless, of course, you don't care what the date looks like.)

Also, every once in a while, you may want dates to be formatted a little differently than Works normally does them. Instead of August 28, 1945, you may want 8/28/45, or maybe even 8/45, ignoring the day; heck, you may just want the month: August. No problem again. Works can do all these tasks.

When you enter a date or time in a format that Works recognizes, Works actually stores a secret serial number and then formats the cell with a date or time format pretty close to the one you typed.

Here's how to format numbers as dates (or reformat dates):

1. Select the cell or cells to format.

2. **Choose Format⇨Number.**

   The Number tab of the Format Cells dialog box appears on-screen.

3. **Click Date in the Format area of the dialog box.**

   Date is already selected if the cell is currently date-formatted; if this is the case, you can skip this step.

4. **Click one of the date formats in the Date area of the dialog box.**

5. **Click the OK button.**

You can also change formatting for time. For example, if you don't like 2:30 PM and prefer 24-hour time, you can change the time to read 14:30. To do so, follow the preceding steps, except make these changes: In Step 3, click Time in the Format area of the dialog box, and in Step 4, choose a time format in the Time area of the dialog box. Among the formats are also choices for displaying seconds, as in 9:56:48 PM, if seconds are important to you.

Changing formatting does not change what's really in the cell — it changes only the appearance. If you reformat August 28, 1945, to appear on-screen as just August, the number in the cell remains 16677. If you aren't convinced, press Alt+V and then *F* to turn on the Formula view. The Formula view shows the true contents of every cell. Press Alt+V and then *F* again to go back to the Regular view.

Adding Borders and Gridlines

You have no excuse for ugly spreadsheets anymore. Pity. Now folks have to spend a lot of time duding up stuff in order for it to be appreciated by anyone else. Fortunately, Works takes much of the pain and strain out of prettying up spreadsheets with its AutoFormat feature (refer to the section "Formatting in One Swell Foop!" earlier in this chapter).

Alas, sometimes you still need a few lines to dress things up further: a line along a column, or across a row, or outlining a table. For this effect, you need borders.

Borders are lines along the top, bottom, or sides of a cell. Combined properly, these lines can create the appearance of a border on or around a single cell, a range, or any given area of your spreadsheet. Used individually, borders are useful for such things as the summation line at the bottom of a column.

If you use borders, notice that some of them are so thin that they're masked by the gridlines that normally cover a spreadsheet. To turn off the gridlines, choose View⇨Gridlines. (Or press Alt+V and then G.) The same action turns the gridlines back on.

Here's the step-by-step procedure for putting a border on cells:

1. **Select (highlight) the cell or cells that you want to apply a border to.**

   You can apply a border to either a single cell or a range of cells at one time.

2. **Choose Format⇨Border.**

   The Border tab of the Format Cells dialog box materializes.

3. **Choose what line style you want for your border(s).**

   Click any of the Line Style examples shown in the dialog box. The top style signifies no line at all; choose it for turning off borders.

4. **Choose what type of border or borders you want in that line style.**

   Click one or more of the boxes in the Border area of the dialog box:

   - Outline applies your chosen line style to all sides of the cell. If you've highlighted a range, you get a border around that range.

   - Choose Top, Bottom, Left, or Right to apply your line style preference to that particular side. When you highlight a range, the border is applied to every individual cell in that range, *not* to the range itself.

   To select a border and turn it on, click its box. The chosen box gets o utlined, and your chosen line style appears there. To turn off the border, click its box again once or twice until no line remains in the box. (If the box becomes shaded, that signifies to Works that a cell in your selected range already has a border, and that Works should not change that border.) Repeated clicking cycles the border through the states of being on, off, and (if a border already exists) no change.

   To choose a color for whatever border is currently outlined, click the down-arrow button to the right of the box marked Color, and choose a color from the list that drops down.

5. **If you want different line styles on other borders, repeat Steps 3 and 4.**

6. **Click the OK button.**

A typical thing to do with borders is to put a line over a row of column sums. To accomplish this, highlight the row of sums and apply a Top border to the range.

Making and Sorting Lists

One of the things that you can do with a spreadsheet — that you can also do with a database — is keep a list. Now, keeping a list may not seem particularly exciting; and if you were just "keeping" a list, you'd be silly to lay out the bucks for a spreadsheet program.

But given a sufficiently long list, you may have several things you want to do with your list: sort it alphabetically or numerically, find particular entries in that list, or do calculations based on things in that list. The Works spreadsheet program can help you do these things. If, however, your list is going to be more than a couple of hundred entries long, or if you want some sort of summary report (such as the total weight of items shipped to each zip code in a shipping list), you may want to consider using the database program instead.

The nice thing about using spreadsheets for lists is that spreadsheets have lots of rows — one row for each item on your list. You can treat these rows the way that you treat file cards, by using one row per "card" and putting the different things that you put on a file card in different columns. In geek-speak (computer gibberish), each row is a *record,* and each column is a *field.*

Look at Figure 19-3 to view a simple list that you can keep in spreadsheet form: a list of pledges and a note of whether they've been paid.

Figure 19-3:
Keeping
a list of
donors in a
spreadsheet.

	A	B	C	D	E	F	G
1	Pledge List						
2	Pledge #	Last Name	First Name	Phone	Pledge Date	Amount	Paid?
3	1	Snodgrass	Mortimer	555-8750	September 15	50	TRUE
4	2	Hostwhipple	Gertrude	555-9165	September 15	40	TRUE
5	3	Meulheuser-Eck	Henrietta	555-1826	September 15	50	TRUE
6	4	Cheeseworthy	Stilton	555-9190	September 16	20	TRUE
7	5	Phoghome	Legolas	555-1725	September 16	15	TRUE
8	6	Towcester	Bill	555-2462	September 16	80	
9	7	Eelgrass	Steve	555-9152	September 16	50	
10	8	Dibblesby	Horst	555-6152	September 19	40	
11	9	Wikketton	Florence	555-4625	September 19	35	
12	10	Smith	Alan	555-4628	September 19	45	
13	11	Smith	Alan, Jr.	555-2451	September 19	25	
14							

Here are some tricks that you can use to create this list. One of the basic tricks is preformatting entire columns, which means applying a number format before any data is entered. (Or "data *are* entered," if you're an unreconstructed classicist.)

✔ Give each pledge (row) a number so that if you later rearrange the rows, you can get them back in the original order. This setup also helps keep the Alan Smiths separate, giving you a unique tracking number for the pledge so that you can, for example, put the right person's name on dunning letters and not harass the wrong guy. (Now if you can just tell their checks apart.)

✔ As each pledge is contacted by phone, the date of the call and the amount pledged are entered. The easy way to enter today's date is to press Ctrl+ : (that is, Ctrl + the semicolon key) in the date column. To preformat the entire column with the kind of date format you want, select the whole column by clicking the column letter (E, in this example) and then applying date formatting.

✔ I chose not to format the Amount column because what else would it be but currency? I don't accept barter pledges in chickens or corn. If you do want to preformat the column in currency, preformat it by clicking the column letter (F, in this example) and then clicking the $ button on the toolbar.

✔ When the pledge is received, you can just make any sort of mark in the Paid? column. I chose to get fancy, preformatting the column with the True/False number format. Typing **1** into that column when someone pays results in a TRUE appearing there.

Sorting lists

One of the nice things that Works can do for you is sort lists. (I'm still working on getting it to sort laundry; I'm starting with laundry lists.) You may, in the example in Figure 19-3, want to alphabetize the list by last name so that you can more easily compare it with, say, a purchased list of prospects. (You don't want to call someone twice.) Or you may want to order the list by amount pledged so that you can single out the generous for special attention next year.

Works can sort your list in alphabetical or numerical order. Before you go running off to sort your list, however, decide on the following sorting options:

✔ Which column to sort by primarily (for example, last name)

✔ Which column to sort by secondarily, for those instances when the primary column has duplicates (for example, first name)

✔ Which column to sort by if duplicates exist in the secondary column (if you care about sorting those duplicates)

✔ What order you want the list in: A–Z and 1, 2, 3, . . . (ascending) or Z–A and . . . 3, 2, 1 (descending)

The order can be different for the primary and secondary sorts — for example, you can have last names in ascending order and dollar amounts pledged in descending order.

In the pledge example, where you want to compare the list with an alphabetical list of prospects, you probably want to sort on column B (last name) primarily, and in ascending order. In case of redundant last names, use column C (first name) as the secondary sort column, also in ascending order. You probably don't care about any tertiary sort.

If you have any calculations or spreadsheet work of any kind (other lists, other tables) off to one side of your list (in the rows that you're going to sort), highlight the area you want to sort before using the Tools⇨Sort command. Then choose Tools⇨Sort, and in the Sort query box that appears, choose Sort Only the Highlighted Information. Otherwise, when you sort the rows of your list, the entire width of each row is reshuffled (all columns), which mangles anything typed off to one side.

The procedure for sorting goes like this:

1. **Save your spreadsheet as a file, in case anything goes wrong.**

   If anything does go terribly wrong and Ctrl+Z doesn't undo it, close the messed-up spreadsheet without saving it and then reopen the original file.

2. **Select (highlight) all the rows in the list.**

   You can use any column or columns in this selection; your choice doesn't matter. Make sure that you don't include any column sum row; otherwise, that row is sorted along with your records. You may include or not include the header row; do as you like. (I deal with header rows in Step 7.)

3. **Choose Tools⇨Sort.**

   The Sort dialog box appears with its first question: Do you want to sort only the columns you selected, or all columns? (You get this question even if you've selected all the columns already.)

4. **Click OK.**

   This action produces the second Sort dialog box, as displayed in Figure 19-4, which asks which column to sort on and whether to sort in ascending or descending order. The Sort dialog box also asks whether one of the rows you've selected is the header row, so it knows to leave the header row alone.

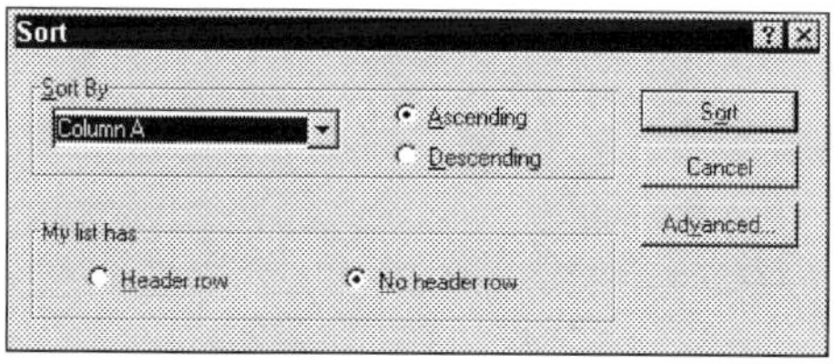

Figure 19-4:
Sorting on one column. Clicking Advanced gets you a triple-decker version.

5. **Choose, from the Sort By list box, the column that you want to sort by.**

6. **Click either Ascending or Descending.**

   Ascending means that rows containing low numbers (or letters) in your chosen column go at the top of the list; rows with high numbers (or letters) go at the bottom. *Descending* means the opposite.

7. **Click either Header Row or No Header Row.**

   If the cells you highlight in Step 2 include a header row, click Header Row. Otherwise, click No Header Row.

8. **If you're concerned about sorting when your chosen column has duplicates (say, sorting the multiple Smiths by their first name), click the Advanced button.**

   You're presented with a sort of triple-decker version of the Sort dialog box, with the top deck containing the column and sort order you just specified. In the second deck from the top (the Then By box), select a second column and sort order (click either Ascending or Descending). If you see duplicate entries in this second column, go to the bottom deck, and choose a third column and sort order in the same way.

9. **Click the Sort button.**

   Works sorts your list (that is, your rows are shuffled around in the order that you specified). To return to the original order, you can press Ctrl+Z as long as you haven't made any other changes. If you're clever enough to create a column in which you give each record (row) a unique number, you can always sort by using that column for Sort By and restore the original order.

You can dress up your list with the AutoFormat feature, just as you can with any other spreadsheet. A couple of formats are even made especially for lists: List Bands and List Ledger. Go back and read the section, "Autoformatting your entire spreadsheet," earlier in this chapter.

Calculating in lists

Putting your formulas in the right place is important if you're using your spreadsheet to keep a list. If you're going to do a calculation based exclusively on data in a single row, put the formula in that row. If you're going to do calculations on multiple rows in a list, doing them in the area above the list is best. If you put them at the bottom, you're going to have to continually insert new rows for data as the list expands. If you put them off to the side, they're likely to be mangled by the sorting process.

In general, don't write formulas that refer to specific cell addresses within your list. (Formulas that refer to complete rows or columns of data are usually okay, however.) When you sort the rows, those specific cell addresses all have new data. Unless you're very clever and that's what you had in mind, the result is nonsense.

Also be very careful about using formulas with ranges that include a group of rows, such as =SUM(F3:F13). If you sort the rows, the range in the formula remains unchanged — (F3:F13) — but it refers to different data.

Keep safe by writing a formula that refers to all the rows — for example, one that sums up the Amount column. But you must be careful to make sure that the range in the SUM formula expands to include any new rows that you add. When you add new rows, insert them (choose Insert⇨Row) above the bottom row. The range in the summing formula expands to include the new row.

Dealing with Printing Peculiarities

Printing spreadsheets is pretty much like printing anything else in Works, so for the general, gory details, hop over to Chapter 4. However, following are a few peculiarities about printing spreadsheets:

✔ To print only a range of the spreadsheet, not the entire spreadsheet, select a range and use the Set Print Area command: Choose Format➪Set Print Area. To go back to printing the entire spreadsheet, select the entire spreadsheet (press Ctrl+A), and repeat the Set Print Area command.

✔ Works splits up your spreadsheet to get it to fit on a printed page. If the spreadsheet is bigger than the page, you literally have to cut and paste pages together to re-create the original layout. Use the Print Preview feature (choose File➪Print Preview) to see how your spreadsheet will print.

To control page breaks yourself, you can split up the spreadsheet horizontally and/or vertically and create page-sized pieces. Here's how:

✔ To split the spreadsheet along a vertical line, begin by selecting a column. Click the column letter (in gray at the top of the spreadsheet) to the right of where you want the break. Now choose Insert➪Page Break. A dashed line appears along the left edge of the selected column, indicating the break. The break runs the entire length of the spreadsheet, although it may not show up on-screen in places where you have fancy formatting.

✔ To split the document along a horizontal line, select the row *below* where you want the page break (click its row number in gray on the left side of the spreadsheet) and choose Insert➪Page Break again. The break runs the entire width of the spreadsheet.

✔ If you forget to select a row or column before choosing Insert➪Page Break, a tiny Insert Page Break dialog box appears. In this dialog box, click Column for a vertical break or Row for a horizontal one, and then click the OK button.

✔ If you click a cell adjacent to an existing vertical page break and insert a new page break, Works assumes that you want a horizontal one now and gives you the horizontal page break you want with no preamble or discussion. Conversely, if you click below a horizontal break and insert a new page break, Works assumes that you want a vertical page break.

✔ To get rid of a page break, put your cursor to the right of the page break (for vertical), or under the page break (for horizontal); then choose Insert➪Delete Page Break.

Part V
Doing Active Duty at the Database

...and so, with a multifunction system like this, whenever you press the DELETE key, you....

OK- this seems like a good time to move on to the UNDO function.

In this part . . .

When you need to get your data to follow orders, march in neat rows and columns, or report on developments in the field, you need a database. When you have large squadrons of names, numbers, or other data, the Works database can help you put your facts into usable form.

The database tool helps you sort, list, find, and report on anything from membership lists to inventories. In this part, you discover how to create a database, interrogate it, and make reports back to headquarters based on the data contained within.

> Therefore, my lords, omit no happy hour
> That may give furtherance to our expedition;

> —*King Henry V,* William Shakespeare

Chapter 20

Reporting for Duty at the Database

*T*he time has come to give your data a little discipline. Have your scraggly collections of names and addresses, inventory lists, and what-have-you report for duty at the database and give them the Works. Here's where your data learns to get organized, march in rows and columns, and respond promptly to your orders and questions.

Using a Database

If you've never used a database before . . . well, actually, you probably have used a database before, but it was probably on paper, a more sense-able (able to be sensed) medium than a computer. If you've ever used a library card catalog, a Rolodex, a dictionary, or a phone book, you've used a database. A *database* is just a collection of information that has some organization to it. (For example, every card in a Rolodex has the same structure: a line for a name, usually last name first; a couple of lines for an address; a line for the phone number; and so on.)

The thing that you may never have used before is a database manager, or (as in Works) a database program. When you put a database on a computer, a *database manager* or *program* is the thing that you use to read the database and to put information into the database. Because database programs always accompany databases, people get lazy and lump the terms together, calling the whole ball of wax a database.

What's the big deal?

The big deal with computer databases and database programs is that not only does the program let you read the database, it also helps you find things quickly. (Not your car keys, though. Sorry.) Making a list of everyone in your Rolodex with the same zip code (postal code) will take you awhile. But use a computer database, and the whole task takes hardly any time at all. Looking for something (or things) in a database is called *querying*.

A database helps you do other things that would be a pain in the wrist to do by hand. Take organization, for example. To organize a meeting of people who live in the same general area, you may want to find everyone whose zip code is one of, say, three possible codes. Or you may want to sort things, such as your organization's membership list by street, so that you can set up neighborhood meetings. A database makes these kinds of tasks a breeze.

Computer databases are also great for storing numerical information because the database program lets you make statistical reports. If you store your business inventory in a computer database and record each item's value and department, you can easily find out the total inventory value for each department. If you record the item number and salesperson for every sale, you can quickly figure out sales commissions and the remaining inventory levels. Analyses such as these are generally called reports, and Works has a special ReportCreator tool in the Tools menu to help you get them just right.

Finally, (and, for most people, most importantly), databases are great for creating mailing labels and bulk addressing envelopes. Works' Envelope tool in the word-processor program can read a Works database file, full of names and addresses. It can then automatically label envelopes or labels. (More about this process in Chapter 7. The word processor can alternatively use Microsoft's Address Book for this purpose.)

Fields and records: How information is stored

Works talks a lot about fields and records, so you need to understand what they are. The Rolodex metaphor is great for understanding fields and records, which are part of every database program.

Each card in your Rolodex is like a record in a database. (If you don't have a Rolodex, think of a recipe card file; each recipe card is a record.)

Each card has the same blank areas to fill out: name, telephone number, and address, at the very least. These blank areas are called fields in computer databases. Each field has a name, such as the Address field in a Rolodex (or Number of Servings if you're thinking of recipe cards). Each record has different entries in those fields, which typically describe a person (as in the Rolodex), a transaction (such as a sale or a phone call), an object, or a location.

Sorting, filtering, and reporting: Finding only the information you want

Although having a lot of information well organized into fields and records is very nice, that benefit alone wouldn't convince *me* to use a database instead of a Rolodex or card file. No, what sells me on databases is that they can help you find the information you want — and only that information. If a database is very small, of course, you can just rummage through it. But the reason that you have a database is that you have a lot of data, and rummaging through it to find the information is just not practical. Three ways in which the Works database helps you find and display data are as follows:

- ✔ **Sorting** lets you organize records alphabetically (by last name, for example) or numerically. Sorting your database records also groups similar records together. For example, when you sort based on zip code, all the records sharing a common zip code are grouped together.

  For the full scoop on sorting, peruse Chapter 23.

- ✔ **Filtering** shows you only certain records in your database. For example, to find all 12-year-olds in your school database, you can create a filter that, using the Age field of your database, screens out every child but the ones that you want. You can also filter based on multiple fields. For example, if you want all the 12-year-olds who are not in your charming town of Mudville, that can be accommodated, too.

  For information on filtering, read through Chapter 22.

- ✔ **Reporting** filters, sorts, and organizes records into a report or summary form for printing. For example, you can create a report of your customers in the state of California, grouped by zip code, with subtotals of sales for each group for the month of December.

  For more on creating reports, check out Chapter 23.

Doing Database Duty

You can start a new document in the database program as you do with any other Works program. (Choose the program you want — the Database, in this case — from the Programs page of the Task Launcher.) To review the method for starting Works, the Task Launcher, and the various ways of starting a new document or opening an existing document, check out Chapter 1. If you're a little vague on using commands, menus, and dialog boxes, flip back to Chapter 2.

Before you start a new database document, however, you should spend a little time thinking about your database design. Check out "Designing Your Database" and then "Creating Your Database" (both sections appear later in this chapter) for details on starting a new database document.

Designing your own database can be time consuming. If you prefer someone else to do the groundwork, Works has a few predesigned databases, listed as Tasks when you choose the Database program on the Task Launcher. For more on using Tasks in general, see Chapter 5.

The database window

In Figure 20-1, you see the window for the database program. Your window looks like this after you create or open a database.

Database toolbar

Menu bar

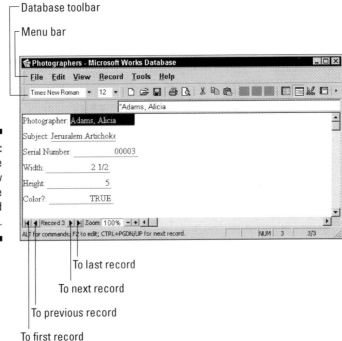

Figure 20-1:
A database
in Form view
shows one
data record
at a time.

To last record

To next record

To previous record

To first record

A slightly modified version of the usual Works menu bar appears near the top of the Works window, and the database toolbar is underneath the menu bar.

Don't try to memorize all the stuff in this figure. Stick a pencil here, or an unused stick of gum, or turn back the corner of the page and come back whenever you need to refresh your memory.

Make a mental note that Figure 20-1 is one of two main views of a database. The view shown here is called Form view; the other, which looks like a spreadsheet, is called List view. (A third view, Form Design view, looks like Form view but functions as an editing feature to let you change how Form view looks. A fourth view, Report view, is confusing as heck and useful only to advanced users.)

The database menu

In the database program, the menu bar (the line with File and all the other command words on it; refer to Figure 20-1) looks almost exactly as it does for the word-processor and spreadsheet programs. The menus display some differences when you go to use them, and they differ slightly among the three views you'll most likely use: Form view, List view, and Form Design view.

Many of the basic commands are the same, however, especially the ones in the menus that drop down when you click File or Edit. The File and Edit menus include commands for starting a new document, opening an existing document file, closing a document, saving a document to a file, and making basic edits. Even the Find command is practically the same as in the word processor or spreadsheet. Most of these commands are discussed in detail in Part I, the basic skills chapters.

I cover the other commands — the commands that are specific to databases — one at a time, throughout this chapter.

The spreadsheet connection

Works' Database program and Spreadsheet program have a great deal in common. The List view of a Works database looks (and can be controlled) very much like a spreadsheet. Also, you can easily cut and paste data between the List view of a database and a spreadsheet without too much confusion. You can even sum up rows (records, that is) by creating a formula field. You cannot, however, sum up columns (except in reports).

You may want to learn about spreadsheets at some point in order to pick up some tricks for working with databases in the List view. Take a look at Part IV for more information on spreadsheets.

The database toolbar

The thing with all the decorative buttons under the menu bar is called the database toolbar. The toolbar is just a faster way than the menu bar to do some of the same things. You click a button, and stuff happens.

Many of the buttons on the database toolbar are similar to those in other Works toolbars (see Figure 20-2). For more on Works toolbars, see Chapter 2.

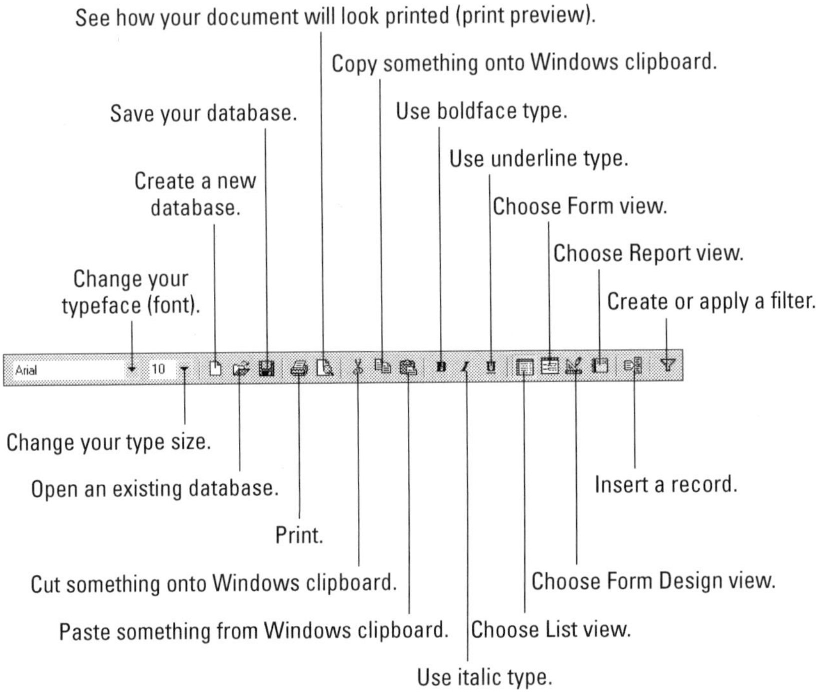

See how your document will look printed (print preview).

Copy something onto Windows clipboard.

Save your database.

Use boldface type.

Use underline type.

Create a new database.

Choose Form view.

Choose Report view.

Figure 20-2: Where database tools hang out when they're on base: the toolbar.

Change your typeface (font).

Create or apply a filter.

Arial 10

Change your type size.

Insert a record.

Open an existing database.

Print.

Cut something onto Windows clipboard.

Choose Form Design view.

Paste something from Windows clipboard.

Choose List view.

Use italic type.

Most of the buttons on the toolbar are the usual suspects mentioned in Part I for starting, saving, printing, doing basic cut-and-paste edits, changing fonts, and getting help. The remaining buttons are specific to databases. Here's where to go for a discussion of what each of these buttons refers to:

- ✔ **List, Form, and Form Design view:** See the section, "Selecting a view," later in this chapter.

- ✔ **Insert a record:** See Chapter 21.

- ✔ **Insert a field:** See Chapter 21.

- ✔ **Create or apply a filter:** See Chapter 22.

- ✔ **Create a report:** See Chapter 23.

To quickly see what a button on the toolbar does, place your mouse cursor over the button (don't click) and wait half a second. A tiny gray sign appears, giving you a tiny gray description of the button.

Designing Your Database

Unless you're using a Task, you do have to design your own database. Well, no, that's not quite right. You don't have to design it — you can slap it together in a devil-may-care fashion — but you will pay a price later as you add or rearrange things and possibly have to reenter data. Use the following procedure as a guideline for designing your database:

1. **Make a list of the things that you want your database to group and describe, and give the list a title.**

    Ask yourself, "What is this list about?" It may be a list of your friends, your clients, your photographs, the houses your real estate business is selling, or your collection of antique Popsicle sticks.

2. **Ask yourself, "What do all these things have in common that is important to include in a description?"**

    Imagine that your database is actually a list on paper and that you are now creating columns. What information would each column contain? What do you want to be able to recall about each thing? If it were a paper list of photographs, you may imagine having columns for Subject, Date, Type (print or slide), and Where Filed. And while you're at it — if you're going to be so nice and organized — you may even consider giving each photograph a serial number in a Serial Number column.

3. **Take a piece of paper (remember paper?) and a pencil (a digital printing instrument) and write down the list of imaginary column headings that you just created.**

    This is your list of field names. Guidelines for choosing fields appear after these steps.

4. **Consider setting up some standards for the way you will enter information in these fields.**

    Standards make finding things and generating reports easier. If you decide to have a field for Color, for instance, write down a list of the color names you will use. If you choose purple as a standard, then shun violet. If you refer to the same thing by two different names, you have to work twice as hard to find all the data again. If you can't think of any standards to begin with, wait until you begin entering data — some standards will occur to you then.

Here are some guidelines for choosing your fields:

✔ Provide a field for anything that you may want to search for or report on: date, manufacturer, color, price, vendor, nickname, neck size, and so on.

✔ Provide a field even if something may not exist in every record. For example, will you always enter the area code for phone numbers, or will you leave it off for local numbers? If you occasionally leave the area code off, it's a good idea to create a separate field for the area code.

✔ If you're not sure whether to separate things — such as a person's first name and last name — the safest solution is to use a separate field for anything that is separable. For example, the names of many people in your database may begin with Mr., Ms., or Mrs.; when you use your database, life is easier if this type of title is listed in a separate field.

✔ Provide a serial number field. This ensures that each record has something unique to identify it, in case the descriptions are otherwise identical. A serial number field also ensures that you can reconstruct the original order in which you entered the data (provided that the serial numbers are sequential).

Now you're ready to take the next step, which is to actually create your database document. Read on.

Creating Your Database

Works bends over backward to help you create your database. First of all, Works offers a few Tasks (inventories and recipes). Second, even when you start without benefit of a Task, Works guides you step by step through the initial database-creation procedure.

To start a fresh database from scratch, do the following:

1. **On the Task Launcher, click Programs.**

   The Task Launcher displays the Programs page.

    If you're already using the database program, you can skip these steps. Instead, just press Ctrl+N or click the New Document button on the far left of the toolbar. Either command opens a new database window and displays the Create Database dialog box.

2. **Click Works Database in the list of programs on the left.**

3. **Click Start A Blank Database.**

   The Create Database dialog box, as shown in Figure 20-3, leaps into view.

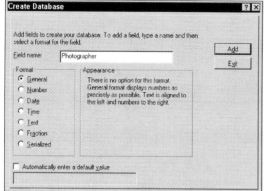

Figure 20-3:
The Create
Database
dialog box
creates one
field at a
time. You
specify
the field
and then
click Add.

Works is now ready for you to begin creating your database fields. Read on!

New fields of endeavor

When you create a new database (without using a Task), your principal job is entering fields. Here in New England, we wear our rubber boots and watch where we step when we enter fields. No such precautions are necessary for your database.

Here's the procedure for creating new fields by using the Create Database dialog box, as shown in Figure 20-3. Repeat this procedure for each field that you think you need. If you discover that you need to change an earlier field, it's easier to wait until you have all the fields done and then go back and make changes.

1. **Enter a name for a field in the Field Name box; the field name must be shorter than 15 characters.**

    For example, in Figure 20-3, I'm starting to create a database of photographs that I use in my business. The first field I want to create is for the photographer's name. (Don't bother to dress up your field name by adding a colon at the end of the name; Works will add one for you in Form view.)

2. **Choose a format for the field (in the Format area of the dialog box):**

    (These formats are very much like the number formats for spreadsheets. Refer to the section on formatting numbers in Chapter 19 of this book.)

    -   **General:** You can use the General format for most fields, but for a few special circumstances (such as fields containing dates, dollars, or fractions) you may want to choose something other than General. Formats can also be changed later, after you have the database built.

You can change the format even after data has been entered, but it's best to decide on the format before you enter your data.

- **Number:** Use this if you want dollar signs, commas, percentages, or scientific notation to appear without having to type them in. A list of examples appears when you choose Number; choose a format from this list. Number format also includes a TRUE/FALSE option for fields like the Color? field in Figures 20-1, 20-4, and 20-5 — type in **1** for TRUE or **0** for FALSE.

- **Date or Time:** Use these if you want the flexibility to change the way dates or times appear in your database. Use these, too, if you need to take advantage of Works' capability to subtract dates or times, such as calculating elapsed time.

- **Text:** Use this if you need to enter data with a mix of letters, numbers and symbols, or codes (like some zip codes) that begin with zero. (Otherwise, the zip code 01776 will turn into 1776.)

- **Fraction:** Use this, and Works automatically rounds off data entered in decimal form into mixed-number fractional form: 2.125 becomes $2\frac{1}{88}$. In the list that appears, choose what fraction you want the number rounded off to. This is useful for listing things in nonmetric dimensions, such as inches. Works will reduce a fraction like $\frac{4}{8}$ to $\frac{1}{2}$ unless you click the Do Not Reduce check box.

- **Serialized:** This is a very useful format when you want to create a serial number field (and most databases do need some unique number for each record, which a serial number provides). Choose this, and you won't even have to enter a number in this field; Works will do it for you automatically each time that you enter a new record. In the Next Value box, enter the number that you want the next record to start with. If you want the number to increment by something other than 1, enter that increment in the Increment box.

3. **Specify a default value for the field, if this field will often contain the same value.**

At the bottom of the Create Database dialog box, you can optionally specify a default value by clicking in the check box and typing the value in the box at the very bottom. A *default value* is data that appears in the field automatically whenever you create a new record, and it saves you time. For example, if most of the photographs in my photography database were taken by the same person — Johnson — I could make Johnson my default value. Then whenever I record a new photograph in my database, Johnson would automatically be typed in. (I could replace it with another name if the photographer were not Johnson.)

Fields that use default values behave oddly when you go to enter data into a record: *The default value will not appear until you enter data in at least one other field.*

4. **Click the A<u>d</u>d button (in the Create Database dialog box).**

   This action adds the field you just specified to the database, and it lets you move on to add the next field. (For instance, my next field in my photograph database is for the photo's subject.) Return to Step 1 if you want to add another field to your database. If you are done creating fields, click the Done button.

When you're done, your database is ready for you to add some data. But wait! Why does it look like a spreadsheet? Shouldn't it look more, um, database-y? Well, the odd thing about databases is that they can look like darned near anything. Read the following section for the details on viewing your database.

Is Works Help panel cluttering up your screen? Clear it from your window by clicking the X button in the upper-right corner of that panel.

Selecting a view

One reason that people sometimes get a bit confused when using a database program is that the program can show your data in different ways, called views. Unlike your Rolodex, which has real cards that you can touch, feel, and scribble notes on, computer databases are pretty ethereal. The computer can display the data in various ways, depending on what you tell it to do.

The Works database has a total of four views. Two of the four are views you will use most often for casually browsing through your records: the Form view and the List view, which are shown in Figures 20-4 and 20-5. Works also has a special Form Design view, which lets you design the page you see in Form view, specifying where each field appears. The fourth view is the Report view, which sounds useful but is a bit too weird for most people to use easily. Chapter 23 guides you in the basics of using the Report view. Some tasks can be done only in one view or another; if you find that you can't do a particular task, consider changing views. For example, you can add fields only while in List view or Form Design view. This book will tell you whether something can be done only in certain views.

Here's what the different views do for you:

✔ **Form view** lets you enter and look at data as if it were entered on a paper form. This view shows data the way you see it on your Rolodex: one record at a time. Figure 20-4 shows a database in Form view. The field names (Photographer, Subject, Serial Number, Width, Height, and Color?) are followed by blank lines on which data is entered. By using Form Design view, you can position your fields anywhere on the Form view page by simply dragging them.

✔ **List view** looks like a pad of lined paper on which you copied all the information from your Rolodex, using columns for the fields of, say, Name, Address, and Phone Number. You can see several records at once. Figure 20-5 shows the same database as Figure 20-4, but in List view. In this view, your database is a big spreadsheet-like table with rows and columns. The rows, which are numbered along the left side, are individual records. (Blank rows are records in which you haven't entered data yet.) The columns are your fields.

✔ **Form Design view** lets you edit the Form view. The Form Design view provides features that let you move, resize, reformat, or otherwise change how the fields will look in Form view. You can also add text, such as headings or explanations, or even add illustrations to your forms by using Form Design view.

✔ **Report view** lets you create printed reports — but only if you are technically inclined. Works gives you a ReportCreator tool that's much easier to use and gives most people what they need.

Figure 20-4: My database for cataloging photographs, in Form view, showing record 6.

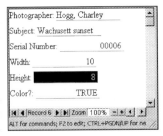

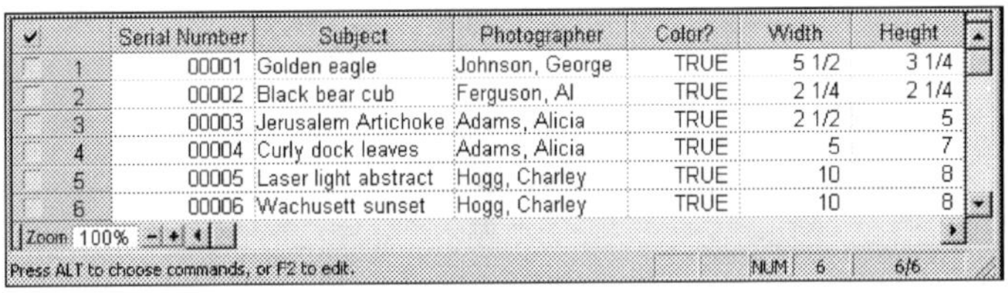

Figure 20-5: Same database as Figure 20-4, but in List view, showing records 1-6.

	Serial Number	Subject	Photographer	Color?	Width	Height
1	00001	Golden eagle	Johnson, George	TRUE	5 1/2	3 1/4
2	00002	Black bear cub	Ferguson, Al	TRUE	2 1/4	2 1/4
3	00003	Jerusalem Artichoke	Adams, Alicia	TRUE	2 1/2	5
4	00004	Curly dock leaves	Adams, Alicia	TRUE	5	7
5	00005	Laser light abstract	Hogg, Charley	TRUE	10	8
6	00006	Wachusett sunset	Hogg, Charley	TRUE	10	8

To switch between views, you can do any of the following:

✔ Click the List view, Form view, or Form Design button on the toolbar. Each button is located to the right of the **B/U** (**Bold**/*Italic*/Underline) buttons (refer to Figure 20-2).

✔ Press the F9 key to go to Form view.

✔ Press Shift+F9 to go to List view.

✔ Press Ctrl+F9 to go to Form Design view.

✔ Choose View⇨List (or View⇨Form, or View ⇨Form Design) from the menu bar.

Moving and resizing fields

If you don't like the position or size of your fields in either Form view or List view, changes are a simple matter. Just remember the following:

✔ To change the size or position of your fields in Form view, you must use Form Design view.

✔ In List view, you can make changes right there; you don't need to change views.

Moving fields in Form Design view

To move the position of a field as you see it in Form or Form Design view, do the following:

1. **Switch to Form Design view, if you're not there already.**

   To switch to Form Design view, click the Form Design button on the toolbar, or choose View⇨Form Design from the menu bar, or press Ctrl+F9.

2. **Click and drag the field where you want it.**

   To move a bunch of fields at once, select them first. One easy way to select a group of fields is to hold down the Ctrl button and click each field that you want to move. Release the Ctrl key, and then click and drag the whole lot of them.

Moving fields in List view

To move a field (column) in List view, do this:

1. **Click the top cell of the column — the one with the field name in it.**

   This action selects the field/column.

2. **Click the top cell of the column and drag the column to the left or the right.**

   The dark vertical line that appears between columns indicates where the column will be placed when you release the mouse button.

Resizing fields in Form Design view

If a field is too small to display your data (as the field appears in Form or Form Design view), you can resize the field. (You may have to move adjoining fields to allow for the change in size.)

1. **Switch to Form Design view, if you're not there already.**

   To switch to Form Design view, click the Form Design button on the toolbar, or choose View⇨Form Design from the menu bar, or press Ctrl+F9.

2. **Click the underlined area to the right of the field name.**

   The field is highlighted, and three tiny, gray squares (called handles) appear in the highlight. See Figure 20-6 for a blown-up view of the highlighted area.

Figure 20-6:
Dragging
handles
helps you
get a handle
on field size.

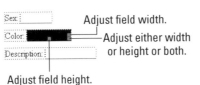

3. **Adjust the field size by dragging the handles.**

   To make a field wider, drag the handle at the center of the right edge to the right. To make the field higher (to add lines), drag the handle at the center of the bottom edge down. The handle at the corner lets you drag both width and height at the same time.

   To adjust field size more precisely, click the underlined area next to the field name; then choose Format⇨Field Size to open the Field Size dialog box. Enter a width (how many characters) and a height (how many rows) for the data entry.

Resizing fields in List view

To resize a field (change column width) in List view, you can either drag a column edge or use the Field Width dialog box:

✔ To change the width of the column by dragging, move your cursor to the gray row at the top of the columns, where the field names are. In this row, slowly move your mouse pointer across the right-hand edge of the column that you want to change. When the pointer changes to a double-headed-arrow-sort-of-deal with the word *Adjust* attached, click and drag the column edge left or right.

✔ To set the width of a column more precisely, use the Field Width dialog box. First click any cell in that column to select the column. Then choose Format➪Field Width from the menu bar. When the Field Width dialog box appears, type a number slightly larger than the maximum number of characters you expect for data in this field and press the Enter key.

To make your field size just large enough to hold the longest entry in your database, double-click the field name (in the top cell of the column).

Navigating in Different Views

An important part of your basic database training is navigation. You don't want your metaphoric half-tracks wandering all over your metaphoric terrain. Here's how to get around with minimal casualties and good gas mileage.

If you've applied a filter, some records will be hidden as you navigate your database. To see them all, choose Record➪Show➪1 All Records from the menu bar. See Chapter 22 for more information on using filters.

Navigating in Form or Form Design view

In Form or Form Design view, you're looking at a representation of a page that is 8½ x 11 inches, unless you've fooled with the Page Setup commands. You can look at any part of the page or type anywhere on the page.

To scroll around vertically or horizontally, use the scroll bars on the right side and bottom of the document window (thumb through Chapter 2 if you don't recall how to use scroll bars).

To move around vertically on the page, you can also use the navigation keys (arrows, Home, End, Page Up, and Page Down).

The dashed lines indicate page boundaries, so you need to keep your fields above and to the left of them.

To advance from one field to the next, press the Tab key. Press Shift+Tab to move in the opposite direction.

To move between records, use one of these methods:

✔ To advance to the next record, press the Tab key after the last entry on the page (record).

✔ Another way to advance one record is to press Ctrl+Page Down. To go backward, press Ctrl+Page Up.

✔ Yet another way to advance or go back one record is to click the inner left or right arrow in the gadget in the bottom-left border of your document window:

✔ To go to the first or last record in your database, click the outer left or right arrow in that gadget.

✔ Or, to go to the first record, press Ctrl+Home; to go to the last record, press Ctrl+End.

Navigating in List view

Navigating a database in List view is almost exactly like navigating a spreadsheet, so if you know how to do that, you're in Fat City. If not, here's the scoop.

To look around your database in List view, use the scroll bars on the right side and bottom of the document window (head over to Chapter 2 if you don't recall how to use scroll bars). To see more fields, use the horizontal scroll bar at the bottom of the window; to see more records, use the vertical scroll bar along the right side of the window.

A cell represents a specific record's data for a specific field. To do anything to a cell (the intersection of a row and column), simply click that cell. (Notice that your mouse cursor is a big, fat plus sign in the database program, as it is in the spreadsheet program.) Around the cell appears a rectangle that Microsoft calls the highlight. This highlight indicates the "active" cell: the one you're about to type in, edit, format, or otherwise muck around with.

After you have clicked a cell, the Tab key, Shift+Tab, and the navigation keys on your keyboard will also move the active cell, just as they do in the Works spreadsheet program. Check out the discussion of moving from cell to cell in Chapter 17.

Entering Data

To enter data into your database, you generally fill out one record at a time, starting with the first record. In a nutshell, the procedure is just to click a cell (List view) or click in a field (Form view) and type.

Use any of the techniques mentioned in the section, "Navigating in Different Views," earlier in this chapter, to move from one field or record to the next. A popular method is to use the Tab key to advance from one field to the next (press Shift+Tab to go backward). If you press Tab at the end of one record, you automatically move to the first field of the next record.

Following are a few tips for entering data:

- ✔ To put a new record into your database, just add it at the end: In Form view, press Ctrl+End; in List view, press Ctrl+End and then Tab.

- ✔ When you use other-than-General formatting for a field, the appearance of the data you enter may change after you enter it. This procedure can be a convenience for data entry. For example, if you choose a Date format of the form *January 5, 1996,* you can enter the date as 1/5/96, but Works will still display it as January 5, 1996.

- ✔ For fields formatted as TRUE/FALSE fields, you can either type the number **1** for True or **0** for False, or you can type the words **TRUE** or **FALSE**.

- ✔ If the symbol ####### appears after you enter some data, the field is not wide enough to display the data. Make it wider! (A quick fix is to double-click the field name in the top cell of the column, if you're in List view. See the section, "Moving and resizing fields," earlier in this chapter.)

Creating an Example Database

It's show time! Here's an example of how to create a database. (The example is a very simple, five-field database for cataloging photographs.) The Rule of This Design, as dictated by its omnipotent creator (me), is that there shall be six fields: Photographer, Subject, Serial Number, Width, Height, and Color?.

The standards for the data are as follows:

- ✔ The Photographer field contains the surname followed by a comma and then the first name.
- ✔ The Subject field contains a short description of what's in the photo.
- ✔ The Width and Height fields give the dimension in whole inches and in one-eighth ($\frac{1}{8}$) fractions of an inch.
- ✔ The Color? field is a TRUE/FALSE field indicating whether the photo is in color (TRUE) or black and white (FALSE).

To be on the safe side, I would use a separate field for the first and last name of the photographer, but I'm feeling reckless. To create this example database, follow these steps:

1. **To start a new database document, start the Task Launcher and click Programs; then, click the Works Database program and click Start a Blank Database.**

2. **A First-Time Help dialog box may appear; if it does, click the To Create a New Database button.**

   The Create Database dialog box arises.

3. **Type** Photographer **into the Field Name box and click the Add button (do *not* press the Enter key).**

   You use the General format for this example, so there's no need to change the format. A new, blank field form appears in the Create Database dialog box.

4. **Type** Subject **into the Field Name box and click the Add button.**

5. **Type** Serial **into the Field Name box. In the Format area, choose Serialized. Click the Add button.**

6. **Type** Width **into the Field name box. In the Format area, choose Fraction. In the Appearance box, choose ⅛. Click the Add button.**

7. **Type** Height **into the Field name box. In the Format area, choose Fraction. In the Appearance box, choose ⅛. Click the Add button.**

8. **Type** Color? **into the Field name box. In the Format area, choose Number. In the Appearance box, scroll to the bottom and choose True/False. Click the Add button and then click the Done button.**

Your database is created! Well, the structure of it, at least. But your database still needs some data.

Now start entering data. You can do this in either List view (which is what you are looking at) or Form view. Simply click a cell (in List view) or a field (in Form view) and type. Or you can use the Tab key to advance to the next field.

Printing Your Database

Printing databases is pretty much like printing anything else in Works, so for the general details, read through Chapter 4. Here are a couple of peculiarities about printing databases, however:

✔ When you print in Form view, you normally print one record on a page. If your records are small, you may prefer to combine them on a page. To do so, choose File➪Page Setup to get a Page Setup dialog box. Click the Other Options card in this box, and then click the Page Breaks Between Records check box to clear the check mark from it. Adjust the spacing between records by clicking the up/down arrows in the Space Between Records box.

✔ When you print in List view, you normally see just data, no headings. You can have the field and record headings print out if you choose. You can also have gridlines printed. Choose File➪Page Setup to get a Page Setup dialog box. Click the Other Options card in this box. Click the appropriate check box — the one marked Print Gridlines or the one marked Print Record and Field Labels (or both).

✔ To force a page break at a particular point in a List view of records, first select the row you want at the top of the next page (click the numbered gray button at the leftmost end of that row). Then choose Format➪ Insert Page Break.

✔ To force a page break between columns in a List view, first select the column you want on the next page (click the gray button with the field name at the top of the column). Then choose Format➪Insert Page Break.

✔ To print only certain records, you first have to mark them: Switch to List view and select the check box in the leftmost column of each row that you want to print. Choose Record➪Show➪2 Marked Records from the menu bar and then print as Chapter 4 describes. Read more about marking and hiding records in Chapter 22.

Saving Your Work

Databases are in dire need of salvation — and yours is no exception. I urge you to save your work promptly because I don't want to be accused of making a "salvator" dally. What I mean to say (having perhaps exercised a little too much artistic license) is that you need to save your database document as a file, regularly, so that you don't lose data. (If you were Salvador Dali, I suppose you would have to save to a floppy disk.)

Saving your database document is very much like saving any other Works document: Choose File➪Save, or press Ctrl+S, or click the toolbar button with the diskette icon (for more information, see Chapter 2). For basic information on files and disks, read through Chapter 1. For more on Salvador Dali, head on down to your local library.

Chapter 21

Making Changes in Your Database

In This Chapter

▶ Editing in the formula bar

▶ Inserting and removing fields

▶ Adding, inserting, and deleting records

▶ Copying and moving data

▶ Fooling around with formats

*A*ll is flux, and before you can say *tempus fugit,* you may need to make some changes to your database: Your friends move, so you have to change your address database; your customers grow successful (thanks to you) and sprout new divisions, so you have to create a Division field in your customer database; or maybe you just decide to make your database a bit more readable. Here's how to keep your database up to date and looking snazzy!

Editing Data and Field Names

When you need to change some data or a field name in your database, use the formula bar, which is present in all views. (See Chapters 20 and 22 if you're unfamiliar with database views.) The formula bar works just the same as the formula bar in the Works spreadsheet program, in case you're familiar with that program. You can see the formula bar located just under the toolbar in Figure 21-1.

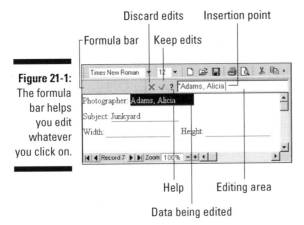

Discard edits   Insertion point

Formula bar   Keep edits

Figure 21-1:
The formula
bar helps
you edit
whatever
you click on.

Help   Editing area

Data being edited

The following list details how to edit data or field names using the various views. (Remember, to switch to a view, choose View and then List, Form, or Form Design from the drop-down menu.)

- ✔ **To edit data in either List or Form view:** Click the data; then click in the text box on the formula bar.

- ✔ **To edit a field name in a form:** Switch to Form Design view, click the field name, and then click in the text box on the formula bar. (You can't edit field names in Form view, only in Form Design view.)

- ✔ **To edit a field name in List view:** Click anywhere in the field's column. Then choose Format⇨Field from the menu bar. Edit the field name in the Format dialog box that appears and then click the OK button.

The formula bar works like this:

1. **When you click a cell, Works copies the data value or field name into the white text box of the formula bar.**

2. **When you click in the text box on the formula bar, you can edit the data value or field name.**

   (Details of editing follow this numbered list.)

3. **When you're done, either click the check mark button on the formula bar or just press the Enter key.**

   The new, edited stuff replaces the old stuff in the database.

The editing process works like this: Use the insertion point — the vertical line that you also see in the Works word processor (refer to Figure 21-1) — to edit text and data. The insertion point is where characters appear when you type and where they vanish when you backspace or delete.

Surviving (or using) the Protection racket

If you find that Works complains when you try to edit data, the complaint probably arises because the field that you're working in is protected against data changes. This situation happens when you use certain tasks. Here's what to do to defeat this protection scheme:

1. Switch to either List view or Form Design view.

2. Click the field you want to change.

3. Choose Format➪Protection from the menu bar to open the Format Protection dialog box.

4. Click the Protect Field check box to clear the check mark.

5. Click OK.

On the other hand, you may want to use this Protection racket yourself. By protecting a field, you can help avoid accidental changes to important data. This protection is especially valuable if you are working with another person who may not realize how important some data value is. To protect a field, you follow the same four steps just listed, only you turn the check mark on in Step 4 by clicking the Protect Field check box.

To move the insertion point, move your mouse pointer over the text box on the formula bar; doing so causes the pointer to change to an I-beam shape. Position that I-beam where you want to type or delete something and then click. The insertion point jumps there. When you type, the characters are inserted at the insertion point. When you press the Backspace key, the character before the insertion point gets deleted. Press the Delete key, and the character after the insertion point gets vaporized.

If the data you're editing is long, you may not be able to click near the end of that data. In that case, click where you can and use the navigation keys (left- or right-arrow keys, Home, or End) to move the insertion point.

The X on the formula bar is the "whoops" button. Clicking this X has the same result as pressing the Esc key. Either one abandons your edits and leaves whatever you were editing in its original state.

Clicking the check mark has the same result as pressing the Enter key. Either one enters the contents of the formula bar into the cell.

In List view, just as in spreadsheets, you don't need the formula bar to edit data. You can edit data right in its cell: Just double-click the cell, and the insertion point that you need for editing appears in the cell.

Conducting Field Exercises

Strategically speaking, there is a time to advance upon a field and a time to retreat from a field. This stratagem is general knowledge (known by generals).

Likewise, in database work, there's a time to add fields and a time to remove them. Well, no problem (as certain teenagers and hotel personnel are tiresomely fond of saying instead of, "You're welcome"). The following few sections detail how to add or remove a field.

Adding new fields

You can add new fields in either the List view or the Form Design view. The advantage of using List view is that the process is very simple. The advantage of using Form Design view is that after you add a field, you are then conveniently in the correct view for positioning or sizing the field. The choice is yours!

Adding new fields in List view

In List view, the fields are columns. New fields are columns that go to the right or left of existing columns. Follow these steps to create new fields in List view:

1. **Click in the column next to which you want to add a new column.**

2. **Choose Record⇨Insert Field from the menu bar; then choose 1 Before (to put a new field to the left of your chosen column) or choose 2 After (to put a new field to the right of your chosen column).**

   An Insert Field dialog box graces your screen, bearing a familiar face: It looks and works just like the Create Database dialog box that you use when you create a database. See Chapter 20 if you need instructions on how to use this dialog box.

3. **Type in a name for the field (and a special format if you need it) and click the Add button.**

4. **For additional fields, repeat Step 3.**

5. **When you're done adding fields, click the Done button in the Insert Field dialog box.**

Adding new fields in Form Design view

Here's how to add fields in Form Design view:

1. **Right-click where you want the field to appear.**

   Don't add a field to the right or below any dashed line that you see at the edges of the window, unless you don't want the field to print when you print this form. That dashed line is the page margin area, which is visible when your Works window is sufficiently large.

   A set of coordinates tells you where you are on the page, if you care. Look in the upper-left corner of the Works window, just under the font box in the text bar. The number after X gives the horizontal position from the left edge of the page; the number after Y gives the vertical position from the bottom edge.

2. **Choose Insert Field from the menu that appears.**

   The Insert Field dialog box shows up again (you've seen this one before).

3. **Type in a field name (and a special format if you need it) and click the OK button.**

   Your new field appears on the form.

Removing fields

Removing a field is so easy it's a little scary. When you remove a field, you also remove all the data that's in it — data that may represent a lot of work on somebody's part. But if removing a field, along with all its data, is what you really intend to do, go for it. If you think that you may want to access the field and its data again sometime, do this: Before you delete the field, save your unmodified database with a new name, using the File↔Save As command.

Removing a field in List view is a little safer than removing a field in Form Design view because you can undo the deletion if you accidentally delete the wrong field. For no particularly good reason that I can think of, Works allows you to undo a deletion (by pressing Ctrl+Z) in List view but not in Form Design view.

Here's how to remove a field in both views:

✔ **Form Design view:** Just click the field name and choose Edit↔Delete Selection from the menu bar. A warning box appears on the scene to ask whether you want to Delete this field and all of its contents? and to warn that you won't be able to undo this delete. If you really do want to delete the field, click the OK button.

✔ **List view:** First, click anywhere in that field's column; then choose Record↔Delete Field from the menu bar. A warning box appears, asking whether you in fact want to Permanently delete this information?. If you really do want to delete the field, click the OK button.

Zap! It's dead, Jim.

Adding, Inserting, and Deleting Records

Many unprincipled people have wished, over the years, that they had the ability to add or delete certain records in their files. If only they knew how easily you can add or delete records when you've got a Works database.

Adding a record

When you've acquired yet another antique Popsicle stick for your collection, you will want to add another record to your Popsicle stick database. The easiest way to add a record is to add it to the end of your database. To get to a blank record at the end, use these commands:

✔ In Form view, press Ctrl+End.

✔ In List view, press Ctrl+End and then press the Tab key.

A record is an entire page or row of related data, not just a datum. (If you are of the pre-compact disc — or vinyl — generation, think of these records as albums, not singles.)

Inserting or deleting a record

To add a record at a particular point in your database, you insert it. First, indicate to Works where you want to insert the new record. In Form view, just move to that record. In List view, click that row. Then do the following:

✔ **To insert a record:** Choose Record⇨Insert Record from the menu bar. Or click the Insert Record button. (If you're uncertain which button that is, slowly move your mouse pointer across the buttons and read the labels that pop up.) A blank record appears for you to fill in.

✔ **To delete a record:** Choose Record⇨Delete Record from the menu bar. The record is then deleted, and you are left gazing upon the next higher record in the database.

All the records following the one you inserted or deleted are renumbered.

You can alternatively delete just the contents of a record rather than the record itself. This trick is useful if you are replacing an item listed in your database (say, a deceased computer in your inventory). In List view, click the row number (in the gray area on the left) to highlight the entire row — or highlight just as much as you want to delete — and then press the Delete key. The record is now blank (except for serialized fields), and you can enter new data into it.

Copying and Moving Data

Years ago, in school exams, the consequences of copying data were severe. That's too bad because copying today is an essential skill for entering data into databases. (So there, Mr. Schweinkopf!) Copying is a great time saver and helps enforce your rules for consistent data, such as always using the word purple and not violet in your Color field.

In any database, many records may have exactly the same data. In a pediatrician's medical database, the term *otitis media* (middle ear infection) would sum up the better part of a week's work. Kids get ear infections the way lawns get dandelions. It's surprising that there aren't fast-food-style drive-through kids' ear exam and dispensary outlets. ("Stick your head in the clown's mouth, Junior; we'll get a toy at the window with our antibiotics.")

Anyway, what a boon to the bored pediatrician-in-a-box to be able to just copy the Diagnosis field data from one patient-encounter record to another, rather than retype it. Copying prevents typos, too. Nine out of ten doctors recommend copying.

Copying with the Clipboard

To copy data from one record to another, switch to List view (choose View⇨ List or press Shift+F9) and use the Windows copy and paste functions described in Chapter 3. To copy a single piece of data, click the cell that you want to copy and press Ctrl+C. Then click the cell where you want a copy and press Ctrl+V.

You can also make multiple copies of that single cell (as you may need if you get a busload of kids at your Doc-in-the-Box, all with *otitis media*). Copy the cell with Ctrl+C; then drag down across the rows (records) where you want copies to highlight those cells. Then press Ctrl+V. Each cell gets a copy of the original cell.

You can also copy data from multiple fields (such as the date and the diagnosis fields) at once, as long as the two fields are in adjoining columns. Highlight any group of cells in the row that you want to copy and press Ctrl+C. Then click the leftmost cell where you want to paste a copy and press Ctrl+V. To paste copies in multiple rows, highlight the leftmost cells in several rows before pressing Ctrl+V.

Copying and moving by dragging

Another way to move or copy data is by dragging — preferably in List view. To copy data by dragging it, first click it. Then position your mouse cursor anywhere on the black outline around the selected data until a tiny tag — Drag — appears. To copy, hold down the Ctrl key, and then click and drag. A black rectangle follows you as you move to any other record or field. To move data, do the same thing without the Ctrl key.

List view is best for dragging copies because you can drag between records (rows). In Form view, you can't drag between records.

Applying and Changing Formats

Just as your mother said, appearances are important. You can do a number of things to change the way your field names and data appear in a Works database. The formats you can change are as follows:

- ✔ **Field:** How Works interprets and displays your data: as a number, time, or text.
- ✔ **Alignment:** Whether data or a field name is left- or right-justified, or centered, for example.
- ✔ **Font:** What typeface and style the data or field name appears in.
- ✔ **Border:** For borders around data or field names.
- ✔ **Shading:** To apply a background color or shade to data or field names.

You set fonts, borders, and shading independently for List view and Form view. Formats you apply in one view do not apply to the other view. For instance, a tasteful magenta shading of a field in List view does not create a magenta background in Form (or Form Design) view. But field and alignment formats do apply to all views, regardless of which view you use to choose them.

To change any of the previously listed formats, do the following:

1. **Choose either List view or Form Design view.**

   To format the appearance of a field name (as opposed to data in a field), choose Form Design view.

2. **Click in a field to select that field (or select several fields by highlighting them).**

   In Form Design view, you can format either the data area (the underlined part of a field) or the field name area. Click either area to format it. To change the Field formatting (formatting of data as text, numbers, or time), click the data area.

3. **Choose Format from the menu bar; then choose Field, Alignment, Font, Border, or Shading.**

   The Format dialog box (as shown in Figure 21-2) appears, displaying the tab that matches the choice you make in this step.

Figure 21-2:
The Format
dialog box,
where
appearance
is every-
thing, has
multiple
tabs for
different
kinds of
appear-
ances.

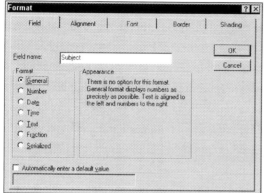

Here is the executive summary of what you can accomplish in each tab of the
Format dialog box:

✔ **The Field tab** lets you specify the same kind of formatting that you specified when you first created the field, telling Works to display the value
as a date, a fraction, or a dollar amount, for example. Changes to Field
formats affect all views.

If you change a field from General or Text to a Date or Time format, you
may have to reenter the data in that field.

✔ **The Alignment tab** enables you to click Left, Right, or Center, respectively, to left-justify, right-justify, or center text in its field. Choosing
General aligns text to the left and numbers to the right. If you are using
List view, you can choose to make text wrap around within a cell in List
view by selecting the Wrap Text check box. If, in List view, your rows are
higher than a single character height, you can also align text vertically:
Click Top, Center, or Bottom.

✔ **The Font tab** works just as it does elsewhere in Works. Check out
Chapter 3 for more on formatting.

✔ **The Border tab** lets you put an outline around a field or data for empha-
sis, if you like. Click a line style from the list presented. Click the top line-
style box (with no line in it) to turn off a border.

✔ **The Shading tab** lets you apply a background color or pattern. Choose a
pattern from the Pattern box; patterns are made up of two colors, given
by your selection of foreground and background colors. Unless you have
a color printer or don't intend to print at all, sticking to Auto for both
colors is best.

When you print in Form view, having a lot of space between fields on the same line can be annoying. For instance, when you print address labels, you probably don't want a big gap between the city and the state. When you design the form, however, you have to use a City field that's wide enough for, say, "Lake Memphremagog," which pushes your State field way over to the right. When you print, if the city's name in a given record is short, like Big Sky, Montana, a lot of open space appears before Montana. (As it does in real life, come to think of it.) Works provides a trick to get rid of this excess space during printing. Using Form Design view, click either the field name or data area of the field that is on the right (the State field, for instance). Choose Format⇨Alignment, click the Alignment tab, and then select the Slide to Left check box. Use print preview to check the result.

Chapter 22

Finding and Filtering Your Data

*W*hen interrogating an enemy prisoner, you expect the prisoner to be reluctant to impart information. When interrogating a database, you have the opposite problem: The database offers too much information — volunteering, as it were, name, rank, serial number, birth date, sock size, and mother's middle name, a thousand times over. Finding out just one piece of data becomes tremendously difficult.

You have three ways to solve this problem and find the data that you're looking for with the Works Database:

✔ **Find:** The simplest solution, if you're looking for those records that contain one particular piece of data (such as the word *tubular*), is to have the database find records containing that specific word, number, or phrase.

✔ **Filter:** If you're looking for the records that contain some combination of information in specific fields (such as *tubular* in the Description field and the number 90210 in the zip code field), you apply a filter.

✔ **Sort:** If you just need an ordered list — ordered alphabetically or numerically by the contents of a particular field — you perform a sort. For information on sorting, see Chapter 23.

If you apply a filter or a find, Works shows you the records that you requested and hides the rest. To see all the records again, choose Record➪Show➪ 1 All Records.

So — those are all the fundamentals you need to know. Now, for the details, read on!

Finding Specific Data

To locate records that contain a specific word, phrase, or number, the simplest thing you can do is to use the Find command. (The Find command is very much like the Find commands in the word processor or spreadsheet, in case you're familiar with those.)

You can tell Works to find either the first instance of that word, phrase, or number, or to show you all instances. Here's how to do it:

1. **Press Ctrl+Home (which takes you to the top of the document) so that Works begins its search with the first record of the database.**

   This precaution ensures that you don't accidentally skip over any records.

2. **Choose Edit⇨Find from the menu bar (or press Ctrl+F).**

   A small but helpful Find dialog box appears.

3. **Type the word, number, or phrase that you're searching for in Find What box.**

   Type only as much as you remember or need. To find copy paper, printer paper, or any kind of paper, type **paper**. (On the other hand, don't type too little: *pa* will also find padding and packing material if those words are hanging out in your database. Also, possibly your long-lost father.)

   The question mark (?) symbol can substitute for a single character and help you find a broad range of records. When searching for zip codes, for example, the number 0792? will find all the zip codes beginning with 0792.

   The asterisk symbol (*) can substitute for one or more characters as long as the * is preceded by at least one other character. For example, *M*.* will find Mr., Mrs., and Ms. (but not Miss — because this particular search specifies that a period must come at the end).

4. **To find all records that contain your word, phrase, or number, click All Records in the Match area of the Find dialog box. To find just the next record, click Next Record.**

5. **Click the OK button.**

If you choose to find All Records in Step 4, Works shows you only those records that meet your search text criterion and hides the others. When you're done reviewing or printing the results, choose Record⇨Show⇨ 1 All Records to reveal all the records in your database again.

Using Selected Records: Marking and Hiding

Do you have certain records that you just don't want to appear on your print-out, on your screen, or in your database report? Well, do as millions do when the auditor comes to call: Hide those records! (Not that I recommend hiding any particular records; auditors know about databases, too!) Works uses three concepts to help you hide or display only the records that you want:

- ✔ **Hiding** is a way to make records invisible in List or Form view, in print-outs, or in reports.
- ✔ **Showing** is the opposite of hiding.
- ✔ **Marking** is a convenient way to identify a group of records for hiding or showing.

To hide an individual record, first either click the record in List view or move to it in Form view; then choose Record➪Hide Record from the menu bar. To show hidden records, choose Record➪Show➪4 Hidden Records.

To hide several records, mark them first: In List view, select the check box in the leftmost column (the marking column) of each row that you want to hide. (To mark a group that's all together, select the top record's check box; then drag down the marking column.) Then, to hide those marked records, choose Record➪Show➪3 Unmarked Records from the menu bar. You can use marking the opposite way, too: to show selected records. Mark the records that you want to show by using the method described in the preceding paragraph. Then choose Record➪Show➪2 Marked Records from the menu bar.

To show all records — hidden, marked, or otherwise — choose Record➪Show➪1 All Records from the menu bar.

To clear all marks, go to List view and click the check mark (thereby clearing it) at the very top of the marking column.

Filtering Your Data

The Find command is a nice, simple way to find records containing a particular word or number. Sometimes, however, you need to find records with certain combinations of data in various fields, such as all the members of your organization who have more than two kids and who live out of town. Or maybe you want to find members who have contributed $100 or more, in the hope of pressing them for another contribution.

Understanding criteria (comparisons)

The trick to applying a filter is figuring out how to describe the data that you're looking for. Having the capability to write regular sentences, such as, "Show me all the records for families with more than two kids and who live out of town," would be nice. It would be nice if we could all go to Barbados for the winter, too, but that's not going to happen any time soon, either. Filters in Works are a little bit like sentences, but not like sentences that your sixth-grade English teacher would approve of. (Excuse me: " . . . of which your sixth-grade English teacher would approve.")

To construct the description of what records you want, you need three pieces of information:

✔ **The field name:** This is the field where you want Works to look. For example, you can tell Works to search the No. Of Children field — if you had such a field and wanted to find families based on the number of children they have.

✔ **The "comparison":** This is the way to test the data in the field. For example, you can test that the data in the No. Of Children field

is greater than, less than, or equal to some value that you enter.

✔ **The "compare to" value:** This is what you want Works to compare the data to — such as *2* for two kids.

For a single criterion, you enter these three pieces of information in the top, three-part line of the Filter dialog box (see Figure 22-1). The Field Name and Comparison boxes enable you to choose from drop-down lists that are available when you click the down arrow adjoining those text boxes.

Some other examples of single-criterion filters follow:

✔ The entry in a No. Of Children field *is equal to* 2.

✔ The entry in a Description field *contains the word* Mikado.

✔ The entry in a Town field *is not* Mudville.

✔ The entry in an Age field *is greater than or equal to* 21.

To find these big givers, you need to filter your data — strain out all the poor of purse. When Works filters your data, Works goes through your database, record by record, comparing what's in those records to certain criteria that you've given it and hiding from view those records that don't meet the criteria. Did Widow Jones give only $50 from her pension? If you are filtering for an amount of $100 or more in your Contributions field, Works hides Mrs. Jones' proud record. (Sorry, there is no filtering for moral character.)

You can create a variety of different filters, each with its own name. Then, when you need one, you can apply it (make it take effect) by name. (See the section, "Applying filters," later in this chapter.) Applying a filter hides records that don't match your criteria, and shows those records that do match.

Here's how to perform a single-criterion filter, step by step. Performing a single-criterion filter is like building a sentence out of three parts; when you're all done, you can read the three parts in sequence, and the parts read like a sentence. Just follow these steps:

1. **Choose Tools⟷Filters from the menu bar.**

   (If the First-Time Help dialog box appears, just click OK.)

   If you have not previously created any filters for this database, the tiny Filter Name dialog box pops up and asks you to type a name for your new filter. Type a name of 15 characters or less, and then click the OK button. Make the name as descriptive as you can; if you create several filters, the name will help you remember what the filter does later.

   The Filter dialog box, as shown in Figure 22-1, now takes up residence on your screen.

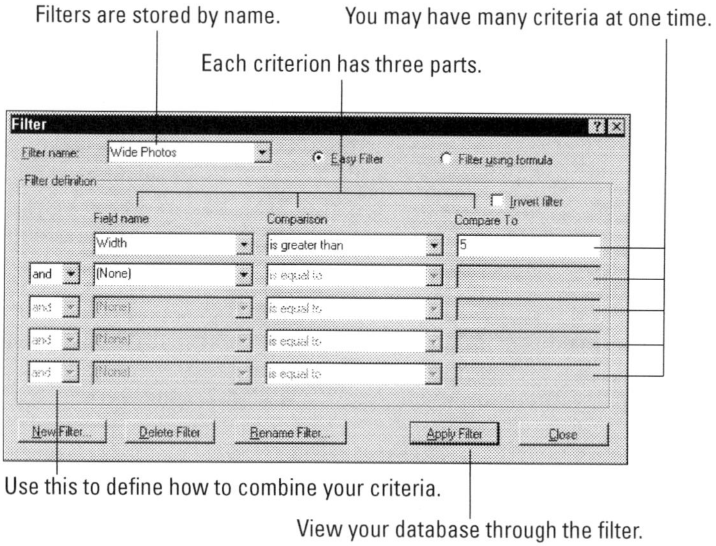

Filters are stored by name.   You may have many criteria at one time.

Each criterion has three parts.

Figure 22-1:
Telling
Works your
criteria for
picking out
certain
records.

Use this to define how to combine your criteria.

View your database through the filter.

   If you have previously created filters, the name of your most recent creation appears in the Filter Name box, and the filter criteria are displayed. You can click the down arrow adjoining the filter name to choose from previous filters. To create a new filter, click the New Filter button in the dialog box and enter a filter name in the Filter Name dialog box that pops up.

2. **Choose a field: Click the down-arrow button next to the box marked Field Name; then click any field name in the list that drops down.**

   Works has tentatively chosen the first field name in your database, and that field name is initially displayed here. Pick whatever field you need Works to search through.

3. **Choose how to compare: Click the down-arrow button next to the box marked Comparison; then click any comparison in the list that drops down.**

   Read the sidebar, "Understanding criteria (comparisons)," elsewhere in this chapter, if what is going on here seems mysterious to you. Works initially chooses *equal to* as your comparison only because *equal to* is the first comparison in the list. Choose any comparison that you like.

   For purposes of comparison:

   - Later dates are greater than earlier dates.

   - Later times are greater than earlier times.

   - Letters that fall later in the alphabet are greater than earlier ones.

4. **Choose a value for the comparison: Click the box marked Compare To and type in a word, phrase, or number.**

   Works doesn't take note of capitalization. The words *Potato* and *potato* are identical as far as Works is concerned.

   You can use the question mark and asterisk (? and *) characters just as you do in a Find command, if you like. (See the section, "Finding Specific Data," earlier in this chapter.)

   When you're done, read across the line that you just entered in the Filter dialog box and combine the three parts of the criterion into a crude sentence, such as "Width . . . is greater than . . . 5." This is your criterion; Works can then find those records in which the Width field contains a number greater than 5.

5. **Press the Enter key or click the Apply Filter button to create the filter and execute the filtering.**

   If you're not in List view at this point, switch to it (press Shift+F9 if you're in Form view). Seeing what's going on is just easier if you're in List view.

   You're done! In List view, you see only those records that meet your criterion. (Your filter has automatically been applied to your data.)

The records that don't meet your criterion are hidden to get them out of your way. When you're done looking over your success, choose Record⇨Show⇨ 1 All Records to make the other records reappear.

Managing Filters

Creating a filter takes a bit of work; so, for your future convenience, Works saves your filters, storing all that criterion stuff you masterfully created in the Filter dialog box. Works saves each filter under the name that you give it.

The reasons that Works saves filters are:

- ✔ You can fool around with them until they're correct.
- ✔ You can easily switch from one to the other, applying them to your database when you need them (check out the section, "Applying filters," later in this chapter).

The idea is that you're likely to want to have a few standard filters that you use on your database regularly.

One quirk is that you can't have more than eight saved filters — any more than eight, and you have to delete one in order to create a new one.

Editing filters

To change a filter, simply return to the Filter dialog box, call up the filter by name, and adjust the criteria. Here's the blow-by-blow description:

1. **Choose Tools⇨Filters in the menu bar (or click the Filters button on the toolbar).**

   The Filter dialog box springs to life.

2. **Click the down arrow adjoining the Filter Name box and choose the filter that you want to edit from the list.**

3. **Change your filter criteria (the other stuff in the Filter dialog box).**

4. **Click the Apply Filter button to see how the filter works.**

To change the name of a filter, click the Rename Filter button. Enter a new name in the Filter Name dialog box that appears.

Applying filters

To apply the filter that you've used most recently, just press F3.

To apply any other filter to your database, follow these steps:

1. **Choose Record⇨Apply Filter.**

2. **Choose any filter in the Filter list that pops out.**

   Zap. You're looking at all the records that match your filter criteria.

To restore all the hidden records, choose Record⇨Show⇨1 All Records.

Deleting filters

If a filter isn't quite right or you don't need it anymore, deleting the filter is easy:

1. **Choose Tools⇨Filters (or click the Filters button on the toolbar).**

   The Filter dialog box forces its attentions upon you.

2. **Click the down arrow adjoining the Filter Name box and choose the filter that you want to delete from the list.**

3. **Click the Delete Filter button.**

   Works puts up a warning box to make sure that you want to do this. Click the Yes button.

4. **Click the Close button of the Filter dialog box when you're done deleting.**

Using More than One Criterion

You can have Works use up to five criteria at one time in a filter, which is why the Filter dialog box has five rows. This five-criteria feature lets you narrow down or expand your search.

For example, if you want only the families in your database that have more than two kids and also live out of town, you create a second row for the Town field, specifying that the town selected should not equal your town of Mudville. Figure 22-2 shows such a two-part filter for a database of photographs.

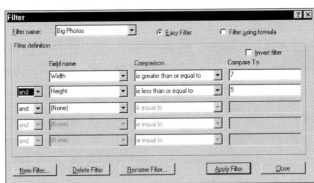

Figure 22-2: Filtering using two criteria.

To request more than one criterion, just fill out the first one as usual. Choose either and or or in the drop-down list box that begins the next line; then fill out the second criterion in a similar fashion. Do the same for any other criteria that you need.

For the example in Figure 22-2, you want Works to find records that meet both criteria:

> The photograph width is greater than or equal to 7 inches.
>
> and
>
> The photograph height is less than or equal to 5 inches.

So you select and from the drop-down list.

You use the or selection to specify that a record can meet either criterion. If and is changed to or in Figure 22-2, the search results in photographs that are at least 7 inches wide (but can be any height) as well as photographs that are less than or equal to 5 inches high (but can be any width).

You can also have multiple criteria lines using the same field, one on each line: for example, width is greater than or equal to 7 on the first line and width is less than or equal to 14 on the second line. This search would find all photos with a width between 7 and 14 inches.

If you set up your logic incorrectly and end up filtering out things that you want to filter in, select the Invert Filter check box in the Filter dialog box to reverse the logic. This method is also a good way to look at the filtered-out crowd and make sure that the filter is working correctly.

Chapter 23

Sorting, Reporting, and Calculating

* * *

In This Chapter

▶ Sorting data

▶ Creating standard reports

▶ Viewing your report

▶ Improving the appearance of your report

▶ Reporting on selected records

▶ Doing calculations on your database

* * *

*T*he real value in a database is not that it lets you amass an army of data on your computer; the real value is that a database helps you find, display, and compute meaningful answers from that army of data. Sorting, reporting, and calculating are Works' key features for extracting order from your chaos.

Sorting enables you to see records in a convenient order, such as alphabetical order. In addition, just as the alphabetical sorting in a telephone book inherently groups all the Smiths together, sorting in a database inherently groups things together, such as all the members of your softball league who have similar batting averages. In the Works Database tool, you can sort on any field; in fact, you can sort on several fields at once. You can sort on all sorts of things (sort of). You'll never be "out of sorts" with Works. . . . (*Whack! Ouch!* Okay, okay, I'll stop with the sordid puns. For now.)

Reports are also an important feature of any database tool. Reports enable you to list records, summarize data statistically (providing sums, averages, counts, and the like), and organize this information in a nice, readable form to print and give to other people. Sorts and reports can also be combined with filters (as I discuss in Chapter 22) so that you can focus on a subset of your database — say, your sales in Sasketoon only — and not have to peruse the whole database at one time.

In addition to the statistical summaries that Works can provide in a report, such as summing up all your sales for the month in a given country, Works can provide other useful forms of automatic calculation. For instance, as you enter a sales order as a record in your sales database, Works can add up the cost of each item to compute your customer's total amount due. You can also add calculations to Works reports, such as dividing the total sales revenues by the total number of orders to compute the average sale per order.

This chapter covers all these features — reporting, sorting, and calculating — in greater detail.

Sorting

Give your data its marching orders. But first, tell the data which order to march in: alphabetical or numerical. Do you want to sort your inventory alphabetically by location or numerically by value? No problem; it's your choice. Do you want to sort your mailing list numerically by zip code and then alphabetically by street name within each zip code? Again, no problem. Works does it all.

If you already know how to sort in Works' Spreadsheet tool, the database sorting process may seem very, very familiar to you.

Before you go running off to sort your database, decide how you want it to be sorted. Works lets you sort by up to three fields, which, in turn, lets you have a list in which your records are sorted by:

Categories (say, by zip code),

Subcategories (by street name within each zip code), and

Sub-subcategories (last names of people living on the street)

You can also choose the order in which you want the various groups to appear: A–Z and 1, 2, 3 . . . (ascending) or Z–A and . . . 3, 2, 1 (descending).

Using List view to see the results of sorting is generally easier, so if you're currently in Form view, I suggest that you switch to List view (press Shift+F9). Now, here's how to sort:

1. Choose Record⇨Sort Records from the menu bar.

The Sort Records dialog box, as shown in Figure 23-1, jumps gaily into your lap (so to speak). In Figure 23-1, you can see how Works makes selecting a field for sorting easy by providing a drop-down list of all your field names.

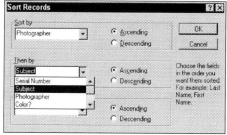

Figure 23-1:
Choosing
what fields
to sort on in
the Sort
Records
dialog box.

2. **Choose the principal field to sort on.**

   Click the down arrow next to the Sort By box and then click a field in that list. In a mailing list database, for example, you may choose zip code as the principal field to sort by. In Figure 23-1, I chose the Photographer field in my catalog of photographs.

3. **Choose a sorting direction for that field:**

   • Click Ascending to go from A–Z or in the order 1, 2, 3. . . .

   • Click Descending to go from Z–A or in the order . . . 3, 2, 1.

4. **Optionally, choose a second and third field to sort on and then choose a sorting direction.**

   If you fill out the information in the first Then By list (for example, choosing the Street Name field in a mailing list), Works sorts based on that field when two or more records have identical data in the first (or primary) field. (Plenty of folks have the same zip code, for example. If your principal field is zip code, the Then By field lets you put the identically zipped records in, say, alphabetical order by street name. If you don't fill out this information, the records won't be in any particular order within each zip code.) The second Then By field does the same thing for duplicate entries in the second field.

5. **Click the OK button.**

   If you're in List view, you see your database with its records shuffled around in the order you specified.

Keep the following points in mind when viewing your database in List view:

   ✔ Note that records don't keep their original record numbers (the number at the far left of each row in List view) when they're sorted. This is one reason why having a serial number field is important: The serial number field enables you to reconstruct the original order by sorting on that field.

✔ You can combine a sort with a filter if you just want to sort a portion of your database. Do the filtering first, which hides all the records you don't want. (Read more on filtering your data in Chapter 22.) Then sort on the remaining records. When you're done, you can bring all the records back into view by choosing Record➪Show➪1 All Records.

In Figure 23-2, you can see the result of sorting a database by photographer's name and then by subject.

Figure 23-2: Sorting groups of records with identical data groups them together.

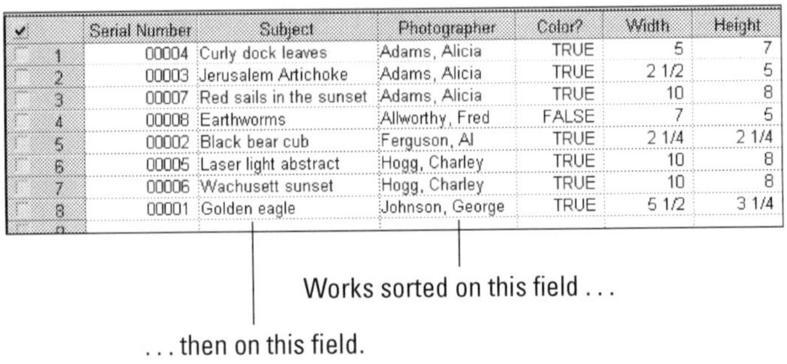

✔	Serial Number	Subject	Photographer	Color?	Width	Height
1	00004	Curly dock leaves	Adams, Alicia	TRUE	5	7
2	00003	Jerusalem Artichoke	Adams, Alicia	TRUE	2 1/2	5
3	00007	Red sails in the sunset	Adams, Alicia	TRUE	10	8
4	00008	Earthworms	Allworthy, Fred	FALSE	7	5
5	00002	Black bear cub	Ferguson, Al	TRUE	2 1/4	2 1/4
6	00005	Laser light abstract	Hogg, Charley	TRUE	10	8
7	00006	Wachusett sunset	Hogg, Charley	TRUE	10	8
8	00001	Golden eagle	Johnson, George	TRUE	5 1/2	3 1/4

Works sorted on this field . . .

. . . then on this field.

Reporting

Reports seem to make the world go 'round in some organizations. If that's true for you, Works is ready to help you make a report "heard 'round the world." But first, let me make sure that you know what I'm talking about when I say report:

✔ A Works report is intended to be printed — not viewed — on your PC screen.

✔ A Works report is made up of two kinds of information:

- A list of records very much like the List view.

- A summary based on your records.

For example, a mailroom may have a database consisting of the packages that have shipped, the date of shipping, the destination zip codes, the package weights, the shipper, and the cost of shipping. (The mailroom may also have a database with the football pool bets, but if the employees are smart, they won't keep their football pool database on the hard drive where the boss can see it.)

From the shipping database, management may want reports on how cost-effective various shippers are, how much product is being shipped by weight every month, how much is shipped to each zip code, the average weight shipped, and other typical, nosy management requests. All these reports require either a summary of some sort or a list, or both.

What's a standard report?

To make creating a report easier for you, Microsoft took some of the basics of report creating and made dialog boxes that help step you through the creation process. The result of using these dialog boxes is what I call a standard report. You can then make a more elaborate report by modifying this standard report.

A standard report from the shipping department's database may show all the packages sent, together with a summary of total weight and total cost of all the records. Such a standard report would look something like the one shown in Figure 23-3.

The report in Figure 23-3 contains lists of shipments grouped by shipper, with total weight and average weight shipped for each group, and total and average weight at the bottom. Not bad for a little database program!

What a standard report doesn't give you

Keep in mind that a standard report doesn't give you a couple of things that you may want:

- First, a standard report doesn't give you a report that provides answers calculated from two or more fields. For example, you may want a report that computes average shipping cost per package by summing all the costs, counting all the records, and dividing the total cost by the total number of packages. You can do this task in Works by modifying a standard report, but a standard report alone will not do the trick.

- Second, a standard report doesn't give you labels and special report formatting to make the report easier to read. But you can use Works' Database tool to modify a standard report, adding a lot of the same formatting features that the spreadsheet and word processor tools have, such as different fonts and styles, alignments, and borders.

In this chapter, I look at how to create a standard report and then show you how to do these few useful modifications.

shipping.wdb - Wt. by Shipper

Shipper	Weight	
CityZIP	0.73	
CityZIP	0.94	
CityZIP	0.21	
CityZIP	0.67	
CityZIP	0.75	
CityZIP	0.95	
CityZIP	0.18	
CityZIP	0.82	
GROUP TOTAL Weight:		5.26
AVERAGE Weight:		0.66
DinEx	0.80	
DinEx	0.44	
DinEx	0.63	
GROUP TOTAL Weight:		1.86
AVERAGE Weight:		0.62
Hercules	0.05	
Hercules	0.03	
Hercules	0.37	
---- (I cut out some stuff here)----		
PSU	0.04	
PSU	0.76	
PSU	0.60	
GROUP TOTAL Weight:		1.40
AVERAGE Weight:		0.47
Rural Xpres	0.87	
Rural Xpres	0.58	
Rural Xpres	0.08	
GROUP TOTAL Weight:		1.53
AVERAGE Weight:		0.51
Zowiefast	0.98	
Zowiefast	0.80	
Zowiefast	0.96	
Zowiefast	0.76	
Zowiefast	0.86	
GROUP TOTAL Weight:		4.36
AVERAGE Weight:		0.87
TOTAL Weight:	14.98	
AVERAGE Weight:	0.58	

Figure 23-3: One of the standard reports Works can make. (I chopped out the middle so that the report would fit on this page.)

Creating a Standard Report

Works makes it fairly simple to create a standard report, but you have to play your cards right! The ReportCreator dialog box deals you six different cards (tabs in the dialog box) that you have to fill out.

To begin your quest for a standard report, awaken the mighty ReportCreator from its slumber: Choose Tools⇨ReportCreator from the menu bar. (If a First-Time Help dialog box appears, click OK.)

A tiny Report Name dialog box requests that you name your report. Use 15 characters or fewer. This name doesn't appear on your report; it just identifies your report so that you can use this report again.

Then the ReportCreator dialog box, as shown in Figure 23-4, swings into action and deals you its six cards.

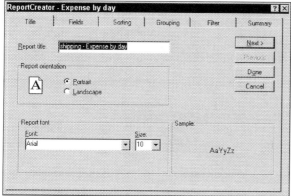

Figure 23-4:
The Report-
Creator's
Title tab. Fill
out all six
tabs to
create a
report.

You don't have to take the six tabs in strict left-to-right order, but Works presents them to you in that order when you use the Next button on the ReportCreator dialog box. To work on a different tab at any time, just click that tab.

First card: Title, orientation, and font

The top card of the hand that the ReportCreator deals you is the Title tab. The title is what appears on the top of your report. Works suggests a title for you, made up of the database file name and the name that you gave the report, but you can come up with a better one. Works also suggests that the report be created in the portrait orientation (taller than it is wide) and in 10-point Arial font, but Works also allows you to change these selections. Follow these steps to fill out the Title tab:

1. **Click in the Report Title text box and enter a title if you don't like Works' suggestion.**

   How about a title like *Commander of North American Operations.* No, just kidding; type in something boring and industrial, such as Shipping Costs.

2. **Choose Landscape orientation, if you are making a w – i – d – e report (that is, a report with a lot of fields on it; the number of fields you can include depends on how wide your fields are). Choose Portrait orientation if your report is long.**

3. **Choose a Font and Size in the Report Font area.**

When you're done, click the Next button or the Fields tab.

Second card: Choose your fields

The second card the ReportCreator deals you is the Fields tab, as shown in Figure 23-5. Here, you choose which of the fields in your database you want to appear in your report and in what order. (In the report, fields appear in columns, going left-to-right in the order you specify here.) Also, you can specify whether you want field names as headings for those field columns.

Figure 23-5:
Copy field
names from
the left box
to the right
box by
clicking the
Add button.

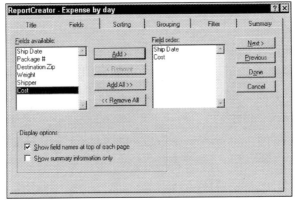

Follow these steps to choose the fields that you want to appear in your report:

1. **Click a field name in the Fields Available box (the left-hand box).**

   The list in the Fields Available box is a list of the fields you have in your database. The basic procedure in this dialog box is to copy field names from the left box to the right box.

   Click a field that you want to appear in your report.

2. **Click the Add button to copy that field to the Field Order box (the right-hand box).**

   The right-hand box is where you accumulate a list of the fields that will appear in the report.

Every time you add a field, the highlight in the left-hand box moves down, for your pleasure and convenience. So, to copy a series of field names, you can just keep clicking the Add button.

3. **Repeat Steps 1 and 2 for each field that you want to include in the report.**

   If you want all the fields, click the Add All button.

   If you change your mind about a field, click that field in the right-hand box and then click the Remove button. To remove all the fields from the right-hand box and start again, click the Remove All button.

4. **If you don't want the field names to appear at the top of each page of the report, click the S̲how Summary Information Only check box.**

   Normally, you want them. Figure 23-3 has 'em.

When you're done, click the Next button or the Sorting tab.

Third card: All sorts of stuff!

The Sorting tab may look familiar to you if you have already done sorting in the Works database tool. *Sorting* is the ordering of records alphabetically, numerically, or by date or time (for more on this, see the "Sorting" section, earlier in this chapter). In Figure 23-3, for example, I sorted by the Shipper field — which is a text field — so Works sorted it alphabetically: The report starts with CityZIP and ends with Zowiefast. In Figure 23-6, I sort by date.

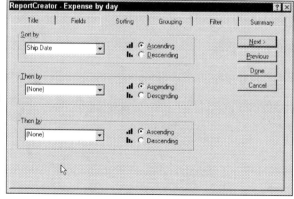

Figure 23-6:
What order do you want your data listed in?

Here's the procedure — bear in mind that you don't have to sort at all. Your report can just display stuff in the order in which it was entered (or previously sorted). You do have to specify sorting if you want groups in your report (see the Grouping tab). But if you don't want to sort (you're feeling "out of sorts"), just click the Next button.

Follow these steps if you want to specify how your data is listed in the report:

1. **Choose the principal field to sort on.**

   Click the down arrow next to the box labeled Sort By and then click a field in that list. In Figure 23-6, I want to see things in order of shipment date; I don't care about ordering shipments within a date, so I don't sort on any other field.

2. **Choose a sorting direction for that field:**

   • Click Ascending to go from A–Z or in the order 1, 2, 3. . . .

   • Click Descending to go from Z–A or in the order . . . 3, 2, 1.

3. **Optionally, choose a second and third field to sort on and then choose a sorting direction.**

   If you want additional sorting, use these fields. (For example, if I wanted shipments listed in order of increasing cost for each date, I would choose *Cost* as my second field.)

When you're done, click the Next button or the Grouping tab.

Fourth card: Groupings

Grouping allows you to summarize within a report. In Figure 23-3, for instance, the report has groups by shipper, listing a total for each shipper. Another example of grouping is to calculate a total for all the shipments on each date; that would be grouping by ship date. You can group only on the fields that you have sorted by on the Sorting tab. (Figure 23-6 shows how sorting is set up.)

Here's the scoop on grouping:

✔ You don't have to group at all. Not feeling groupish? Just click the Next button.

✔ To create a group, click the When Contents Change check box, as Figure 23-7 shows. The other check boxes then come alive because they all control things that you can do to a group. The When Contents Change check box is so called because Works puts blank lines between groups when the contents of the specified field change (for example, when the date changes in the Ship Date field).

✔ You can group only on fields that you select to appear on this report (on the Fields tab) and choose for sorting (on the Sorting tab). If I want to group on, say, the Cost field, I have to go back to the Sorting tab and add that field. Each field you select for sorting appears on the Grouping tab.

✔ You can have groups, subgroups, and sub-subgroups — that's why three identical areas are on this tab. For example, I can group shipments by date, then by shipper, and then by zip code. The order in which you choose your fields on the Sorting tab determines the order in which your fields appear on this tab; that order, in turn, determines whether you can use a field as a group (top area), subgroup (middle area), or sub-subgroup (bottom area).

✔ You can create groupings based strictly on the first character of a data entry. For example, if you had a list of last names, you probably wouldn't want to group by each name (many groups would be only one name long), but rather by initial name letter — all the As together, the Bs together, and so on. To do this type of grouping, click the Use First Letter Only check box.

✔ You can use a heading to identify each group. For example, if you are grouping by zip code, you can head each group with its zip code. Heading each group with its zip code is somewhat redundant, however, because the zip code appears in every line of that group anyway, making it rather obvious what group it is. Nonetheless, if you like this sort of thing, click the Show Group Heading check box.

Works' ReportCreator doesn't properly handle dates as group headings. The ReportCreator doesn't format them correctly, so the dates appear as numbers (the number of days since January 1, 1900)!

✔ For some reports, you may want to print each group on a separate page. For example, in a national sales database, you may need to send a separate page to each region's sales office. To do this task, click the Start Each Group on a New Page check box.

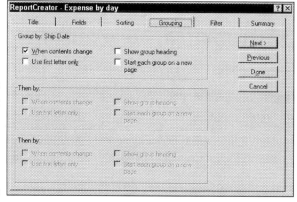

Figure 23-7:
Choosing
to create
a group
for each
Ship Date.

When you're done, click the Next button or the Filter tab.

Fifth card: Filters

Filters enable you to separate the sheep from the goats, so to speak (or the wheat from the chaff, in case you are a vegetarian). Filters are a bit lengthy to discuss right here, but I go into more detail on filters in Chapter 22. The filters that you can use here are exactly the same as the ones I discuss there.

The executive summary on filters is that filters enable you to selectively hide certain records from your report. For example, packages shipped by the regular postal service may not belong in this report, so you would create a filter that says (in filter-ese) *Shipper . . . is not equal to . . . U.S. Postal Service.*

To create a filter, click the Create New Filter button and see Chapter 22 for further instruction. After you create a filter, the filter appears in the Select A Filter text box. You can modify that filter with the Modify Filter button, if you need to.

If you have not created any filters, the ReportCreator gives you two options anyway, in the Select A Filter text box. Choose one of these options:

- ✔ **(Current Records)** means that you want to display only the records that are not hidden in your database. For instance, you may have manually hidden certain records, and by choosing this option, you make sure those don't appear in your report.
- ✔ **(All Records)** means just that: include all the records (hidden or not) in the report.

Be brave; you are almost done. Click the Next button, or click the Summary tab of the ReportCreator, to wrap up your report with a few summaries.

Sixth card: Statistical summaries

At this point, you are gazing (glassy-eyed) at the Summary tab of Figure 23-8.

Statistical summaries are useful things. Statistical summaries are how you get the answers to such questions as, "What are the total sales for January in the Eastern region?" or "What is the batting average for each team?" or "Why are my eyes glazing over?" (Just kidding about the last one. The answer is your eyes are going buggy from staring at your computer screen or reading this book too long.)

Summaries are optional. If you don't specify any summaries and you just click the Done button in the ReportCreator, you get a report that simply lists all the records in your database, displaying the fields that you chose on the Fields tab — sorted and grouped, if you chose those features.

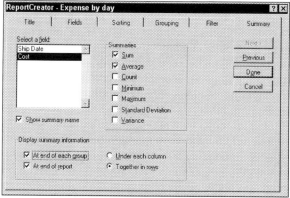

Figure 23-8:
Time to
sum up,
counselor!

If you want statistics (including sums) on a certain field or fields, here's what to do:

1. **Click the field in the Select A Field box.**

2. **Choose the kind of statistical summary (or summaries) that you want for that field.**

   Click a check box in the Summaries area to select a particular kind of summary. Heck, click a batch of 'em if you want several different kinds of summaries.

   Average computes the average of all the numbers in the field. *Minimum* shows you the smallest (or most negative) value, and so on.

3. **Repeat Steps 1 and 2 for each field that you want summarized.**

   Each field can have its own set of summaries.

   Be careful as you enter information on this tab because summaries can't easily be changed after you've clicked the Done button. Be careful that you don't sum when you want to count. *Sum* adds up the numerical value of all the records in the selected field. *Count* just counts the records that have data in a field. Also, don't accidentally sum up the wrong field (such as the date field)!

4. **Click Show Summary Name.**

   This option makes Works label the summary as a sum, or an average, or whatever you choose.

5. **If you create groups on the Grouping tab, you can have a summary appear under each group by clicking At End of Each Group.**

6. **Choose where you want your summaries to appear in the report. Click:**

   - Under Each Column to put your field summaries at the bottom of their respective columns.

   - Together in Rows to put each of your field summaries in a separate row at the bottom of the report (or at the bottom of each group, if you chose that option).

7. **Click the Done button.**

   Things whiz around on your screen, ultimately delivering . . .

   . . . a big, confusing mess, and then one of those little boxes with the exclamation point in it! What the heck?!? This isn't what you had in mind! Where's that nice report??

Hang in there. Read the little dialog box, which reads `The report definition has been created`; it asks whether you want to preview the report or modify it. I suggest that you choose Preview. Choosing Modify doesn't gain you much — it just leaves you gazing at the big, confusing mess (called the Report view).

Click the Preview button, and Works shows you your report in Print Preview mode. Remember that the main purpose of a report is to make a nice report to print — not to view on your screen. (For details on how Print Preview works, check out Chapter 4.) Click the Cancel button when you're done viewing.

Read on to figure out exactly what's going on here.

Laying your cards on the table: Viewing your report

After you leave Print Preview, what's on your screen at this point is not your actual report. Instead, what is on your screen is the Report view — a view most people don't find very comprehensible, and a view that's not necessary for most work. This view displays the rather intimidating report definition that tells Works how to construct your report. Don't be too upset — if it weren't for that nice ReportCreator dialog box, you would have had to enter all that intimidating stuff by hand.

You probably want to get out of the Report view and go back to List or Form view. To go back, just click View and then click either List or Form in the menu that drops down.

Now that you defined your report, it exists as part of your Works database document. As with filters, you can call up this report at any time, and the report takes into account any new or changed data in your database. Also, as with filters, you can have only eight reports; any more, and you have to delete one by choosing Tools⇨Delete Report and double-clicking the report name in the dialog box that appears.

You can reuse this report over and over as you add data. Just choose View⇨ Report and double-click the report name in the dialog box that appears.

Modifying Your Report

Works makes modifying your report easy — within limits. But if you can't make the changes that you want in the Report Settings dialog box (the easy way), or if you want to get a better-looking report than the standard one, you need to go the hard way by using the Report view.

The following two sections detail the easy way and the hard way to modify your report.

The easy way

You can easily modify the sorting, grouping, and filtering of your report. However, you can't as easily change fields or summaries. Here's the scoop on how to modify report settings:

- ✔ **Sorting:** Choose Tools⇨Report Sorting
- ✔ **Grouping:** Choose Tools⇨Report Grouping
- ✔ **Filtering:** Choose Tools⇨Report Filter

All these steps take you to a Report Settings dialog box, where the tabs look exactly like the tabs in the ReportCreator, except that only these three functions (rather than six) are available. Refer back to the preceding discussions of sorting, grouping, and filtering for instructions.

The hard way

You can use Report view to create the report you need in one of two ways:

- ✔ Create a report from scratch by writing one of those scary-looking report definitions you see in the so-called Report view.
- ✔ Modify the standard report definition.

My money's on the second option.

Using Report view is not for the easily confused! Explaining how to use the Report view in detail would take too long in this book, so I give you only the executive summary and a few instructions on how to change things. Fortunately, you should rarely need to resort to editing this report definition to create the reports you need.

To modify an existing report definition, switch to the Report view: Choose View➪Report, click the report name in the View Report dialog box that appears, and then choose the Modify button. You are confronted with a strange-looking spreadsheet kind of thing.

Each row in the Report view has a special function. Down the leftmost side are special labels that identify what part of the report is being controlled by that row. For example, report titles are entered in a row labeled Title; blank rows of any type just provide extra space.

The vertical position of the row corresponds to the position of that row in the final report. Title rows, for example, are at the top; summary rows are at the bottom.

Anything you see displayed in bold text in Report view is text that literally appears on the report. Anything else is a special term referring to fields, calculations, and other parts of the database and its report.

The following are several types of rows you will find. You identify them by the text shown below in bold, which appears in the leftmost column (the gray column):

- **Heading** rows contain text used for column headings.

- **Intr** *fieldname* rows (such as Intr Photographer, if Photographer is a field name) appear if the report is divided into groups. These rows mark the line in the report where the group begins and usually display some text to identify the group. That text is typed into any of the cells of that row.

- **Record** rows print the field contents of each individual record in the report. They contain the formula =*fieldname,* where *fieldname* represents the name of the field.

- **Summ** *fieldname* rows print summaries that appear for groups.

- **Summary** rows print summaries for all the data in the report.

You can add these sorts of special rows if you think that you understand their functions from these very brief descriptions and the descriptions that follow in this chapter. (Or, try to understand them by playing around with them.) Click the row above which you want to add a row and then choose Insert➪Insert Row from the menu bar. Choose a row type from the list in the Insert Row dialog box that appears and click the Insert button.

Adding or deleting fields

A typical standard report displays only a few of the many fields in your database. To add a new field to your report in Report view (which is the only view in which you can do this task), see Figure 23-9 for an example, and do the following:

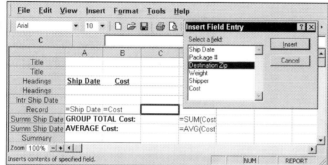

Figure 23-9:
Adding a
field to your
report
requires
using the
rather icky
Report view.

1. **Locate the row labeled** `Record` **in the leftmost column.**

2. **Find the first blank cell available in that row and click it.**

   A black border appears around that cell, as shown in Figure 23-9.

3. **Choose** **Insert**⬧**Field Entry from the menu bar.**

   The Insert Field Entry dialog box appears, as shown in Figure 23-9.

4. **Choose the field that you want to add to your report from the list in the Insert Field Entry dialog box.**

   In Figure 23-9, I'm adding the Destination Zip field.

5. **Click the Insert button.**

6. **Add a heading, if you want.**

   Find a row above the current cell labeled `Headings` (which probably has other headings in it), and simply type in a heading. (If no row is labeled `Headings`, choose **Insert**⬧**Insert Row** from the menu bar and choose Headings from the Insert Row dialog box that appears.) Format the text that you type with bold, underline, or any other font, style, or alignment formatting that you like. If a *Summ* something-or-other field appears under the cell that you type, you want an underline. (Read through the section, "Adding or deleting summaries," later in this chapter, for more information about adding summaries.)

7. **Add an underline by choosing** **Format**⬧**Border, choosing Bottom in the Format dialog box, and then clicking OK.**

To delete a field from the report, look in the row labeled Record for a cell containing an equal sign (=) followed by the field name. Click that cell and then press the Delete key.

To see whether these mysterious actions really gave you what you wanted, go to Print Preview. (Click the document-with-a-monocle icon button or choose File➪Print Preview.)

Adding or deleting summaries

A report may have two kinds of summaries: group summaries and overall summaries. In Report view, group summaries are controlled by rows labeled Summ (and then the field name). Overall summaries are controlled by rows labeled Summary.

You can put your new summary in a row by itself, or add your summary to an existing summary row.

To put your new summary in a row by itself, follow these steps:

1. **Click any row above which you want to add a summary.**

   A good choice is the row below an existing Summ or Summary row.

2. **Choose Insert➪Insert Row from the menu bar.**

3. **Select Summary or Summ *fieldname* from the list of row types in the Insert Row dialog box, and click the Insert button.**

   For example, if you are adding a new summary to a group grouped by the Zip Code field, you choose Summ Zip Code.

4. **In the A column of your new row, type a label for this summary, such as** TOTAL: Weight.

5. **Click in the column where you want the summary to appear in this row.**

   You can choose any column of this row (column D, for example) that is not overlapped by the label that you typed.

6. **Choose Insert➪Field Summary from the menu bar.**

   The Field Insert dialog box appears.

7. **Choose a field from the list and click the kind of summary you want in the Statistic area of the dialog box; click the Insert button when you're done.**

To see whether you really created the summary you wanted, go to Print Preview. (Click the document-with-a-monocle icon button or choose File➪Print Preview.)

To add a summary to an existing Summary row, start with Step 5 in the preceding list, in which you select an unused cell in that row. That cell is where your new summary appears.

To delete an entire Summary row, click the row to be deleted, and then choose Insert⇨Delete Row from the menu bar. To delete a single summary from a row with several summaries, first use Print Preview to see which column the summary is in. Then click Cancel in Print Preview to return to the Report view. Click in that column of the Summary row (you find there a formula beginning with the equal sign) and press the Delete key.

Fixing up appearances

When most reports first appear, they don't look any better than I do when I first appear in the morning. However, you can do a few things in Report view to improve your report's appearance. To switch to Report view, choose View⇨Report, click the report name in the View Report dialog box that appears, and then choose the Modify button.

Much of the report's appearance can be set the same way that spreadsheet appearances are set. The commands and procedures are similar, if not identical. If you're already familiar with Works' spreadsheets, you probably know how to do many of the formatting tasks in the following list. If you are not familiar with Works' spreadsheets, here is a quick summary:

- ✔ **Adjust report column widths:** Click and drag the line between the column letters (the gray cells with the letters A, B, C, and so forth, across the top of the columns).

- ✔ **Align data within the report columns:** Click the column's letter to select the column. (Click and drag across the column letters to choose multiple columns.) Choose Format⇨Alignment to get to the alignment page of the Format dialog box. Click the Alignment you need. (Typically, Left, Right, Center, or Center Across Selection does the job.) Then click OK.

- ✔ **Edit the column headings:** Click a report heading (in a row labeled Headings) and make edits to the heading text by using the formula bar.

- ✔ **Change font, font size, or style:** Select either a report heading (click it in a row labeled Headings), an entire column (click its column letter), or the entire report (press Ctrl+A). Then choose a new font, type size, or style (bold, italic, or underline) by using either the toolbar or the Format⇨Font and Style command.

- ✔ **Change number formats:** To make your numbers look right — with dollar signs preceding monetary figures and zeros leading zip codes — you need a number format. Select the column that needs fixing (click its column letter) and choose Format⇨Number from the menu bar. The Number tab of the Format dialog box appears. Click a Format, choose any Options, and then click OK. Check out Chapter 20 for more information on number formats.

✔ **Borders:** To put lines and borders around rows and columns, first select the row (click its label, such as Headings, in the gray column at the left of the row) or column (click its column letter) and choose Format⇨Border. Click a Line Style, click a Border, and then click the OK button. You can find more information on applying and changing formats in Chapter 21.

Calculating

The Works database tool can perform calculations that you may find useful, but also somewhat confusing to perform without some study. Works' Database tool can perform calculations for you in two locations:

✔ **You can make a calculating field.** For instance, while entering a shipping record, you may enter an item's weight in pounds; in the calculating field, Works computes the item's weight in kilograms.

✔ **You can add calculations to a report (in addition to the calculations already provided by summaries).** For instance, a report in a manufacturing and sales database could compute profit margins by adding up the total cost from several cost fields (parts, labor, and so forth) and then subtracting the total from the total sales.

Calculations in fields provide results based on a single record. Comparatively, calculations in reports provide results based on all records or a group of records in your database.

In Works' Database tool, calculations are similar to calculations performed in the Spreadsheet tool. You may find the discussions of formulas and functions in Chapter 18 useful if you haven't performed calculations in Works before.

You write formulas for Works databases by using the same sort of terms you use in spreadsheets, but with some important differences:

✔ As in spreadsheet formulas, you use various *operators* such as + (add), – (subtract), * (multiply), and / (divide) together with constants, such as the number 2.04.

✔ Use field names to represent values instead of using cell addresses or ranges as you do in a spreadsheet — for instance, you may write the formula =Price-Cost to calculate an item's profit margin in a database, whereas you would write =B2-B1 in a spreadsheet.

If your field names are the same as Works function names, such as Date, enclose the field name in quotation marks ("Date") in your formula. Otherwise, Works may think you intend to use a function.

✔ Use Works functions, such as if( ), sum( ), or avg( ). In reports, because they summarize the results of many records, you can use only statistical functions, such as sum( ) or avg( ). In fields, you can use a much larger variety of functions.

Following are a few examples of calculations for a database in which Cost and Weight are the names of two fields:

✔ **=Cost/Weight:** If used in a field, this provides each record with a computed field that displays the cost per pound of that item (that record).

✔ **=sum(Cost)/sum(Weight):** If used in a report, this divides the total of all entries in the Cost field by the total of all entries in the Weight field, giving average cost per pound for all items (records) in the database.

✔ **=if(Weight>10, "Overweight!" , ""):** If used in a field, this provides each record with a field that displays the warning "Overweight!" if the item weighs over ten pounds. You cannot use the if( ) function in a report because it is not a statistical function.

To better understand what is going on in Works calculations, read on.

Adding a calculating field to your database

To add a field to your database that does calculations, follow these steps:

1. **Switch to List view, if you're not already using that view (choose View➪List).**

2. **Add a field using the Record➪Insert Field command.**

   For a review of inserting fields, read more about adding new fields in Chapter 21.

3. **Click the name of the new field at the top of the column to select that field.**

4. **Type the equal (=) sign to begin entering a formula.**

5. **Type the remainder of the formula, using field names, constants, functions, and operators.**

   For instance, to compute an item's cost per pound, you divide that item's cost by its weight: Assuming your field names are Cost and Weight, you would type **=Cost/Weight**. As you type your formula, instead of actually typing field names, you may "point and shoot:" Click the columns corresponding to the fields.

If you need help remembering how to write a function, choose Help⇨Works Help; as you type the function's name (such as **=date**) into your field, Help displays an Overview window.

If you are using statistical functions such as sum(Cost) in field calculations, you probably misunderstand how field calculations work. Field calculations work on only one record at a time, so sum(Cost) is the same as Cost. To sum the values in the Cost field, you must put your calculation in a report, not a field.

6. **Press the Enter key when you're done, or click the check mark button on the formula bar.**

To see the result of your new field, choose File⇨Print Preview.

Because List View looks a lot like a spreadsheet, you may be tempted to try to sum data in columns or write a formula that uses data from various cells in various rows. A database doesn't work that way. A formula can refer only to the data in the same row (or record), which it does by using the field name of that data.

Adding or modifying calculations in reports

Why add or modify a calculation? The standard report you get from the ReportCreator doesn't provide any calculations other than a statistical summary of a single field. So, although your shipping department report may contain total weight shipped and total shipping charges, the report isn't able to print the average cost per pound of shipping (total shipping charges divided by total weight shipped) unless you create your own formula to perform the division.

To add or modify calculations in your reports, you must use Works' rather confusing Report view. Choose View⇨Report, click the report name in the View Report dialog box that appears, and then choose the Modify button.

Your standard report probably already performs calculations, which are a good place to start to understand report calculations. If, for instance, you include any summaries when you use the ReportCreator, those summaries are the result of the ReportCreator writing formulas that use Works' statistical functions. If you sum up the numbers in a field, for instance, the ReportCreator writes a formula that uses the sum() function.

To see these existing calculations, click a cell in any Summ or Summary row. When you click a cell, the formula bar displays the cell's contents. Any cell where the contents begin with an equal sign (=) contains a formula. The formula contains one of Works' statistical functions: sum(), avg(), max(), min(), max(), count(), std(), or var(), depending on the type of Summary you chose in the Summary tab (shown in Figure 23-8).

You can write similar formulas to perform more complex operations. For instance, to compute the range of values in the Cost field of your database, you would use the formula =max(Cost)-min(Cost). When writing report formulas, you do not use field names alone, such as =Cost; instead, use the field names within Works' statistical functions, such as =max(Cost).

Where do you write these formulas in Report View? You can write them in a Record, Summ, or Summary row. Enter the formulas in any blank (empty) cell in that row; whatever column you write the formula in is the column in which the result will appear on your report. You can also edit an existing formula: Start by simply clicking the formula, and edit it as you would a spreadsheet formula. (See Chapter 18 for details.) Here's how to choose which row to use:

✔ To perform a calculation on all the records in the report, enter the formula in the Summary row. For instance, to compute the shipping cost per pound for all the shipments in your report, enter your formula in any available (blank) column of the Summary row. You can also add a new Summary row by choosing Insert⇨Insert Row and selecting Summary from the list that appears.

✔ To perform a calculation on each group (or subgroup) of your report, enter the formula in a Summ row for some field name. For instance, if you group by Shipper (as in Figure 23-3), enter your formula in the Summ Shipper row to create a calculation of shipping cost per pound for each shipper. (If your report uses subgroups, such as zip code groups within each shipper, you have additional Summ rows. If you want to compute cost per pound separately for each zip code handled by the shipper, you enter your formula in the Summ Destination ZIP row.)

✔ To perform a calculation on each record of your report, enter the formula in a Record row. Because this calculation is performed on each record, it appears on every line of the report and looks like a calculating field. For instance, if you want to display weight in kilograms for each shipment — but your data is in pounds — you enter the formula =Weight*2.204 in a blank cell of the Record row.

Feel free to add text in any blank cell that you want to appear on the printed report. Figure 23-10 shows an example Report view with additional calculations for cost per pound, and Figure 23-11 shows the resulting report. The text and summaries that I added are in italics.

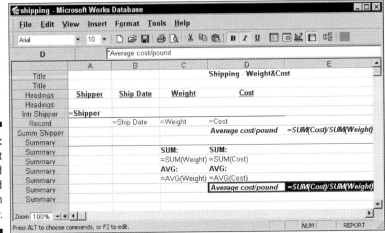

Figure 23-10:
Adding Cost
per Pound
labels and
formulas in
Report view.

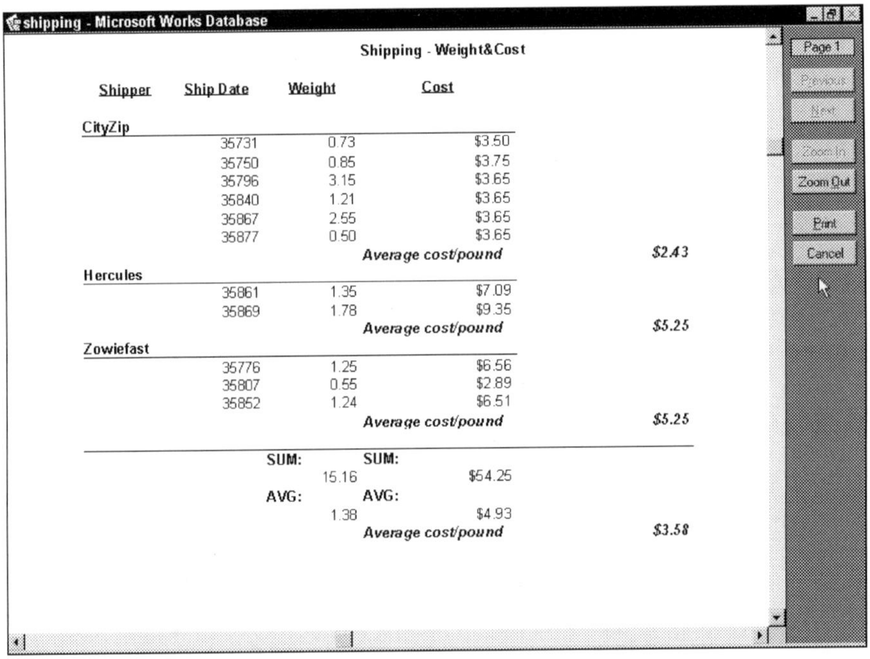

Figure 23-11:
Viewing the
new cost
per pound
results
in Print
Preview.

Part VI
Being Online and On Time

The 5th Wave — By Rich Tennant

"SINCE WE GOT IT, HE HASN'T MOVED FROM THAT SPOT FOR ELEVEN STRAIGHT DAYS. ODDLY ENOUGH THEY CALL THIS 'GETTING UP AND RUNNING' ON THE INTERNET."

In this part . . .

*G*et ready for a shocker: Life is more than word processing, spreadsheets, and databases! (Oh, you
already suspected that?) Yes, indeed. Works comes with
Internet programs and a calendar program that will fill
your life with all kinds of intriguing new adventures.

(Technically, these programs aren't part of Works. They
come with Works, and the Works Task Launcher makes
use of these guys as if they were part of Works, but they
are really independent programs that Microsoft distrib-
utes in many other ways besides Works. Then again, who
cares?)

Going online is a fine adventure. But if, to you, online is
where the laundry goes when the clothes dryer breaks,
never fear. No clothespins will be applied to your neck.
This part tells you how to get online without being hung
out to dry; how to browse the Web without getting spiders
in your hair; and how to send and receive messages
through this mysterious medium of the Internet without
resorting to smoke signals.

For many of us, just keeping our lives organized is an
adventure. Microsoft Calendar takes away our final excuse
for organizing our lives with desiccated sticky notes, a
free Poodles of Pennsylvania calendar, and a tattered Star
Wars school notepad. Give it up, people. The software
is here, and it works: personal appointments, birthdays,
meetings — the (you should excuse the expression)
works. The excuses are gone. Boldly into the future
with you!

How now, wit! Whither wander you?

—As You Like It, William Shakespeare

Chapter 24

Exploring with Internet Explorer

* *

In This Chapter

▶ Finding an ISP (Internet service provider)

▶ Going online

▶ Browsing and searching the Web

▶ Printing Web pages

▶ Downloading from the Web

▶ Disconnecting

* *

*I*nternet Explorer is Microsoft's sport utility vehicle for a safari on the World Wide Web (or just *the Web*). This chapter gives you basic driving instructions and a few tips for navigating this online wilderness.

Note: Many computer writers, myself included, tire of typing *Internet Explorer* all the time, so we use the abbreviation *IE* (and sometimes add the version number, such as IE 5.5, which is the version I use) instead. I use the abbreviation here so that you get used to seeing it elsewhere.

Setting Up a Connection

Before you can explore the Web or send e-mail, you need an Internet connection service. Companies known as Internet service providers — or *ISPs* — provide Internet connection service. Microsoft would love to be your ISP, offering you an Internet Connection wizard to help you set up service either with The Microsoft Network (MSN) or with any of several nationwide ISPs such as MindSpring, EarthLink, or Sprint, by choosing from a referral service that Microsoft has put together. Check out your local ISPs for their options; they may offer more local connections or better service. Contact them individually for connection information. After you do your homework, the connection wizard can hook you up to a local ISP or a national ISP that's not listed in Microsoft's referral service.

To set up online service using the connection wizard, follow these steps on the Programs page of the Task Launcher:

1. **Choose Internet Explorer from the list on the left and click New Internet Connection in the list of tasks on the right.**

2. **Click the link, Start This Task (on the far right).**

   The Internet Connection wizard screen appears.

3. **To choose an ISP from Microsoft's referral service, just click Next; if you contract your own ISP service, click the option box labeled** I want to set up my internet connection manually **and then click Next.**

4. **Follow the wizard's directions, and soon you'll be ready to roll.**

Going Online and Offline: The Dialing Process

After signing up with an ISP (refer to the preceding section, "Setting Up a Connection"), you can start your Web-surfing safari by following these steps:

1. **Start Internet Explorer by using one of these methods:**

   - Click the *e* icon on the Windows taskbar (where the Start button is).

   - Double-click the globe icon labeled Internet Explorer on your Windows desktop.

   - Use the Works Task Launcher. On the Programs page of the Task Launcher, choose Internet Explorer from the list on the left-hand side, and then click Start Internet Explorer, found on the right-hand side. (All the tasks listed for IE, by the way, also launch IE and take you to various services on the Web.)

   After you launch an Internet program, such as Internet Explorer or Outlook Express, Windows begins a process of automatic dialing. No, it's not surreptitiously dialing Bill Gates with your credit card number. Windows is dialing your ISP so that you can go online to the Internet.

2. **In the Connect To or Dial-Up Connection dialog box that appears, enter the account name (your ID) in the User Name box (unless it's already filled in).**

3. **In the Password box, enter the password assigned to you by your ISP (unless that box is filled with ****).**

   As you type your password, asterisks (****) appear in place of the characters you type; this is a safety measure used to thwart any would-be spies who may be looking over your shoulder.

To avoid having to retype your password in the future, select the Save Password check box if it's not grayed out. (For strange and complicated security reasons, this check mark is grayed out unless Windows is set up to request a Windows password when you start your computer.) If the dialog box you see is the Dial-Up Connection dialog box, you can avoid having to interact with it in the future by selecting the Connect Automatically check box.

4. **Click the Connect button.**

   After your PC connects, an icon (or, in Windows 95, a button with an icon) appears on the Windows taskbar. The icon features two PCs with a line (or a line and telephone) between them. The icon is tiny and lurks at the opposite end of the taskbar from the Start button. You're now online!

When you close IE or Outlook Express, Windows automatically asks whether you want to disconnect. To manually disconnect, double-click the icon in the taskbar. In the dialog box that appears, click Disconnect. (You may also right-click on the icon and choose Disconnect from the menu that appears.)

Internet Explorer and Outlook Express can both do certain work offline (not connected to the Internet), which saves you the cost of connection time to your ISP. Offline, both programs can read documents and messages that you have downloaded or viewed previously. To work offline, click the Cancel button when the Dial-Up Connection dialog box appears, wait until the call is disconnected, and then click the Work Offline button that now takes the place of the Cancel button. To return Internet Explorer or Outlook Express to online operation, choose File➪Work Offline from the menu bar of that program. (Working offline causes the Connect Automatically check box mentioned in Step 3 to be cleared, so you'll need to select it again the next time you connect.)

Home, Sweet Home Page

Each time you start up Internet Explorer, it displays a Web page located somewhere on the Internet. The page that Internet Explorer turns to first (no matter where it is) is called Internet Explorer's home page. *Home page* just means the starting page.

Microsoft initially sets IE's home page to be the Microsoft Web site. If you prefer to have IE first go to another page on the Internet, such as a search engine or your company or university's home page, browse to that page. Then in IE, choose Tools➪Internet Options, click the General tab in the Internet Options dialog box that appears, and click the Use Current button.

Browsing the Web

Browsing is the trendy activity of the day, whether you're into computers, shopping, or eating. Applied to the Web, *browsing* means viewing the documents (together with their graphics and sounds) located at various Web addresses around the world. The term *Web site* refers to a collection of documents representing some organization or person.

Viewing a distant Web document isn't quite like viewing a distant mountain through a telescope; it's more like having a copy of the distant mountain shipped to your doorstep piece by piece. The entire document is transmitted to your Web browser, and this transmission can take a while.

Browsing by typing an address

One way to browse the Web is to specify a document's address, called a *URL* — short for Uniform Resource Locator, and pronounced "earl" or "You Are Ell." Addresses on the Web are a bit cryptic; you've undoubtedly seen them on TV and elsewhere. They typically look like the following:

- `http://www.snogglepuss.com`
- `www.snogglepuss.com`
- `home.snogglepuss.net/users/barney.html`

Web sites all have a starting page — their own home page — which is the main address from which you can reach all the other pages of that site. Addresses that end in `.com`, `.org`, or `.edu` take you to the home page of a Web site.

Technically speaking, all Web addresses should begin with `http://`, but Internet Explorer lets you omit it and just type the rest of the address: `www.brightleaf.com/tracking`, for instance. For many addresses, you can even omit the `www` portion. The single forward slash (as in `/tracking`) indicates folders under the main address (`brightleaf.com`). Individual Web documents typically end in `.htm`, `.html`, `.shtml`, or `.asp`.

If you know the URL of the Web site you want to see (for instance, `www.dummies.com`), you can type that address (or paste it with Ctrl+V, if you've copied it from elsewhere) in one of two places:

- **In the white area (text box) of the Address bar.** If an address is currently listed, replace that address with whatever you type. Press Enter when you're done or click the Go button at the right end of the Address bar.

- **In the Open dialog box that appears when you choose File⇨Open (or press Ctrl+O).** Press Enter when you're done or click OK.

After the Web page is loaded, its title appears in the title bar of the Internet Explorer window, and its full address (URL) appears in the Address text box. (See Figure 24-1.)

Graphics are often links.

Type an address, then press the Enter key.

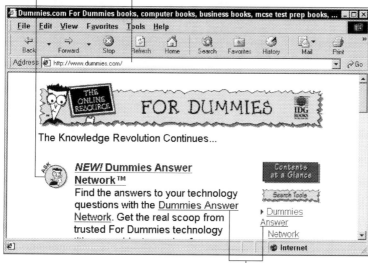

Figure 24-1:
Tell Internet Explorer where to go by typing an address or clicking a link.

Underlined text is usually a link.

Browsing with buttons

The IE toolbar gives you some helpful controls for browsing and other jobs. In Figure 24-2 you can see what each button does.

Backward in viewing history

Stop downloading page

To pages you marked as Favorites

To the IE home page

To read or send e-mail

Figure 24-2:
A bellyful of buttons bolsters your browser.

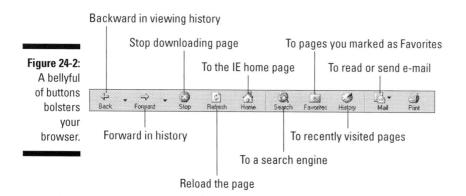

Forward in history

To recently visited pages

To a search engine

Reload the page

Some of the button descriptions in Figure 24-2 use special terms — such as downloading and reloading — which I explain in other sections of this chapter. Clicking the Mail button gives you a list of choices that will cause Windows to run Outlook Express and do various things with it, like reading mail or sending a message.

Browsing by clicking links on Web pages

When you view a Web document in Internet Explorer, you can switch to different documents by clicking links within the current document. Links may take the form of buttons, specially marked text, or certain graphics on the page (refer to Figure 24-1).

The best way to tell whether a word, a graphic, a button, or some other element on the page is a link is to move your cursor over that element without clicking. The cursor changes from an arrow to a little hand if the element is a link. The address that the link takes you to appears at the bottom left margin (status bar) of the Internet Explorer window.

Text links are easy to spot. They're usually underlined and often appear in a distinctive color (typically, bright blue). If you've already visited a page that a text link connects to, the color of the text usually changes to a darker or fainter color so that you know you've already visited that link.

Clicking some links initiates downloading a file instead of taking you to another Web page. If that happens unexpectedly, simply press the Esc key to exit from the File Download dialog box that appears. For more information, read the section, "Downloading Programs and Other Files from the Web," later in this chapter.

Returning to a page in History

Don't know much about History? Well, Internet Explorer does. Each time you use IE, it keeps a record of the Web pages you've visited so that you can return to them. Several buttons on the toolbar can help you travel through time:

- **Back:** To return to the last Web page you visited, click the Back button on the toolbar. Keep clicking the Back button to move backward in History.

- **Forward:** After moving back in History, you can move Forward again by clicking the Forward button.

✔ **Down arrows:** To go back to any recently visited page in History, click the tiny down arrow adjoining the Back button and choose a page title off the list that appears. Likewise, to move forward in History, click the tiny down arrow adjoining the Forward button. Click the down arrow at the far right of the Address bar and you can revisit a previously visited site by clicking its address in the drop-down list.

✔ **History:** To revisit any Web page you visited in the past 20 days, click the History button. (You can change this time frame by choosing Tools⇨Internet Options. Then in the General tab of the Internet Options dialog box that appears, enter a new value less than 99 in the Days To Keep Pages In History box.)

Click the History button to see a History menu appear on the left side of the IE window, as shown in Figure 24-3. Your browsing history is organized by the day and week in which you visited a Web site. The Web sites you visit today, for instance, are in a Today category. Earlier sites are grouped by the day of the week (such as Monday), or how many weeks ago you visited (such as 2 Weeks Ago). Any Web sites you visit are shown as folder icons.

Figure 24-3:
Back to the future (or past) with the History panel of Internet Explorer.

Change the way sites are listed.

Remove History panel.

Search for a word in an address.

Click to expand/collapse list.

Here's how to use the History panel:

✔ **To view sites visited earlier:** Click the icon for the day or week when you visited a site. (The icons look like tiny calendar pages. Really.) The icon spews forth (*expands* into) a list of folders for all the sites you visited. To *collapse* the list (stuff it back into the icon, so to speak), click the icon again. IE keeps track of your browsing for the past 20 days (or however long you specify; go back and read the preceding History bullet).

✔ **To open a folder for a given Web site:** Click it. Pages you visit on that site appear indented under the folder. (Click the folder again to close it.)

✔ **To return to any page listed in a folder:** Just click it. That page appears in the remainder of the IE window on the right side.

✔ **To view history in a different order:** Click View on top of the history list and choose By Date, By Site, By Most Visited, or by Order Visited Today.

✔ **To remove the History panel altogether:** Click the X in the upper-right corner of the panel.

Returning to your favorite pages

Now, just where was that recipe for tripe soufflé? The Web is so vast that you may never find it again, much to the dismay (or joy) of your dinner guests. The Favorites feature helps you rise above absentmindedness.

Adding to Favorites

When you view a Web page that you think you may want to revisit, tell IE to add it to your list of favorites. Just follow these steps to add a favorite:

1. **Choose Favorites⇨Add to Favorites from the menu bar.**

   The Add Favorite dialog box appears, offering some nit-picky options.

2. **Make sure that the text in the Name box (which starts out as the title of the Web page) is descriptive enough that you can recognize the page by that text. If not, type in a better, more recognizable name.**

3. **Click OK or press the Enter key to enter the page in the basic Favorites list.**

You can keep your favorite pages in various folders, too. The Favorites list already has several folders. Click to open a folder, or click New Folder to create your own folder. When you click OK, your favorite goes into that folder.

Returning to Favorites

To return to a favorite page, click the Favorites button on the menu bar. In the list of Favorites that drops down, click your favorite's name. Click a folder to see additional favorites in that folder.

You can return to a page without even going online! Choose File⇨Work Offline. When you choose a Favorite, Internet Explorer retrieves the page from your PC's hard drive instead of the Internet. The page may not be up to date, but many pages don't change that often, anyway, or you simply may not care about updates.

Organizing Favorites

After you have a dozen or so favorites in this list, you may want to add folders so that you can organize them or change the names of your existing favorites. Choose Favorites➪Organize Favorites to open the Organize Favorites dialog box.

To move a favorite to a folder, you can drag it. You can rename or delete favorites and folders or create new folders just as you would in an Open or a Save As dialog box, as I describe in Chapters 1 and 2, respectively. Or you can click the favorite or folder, and then click the Move, Delete, or Rename button.

Searching the Web for Information

Don't know something? Check the Web. The Web is turning into a vast library of information. But unlike your town library (or so I hope), the librarians of the Web are computer programs, and the quality of information ranges from timeless and irrefutable truths to complete and utter Biscuit Sauce (BS). It is up to you to determine which is which.

What I call librarians are called *search engines* by most people. These search engines all live at different addresses (URLs), and they all have different strengths and weaknesses. Two popular ones, for example, are AltaVista (`www.altavista.com`) and Yahoo! (`www.yahoo.com`). Although these search engines differ in the details, in general they enable you to choose a subject, and then they present you with a page of links to various pages on the subject. A brief excerpt from the page accompanies each link so that you can decide if the page is of interest.

Because you have your choice of so many search engines, Microsoft designed Internet Explorer with a Search Assistant feature that lets you search several of these engines at once. Follow these steps to use this feature:

1. **Click the Search button on the toolbar.**

    A Search panel opens on the left-hand side of the IE window.

2. **Choose a search category — Web page, address, business — if you want and then type one or more search terms in the text box or boxes that appear.**

3. **When you are finished typing, click the Search button.**

    A list of links to pages that meet your search criteria appears in the Search panel. Click one of those links, and the page appears on the right side of the IE window.

To try again with a new search, click the New button at the top left of the Search panel. Or, you may close the Search panel by clicking the X at the panel's top, right corner.

To see Microsoft's listing of search engines or to choose a different search engine, click the Customize button near the top of the Search panel. The Customize Search Settings dialog box maintains a list of engines that you are using and the order in which the Search Assistant uses them. Select and deselect search engines by clicking their check boxes. You can set the order in which they are used by selecting an engine and clicking the arrow buttons (Move Up and Move Down) below each list.

Printing Web Documents

You can print most Web documents just as easily as you print Works documents. In fact, the print command — File⇨Print — is the same in all those programs, and the associated Print dialog box is very similar. The printed page includes graphics and, if you have a color printer, color. (Colored backgrounds, however, are not printed. Thank goodness, or your ink cartridge would be depleted in about a minute.)

Some pages on the Web use frames, which complicate the printing process slightly. If you want to print a single frame, click in that frame before giving the print command. If you want to print just selected text, drag your mouse cursor across that text. Then choose File⇨Print, as usual, and at the bottom of the Print dialog box, select one of these choices for printing:

- **As Laid Out on Screen:** Your printout looks like your screen, except that any documents in any frame that go below the screen are included as well.
- **Only the Selected Frame:** The entire document of the frame that you clicked in (or in which you selected text) prints.
- **All Frames Individually:** Each frame prints separately, as a full document.

If you want to print only selected text, choose Selection in the Print dialog box.

Downloading Programs and Other Files from the Web

A Web browser such as Internet Explorer enables you to acquire (download) all kinds of stuff. Many companies and individuals offer programs for free on the Web. From Microsoft, you can download enhancements to Windows or to

Internet Explorer itself. Various companies offer add-on software or special viewers for special purposes. You can also download graphics files, music, audio, and video files that can play on properly equipped PCs!

If you look around carefully, you can find one or more download areas on the Web sites of Microsoft and most other PC software vendors. Use search engines to find free graphics (also called clip art), music, and video files. Follow the links and instructions, and eventually you click a link that causes Internet Explorer to download the file you choose.

To avoid computer viruses, be careful to download files only from reputable sources. If you have a virus-scanning program, scan any file that you intend to double-click or otherwise open.

After you click a link that starts a download, a File Download dialog box briefly appears, and then an Internet Explorer dialog box asks what you want to do with the file. Depending upon the type of file, you have two or more choices:

- **Run this file from its current location:** I don't recommend this choice unless you are certain you are downloading from a reliable source (say, a major corporate Web site). When you choose this option, the file is downloaded into a temporary storage area on your PC and then immediately opened, which may preclude your being able to virus-check the file.

- **Save this file to disk:** Click this button, and a Save As dialog box appears so that you can choose where you want to save the file. Choose a folder (and remember what folder you choose) and then click the Save button.

After making your selection, the File Download dialog box reappears, usually displaying an estimate of how long the downloading process may take. To stop the download, click the Cancel button. You can browse to other locations using IE while a file is downloading; you can also use other programs, such as the Works word processor, or do other Internet tasks, such as checking for e-mail — but expect your PC's response to be slower.

After downloading is complete, use your virus-scanning software (if you have it) on the downloaded file. You can browse to the folder where you downloaded the file by double-clicking the My Computer icon on your screen. Then, to begin installing the software, double-click the downloaded file. Sometimes, double-clicking the downloaded file only uncompresses the installation files. In that case, find the file named `install.exe` — typically in the same folder as your downloaded file — virus scan that file, and then double-click it to install the software.

Secure and Insecure Sites

What about doing business on the Internet? Increasingly, businesses that accept orders and credit card numbers over the Web use secure sites. *Secure sites* work with Internet Explorer to encrypt the data between your PC and their sites in a very secure way. The risk of doing business over a secure site is generally considered to be less than that of using a credit card in person.

If you're browsing a secure site, Internet Explorer displays a lock icon on the status bar at the bottom of its window. When you move from a secure site to an insecure site, Internet Explorer warns you.

Disconnecting and Quitting

When you're done Web browsing — or if you're simply reading a document and not planning to click any of its links — disconnect by choosing File⇨ Work Offline from IE's menu bar.

To reconnect, click the Refresh button in Internet Explorer's toolbar. (Your PC goes online automatically when any program demands information from the Internet. The Refresh button demands fresh information.)

To quit Internet Explorer, choose File⇨Close or click the button with the X in the upper-right corner of the Internet Explorer window.

Chapter 25

Reaching Out with Outlook Express

*H*ear that distant drumming? It's the sound of e-mail and news messages being pounded out on PCs and wafting their way across the Internet wilderness. Now you have your turn to join in the fun, using Outlook Express.

Send e-mail to family members. Subscribe to a newsgroup of fellow newt breeders (or whatever your vocation or hobby may be), and catch up on the latest news. You can do it all using Microsoft Outlook Express, which is Microsoft's cheaper version of its Outlook software for e-mail and news.

Note: If you haven't yet set up your PC to cruise the Internet or to deal with e-mail and newsgroups, you'll encounter an Internet Connection wizard if you try to use Outlook Express. You can read more about this wizard at the beginning of Chapter 24.

Launching Outlook Express

You can start Outlook Express several different ways:

  ✔ Look for an envelope-with-arrows icon on the taskbar and click it.
  ✔ If you see the Outlook Express icon labeled on your desktop, double-click it.

> ✔ Go to the Programs page of the Works Task Launcher, click Outlook
> Express in the list on the left, and then click Start Outlook Express on
> the right.

When you first launch Outlook Express, it may display a Browse for Folder
dialog box and ask you to choose a folder to keep your messages in. Just
click OK; that folder's file name should be `C:/Windows/Application
Data/Microsoft/Outlook Express`. Outlook Express may also ask whether
you want it to be your default mail client. That means, will Outlook Express
be your main e-mail program? If you like this arrangement, click to clear the
Always Perform This Check When Starting Outlook Express check box, and
then click Yes. (Click No if you usually use a different e-mail program.)

Going Online — or Not

When you launch Outlook Express, it displays a Dial-up Connection dialog
box, meaning that your PC is about to call your Internet Service Provider
(ISP) and go *online* — that is, connect to the Internet. (You can read more
about the Dial-up Connection dialog box, ISPs, and going online and offline in
Chapter 24.) You don't have to be online to read or compose messages —
only to receive and send them.

After you are online, how do you go offline? Choose File⇨Work Offline in
Outlook Express. Outlook Express asks whether you want to hang up the
modem; click Yes — otherwise, you're wasting your money on connection
time or tying up your phone line! Outlook Express automatically goes online
again when you send or receive messages.

What's What in the Outlook
Express Window

See Figure 25-1 to check out the Outlook Express window. The window looks
like this most of the time — except when you first start Outlook Express. When
you start Outlook Express, the right-hand window contains icons for e-mail,
news, and contacts. You can click these icons to do the same tasks as many of
the buttons and menu choices I describe in this chapter. To see the initial
window at any time, click Outlook Express at the top of the left-hand panel.

Look for various message boxes and folders on the left side of the window.
Click a box or folder to view its contents on the right side of the window. (In
Figure 25-1, I clicked the Inbox and then I clicked a message from me, Dave
Kay, to myself.) The bold type indicates unread messages. The numeral *1*
next to the Inbox icon tells me that I have one unread message.

Reply to
chosen message

Click a message to choose it

Create new
message

Unread message (bold)

List of messages

Send messages and check e-mail

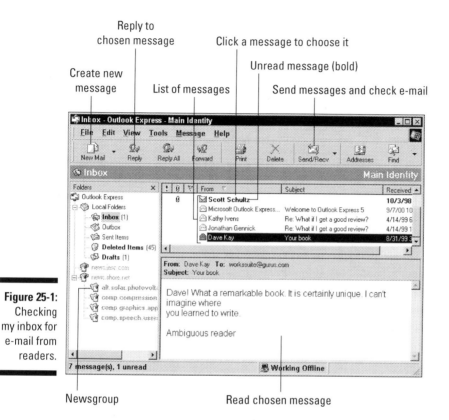

Figure 25-1:
Checking
my inbox for
e-mail from
readers.

Newsgroup

Read chosen message

Exchanging E-Mail Messages

Outlook Express enables you to send and receive e-mail from family, friends, business associates, and so on. The following three sections offer the step-by-step details for exchanging e-mail messages.

Creating e-mail messages

To send an e-mail message to someone, you need that person's address, usually in the following form: name@organization.com (or some other suffix, such as .edu, .net, or .org). Be careful to get all characters exactly right, or your message probably won't go through.

To create an e-mail message, do the following:

1. **Click the New Mail button at the far left of the Outlook Express toolbar.**

   If the New Mail button is not on the toolbar, click Inbox in the left panel to make it appear.

A New Message window appears.

2. **Click in the To text box and type your recipient's e-mail address.**

   To send e-mail to several people, type their e-mail addresses one after the other, separating each address with a comma or semicolon.

   Instead of typing the address, you may choose an address from your Address Book. Read the "Contacts and the Address Book" sidebar in this chapter, and also peruse Chapter 6, for help.

3. **To send a copy of your message to someone else, click the Cc line and enter an address as you did in Step 2.**

4. **Click the Subject line and type a short description of your message subject.**

   That subject line is the title of your message window.

5. **Click the message area and type your message. You don't need to press Enter at the end of a line; just keep typing.**

6. **Click the Send button in the message window to send the message now, or choose File➪Send Later to place the message in your Outbox.**

   The Outbox is one of the message boxes on the left-hand side of the window. Your messages reside there until you send them.

You can send a file of any kind (an image, a document, a Microsoft Greetings file, and so on) by *attaching it* to an e-mail message. In the message window, click the button with the paper-clip icon, or choose Insert➪File Attachment. In the Insert Attachment dialog box that appears, browse through the files, choose the file you want to send, and then click the Attach button.

Sending and receiving e-mail messages

To check your e-mail — and, at the same time, send any messages you've written but not yet sent — click the Send/Receive button on the Outlook Express toolbar. (If the Send/Receive button isn't visible, click Inbox in the left panel of the window.)

If you aren't already online, Outlook Express goes online now. If any dialog boxes appear, just click OK or Connect. If a Dial-up Connection dialog box appears, select the Save Password check box and then click the Connect button. You remain online until you exit Outlook Express or until you choose File➪Work Offline from the menu bar.

Messages are stored in boxes and folders, which are displayed in the left-hand panel; click a box or folder to see the messages stored there. Any new messages that you receive go into the Inbox. Any messages that you send are stored in the Sent Items box. Your Outbox is empty after sending messages.

If someone sends you an attached file, a paper-clip icon appears at the top-right corner of the panel displaying the message text.

- ✔ If you want to save that file and open it later, click the paper-clip icon, and in the drop-down menu, choose Save Attachments. A dialog box also appears that lets you choose a folder for the file. (This process works just like using the Save As dialog box in Works — see Chapter 1 for details.)

- ✔ If you want to open the attachment, click the paper-clip icon, and in the drop-down menu, choose the top item, the file's name. In the Open Attachment Warning dialog box that appears, select the Open It option, and then click OK.

Don't be too fast to open that attached file. Never, ever open an attachment that you aren't expecting — even if it's in a message from a friend. The attachment may be a virus. A number of notorious viruses have spread because they lurk in innocent-looking attachments that someone unwittingly opens. Then the virus is free to scour that person's Microsoft Address Book and e-mail its viral attachment to all that person's contacts, along with an innocuous-sounding message and subject line. When in doubt, delete the message. Then create a new message to the sender, checking the validity of the attachment.

Contacts and the Address Book

Outlook Express and some of the tasks in Microsoft Works use the Microsoft Address Book, a kind of database that you create of people (well, their names and addresses) you want to send stuff to. See Chapter 6 for help creating the Address Book.

To use an address from the Address Book, open a message window and follow these steps:

1. **Click the To or Cc button (displaying a book icon) located to the left of the To or Cc field.**

   The Select Recipients dialog box appears.

2. **Click the name of the person you want to e-mail in the column on the left.**

3. **Click the To, Cc, or Bcc button to add the name to any of the Message Recipients lists on the right.**

   (Bcc stands for Blind Carbon Copy, which means that person gets a copy, but nobody else knows that he or she has received a copy.)

4. **Click OK when you're done.**

To add someone to your Address Book who has sent you e-mail, right-click on a message from that person in the list of messages. Choose Add Sender to Address Book from the menu that pops up.

Reading, deleting, and replying to e-mail messages

To view the e-mail you receive, click the Inbox in the left panel of the Outlook Express window. Outlook Express lists your new, unread messages (distinguished by bold type and a sealed-envelope icon) in the upper right-hand panel of the Outlook Express window, as shown in Figure 25-1. Click any listed message to view its contents in the lower right-hand panel.

To reply to a message, first click the message to open it. Then click the Reply button on the Outlook Express toolbar. The Reply button opens a message window just as if you were creating a new message, but with the text of the original message already included. Just type and send the e-mail as you would any new message.

To move a message to the Deleted Items box, click the message in the upper right-hand panel, and then press Delete on your keyboard (or click the Delete button on the Outlook Express toolbar). To permanently delete the message, click the Deleted Items box, click the message (or Ctrl+click — that is, press the Ctrl key and click the mouse to choose several messages), and then press Delete.

Getting Started with Newsgroups

Newsgroups are like giant bulletin boards where people with common interests post messages. The Internet has thousands of newsgroups; some of them are good, some are bad, and some are downright ugly. As with e-mail, newsgroup messages (called postings) can contain attachments such as pictures, sounds, programs, and other stuff. You can read postings without participating (called lurking), or you can contribute material yourself.

Many newsgroups contain extremely useful material from fellow enthusiasts in a given subject. But others contain material that non-enthusiasts may find offensive in the extreme. Also keep in mind that a posting can have a computer virus attached, so never open any files attached to a newsgroup posting without screening them with a virus checker first.

Setting up your news account

Before you can do any of the cool stuff with newsgroups, you need to set up Outlook Express to read newsgroups from your ISP's news server. Fortunately, the Internet Setup wizard comes to your aid, as it did for setting up a mail account. Just follow these steps:

1. **Choose Tools⇨Accounts from the Outlook Express menu bar.**

   The Internet Accounts dialog box shows up, listing all your e-mail and newsgroup (news) accounts.

2. **Click the Add button and choose News from the menu that pops up.**

3. **From here on, the wizard prompts you to fill in information from your ISP about newsgroups and servers.**

   You may need some help from your ISP for this!

Listing and subscribing to newsgroups

Newsgroups cover thousands of topics, so your first task is to decide which newsgroups to subscribe to. Choose Tools⇨Newsgroups to begin the process. When you set up your news account (refer to the preceding section), you probably told Outlook Express to download a list of all the newsgroups available on your ISP's news server. If you didn't download the list then, Outlook Express now offers to do so. To trim the list, try typing a word you're interested in (**dog**, for example) in the Display Newsgroups Which Contain text box.

To read or contribute to the messages in a newsgroup, you must first *subscribe* (sign up). To do so, click a newsgroup name, and then click the Subscribe button. Subscribe to as many newsgroups as you like. To see which ones you already subscribe to, click the Subscribed tab at the bottom of the Newsgroups dialog box. To unsubscribe, click a newsgroup, and then click the Unsubscribe button.

To quit the Newsgroups dialog box, click its OK button. To return to the Newsgroups dialog box, choose Tools⇨Newsgroups or click News Groups (if it appears on the Outlook Express toolbar). The button appears only when you are viewing news. To update the list of newsgroups, click the Reset List button.

Downloading and reading newsgroup messages

To download and read newsgroup messages, choose Tools⇨Newsgroups or simply click your newsgroup in the left panel in the Outlook Express window. (In Figure 25-1, the newsgroup is entitled `news.shore.net`.) Here you see your subscribed newsgroups in a list indented under your news account.

To download all of the latest messages in a newsgroup, click the newsgroup. (In Figure 25-1, one newsgroup begins with `comp.speech`.)

In the same way that you click the e-mail Inbox to list mail messages, you click a newsgroup to list its messages in the upper-right panel. Click a newsgroup message to read its text in the lower-right panel.

Unlike e-mail messages, newsgroup messages are organized into *threads*. When someone *posts* a reply (sends a response) to a message, that reply is grouped with the original message and a plus sign (+) appears to the left of the original message. Click the plus sign to display the replies, which are indented underneath the message.

Posting newsgroup messages

Posting (sending) and replying to newsgroup messages is very similar to sending and replying to e-mail — just click the magical buttons on the Outlook Express toolbar, as follows:

- **To create a message on a new topic for the newsgroup:** Click the newsgroup that you want to post to; then click the New Post button.

- **To post a reply to a previously received message:** View that message and then click the Reply Group button.

- **To reply by private e-mail to the author of a newsgroup message:** Click that message and then click the Reply button. Many posts do not include the correct return e-mail address in the From field, so the Reply button won't work. Sometimes, these people do give a valid e-mail address elsewhere in the message, however, so you can compose an e-mail message to them the regular way. Their intention is to make spammers work harder.

Fill out the message window that appears after you click any of the buttons just listed, just as you would for an e-mail message. Be sure to type a subject line for messages on new topics, but not for replies. You don't need to fill out an address; the message is already addressed.

Click the Send button in the message window to send the message now or choose File⇨Send Later to place the message in the Outbox. If you send the message now and you aren't already online, Outlook Express goes online. If you choose instead to send the message later, the message goes into the Outbox and is sent the next time you go online.

Chapter 26

Time Traveling with Calendar

*P*ersonally, I have trouble remembering the old rhyme, "Thirty days hath whatever, April, March, and whenever, and all the rest have something different." But all Works Calendar needs to help you take over the world is for you to put your business, personal, and other appointments or day-long events into its calculating little brain. Do so and you not only can see all your upcoming happenings displayed by day, week, or month, but you also get automatic reminders of appointments, review your notes before meetings, and print out calendars for business associates.

Starting Works Calendar

You can start Works calendar in either of two ways: from the Works Task Launcher, or from the Windows taskbar (as you would for any other program).

✔ From the Windows taskbar, choose Start⇨Programs⇨Microsoft Works⇨ Microsoft Works Calendar.

✔ From the Works Task Launcher, click Programs at the top of the window. Click Works Calendar in the list of programs that now appear along the left side of the window. Click Start the Calendar (in colored text) in the right-hand panel.

This same page of the Task Launcher also gives you shortcuts so you can either create a new appointment or find an existing one:

- To create a new appointment, click the task, Calendar, Set Appointment, and then click the <u>Start This Task</u> link. This delivers you to the New Appointment dialog box that you can read about in the section, "Setting Up Appointments or Events," later in this chapter.

- To find an appointment by looking for some text in it, click Appointment Search and then click Start This Task. Enter some text of the appointment title you're looking for in the Find dialog box that appears and click Find Now.

After you start it up, Works Calendar may ask you whether you want to give it the honor of being your default calendar. If you're not currently using another calendar, click Yes. If you're using another calendar but want to check out Works Calendar before deciding which to use, click No. To get it to stop asking the question, click to clear the check mark labeled `Always perform this check when starting Works Calendar`.

What's What in the Calendar Window

The calendar window displays the kind of menu bar and toolbar that you find in any Windows program, plus one of the several views of your calendar among which you can choose (look at Figure 26-1). Initially, you see an entire month, but you can choose to view a single day or week instead. (Jump ahead to the following section, "Viewing by Month, Week, or Day," for details.) You can also view your appointments by different categories — displaying, for example, just personal or just business appointments. (See the section, "Using categories," later in this chapter, for details.)

As do most Windows programs, Calendar offers you several alternative ways to perform any given task: toolbar buttons, keyboard shortcuts, a pop-up menu that appears after you right-click on a date, or the menu bar. The method you use is up to you. I find that using the toolbar buttons and the right-mouse menu are the most convenient methods, but you may prefer to use a different method.

Viewing by Month, Week, or Day

Calendar enables you to choose your view: month, week, or day. (I prefer an ocean view, but they refuse to give me a room with a window.) Click the appropriate button on the toolbar, as shown in Figure 26-1, or choose <u>View</u>⇨ <u>D</u>ay, <u>W</u>eek, or <u>M</u>onth from the menu bar.

New appointment

Find appointment

Delete current appointment

Print calendar as shown

View today

View selected day

View week of selected day   ⌐ Check for open reminders   Next month

View month   View appointments by category

Toolbar ⌐

Menu bar ⌐

Figure 26-1:
Viewing an
entire
month. Click
a date
before trying
to schedule
anything on
that date.

Built-in holidays   Currently selected day   A personal recurring event

Here are a few tips for choosing views; I find Day and Month views to be the
more useful ones:

✓ Choose Day view for easiest scheduling of appointments at particular
hours. Day view displays all-day events in light gray above the list of
time slots.

> ✔ Choose Month view for easiest scheduling and viewing of all-day events. If an appointment title isn't fully visible in Month view, position your mouse cursor over it and wait a second. The title appears in full (as shown in Figure 26-1 for Steven Smednoff's birthday).

Looking Ahead or Behind

If you're like me (and I don't say that you are), you're always nervously looking ahead and behind to see what's coming or what you forgot to do. In Calendar, each view provides the following two ways to move your view forward or back in time:

> ✔ Click the Previous *whatever* or Next *whatever* arrows at the left and right sides of the calendar, respectively, just under the toolbar. (By *whatever*, I mean *Day* in Day view, *Week* in Week view, or *Month* in Month view.)

> ✔ Click the month or date text that appears in large type just under the toolbar. Choose a new date from the list of selections that drops down.

Setting Up Appointments or Events

Works' Calendar program distinguishes appointments, such as meetings or lunch dates, from all-day events (or events for short). (The program is superior to some business people I've known in that regard.) Appointments are happenings that begin and end at particular hours. All-day events are happenings that include holidays, birthdays, or casual day at work. I use the term *happenings* in this chapter if the text applies to both events and appointments.

The key Calendar feature you use to set up happenings of either kind is the New Appointment dialog box (or its nearly identical twin, the Edit Appointment dialog box). Calendar also offers a few shortcuts for creating and editing happenings. I show you how to use all these features in the following sections.

Making happenings happen

Works Calendar gives you lots of ways to enter various happenings. Some ways are obvious because they appear right on-screen and read `Click here to add`. If you click where Calendar indicates, a blank line and cursor appear so that you can type a title for the happening.

In Week or Month view, always click the date of the appointment or event first to select it. (To enter a multi-day event, drag across several dates.) In the Day view, click the half-hour time slot first. (To enter an event that takes longer than one half hour, drag across several time slots.) Then, use either of these methods to enter a happening of any kind:

✔ Click the New Appointment button (or press Ctrl+N or choose File⇨New Appointment).

✔ Right-click directly on the selected date (or time slot in Day view). (Right-click the date itself, not an appointment or event on that date.) Then choose the top selection in the list that drops down, which is either New Appointment or New All Day Event. Don't worry about the difference right now; you can choose the type of happening you want in the New Appointment dialog box that appears.

Whichever of those two ways you choose, you end up gazing at the New Appointment dialog box, as shown in Figure 26-2.

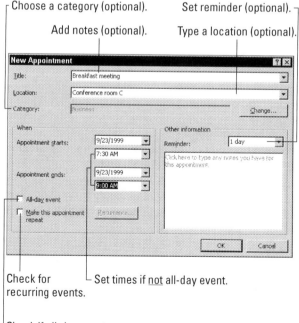

Choose a category (optional).   Set reminder (optional).

Add notes (optional).   Type a location (optional).

Figure 26-2:
Specifying
everything
about an
appoint-
ment,
including
any
reminder.

Check for recurring events.   Set times if not all-day event.

Check if all-day event.

If you edit an appointment, you use a nearly identical dialog box known as the Edit Appointment dialog box.

The following steps are the only essential ones for entering an appointment or event in the New Appointment dialog box (refer to Figure 26-2):

1. **Click in the Title box and type a descriptive title for the appointment or event.**

   This title is what appears in the calendar.

2. **Select or deselect the All-Day Event check box, if necessary.**

   If you're entering an all-day event (such as a birthday or holiday), make sure that the All-Day Event check box contains a check mark. (Click the check box if it doesn't contain one.)

   If you're entering an appointment (which needs starting and ending times), make sure that the All-Day Event check box does not contain a check mark. (Click the check box to remove the mark if it does.)

3. **Adjust the dates and/or times for this happening, if necessary.**

   To change the date or make a multiday event, you can edit the dates in the Appointment Starts and Appointment Ends drop-down list boxes. If you prefer to pick dates from a calendar, click the down arrows adjoining those boxes.

   For appointments, type a starting and ending time for the appointment, as shown in Figure 26-2. If you prefer to pick half-hour intervals from a list, click the down arrows adjoining those boxes. You may also enter a new date above the time boxes. (If you make an appointment span more than one day, it appears in its time slot on each of those days.)

4. **Click the OK button when you're done.**

Some of the options you can choose in the New Appointment dialog box are as follows:

- ✔ Select the Make This Appointment Repeat check box to make your happening repeat every day, week, month, or year. See the following section, "Entering birthdays and other recurring events," for details.

- ✔ Click in the Location box and type a location for the event. Calendar keeps a list of locations you've used in the past. To choose from that list, click the down arrow at the far-right end of the Location text box.

- ✔ Click the Change button to categorize your happening. Check out the section, "Using categories," later in this chapter, for instructions.

- ✔ Click the Reminder drop-down list box and type a time interval (or click the adjoining down arrow and choose a time interval from the list) to have Works remind you in advance of the happening. See the section, "Setting up reminders," later in this chapter, for details.

- ✔ Click and type notes about the event in the large white box under the Reminder box.

Entering birthdays and other recurring events

If your event or appointment occurs once a year, a month, a week, the second Tuesday of each month, or Mondays through Fridays, you're in luck (unless you're talking about dental surgery appointments). Calendar enables you to enter the happening just once and make it repeat on any of those intervals. Follow these steps to success:

1. **To enter a new, repeating event or appointment, either click the New Appointment button (or press Ctrl+N or choose File➪New Appointment), or, in Month or Week view, right-click on the date you want and choose New Appointment from the menu that drops down.**

   Or

   To change an existing event or appointment to a repeating one, begin by right-clicking on it. Then choose Open from the pop-up menu that appears.

   You see an Edit Appointment dialog box, which is identical to the New Appointment dialog box. (If this existing event is a recurring one, the Open Recurring Event dialog box appears first. Choose Open This Occurrence to make a change for the date you chose. Choose Open the Series to make a change that applies to all dates on which the event recurs.)

2. **Select the Make This Appointment Repeat check box in the New Appointment (or Edit Appointment) dialog box.**

3. **Click the Recurrence button.**

   The Recurrence Options dialog box appears, as shown in Figure 26-3.

Specify how often your happening occurs and for how long it continues to recur, by following these steps in the Recurrence Options dialog box:

1. **Click the option button for your choice of interval: Daily, Weekly, Monthly, or Yearly.**

2. **Choose from among the options that each different interval offers by clicking option or check boxes:**

   - **Daily options:** Every Day (seven days a week) or Every Weekday (Monday through Friday).

   - **Weekly options:** Choose a day of the week.

     For happenings that occur several times a week, you can choose multiple days.

   - **Monthly options:** Choose by day number (on the 6th day, for example) or by the day and week (such as Every Second Thursday).

   - **Yearly options:** Choose by date (August 13, for example) or by day, week, and month (such as Every Second Thursday in August).

Choose a recurrence interval.

Refine the interval here.

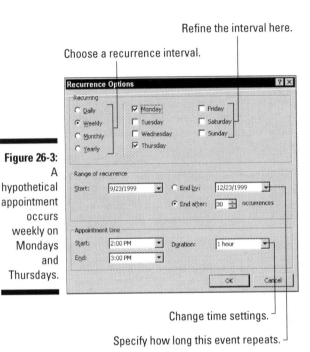

Figure 26-3:
A
hypothetical
appointment
occurs
weekly on
Mondays
and
Thursdays.

Change time settings.

Specify how long this event repeats.

3. **Specify how long this happening is to repeat by giving a beginning date and either an end date or a number of occurrences.**

   Type a beginning date in the Start drop-down list box.

   Type an ending date in the End By box, or click End After and enter a number of occurrences.

   By editing the values in the Start, End, or Duration boxes (or all of these), you can also adjust the appointment times if necessary.

4. **Click OK in the Recurrence Options dialog box when you're done there.**

5. **Review — and, if you like, change — the information in the New Appointment (or Edit Appointment) dialog box to which you return.**

   If you need to adjust appointment times, click the Recurrence button again.

6. **Click OK when you're done.**

To automatically enter birthdays and anniversaries stored in your Windows address book, choose Edit⇨Birthdays.

Editing and moving appointments and events

If you're like me, your appointments change and move even faster than those giant man-eating chameleons. (You know — the ones crawling up your walls?) Well, maybe you're not like me — you may have fewer mental health appointments — but I bet your appointments change. Here's the lowdown on editing and moving appointments and events:

- ✔ **To edit the title** of an appointment in any view, simply click the appointment. A blinking cursor appears, and you can type, backspace, select text, and delete text just as you do in the text box of a dialog box. Click any date (or any hour, in Day view) to close the text box.

- ✔ **To edit any aspect of an appointment**, including its dates, times, notes, or title, right-click on the appointment and choose Open from the pop-up menu that appears. The Edit Appointment dialog box appears, which works identically to the New Appointment dialog box (refer to Figure 26-2) and enables you to change any aspect of the appointment. If the appointment is a repeating one and you need to change its date or time, click the Recurrence button and make the changes in the Recurrence Options dialog box.

- ✔ **To move** any happening (appointment or event) to another date or time, dragging is the easiest method. Click that happening and, holding down the mouse button, drag the happening to another date on the Calendar.

- ✔ **Copying** an appointment or event is similar, except that you press and hold the Ctrl key on your keyboard while you drag the appointment.

- ✔ **To move** an appointment or event to a date farther in the future than you care to drag it, edit the appointment or event (as I describe in the second bullet) and change its date.

- ✔ **To delete** an appointment or event, right-click on it and then choose Delete Item from the context menu that appears.

Using categories

If you get really serious about using Calendar to manage your life, consider using the Calendar categories. (Or consider getting a simpler life!) If you have lots of happenings in Calendar — meetings, trips, lunches, therapies, kids' activities, holidays, classes, or the Ludlow, Vermont Zucchini Festival — your calendar gets pretty cluttered.

By using Calendar's categories, you can assign any happening to one or more categories: business, education, medical, personal, and so on. Then you can restrict (or filter) the display to show only certain categories of happenings at a time. Calendar comes with a set of standard categories among which you can choose, and you can create, rename, or delete categories as well.

Assigning categories

The place to go to assign categories is the Choose Category dialog box. You can access this dialog box in any of the following several ways — whichever is most convenient for you:

✔ To assign a category while you're creating or editing a happening, click the Change button in the New Appointment or Edit Appointments dialog box (refer to Figure 26-2).

✔ To quickly assign a category to an existing happening, right-click that appointment or event and choose Categories from the pop-up menu that appears.

The Choose Categories dialog box that then appears consists simply of a list of check boxes, one for each category. Check one or more categories for your happening and then click OK.

Creating your own categories

To add a category of your own design or to delete or rename a category, you need to access the Edit Category dialog box. Choose Edit↪Categories from the menu bar or click the Edit Categories button in the Choose Categories dialog box.

In the Edit Categories dialog box, click a category to delete or rename and then click the Delete or Rename button. To create a new category, click the blank text box at the bottom of the dialog box, type a new name, and then click the Add button.

Filtering happenings

To make your calendar display only certain categories of appointments or events (say, medical appointments), you *filter* out the other happenings by using the filter control panel. Click the Category Filter button (the right-most button in the toolbar, as shown in Figure 26-1) to display or hide that panel.

A list of check boxes appears to the left of your calendar; check marks indicate which categories Calendar is displaying. Click to clear the check marks for categories that you don't want to see, and your calendar changes accordingly.

To restore all happenings to your calendar, click the words Category Filter at the top of the filter panel, and choose Show Appointments in All Categories from the menu that appears. To hide the filter panel, click the Category Filter button again.

Hiding the filter panel doesn't remove filtering. Only by choosing Show Appointments in All Categories do you remove filtering.

Setting up reminders

Calendar can remind you of upcoming happenings (events or appointments) by popping up a reminder window and, optionally, making a sound. All you need to do is tell Calendar how far in advance to remind you. Here's how:

1. **Start a new appointment or begin editing one as I describe in earlier sections of this chapter.**

2. **In the New Appointment (or Edit Appointment) dialog box that appears (refer to Figure 26-2), type an interval in the Reminder drop-down list box that reflects how long before the happening you want Works to remind you about it.**

   Either type an interval (in minutes, hours, days, weeks, months, or years) or click the down arrow adjoining the Reminder text box and choose a standard interval from the drop-down list that appears.

3. **You can now exit Calendar by choosing File⇨Exit.**

   Calendar doesn't need to be running for the reminder to work.

At your specified interval before the appointment or event begins, a View Reminders dialog box appears. You may leave the View Reminders dialog box on-screen to help you remember the appointment. The dialog box displays all current *(active)* reminders in its Reminders text box. To view your notes on a given happening, click the happening in the Reminders text box, and then click the Open button.

After you're sure you're going to remember an upcoming happening (or after it passes), you may clear (dismiss) its reminder in the View Reminders dialog box. Click that happening and then click the Dismiss Item button. To dismiss all current reminders, click Dismiss All; they don't appear again. Dismissing a reminder is the same as deleting or canceling it.

Click the Close button to remove the View Reminders dialog box from your screen. You can check your reminders at any time by choosing View⇨ Reminders from the Calendar menu bar or by clicking the Reminders button on the toolbar, which sports a bell icon.

Printing Calendars

Computers — phooey! Nothing beats a paper calendar or appointment book for keeping you current with events and appointments and for sharing a schedule with others. Works Calendar gives you more ways to print your schedule than you probably can ever use. Follow these steps to print a calendar:

1. **Choose File⇨Print (or click the Print button on the toolbar or press Ctrl+P).**

   The Print dialog box appears.

2. **Begin by selecting a calendar style.**

   To print out a day's appointments, choose one of the following Day styles from the Style box:

   - **Day by appointments:** Similar to Day view; shows a space covering each appointment's duration.

   - **Day by hours:** Similar to Day view but lists every half-hour time slot and shows what appointment begins in that half-hour.

   - **Day list:** Lists each appointment in order and its start and end times; shows no time slots.

   - **Day list by sections:** Groups appointments into Morning, Afternoon, and Evening, showing start and end times for each appointment.

   Calendar also offers Week and Month calendar styles in the Style box. Choose Month-Portrait for a calendar that prints vertically on a page or Month-Landscape for the horizontal orientation that you usually use for calendars.

3. **Enter a Start and End date and time in the Range area of the Print dialog box. (Or use the default dates and times that Calendar suggests.)**

4. **Make sure that Calendar applies any filtering the way you actually want it to appear. If you want to print all appointments and events instead, click All Appointments.**

   In the Include area of the Print dialog box, Calendar assumes by default that any filtering you're currently applying (displaying Personal appointments only, for example) also applies to this printed calendar.

5. **Click OK to close the Print dialog box and print the calendar.**

Part VII
The Part of Tens

The 5th Wave   By Rich Tennant

"MY GIRLFRIEND RAN A SPREADSHEET OF MY LIFE, AND GENERATED THIS CHART. MY BEST HOPE IS THAT SHE'LL CHANGE HER MAJOR FROM 'COMPUTER SCIENCES' TO 'REHABILITATIVE SERVICES.'"

In this part . . .

As on *Sesame Street,* this part is brought to you by the number ten: "Ten Things NOT to Do" and "Ten Solutions to Common Problems." If you can't find what you want in the rest of this book, you may just find it here.

If chapters be the food of comprehension, write on;
Give me excess of it, that, surfeiting, the appetite may
sicken, and so die.

—*Tenth Night,* early play by William Shakespeare

Chapter 27

Ten Things NOT to Do

*E*veryone has an idea about how things ought to work. Unfortunately, computers don't usually work that way. You can easily fall into old typewriter habits or form a mistaken impression that Works makes you do something that you don't really have to do. Here's my list of the top ten errors, misconceptions, or just plain boo-boos that you should avoid.

Do Not Use Extra Spaces, Lines, Tabs, or Line-Ends

If you're using multiple, consecutive spaces, tabs, or line-endings in a word processing document, you're probably making your life difficult. If you're using multiple tabs in every line, it's probably because you haven't set your tab stops or you forgot that you can indent a paragraph with a toolbar button. If you're using blank lines to separate paragraphs, try pressing Ctrl+0 (that's the numeral zero, not the letter *O*) to put space above the paragraph instead. Read Chapter 15 for additional better ways to do things.

In particular, do not keep pressing Enter to begin a new page. This trick may work nicely on your Royal typewriter, but in Works word processing documents, it creates a royal mess. Instead, press Ctrl+Enter to start a new page.

Do Not Open Too Many Windows

Open too many windows at home, and your house gets buggy. Open too many windows in Works, and it, too, may get a little buggy. (In particular, it may get a bit slow and be confusing to you.) In Works, whenever you open a new document, you get a new window and button on the toolbar! If you don't need all those documents open, close them! Click the X in the upper-right corner of the window to close it. You can get rid of the Task Launcher window that way, too, if you like.

If you do need multiple documents open, you can avoid confusion by *minimizing* their windows. Click the "_" button in the upper-right corner of the window; the window shrinks to a button on the taskbar. Click the button to re-open the window.

Do Not Press Enter at the End of Each Line

I know, I've said this before, but it pains me greatly to see people fighting their word processors. If you press Enter at the end of every line in a word processing document, Works can't word-wrap for you. As a result, every time you edit a line, you have to manually readjust every line! AAAAAGGGH!! JUST DON'T DO IT, YOU HEAR ME?!! (Notice how annoying text is when it's all in capital letters? If you want to know why adults shouldn't shout at each other like this, skip down to the tenth thing not to do in this chapter.)

Do Not Type Your Own File Extensions When Saving Files

When you save a file, just type the filename, not the .wks or any other extension. Works automatically puts the proper extension on. If you use your own special extension, it's harder to get Works to display the file in the Open dialog box, and the file is therefore harder to open.

Do Not Number Your Pages Manually

Works can automagically number your word processing pages, positioning the numbers where you want them. What more could you want? If you try to number your own pages by simply typing a number on each page, you'll be continually adjusting them as you edit the document.

Do Not Turn Off Your PC Before Exiting

Hey! It's time for dinner! But don't just flip the power switch on your PC. Exit Works and exit Windows first. (If your PC is one that suspends the state of all your programs — and of Windows — as you turn the PC off, you don't need to exit Works and Windows first. Some laptops also have a suspend feature.) If you don't exit before you turn off your computer, Windows and Works can become confused the next time you try to do things. At the very least, your hard drive fills up with little Windows temporary files.

Do Not Use Spaces for Blank Cells

In your spreadsheet documents, when you want to remove an entry, don't type a space; press the Delete key instead. If you put a space in the cell and use a COUNT, AVG, or other statistical function, the cell is counted.

Do Not Work in Tiny Windows Unnecessarily

Just because Works starts out with a smallish window doesn't mean that you have to stay with it. Click and drag a corner or side of the Works window to enlarge it. Do the same with your document windows. Better yet, maximize the Works or document window. Check out Chapter 2 for a refresher on doing this.

Do Not Stuff All Your Files in the Same Folder

See Chapter 2 for ways to make new folders. When you save files, put them in different folders. If you stuff them all in the same folder, you'll eventually get very confused.

Do Not Type in ALL CAPITALS

Particularly when you're using Outlook Express to send mail to somebody, don't type in all capital letters (uppercase letters). It's considered shouting. In other tools, using all capitals makes your documents harder to read.

Chapter 28

Ten Solutions to Common Problems

*G*etting e-mail from readers is a very enlightening and humbling experience for an author. You discover that people have problems you never thought about, or at least never thought would be a problem. Some problems actually have their roots in software other than Works — most commonly in Microsoft Windows, the foundation software that your PC runs on. In this chapter, you find a mixed bag of the most common questions I get, and some answers.

How Do I Send and Receive Documents by E-Mail?

Not only can you send messages by e-mail, but also you can attach files of any kind to an e-mail message: word processor documents, spreadsheets, databases, pictures. To attach a document for sending, do this:

1. **Save the document as a file (if you have not already done so), remembering what folder you saved it to.**

2. **Create a new message in Outlook Express (see Chapter 25).**

3. **Click the Attach button on the toolbar (with the paper-clip icon).**

4. **In the Insert Attachment dialog box that appears, browse to the folder that contains your file.**

   Read through Chapter 2 for a description of how to browse through folders in the Open dialog box, which works the same way as the Insert Attachment dialog box.

5. **Click your file and then click the Attach button.**

To open a file received by e-mail, take these steps:

1. **Open the message to which the file is attached.**

   Click the message in Outlook Express.

2. **Click the paper-clip icon in the gray bar above the message text, to the right of where it reads** From:, To:, **and** Subject:.

3. **Click the top line of the two-line menu that appears, which contains the name and size of the attached file.**

   The Open Attachment Warning dialog box appears, warning that attachments may contain viruses.

4. **If you are sure that the attachment does not contain viruses, click the Open It option box. Otherwise, run your virus-scanning software if it has not already run. (Some virus checkers can be set up to check your mail attachments automatically as they arrive.) Then click OK.**

   If your PC is equipped with a program that can read the file, that program runs now and opens the file. If your PC doesn't have (or doesn't know that it has) software that can read the file, the Open With dialog box appears. If you know of a program that can read the file, choose it in this dialog box (which lists all the programs on your PC) and then click OK. Otherwise, click the Cancel button; you won't be able to open this file. Ask the person who sent the file to try again with a different format (type) of file.

Outlook Express holds received files in a temporary storage area. If you want to make a permanent copy of the file somewhere more convenient, click the Save It To Disk option box in the Open Attachment Warning dialog box before clicking OK in Step 4 of the preceding steps. The Save Attachment As dialog box that appears works just like the Save dialog box I discuss in Chapter 2. If you save the file to disk, the file is not opened.

The world of e-mail can be very complicated, so if you're really interested in figuring out what's going on with your e-mail, try picking up *E-Mail For Dummies,* an excellent book by Margaret Levine Young.

Why Can't 1 Read Others' Documents?

Many people use different programs than you do, and you may have trouble reading — or perhaps even finding — their documents in Works. Here are a couple of things to try:

- ✔ Choose File➪Open in a Works program; in the Open dialog box, click the Files of Type list box. A list of file types that your Works program can read appears. Click a type that seems to match the file you were sent, or choose All Files (*.*).

    In the word processor, try choosing Recover Text From Any File (*.*). Then browse to the folder containing the file and try to open the file.

- ✔ Ask the sender to send you a different file type (format). The last resort is a text file. For databases and spreadsheets, ask for a comma-delimited text file (one where data is separated by commas); then in the Open dialog box of your program, choose a file type of Text (*.txt).

If, on the other hand, people have trouble reading your files, try saving the document by choosing File➪Save As. In the Save As dialog box, click the Save As Type list box and choose a different file type. You might do this with the other person on the phone, so you can discuss the options.

How Do 1 Turn a Spreadsheet into a Database?

People often use a spreadsheet program called Microsoft Excel to collect data. You may prefer to have that data in a database file. The Works spreadsheet program can read Excel data, but the database program cannot. What to do?

Open the Excel file in the Works spreadsheet program and choose Excel SS (*.xl*) in the Files of Type list box as described in the preceding section. Leave that spreadsheet window open, and create a new, blank database with as many fields as there are columns in the spreadsheet. Then select the data in the spreadsheet window, copy it by pressing Ctrl+C, switch to the database window, and paste by pressing Ctrl+V.

You can use the same technique to turn your Works spreadsheets into databases. Also, by copying from a database in List view, you can paste database data into a Works spreadsheet.

How Do I Make a Backup Copy of a File?

People have different ideas about what having a backup copy of a file means. Some people want a copy on a floppy disk, so if the hard drive on their PC crashes (fails), they haven't lost the data. (Not a bad idea.) To do that, see the instructions for making a copy to a floppy in Chapter 2.

Another interpretation of backup is a copy that allows you to, in effect, "back up" or return to the version of a document just before the current version. If you keep a copy on a floppy, as in the preceding paragraph, you have done just that.

How Do I Delete or Rename a File?

Windows lets you delete or rename a file nearly any time you see it listed — in the Save As or Open dialog box, or in Windows Explorer, or in the windows you get when you double-click the My Computer icon on your desktop. You can always open the Open dialog box, for instance, just for the purpose of deleting or renaming a file, by choosing File⇨Open. After renaming or deleting the file, click the Cancel button.

In those environments, you can delete a file by clicking its icon to select the file, and then pressing the Delete key on your keyboard. A dialog box will ask if you are sure you want to send the file to the Recycle Bin; click Yes.

To rename the file, click its icon first, and then click its name. Type a new name. If you see the three-letter ending (the file extension) — .wdb, for instance — make sure to include that same ending; if no such ending is visible, leave it off. Click the file's icon again when you're done typing.

Works also enables you to delete a file from the History listing on the Task Launcher — but that action does not delete the file from your PC. Click History on the Task Launcher menu bar, and the History page lists your files. Right-click any file, and choose Delete from the menu that pops up. Works asks if you really want to do this; click Yes.

Why Do the Lines in My Document Have Funny Breaks and Gaps?

When lines in a word processor document have peculiar breaks and gaps, the problem is invisible line-break or tab characters. Often, the problem arises when you copy text from an e-mail message in Outlook Express. To see these troublemakers, click the Show All button (the ¶ mark) on the toolbar. Then delete them as you would any character. A fast way to clean up these marks is to replace them with spaces using the word processor's Replace feature. Thumb through Chapter 14 for more on finding and replacing white-space characters.

How Do I See (Freeze) Spreadsheet Headings?

When spreadsheets become larger than one screen's worth, you have a hard time seeing your column and row headings anymore. So lock — or freeze — them in place. Click the cell that's just under your column headings and just to the right of your row headings. Then choose Format⇨Freeze Titles from the menu bar. Now you can scroll all over the place and those headings will stay in place.

To undo your freeze, repeat the action. To freeze just horizontally, select a row (click the row number) before choosing Format⇨Freeze Titles; to freeze just vertically, select a column first (click the column letter).

Why Can't I Sum Up Columns in a Database?

Well, it's true. You can't sum up columns in a database, at least not in List view, which looks so much like a spreadsheet that people always want to treat it like one and put sums at the bottom of columns. If you want sums at the bottom of columns, copy the data into a spreadsheet. Or, check out Chapter 23 for a discussion of reports, which can sum up fields across many records. If you want to sum up the data in a row (a record), you *can* do that: You need a calculating field. See Chapter 23 for details.

Why Doesn't Works Run Like This Book Says?

The usual reason that people find discrepancies between this book and real life is that they're using Works Suite. Microsoft currently puts out two versions of Works: Works itself, and its big brother, Works Suite. Works Suite includes, among other programs, Microsoft Word *in place of* the Works word processor. Note that *Word* is not *Works!* To run that program, pick up a copy of *Microsoft Word For Dummies.* This book is about Works 6.0, so if you're using an earlier version, you may also find discrepancies.

What Do I Do if I'm Still Horribly Frustrated by My PC?

Throw a brick through the monitor. Very satisfying. No, just kidding. That would be a waste of a perfectly good brick and would scare the cat sitting on your monitor.

Your problem most likely comes from inexperience with Microsoft Windows, the underlying foundation garment upon which all programs (including Works) rely. Consider picking up a copy of *Microsoft Windows X For Dummies* (where X is whatever version of Windows you're running) or get a Windows training CD. Also, software is just plain weird. It doesn't follow natural laws and takes getting used to. Try a more careful approach: Don't watch your fingers, but take careful note of exactly what happens on the screen as you do things. Every change in shading of buttons or icons is a clue. Be very careful exactly where you click: Clicking on an icon may not do the same thing as clicking on a file name, for instance.

Index

FOR DUMMIES®

Helping you expand your horizons and realize your potential